TEST DESIGN
Developments in Psychology and Psychometrics

BF
176
.T42

TEST DESIGN

Developments in Psychology and Psychometrics

Edited by

SUSAN E. EMBRETSON

Department of Psychology
The University of Kansas
Lawrence, Kansas

1985

ACADEMIC PRESS, INC.

(Harcourt Brace Jovanovich, Publishers)
Orlando   San Diego   New York   London
Toronto   Montreal   Sydney   Tokyo

COPYRIGHT © 1985, BY ACADEMIC PRESS, INC.
ALL RIGHTS RESERVED.
NO PART OF THIS PUBLICATION MAY BE REPRODUCED OR
TRANSMITTED IN ANY FORM OR BY ANY MEANS, ELECTRONIC
OR MECHANICAL, INCLUDING PHOTOCOPY, RECORDING, OR
ANY INFORMATION STORAGE AND RETRIEVAL SYSTEM, WITHOUT
PERMISSION IN WRITING FROM THE PUBLISHER.

ACADEMIC PRESS, INC.
Orlando, Florida 32887

United Kingdom Edition published by
ACADEMIC PRESS INC. (LONDON) LTD.
24–28 Oval Road, London NW1 7DX

Library of Congress Cataloging in Publication Data

Main entry under title:

Test design.

  Bibliography: p.
  Includes index.
  1. Psychological tests. I. Embretson, Susan E.
BF176.T42   1984   153.9'3   84-2919
ISBN 0-12-238180-7 (alk. paper)

PRINTED IN THE UNITED STATES OF AMERICA

85 86 87 88   9 8 7 6 5 4 3 2 1

Contents

Contributors   ix

Preface   xi

I. INTRODUCTION TO TEST DESIGN

1. Introduction to the Problem of Test Design
Susan E. Embretson (Whitely)

Introduction	3
Desiderata for Test Design	3
Current Practices in Test Development	5
Current Issues in Testing and Test Design	6
Organization of the Book	7
References	16

II. DESIGN VARIABLES FROM PSYCHOLOGICAL THEORY

2. The Representation and Processing of Information in Real-Time Verbal Comprehension
Robert J. Sternberg and Timothy P. McNamara

Introduction	21
Alternative Approaches to Analyzing Verbal Comprehension	22
Theory of Representation and Information Processing	27
Implications for Test Design and Analysis	36
Conclusion	40
References	41

3. Analyses of Spatial Aptitude and Expertise
James W. Pellegrino, Randall J. Mumaw, and Valerie J. Shute

Introduction	45
Spatial Aptitude Analysis	46
Analysis of a Spatial Visualization Task	49
Engineering Design and Graphics	61
Conclusions and Future Directions	74
References	76

4. Theoretically Based Psychometric Measures of Inductive Reasoning
Earl C. Butterfield, Donn Nielsen, Kenneth L. Tangen, and Michael B. Richardson

Introduction	77
Describing and Generating Letter Series	78
Two Theories of Letter Series Continuation	93
Experimental Tests of Theories of Letter Series Continuation	101
Five Conclusions	123
Two Theoretically Derived Psychometric Measures of Inductive Reasoning	125
Summary	133
Appendix	134
References	147

5. Cognitive Analyses of Tests: Implications for Redesign
Richard E. Snow and Penelope L. Peterson

Introduction	149
Basic Examples	150
Recent Advances	155
Conclusion	163
References	164

III. LATENT TRAIT MODELS FOR TEST DESIGN

6. The Assessment of Learning Effects with Linear Logistic Test Models
Hans Spada and Barry McGaw

Introduction	169
The Linear Logistic Test Model	170

Four Logistic Models of Learning between
  Tests   181
Learning and the Validity of Logistic Test
  Models   189
References   191

7. Multicomponent Latent Trait Models for Test Design
Susan E. Embretson (Whitely)

Introduction   195
Test Design and Construct Validity   196
Component Latent Trait Models   200
Conclusion   216
References   217

8. Psychometric Models for Speed-Test Construction:
The Linear Exponential Model
Hartmann Scheiblechner

Speed in Psychological Research   219
The Model   225
Simplification and Generalization of the
  Model: Monotone Probabilistic Additive
  Conjoint Measurement Structure (MPAM)   236
Appendix I   239
Appendix II   242
References   243

9. A Latent Trait Model for Items with Response
Dependencies: Implications for Test Construction and
Analysis
David Andrich

Introduction   245
The Rating Mechanism and Associated
  Models   247
An Elaboration of the Dispersion Location
  Model   251
Two Contexts for the Application of the
  DLIM (DLM of Items)   254
The DLIM and Dependence among
  Responses   257

The Illustrative Data Sets   262
Discussion and Implications for Test
Construction   271
Acknowledgments   273
References   273

IV. TEST DESIGN FROM THE TEST
     DEVELOPMENT PERSPECTIVE

10. Speculations on the Future of Test Design
     Isaac I. Bejar

               Introduction   279
               Technology and Test Design   279
               Cognitive Science and Psychometrics   284
               Concluding Comments   292
               References   292

Author Index   295
Subject Index   299

Contributors

Numbers in parentheses indicate the pages on which the authors' contributions begin.

David Andrich (245), Department of Education, The University of Western Australia, Nedlands, Western Australia 6009

Isaac I. Bejar (279), Division of Measurement Research and Services, Educational Testing Service, Princeton, New Jersey 08541

Earl C. Butterfield (77), Cognitive Studies GS-27, University of Washington, Seattle, Washington 98195

Susan E. Embretson (3, 195), Department of Psychology, University of Kansas, Lawrence, Kansas 66045

Barry McGaw (169), Murdoch University, Western Australia 6150

Timothy P. McNamara[1] (21), Department of Psychology, Yale University, New Haven, Connecticut 06520

Randall J. Mumaw (45), School of Education, University of California, Santa Barbara, California 93106

Donn Nielsen (77), Cognitive Studies GS-27, University of Washington, Seattle, Washington 98195

James W. Pellegrino (45), School of Education, University of California, Santa Barbara, California 93106

Penelope L. Peterson (149), Department of Educational Psychology, University of Wisconsin-Madison, Wisconsin Center for Education Research, Madison, Wisconsin 53706

Michael B. Richardson (77), Cognitive Studies GS-27, University of Washington, Seattle, Washington 98195

Hartmann Scheiblechner (219), Fachbereich Psychologie, Universität Marburg, D-3550 Marburg (Lahn), Federal Republic of Germany

---

[1] Present address: Department of Psychology, Vanderbilt University, Nashville, Tennessee 37240.

Valerie J. Shute (45), School of Education, University of California, Santa Barbara, California 93106

Richard E. Snow (149), School of Education, Stanford University, Stanford, California 94305

Hans Spada (169), Psychologisches Institut, Universität Freiburg, D-7800 Freiburg, Federal Republic of Germany

Robert J. Sternberg (21), Department of Psychology, Yale University, New Haven, Connecticut 06520

Kenneth L. Tangen (77), Cognitive Studies GS-27, University of Washington, Seattle, Washington 98195

Preface

That psychological and educational tests have been sharply criticized is amply documented by the number of articles and lawsuits that concern test validity. Although the test publishers point to correlations of tests with socially important criteria to support their own tests, the critics are concerned more directly with the skills, knowledge, and processes that are involved in solving the test items. Unfortunately, test developers cannot be certain that they have this kind of information about their tests. The traditional approach to psychological measurement has had neither the theoretical foundation nor the psychometric models that could specify explicitly those substantive qualities of test stimuli or of persons that underlie responses.

However, more recent developments in psychology and psychometrics offer a new approach to psychological measurement known as test design. The assumption underlying this approach is that the qualities to be measured can be elicited by the design of the test stimuli. The purpose of this volume is to make available to a wide audience the diverse developments that contribute to a psychometrics of test design. Each of the chapters is an original scholarly contribution and should interest the experts in the field. However, each chapter is addressed to a broad audience and is intended to make test design accessible to a reader with a general background in psychological or educational research. The volume is intended both as a professional book and as a supplementary textbook for a graduate-level course in psychological and educational measurement.

The introductory chapter examines the problem of test design and integrates the topics of the chapters. The first major section of the book presents substantive developments that can be used for test design. The authors of the chapters in this section seek to span the gap between theory and measurement by providing examples of concepts and methods that can be implemented in test design. Three chapters discuss task characteristics and research on the design of test-item stimuli according to theoretical properties. The fourth reviews the relevance to test format, instructions, and stimulus content of the research on learner characteristics and their interactions with treatments.

The second section of the volume presents several psychometric models that quantify the theoretical variables in the test stimuli. Like the latent-trait models that are now popular in American psychometrics, these models offer many statistical advantages for such problems as item banking, test equating, and computerized adaptive testing. However, these models differ from other latent-trait models in that they (1) contain parameters to represent the substantive qualities of items that have been specified in the design of the test and (2) provide statistical tests for alternative hypotheses about the nature of the theoretical mechanisms that contribute to test performance. Although some of these models were influential in European psychometrics in the 1970s, nontechnical presentations of the models have not been available to American psychometricians. The chapters in this section provide a nontechnical introduction to each model and several examples to illustrate applications to design features of tests. The authors of the chapters are the primary developers of these models.

The last section consists of a single chapter, which discusses the contribution of the chapters to psychological testing.

I

Introduction to Test Design

1

Introduction to the Problem of Test Design

Susan E. Embretson (Whitely)

INTRODUCTION

The goal of this book is to present recent developments in psychology and psychometrics that can contribute to the design of psychological tests. Test design has a very explicit meaning in this book. Test design is specifying the aspects of individual differences that a test measures by constructing and/or selecting items according to their substantive properties.

DESIDERATA FOR TEST DESIGN

The preceding definition of test design envisions the test developer as an experimenter who controls the theoretical variables that are represented in the task by carefully selecting, controlling, or counterbalancing the stimulus content. Historically, such test design has seemed to be an impossible goal. Cronbach's (1957) article on the two scientific disciplines of psychology noted that the test developer is trained in a different discipline (i.e., correlational psychology) than is the experimentalist.

Today, however, although the goals of correlational and experimental psychology may still differ substantially, their methods are becoming more similar. Experiments, particularly those influenced by information-processing theory, often use within-subject designs in which the person is presented several tasks that operationalize various theoretical constructs. Increasingly, the tasks consist of meaningful material, such as reading

Copyright © 1985 by Academic Press, Inc.
All rights of reproduction in any form reserved.
ISBN 0-12-238180-7

problems, analogies, or series completions that are systematically varied to reflect differences in the relevant constructs. Correlational studies also present several tasks to each subject, such as reading problems, analogies, and series completions. The goal, however, is to measure individual differences.

The similarity of methods and tasks between contemporary experimental psychology and correlational psychology makes test design a feasible goal. That is, a set of tasks both can measure individual differences and can be designed to represent specified theoretical constructs. But test design requires that substantive theory and psychometric methods be applied *jointly*. Tests cannot be designed by their substantive properties unless the variables that determine item responses have been explicated. In essence, understanding item responses requires a theory of the variables that are involved in item performance. Thus, psychological theory (and thus experimentation) is a fundamental aspect of test design.

Psychometric methods for linking the substantive properties of items to individual differences are equally crucial for test design. The theoretical variables that influence item responses do not necessarily contribute to individual differences. Therefore a psychometric model is needed to clarify how manipulating a specified aspect of the item task influences the attributes that are measured by a person's test performance. Because psychological theories typically postulate *several* variables that influence task performance, psychometric methods that can assess the contribution of multiple independent variables are required. Further, to be useful for test design, the impact of each independent variable should be assessed for individual items.

Test design is strongly related to construct validity. As I have elaborated elsewhere (Embretson,[1] 1983), the construct validity of a test depends on both construct representation and nomothetic span. *Construct representation* concerns the theoretical constructs that explain responses to the item task. Experiments designed to decompose tasks can explicate these constructs. By selecting items according to the relative impact of various constructs, tests can be designed to represent specified aspects of individual differences.

However, it is important to note that any given construct may or may not have implications for the measuring individual differences. Individuals may not vary on the construct or the construct may be too highly correlated with another construct in the target population. Or, perhaps the given construct does not contribute to the validity of the test to predict external variables. Thus, nomothetic span must be assessed. *Nomothetic span*

---

[1] S. E. Whitely is now S. E. Embretson.

measures the utility of the test for measuring individual differences. It is supported by the frequency, pattern, and magnitude of correlations of test scores with other variables.

A joint analysis of construct representation and nomothetic span has real advantages for construct validation research. That is, the external validity of the test can be explained from the theoretical constructs that are operationalized in the item task. Elsewhere (Embretson, 1983), I have shown how explanation is achieved when measurements of individual differences on the underlying constructs account for the test variance and its validity for predicting external measurements.

CURRENT PRACTICES IN TEST DEVELOPMENT

Standard practice in test development is not much like test design as defined here. Item writing is more of an art than a science. Test development units typically are not staffed by persons who have expertise in either the psychological theories that are relevant to the items or the research methods that can test such theories. Instead, test developers tend to have expertise in content areas, such as English or history, or in curriculum development.

The item specifications that guide the actual generation of items reflect the nonpsychological background of the test development units. These specifications often consist of some general guidelines about item structure and format and some rules of thumb and desiderata for the subject matter of the items. For the most part, the specifications are not based on empirical research. An exception are guidelines that are based on Millman, Bishop, and Ebel's (1965) analysis of test-wiseness principles. These principles provide guidelines for item writers, such as avoiding giving away the answer by the wording of the stem and avoiding distractors with the terms *always* or *never*.

In general, the test developer's specifications have little connection with psychological research. First, the relationship of the specifications to psychological theory of the item task is, at best, tenuous. The variables that are contained in typical item specifications clearly are not the variables of psychological theories. Second, the effect of the item specification variables on item difficulty and item quality often has little or no empirical support.

To be fair to current test development staff, it must be noted that their item-writing practices, in conjunction with psychometric analysis of item responses, have produced tests with good predictive validity. It is the link of the test to psychological theory, and hence its construct validity, that has been problematic and that is at issue here.

CURRENT ISSUES IN TESTING AND TEST DESIGN

Several pressures on the field of psychological testing indicate that test design may be quite important in the future. The individual test item and its properties are increasingly becoming major focuses in testing. Due to litigation regarding testing and to public pressure, many test developers routinely disclose the items on which selection or admissions decisions are made. Because the disclosed tests cannot be reused, new items must be constructed for future forms of the test. The equivalence of these items across forms is essential for equating scores among the many resulting test forms. The stimulus features of the items and the constructs that they operationalize can have major importance for test equivalence.

Another development that focuses on the individual item is computerized adaptive testing. In computerized adaptive testing, an individual receives a subset of test items that are optimal for precisely measuring his or her ability level. Computerized adaptive testing will most likely be operationalized soon on the Armed Services Vocational Aptitude Battery (see Green, Bock, Humphreys of Reckase, 1982 for an evaluation plan). If the past history of psychological testing repeats itself, the military developments in computerized adaptive testing will be followed in the private sector within a few years.

A major implication of adaptive testing is that tests no longer have a fixed content for all persons. Instead, items are selected from a large bank according to the information they yield about the person's ability level.

Computerized adaptive testing is made feasible by latent-trait models. Item banking and equating scores from the subsets is accomplished by latent-trait models, which calibrate both the person and the item on the ability or abilities that underlie performance. Latent-trait models also specify the degree of precision that is obtained for each person, given the items that have been administered. For the Rasch (1960) latent-trait model precision depends only on item difficulty, which is optimal when the person has a probability of .50 of passing the item.

However, flexible content tests may change the aspects of individual differences that are measured in at least two ways if the substantive features of items are not considered. First, a small item subset, although optimally selected to provide efficient information about the person's ability level, may not represent the various facets of task performance as compared to the item bank as a whole. Thus, the aspects of individual differences that are reflected in different subsets may vary. Although items are examined for goodness of fit to the latent trait model during the basic calibrations, the adequacy of these goodness-of-fit tests are controversial. Inadequacies in assessing model fit can have important implications for how item subsets vary in assessing individual differences.

Second, the mixture of items in the subset may change the task demands. The context of a specific subset may be quite unrepresentative of the item bank as a whole. Perhaps the subset contains a much broader or much narrower mixture of item types. Results from cognitive component analysis of aptitude (R. J. Sternberg, 1980) shows that an item set can be constructed either to require different strategies from item to item or to require only a single strategy. Choosing the optimal strategy is a critical aspect of performance in the former item set but not in the latter.

In current implementations of computerized adaptive testing, unfortunately, neither the representativeness of the item facets nor the mixture of items is controlled during item selection. It is hoped that by bringing together recent developments in the cognitive analysis of aptitude and in latent-trait theory that the reader may be able to develop a format with which to understand this issue.

ORGANIZATION OF THE BOOK

Two major sections in the book contain most of the chapters: Part II, Design Variables from Psychological Theory, and Part III, Latent-Trait Models for Test Design. The last section, Part IV, Test Design from the Test Development Perspective, contains a single chapter that considers the future of test design.

The section "Design Variables from Psychological Theory" contains four chapters that focus on understanding aptitude tests by explicating the cognitive variables that determine performance. Methods for identifying the impact of theoretical variables in a task (i.e., task composition methods) are crucial for linking aptitude to cognitive theory. Three chapters were invited to illustrate task decomposition on specific item types. The item types that were selected include vocabulary, spatial constructions, and series completions. Although these chapters examine only a few of the many item types that appear on tests, three major abilities are included — verbal ability, spatial ability, and inductive reasoning, respectively.

The authors of the chapters were encouraged to summarize the cognitive literature on the task so that someone with little formal background in cognitive psychology would have access to the relevant findings. However, the major emphasis is to show illustrations of the authors' own research as applied to the item type. Thus, each chapter contains specific design variables for the item type that can be implemented in test construction.

It should also be noted that the task decomposition methods that are shown in the chapters are by no means exhaustive. The chapters focus on decomposing a single task to illustrate basic principles. It is hoped that by understanding these tasks thoroughly the reader will be able to generalize to other item types and other task decomposition methods.

Each chapter shows a different aspect of test design and illustrates a cognitive analysis of an item type. Sternberg and McNamara (Chapter 2 in this volume) decompose both the *cognitive representation* and *cognitive processing* of vocabulary items. Although vocabulary is a good single index of verbal intelligence, a cognitive explanation of performance on these items has received little attention. Sternberg and McNamara's chapter innovatively operationalizes into mathematical models the various theories of how word meaning is represented cognitively. They show how items vary in representing characteristic attributes and defining attributes, which in turn influences the difficulty of the various processing events that are involved in item solving. The chapter also examines strategies for processing vocabulary items, which are defined by the sequences and types of comparisons of the target word to the alternatives.

The reader should consider two major implications of Sternberg and McNamara's analysis of vocabulary items for test design. First, the variables of Sternberg and McNamara's theory of the task can be used to control the difficulty of representation and processing for each item. Second, the construct validity of vacabulary items is further explicated by understanding the representation and processing variables involved in item solving. This information can be used to evaluate the item type as a whole with regard to the intended goals of the test.

The chapter by Pellegrino, Mumaw, and Cantoni (Chapter 3 in this volume) examines the processing on a task that measures spatial visualization ability, the Minnesota Paper Form Board task. This task requires the examinee to compare two figures for identity. Like Sternberg and McNamara's analysis, Pellegrino *et al.*'s process decomposition of the task contributes to test design by providing item selection information and by explicating construct validity.

Some interesting issues emerge in Pellegrino *et al.*'s methods for task decomposition. Their results includes a parallel analysis of response times and response errors. The reader should be aware that combining the results from the two analyses can be complex. The error modeling seems most directly relevant to the goals of testing, since the most popular psychometric index (i.e., total score) is inversely related to number of errors. The results on response errors answer the question of which processes contribute to errors in performance and, hence, which processes are important in individual differences in ability. However, the response time data are needed to support a theoretical variable as a real-time event in processing.

The relationship of response time to error is very complex. An event that is identified by response time analysis may or may not contribute to errors. Further, speed and accuracy often trade off so that a response that is executed too fast is more likely to be inaccurate (Scheiblechner, Chapter 8 in this volume, elaborates on this relationship). Or, time can influence the strategies that are feasible for item solving. In spatial items, for example, several findings suggest that verbal–analytic strategies are ineffective under highly speeded conditions.

Another issue the reader should keep in mind regarding Pellegrino *et al.*'s discussion is that of the isolation of effects versus psychometric quality. In psychometric items, the theoretical factors are usually confounded and thus correlated so that it is impossible to separate fully the independent effects of the design variables. To analyze the task, items that are similar in content to the Minnesota Paper Form Board task are created, but the set is counterbalanced for the primary factors that are postulated to underlie performance. However, their comparability to psychometric items is not fully assured by this procedure.

An important feature of the Pellegrino *et al.* results is an analysis of a criterion task that the spatial visualization task predicts. Although the data are from small samples, the results are suggestive in that they indicate that the efficiency of a strategy for processing engineering drawing tasks depends on a complex interaction of the task demands and the person's ability level. These data suggest that the validity of spatial ability tests to predict this criterion depends on the correspondence of the components that are involved in performance. This is another important aspect of test design. Specifying the components to be measured that yield the maximum validity or differential validity.

Butterfield, Nielsen, Tangen, and Richardson (Chapter 4 in this volume) present a model that predicts the difficulty of series completion tasks. The series completion task has been important in measuring inductive reasoning, as shown by its inclusion on the Primary Mental Abilities Test (Thurstone & Thurstone, 1941). The series completion task has also been studied by several cognitive theorists (e.g., Simon & Kotovsky, 1963) because the task requires basic reasoning but is relatively content-free. Butterfield *et al.*'s model is so successful in predicting accuracy that it may be useful to anticipate item difficulty before empirical tryouts.

A very intriguing aspect of Butterfield *et al.*'s chapter (in this volume) is the possibility of objectively constructing a whole domain of literally millions of series completions. The design variables are sufficiently well specified that items to fit can be generated by computer. Thus, item construction can be wholly objective.

The issue of isolation of effect versus psychometric quality achieves new clarity in Butterfield *et al.*'s chapter. They note the need for counterbalanced designs to isolate effects, which is readily achievable from their item specification system. However, they note that the objectivity of the item specifications allows a direct analysis of the domain representativeness of psychometric items. Butterfield *et al.* suggest that psychometric items may be a very special subset of the task domain.

Snow and Peterson (Chapter 5 in this volume) examine test design on a different level from the preceeding three chapters. They are concerned with molar variables rather than molecular variables. That is, they are concerned about manipulations that influence performance on a related block of items, rather than about differences between individual items. They postulate that what is reflected by a score over a block of items depends substantially on conditions that influence the whole item set, such as format, instructions, practice, or strategy training.

Snow and Peterson suggest that combining aptitude treatment interaction (ATI) research methods with cognitive information processing analysis (CIP) is needed to understand fully the cognitive basis of scores. They present examples of studies in which global conditions, such as permitting note taking during testing or providing more concrete items, influence the cognitive processes that are reflected in the score. They recommend that such manipulations can be used systematically so that differences in performance between conditions can be scored to represent the processes that are manipulated. Systematic manipulation of item blocks represents a challenge to psychometrics because score differences (which have been controversial) may be the primary data.

Snow and Peterson review CIP research in four areas—cognitive correlate, cognitive component, cognitive content, and cognitive training—for relevance to global features of the test. This review suggests some interesting new directions for research on psychological tests.

LATENT-TRAIT MODELS FOR TEST DESIGN

Rather than focus on general test theory models, Section III specializes in latent-trait models that can be used in test design. Theoretically, interest in latent-trait models (also called item response theory) has replaced classical test theory in psychometrics. Latent-trait models explain many of the relationships contained in classical test theory. Most importantly, however, latent-trait models are crucial in item banking and equating test scores across different item subsets. As indicated earlier, latent-trait models are crucial for computerized adaptive testing, which may be a major method of testing in the future.

Interestingly, the use of latent-trait models for test design preceded the impact of cognitive psychology on testing that is exemplified by several chapters in the section on psychological theory. Several European psychometricians (Fischer, 1973; Scheiblechner, 1972; Spada, 1973) developed and applied the linear logistic latent-trait model (LLTM), which is an extension of the Rasch latent-trait model. The LLTM links item responses to theoretical variables that are scored for each item. Most of this work was published in German (e.g., Scheiblechner, 1972; Spada, 1976). The few English-language publications that resulted were not readily available (e.g., Spada & Kempf, 1977). Furthermore, most applications were linked to theories that have had little impact on psychological testing (i.e., structural learning theory and Piaget's developmental theory). Although this work has become more available to U.S. researchers (Fischer, 1978, Fischer & Forman, 1982), it has not been linked to current substantive influences on psychological testing. I hope that the application of LLTM will be encouraged by bringing together discussion of both the substantive influences on testing and these psychometric methods in the same volume.

More recently, a family of latent-trait models has been developed and applied that complements the information-processing approach to understanding aptitude. The multicomponent latent-trait model (MLTM) (Whitely, 1980) measures item and person differences in component difficulties. These models have been applied to several item types (Whitely, 1981) that have been studied by cognitive component theory. More recently (Embretson, in press), a generalization of MLTM has been developed: the general component latent-trait model (GLTM), which combines MLTM and LLTM. Research for applications of these models is in progress.

This section includes chapters by two of the original developers of LLTM, Hans Spada (Spada & McGaw, Chapter 6) and Hartman Scheiblechner (Chapter 8), and by myself, the developer of MLTM (Susan Embretson [Whitely] Chapter 7). A chapter by David Andrich (Chapter 9) was also invited. Andrich has developed some extensions of the Rasch model to handle special types of data. The current selection is a new model that handles the problem of linked items within the test. Used in a hypotheses-testing framework, as emphasized by Andrich, the model complements the other models.

Spada and McGaw (Chapter 6, this volume) devote about half of their chapter to summarizing LLTM. The LLTM can be readily applied to item accuracy response data, such as presented by Pellegrino *et al.* and Butterfield *et al.* To summarize, LLTM basically regresses item difficulty (scaled by a latent-trait model) on scored predictors. The predictors may be dichotomous variables to represent the presence or absence of operations in an item. For example, different operations are represented by spatial items that vary in rotation, separation, and displacement in Pellegrino *et al.*'s

.chapter. Or the predictors can be a scored variable that represents the level
or difficulty of a postulated operation, such as Butterfield *et al.*'s number of
moving strings or level of knowledge variable.

The LLTM is important for test design in two ways. First, calibrating
parameters for LLTM in an item set can permit selection of items that have
specified sources of effects on item responses. The LLTM calibrations can
be used to bank items by the scored variables. If the scored variables operationalize a theory, then the items can be selected by the contribution of
underlying theoretical components. Second, it may be possible to construct
items having specified sources of difficulty. Spada and McGaw note that
good prediction of item difficulty has been obtained for newly constructed
items from the scored variables weighted by the LLTM parameters for contribution to item difficulty.

However, Spada and McGaw continue beyond LLTM to present four
additional extensions of the Rasch latent-trait model that measure learning
effects. At the time they wrote the chapter, the major developments for
LLTM were already a decade old. And, of course, these psychometricians
had moved to new problems, which were the topics that they wanted to
contribute to the book—rather than summarizing LLTM again, in English. The complete elaboration of these models as a set has only recently
been published (Rost & Spada, in press) in German, although some of the
models appear in Spada and Kempf (1977). The structural form of the
models originates with Scheiblechner (1972).

Interestingly, the learning models presented by Spada and McGaw complement the new substantive directions envisioned by Snow and Peterson.
That is, Snow and Peterson discuss manipulations of instructions, practice,
and the set surrounding testing to measure different aspects of individual
differences. Spada and McGaw's model for person-specific learning effects
could be a means for measuring the changes in ability that are due to manipulating conditions, yet retain the item-banking properties of a LLTM
model.

My chapter (Chapter 7) begins with a conceptual model for test design.
Ability, as measured by test scores, is conceptualized as an intervening
variable that summarizes relationships between underlying cognitive-processing variables and external measures. The weights of the various cognitive variables in the test score determine the nature of the ability. Ability is
then linked to test design. The stimulus features of items are conceptualized
as controlling the components that are involved in performance. These
components combine into one or more strategies that can be applied to solve
an item. Thus, ability to solve items depends on the person's performance
on the various strategies, which, in turn, depend on performance of the
component-processing events. The test developer can control the difficulty
of the components by the stimulus features.

Several extensions of the Rasch model for measuring cognitive processing variables are presented. The MLTM contains a mathematical model of the relationship of the component events to item solving and a psychometric model that locates both persons and items on each component event. The components are measured by responses to item subtasks that are postulated to represent the component. A new MLTM for items with multiple strategies is also presented.

The GLTM links the components to the stimulus features of the items. In essence, GLTM models the difficulty of a component in an item from scored variables that reflect varying stimulus features. Taken together, the various component latent-trait models can operationalize the conceptual model of test design. Chapter 7 gives examples of controlling component difficulty by stimulus features and of how to select items to reflect individual differences only on specified components and strategies.

Scheiblechner (Chapter 8) presents a psychometric model for response-time data, the linear exponential model (LEM). Rather than model accuracy probabilities, LEM predicts response time. Because response time is a continuous variable, though, a probability distribution for a range of response times is predicted rather than the single probability, as predicted by the accuracy models.

Like other psychometric models, LEM predicts individual response times in a psychometric model in which both persons and items have parameters. The LEM gives a prediction for a person with a certain ability to respond quickly to a specified item that has a certain propensity to be solved rapidly.

The LEM gives these parameters for persons and items in the context of a psychometric model that has the specific objectivity properties of the Rasch latent-trait model. That is, the total response time is a sufficient statistic for estimating an ability and the item parameters do not depend on the ability level of the sample. Thus, LEM is useful for item banking and equating measures, just as is a latent-trait model.

Scheiblechner also notes that LEM has the capability of using stimulus design features to predict item difficulty in the model, just as LLTM has. For example, the predictors of the item easiness parameters could be a model such as given by Sternberg and McNamara for real-time processing of vocabulary items. Or traditional laboratory tasks such as the S. Sternberg task (1970) or the Posner (1971) could be modeled. Scheiblechner elaborates an example of applying LEM to the Posner task, where the design features categorize the item as to type. However, the reader should note that design structures with continuous variables are also possible. For example, a major variable that determines response time for the S. Sternberg task is the number of digits presented. This may be easily incorporated into LEM as a single predictor of item response time.

The reader should note that LEM postulates a definite relationship between time and accuracy. That is, the response is correct if sufficient time is available. Errors arise from insufficient time, not lack of knowledge. Thus, this model is appropriate for items that appear on "speeded" tests or over-learned tasks that are often used to study real-time processing in cognitive psychology.

Andrich (Chapter 9) presents an extension of the Rasch latent-trait model that can be applied to linked dichotomous response items, such as items with a common stem (e.g., multiple questions to a common reading passage) or subtasks of the same item. The lack of models for linked items has had some unfortunate effects on test design. Stems with multiple questions have been treated as if the questions were independent items. Unfortunately, the items have dependencies (i.e., due to having the common stem as a prerequisite) so that the local independence assumption for latent-trait models is violated. Because the models do not provide adequate description of the data, item banking for linked items is a problem. This has led to eliminating linked items from tests. However, the longer stems of linked items may operationalize somewhat different cognitive processes than the shorter stems of independent items.

Subtasks also have not been used due to inadequate psychometric models. Two types of subtasks that are particularly interesting from the perspective of cognitive theory are both multiple-stage items, in which several separate outcomes are needed to solve the item. If the item is the completion type, then the number of correctly completed subtasks can be counted. If the item is multiple choice, an intriguing possibility is to design distractors to give maximum information about the person's performance. That is, the distractors can reflect answers that result from responding correctly to only some of the stages.

However, neither of the subtask item formats has been used extensively in psychological tests, presumably because no adequate model for treating the dependencies among solving the subtasks had been postulated. Andrich's model for linked items is an extension of Andrich's earlier model for ordered response categories. The model gives the probability that a person with a certain ability will respond in a particular category to a specified item. Given that the linked items or subtasks have sequential dependencies, the model gives the probability of solving the given item or subtask and, consequently, its prerequisites.

Andrich's model includes an ability parameter for each person and a location (i.e., overall difficulty) for the item. The specific category probability depends on the distances between the category thresholds, which are added to ability and location in the exponent of the latent-trait model. Thus, if ability is lower than the location of the item, the person will have the highest response probability in a lower category.

The reader should note that the probabilities for the middle categories are shaped like normal curves. Thus, a person with an ability that is at the location of the item will have a high probability for a middle category and a low probability for responding to *either* of the extreme categories.

The DLM (dispersion location model) that is presented for the first time here assumes equal distances between the thresholds. Thus, the category response model requires only two parameters for each item — location and dispersion (which is also a scaling parameter for threshold distances).

The last chapter in the book (Chapter 10) constitutes its own section. Isaac Bejar speculates on the future of test design and the possible contribution of the psychological and psychometric developments that are contained in this book. Bejar examines test design from the perspective of actual implementation by major test publishers. Bejar notes that, in fact, testing has been changing rapidly. Computers are changing testing in three areas: (1) test administration, (2) test assembly, and (3) test generation (i.e., item writing).

According to Bejar, changes due to computer technology can be superficial. However, computerized test administration has led to fundamental changes resulting from the development of the latent trait models. Computerized testing can use latent-trait models to adapt the items to a person's ability level. This permits precise measurements to be obtained from the fewest possible items. Computerized adaptive testing also means that fixed content tests will be less prevalent in the future. Thus, Bejar views latent-trait models as becoming increasingly important.

Test assembly is the selection of items to compose a test by their various properties, including difficulty, discrimination, and content. Test assembly by computer is just beginning, according to Bejar, and should lead to more objective and well-specified tests. I see test assembly by computer as particularly intriquing because complex counterbalancing of the various stimulus features is possible. The theoretical variables noted in Part II can provide criteria for test assembly if the impact of the features on performance is known. The various psychometric models that are presented in the book (LLTM, MLTM, GLTM, LEM, DLM) provide parameters from which tests can be assembled by their substantive features.

Test generation by computer seems futuristic. Bejar notes that the item form (Hively, 1974) is sufficiently objective for test generation, but its applicability is too limited. Interestingly, Butterfield *et al.* (Chapter 4 in this volume) have developed a system that could, indeed, be implemented by computer. Perhaps cognitive theories for other item types could be sufficiently precise to specify the item domain as for the Butterfield *et al.* type. Computerized test generation, in a sense, seems to be a utopia for test design.

Bejar's chapter is particularly useful for understanding the innovations in, and the constraints that surround, test development. In the various sections, current and recent past practices are noted. If test design as envisioned in this volume is to become a reality, the goals, practices, and constraints of the test developers must be fully considered.

I must conclude this introduction with a disclaimer. The volume certainly is not the last word in test design. It represents the state of the art rather than an integrated conclusion. But I hope that the book helps the reader to ask new questions about tests and to find new ways of addressing old problems in tests. The reader should view the book as an invitation and a challenge for future work in test design.

REFERENCES

Cronbach, L. (1957). The two disciplines of scientific psychology. *American Psychologist, 12,* 671–684.
Embretson, S. E. (1984). A general latent trait model for response processes. *Psychometrika, 49,* 175–186.
Embretson, S. E. (1983). Construct validity: Construct representation versus monothetic span. *Psychological Bulletin, 93,* 179–197.
Fischer, G. (1973). Linear logistic test model as an instrument in educational research. *Acta Psychologica, 37,* 359–374.
Fischer, G. (1978). Probabilistic test models and their applications. *German Journal of Psychology, 2,* 298–319.
Fischer, G., & Forman, A. K. (1982). Some applications of logistic latent trait models with linear constraints on the parameters. *Applied Psychological Measurement, 6,* 397–416.
Green, B. F., Bock, R. D., Humphreys, L. G., Linn, R. L. & Reckase, M. Evaluation plan for the computerized adaptive vocational testing battery. Technical Report 82-1 for Office of Naval Research. Department of Psychology, Johns Hopkins University, Baltimore: May, 1982.
Hively, W. (1974). Introduction to domain referenced testing. *Educational Technology, 14,* 5–7.
Millman, J., Bishop, C. H., & Ebel, R. (1965). An analysis of test-wiseness. *Educational and Psychological Measurement, 25,* 707–726.
Posner, M. I., & Boies, S. (1971). Components of attention. *Psychological Review, 78,* 391–408.
Rasch, G. *Probabilistic models for some intelligence and attainment tests.* Copenhagen: Pedagogiske Institut, 1960.
Rost, J., & Spada, H. (in press). Die Quantifizierung von Lerneffeckten Anhand von testdaten [The quantification of Learning effects with the aid of test data]. *Zeitschrift für Differentielle und Diagnostische Psycholgie [Journal for differential and diagnostic psych.].*
Scheiblechner, H. (1972). Das Lernen und Losen Komplexer Denkaufgaben [Learning & Solving of complex (thought or mental) problems]. *Zeitschrift für Experimentelle und Angewandte Psychologie [Journal of experimental and applied psychology], 19,* 476–506.
Simon, H. A., & Kotovsky, K. (1963). Human acquisition of concepts for sequential patterns. *Psychological Review, 70,* 534–546.
Spada, H. (1973). Die Analyse kognitivier Lerneffekte mit Stichprobenunabhängigen verfahren [The analysis of cognitive learning effects with procedures independent of random

samplings]. In K. Frey & M. Lang (Eds.) *Kognitronspsychologie und naturwissenschaftlicher Unterricht [Cognitive Psychology and Scientific-Instruction]*, (pp. 94–131). Bern: Huber.

Spada, H. (1976). *Modelle des Denkens und Lernens, [Models of thinking and learning]*. Bern: Huber.

Spada, H., & Kempf, W. F. (Eds.) (1977). *Structural models of thinking and learning*. Bern: Huber.

Sternberg, R. J. (1980). Sketch of a componential subtheory of human intelligence. *Behavioral and Brain Sciences, 3*, 573–614.

Sternberg, S. (1970). Memory scanning: Mental processes revealed by reaction time experiments. In S. S. Antrobus (Ed.), *Cognition and affect*. Boston: Little, Brown.

Thurstone, L. L., & Thurstone, T. G. (1941). Factorial studies of intelligence. *Psychometric Monographs* (Whole no. 2).

Whitely, S. E. (1980). Multicomponent latent trait models for ability tests. *Psychometrika, 45*, 479–494.

Whitely, S. E. (1981). Measuring aptitude processes with multicomponent latent trait models. *Journal of Educational Measurement, 18*, 67–84.

II

Design Variables from Psychological Theory

ehension should serve as the cornerstone for an understanding of
ence. Behind such a contention would be the well-known fact that
st widely used test of verbal comprehension ability, vocabulary, is
the best indicators—if not the single best indicator—of a person's
level of intelligence (see, e.g., Jensen, 1980; Matarazzo, 1972). Yet
derstanding of verbal comprehension skills is minimal. Certainly, we
ery little idea, at present, why vocabulary, which is about as explicit a
re of achievement as can be provided, should furnish such a good
f intelligence, which is supposed only to be mirrored in achievement.
chapter presents a description of a theory and data from a newly
ated research program that seeks to understand real-time verbal com-
sion. In particular, the research seeks an understanding of what
is in real time when a person processes verbal relations, as in a syn-
test. The chapter is divided into three major parts. First, we review
alternative approaches to understanding the nature of verbal com-
sion, discussing some of the positive contributions but also some of
itations of each. Next, we present our theory of real-time verbal
ehension (which is an exemplification of one of the approaches de-
in the first part of the chapter) and provide some data supporting the
. Finally, we discuss the implications of the theory and data for the
and analysis of mental ability tests.

ERNATIVE APPROACHES TO LYZING VERBAL COMPREHENSION

rnative approaches to analyzing verbal comprehension skills can be
d up in many ways, but for our purposes, we choose to divide them
vo major groups: those approaches that seek to understand anteced-
f developed verbal ability and those that seek to understand current
functioning. We consider here a highly selected sample of research
ms following each of these two approaches.

OACHES EMPHASIZING ANTECEDENTS OF RENT FUNCTIONING

roaches emphasizing antecedents of current functioning can in turn
ided into three subapproaches—a bottom-up one, a top-down one,
knowledge-based one. We consider each of these three subapproaches
n.

om-up Subapproaches

tom-up research has emerged from the tradition of investigation ini-
by Hunt (e.g. Hunt, 1978; Hunt, Lunneborg, & Lewis, 1975) and

2

The Repr
Processing of
Re
C

comp
intelli
the m
amon
overa
our un
have
measu
index

Thi
form
prehe
happe
onym
severa
prehe
the li
comp
scribe
theor
desig

ALT
ANA

Alt
divid
into
ents
verba
prog

APP
CUR

A
be di
and a
in tu

Bot

Bo
tiate

INTRODUCTION

Verbal comprehension has played a central part i
gence, albeit in different guises. Thurstone's (19
(V) factor, Cattell's (1971) crystallized ability fac
verbal–educational factor, for example, all deri
measure people's ability to comprehend verbal
large majority of intelligence tests, whether theore
sure verbal comprehension skills either directly (e
or reading comprehension) or indirectly (e.g., by
gies or classifications that require fairly sophistic
solution of problems explicitly constructed to mea
as reasoning). An understanding of intelligence s
standing of verbal comprehension skills as one of
One might even go so far as to contend that an

* Preparation of this chapter and the research described in
N0001478C0025 from the Office of Naval Research and Con
Office of Naval Research and Army Research Institute.

All ri

followed up by a number of other investigators (e.g., Jackson & McClelland, 1979; Keating & Bobbitt, 1978; Perfetti & Lesgold, 1977). The basic idea underlying much of this research is that individual differences in developed verbal ability are derived from differences in the speed with which individuals can access overlearned codes in intermediate- and long-term memories. Faster access to those codes results in more efficient and efficacious processing of verbal information, which over the long run results in higher levels of developed verbal skills. In a typical experiment, subjects are presented with the Posner and Mitchell (1967) letter-matching task, which requires rapid recognition of either a physical match (e.g., AA) between two letters or a name match (e.g., AA or Aa) between them. Lexical access time is measured as the difference between name match and physical match time. The typical finding in these experiments is that this difference score correlates about $-.3$ with scores on standardized verbal ability tests.

This subapproach is attractive in its seeking to provide an understanding of current verbal ability in terms of the life-span functioning of basic cognitive processes: Current complex behavior is understood in terms of simpler past behaviors (Hunt, Frost, & Lunneborg, 1973). But there are some problematic aspects of the bottom-up view. We have been and remain concerned that .3-level correlations are abundant in both the abilities and the personality literatures (indeed, they are rather low as ability correlations go), and provide a relatively weak basis for causal inference. A further concern is that most of the studies that have been done on the name minus physical match difference have not used adequate discriminant validation procedures. When such procedures are used, and perceptual speed is considered as well as verbal ability, this difference seems to be much more strongly related to perceptual speed than it is to verbal ability (Lansman, Donaldson, Hunt, & Yantis, 1982; Willis, Cornelius, Blow, & Baltes, 1981), although these findings are subject to alternative interpretations (Earl Hunt, personal communication, 1982). Thus, obtained correlations with verbal ability may reflect, at least in part, variance shared with perceptual abilities of the kind that the letter-matching task seems more able, at least on the surface, to measure. But whatever may be the case, it seems likely that speed of lexical access plays *some* role in verbal comprehension, and what remains to be clarified is just what this role is.

Top-down Subapproaches

The top-down subapproach can be attributed to Werner and Kaplan (1952), who proposed that individual differences in verbal skills can be traced back at least in part to individual differences in the ability of children to acquire meanings of words presented in context. Werner and Kaplan devised a task in which subjects were presented with an imaginary word followed by six sentences using that word. The subject's task was to guess the meaning of the word on the basis of the contextual cues they were able to infer. For example, the imaginary word *contavish*, meaning "hole," was presented in six different contexts, such as "John fell into a contavish in the road." Werner and Kaplan found strategy differences in children ranging in age from 8 to 13 years. The Werner – Kaplan approach was followed up by Daalen-Kapteijns and Elshout-Mohr (1981), who had adult subjects think aloud as they solved Werner–Kaplan-type problems. These investigators proposed a process model of how individuals acquire the word meanings. Of particular interest for present purposes is their finding that high- and low-verbal subjects proceeded through the task in different ways, with the low-verbal subjects using only a subset of the full strategy used by the high-verbal subjects.

Sternberg, Powell, and Kaye (1982) have also used a variant of the top-down subapproach to understand the acquisition of meanings of words presented in context. These investigators used two basic tasks. In one task, subjects were presented with extremely low frequency words embedded in the context of a paragraph in the style of a newspaper article, a history text, a science text, or a literary passage. The subjects' task was to figure out the meanings of the low-frequency words from the context of the passage. In the other task, subjects were presented with single low-frequency affixed words, such as *exsect*. The subjects' task was to figure out the meaning of each word as best they could, and then to choose the best of four possible synonyms. In the former task, the emphasis was on a theoretical account of contextual cues external to the low-frequency word; in the latter task, the emphasis was on a theoretical account of contextual cues internal to the low-frequency word. Their proposed models of cue utilization provided good accounts of how subjects used external and internal cues to infer word meanings. Correlations of scores on the external decontextualization task with verbal intelligence test scores were at the level of about .6.[1]

The results of these investigations provide backing for the claim that vocabulary is a good measure of intelligence because, as Jensen (1980) put it, "the acquisition of word meanings is highly dependent on the *eduction* of meaning from the contexts in which the words are encountered" (p. 146, original emphasis). But although the correlation of task performance with verbal comprehension test scores is higher than that which has been obtained with the (bottom-up) letter-matching task, the nature of the causal link between learning from context and verbal ability has yet to be established. It could be argued that both learning from context and vocabulary level are

---

[1] No psychometric test scores were available for subjects who received the internal decontextualization task.

dependent on some higher-order verbal factor, the nature of which is as yet unknown. And there also seems to be no doubt that a higher level of vocabulary can facilitate the learning of words in context, just as learning from context can facilitate vocabulary development. In sum, this approach, like the bottom-up one, is still in need of a better-articulated and better-demonstrated link between theory and data regarding the development of verbal comprehension skills.

Knowledge-Based Subapproaches

The knowledge-based view assigns a central role to old knowledge in the acquisition of new knowledge. A fairly strong version of this view was taken by Keil (1981), who argued that "structure plays a more important role in understanding many instances of cognitive change in process" (p. 9). Proponents of this approach usually cite instances of differences between expert and novice performance — in verbal and other domains — that seem more to derive from knowledge differences than from processing differences. For example, Chi (1978) has shown that whether children's or adults' recall performance is better depends on the knowledge domain in which the recall takes place and the relative expertise of the children and adults in the respective domains. Children who are outstanding chess players are better at recalling meaningful chessboard positions than are adults who are not chess experts.

We have no argument with the position that the knowledge base is highly important in understanding differences in current performance between experts and novices in both verbal and nonverbal domains. But accounts such as Keil's seem to beg an important question, namely, that of how the differences in knowledge states came about in the first place. For example, why do some people acquire better vocabularies than others? Or in the well-studied domain of chess, why is it that of two individuals given equal intensive and extensive exposure to the game, one will acquire the knowledge structures needed for expertise and the other will not? It seems to us that however important knowledge differences may be in the development of verbal skills, such differences must result at some step along the way from differences in the way information was processed; and it is this kind of difference that bottom-up and top-down subapproaches seek to understand.

APPROACHES EMPHASIZING CURRENT FUNCTIONING

Approaches emphasizing current functioning seem divisible into two subapproaches — those that are essentially molar, dealing with information processing at the level of the word, and those that are essentially molecular, dealing with information processing at the level of word attributes. We shall consider each subapproach in turn.

A Molar Subapproach

Marshalek (1981) administered a faceted vocabulary test along with a battery of standard reasoning and other tests. The facets of the vocabulary test were word abstractness (concrete, medium, abstract), word frequency (low, medium, high), item type (vague recognition, accurate recognition, definition), and blocks (two parallel blocks of words). Marshalek found that vocabulary item difficulty increased with word abstractness, word infrequency, item formats requiring more precise discrimination of word meaning, and with task requirement (such that word definition was harder than word recognition). He also found that partial concepts are prevalent in young adults and that word acquisition is a gradual process. Vocabulary level seemed to be related to reasoning performance at the lower but not the higher end of the vocabulary difficulty distribution. These results led Marshalek to conclude that a certain level of reasoning ability may be a prerequisite for extraction of word meaning. Above this level, the importance of reasoning begins rapidly to decrease.

Marshalek's approach to understanding verbal comprehension is of particular interest because it breaks down global task performance into more specific facets. It is possible, in his research, to assign each subject scores for the various facets of performance as well as for the overall level of performance. We believe this to be an important step toward understanding current verbal functioning. One concern we have, though, is with whether the experimenter-defined facets correspond to important psychological (subject-defined) aspects of performance. Although these facets may differentiate more and less difficult items as well as better and poorer scorers, it is not clear that they do so in a way that bears any resemblance to the psychology of verbal comprehension. In other words, it is not clear how understanding these facets of performance gives what could in any sense be construed as a causal–explanatory account of verbal comprehension and individual differences in it. The causal inferences that can be made are, at best, highly indirect.

A Molecular Subapproach

We have taken the molecular approach in our work on the real-time representation and processing of information during verbal comprehension. The idea is to understand verbal comprehension in terms of how attributes of words are encoded and compared. For example, understanding of performance on a synonyms test would be sought in terms of actual comparisons between the attributes of a given target word and the attributes of the potential synonyms given in a multiple-choice list. At the minimum, it would be necessary to know what kinds of attributes are stored, how these attributes are accessed during verbal comprehension performance, and how these attributes are compared between the target and the options. Our theory of these phenomena and some data testing the theory are presented in the next section of this chapter.

THEORY OF REPRESENTATION AND INFORMATION PROCESSING

ALTERNATIVE MODELS OF WORD REPRESENTATION

Several alternative models have been proposed for how word meaning is represented mentally. We consider here some of the major models that have been proposed.

Defining Attribute (Nonadditive) Models

Traditional models of word meaning make use of necessary and sufficient (i.e., defining) attributes of words (Frege, 1952; Russell, 1956). Such attributes are also sometimes referred to as semantic markers (Katz, 1972). The idea is that the meaning of a word is decomposed into a set of attributes such that the possession of these attributes is necessary and sufficient for a word to refer to a given object or concept. For example, a bachelor might be represented in terms of the attributes *unmarried, male,* and *adult.* Being an unmarried male adult is then viewed as necessary and sufficient for being labeled as a bachelor. (Some might add never-before-married as an additional required attribute.) Traditional models can be viewed as nonadditive in the sense that either a given word has the attributes necessary and sufficient to refer to a given object or concept or it does not have them; there are no gradations built into this model of representation in referring.

Characteristic Attribute (Additive) Models

A second class of models, one that has been more in favor in recent times, might be referred to as the class of characteristic attribute models. In these models, word meaning is conceptualized in terms of attributes that tend to be characteristic of a given object or concept but are neither necessary nor sufficient for reference to that concept. A well-known example of the usefulness of this kind of model stems from Wittgenstein's analysis of the concept of a *game*. It is extremely difficult to speak of necessary attributes of a game. Similarly, it is difficult to speak of any attributes that guarantee that something is a game; hence, it is difficult to find any sufficient attributes of a game. Yet, games bear a family resemblance to each other. Various games can be said to cluster around a prototype for the concept of a game (Rosch, 1978), with games being either closer or further from this prototype depending on the number of characteristic attributes of a game they have. A game such as chess might be viewed as quite close to the hypothetical prototype, whereas a game such as solitaire might be viewed as farther away from the prototype.

The class of additive models can be divided into at least three submodels according to how attributes are used to refer:

1. The referent of a word might be determined by the *number of attributes* possessed by an object that match attributes in the word's definition (Hampton, 1979; Wittgenstein, 1953). If the number of matching attributes exceeds some criterion, then the object is identified as an example of a word; otherwise, the object is not so identified.

2. The referent of a word might be determined by a *weighted sum of attributes*. This submodel is like the first one, except that some attributes are viewed as more critical than others and hence are weighted more heavily (Hampton, 1979). For purposes of our analyses, the first submodel is viewed as a special case of the second (the weighted case) and not treated as qualitatively distinct.

3. The referent of a word might be determined by a *weighted average of attributes*, in which case the sum of the attributes is divided by the number of attributes.

The second and third submodels are distinguished by whether or not a given sum of weights counts equally without respect to the number of weights entered into the sum. To our knowledge, the difference between summing and averaging models has not been addressed in the literature on word meaning and reference, although it has certainly been considered in other contexts, such as information integration in impression formation (e.g., Anderson, 1979).

Mixed Models

A third class of models specifies words as being decomposable into both defining and characteristic attributes. An example of such a model is that of Smith, Shoben, and Rips (1974), who proposed that words can be viewed as comprising both defining and characteristic attributes. Consider, for example, the concept of a *mammal*. Being warm-blooded would be a defining attribute of a mammal, whereas being a land animal would be a characteristic attribute in that most, but not all, mammals are land animals.

In a mixed model (or at least the proposed variant of it), not all words need be composed of both defining and characteristic attributes (Clark & Clark, 1977; Schwartz, 1977). For example, some words, such as *game*, might be viewed as comprising only characteristic attributes. Intuitively, it seems much easier to find defining attributes for some kinds of concepts than for others, and this class of models capitalizes on this intuition. It seems less likely that any words comprise only defining attributes. At least, we are unable to think of any words that do not have at least some characteristic attributes that are neither necessary nor sufficient for referring.

TESTS OF ALTERNATIVE MODELS OF REPRESENTATION

We conducted three initial experiments to test the alternative models of word-meaning representation (see McNamara & Sternberg, 1983). Our concern in these experiments was with how word meaning is represented psychologically. The psychological issues of interest to us are not necessarily the same as those issues concerning philosophers of meaning or linguists.

The first experiment was intended (1) to determine whether people identify necessary and/or sufficient attributes of concepts and objects and (2) to collect rating data needed for the second experiment. Ten Yale University students participated in the study. The study involved three kinds of nouns: (a) natural-kind terms (e.g., *eagle, banana, potato*), (b) defined-kind terms (e.g., *scientist, wisdom*), and (c) proper names (e.g., *Queen Elizabeth II, Aristotle, Paul Newman*). Proper names were included because they have been heavily used in the philosophical literature, often serving as the basis for generalization to all nouns. The main independent variables in the experiment were the type of term about which a rating was to be made (natural kind, defined kind, proper name) and the type of rating to be made (necessary attributes, sufficient attributes, importance of attributes; see subsequent discussion). The main dependent variable was the value of the assigned ratings. Subjects were first asked to list as many properties as they could think of for various objects of the three kinds just noted. Then they were asked to provide three kinds of ratings (with the order of the kinds of ratings counterbalanced across subjects). The first kind of rating was one of necessity: Subjects were asked to check off those attributes, if any, that they believed to be necessary attributes for each given word. The second kind of rating was one of sufficiency: Subjects were asked to check off those attributes, if any, that were sufficient attributes for each given word. They were also asked to indicate minimally sufficient subsets of attributes (such that the subset in combination was sufficient to define a word). The third kind of rating was one of importance: Subjects were asked to rate how important each attribute was to defining each of the given words.

The major results of interest were these:

1. All subjects found at least one necessary attribute for each of the eight natural-kind and proper-name terms. All but one subject found at least one necessary attribute for each of the defined kinds. One could therefore conclude that individuals conceive of words of these three kinds as having at least some necessary attributes. Examples of some of these attributes are for *diamond* that it scratches glass, is the hardest substance known, and is made of carbon; and for *Albert Einstein* that he is dead, was a scientist, was a male, and that he derived the equation $E = mc^2$.

2. All subjects found at least one sufficient attribute or subset of attributes for all natural-kind terms. Almost all subjects found at least one sufficient attribute or subset of attributes for defined kinds and proper names. It could therefore be concluded that most individuals conceive of most words as having at least some sufficient attributes or subsets of attributes. Examples are for an *eagle* that it is a bird that appears on quarters and for *lamp* that it is a light source that has a shade.

3. Roughly half of the natural-kind and defined-kind terms were conceived of as having necessary and sufficient attributes. More than three-fourths of the proper names were conceived as having such attributes. Examples are for *sandals* that they are shoes that are held on with straps and that do not cover the whole foot and for *diamond* that it is the hardest substance known.

4. Internal-consistency analyses revealed that subjects agreed to a great extent as to which attributes were important, necessary, sufficient, and necessary and sufficient (with internal-consistency reliabilities generally around .85; for necessity and sufficiency, reliabilities were generally a bit lower, usually around .75).

The second experiment was intended (1) to determine the extent to which people use defining (necessary and sufficient) and characteristic (neither necessary nor sufficient) attributes when deciding whether or not an object is an exemplar of word, (2) to test four simple models and three mixed models of word meaning, and (3) to determine how generalizable the results were across word domains. Nine of the 10 subjects from the first experiment participated in this experiment. A within-subjects design was used in order to control for possible individual differences in the representation of meaning of specific words. The subjects received booklets with a given word at the top of the page, followed by a list of attributes. The subject's task was to give a confidence rating that the attributes actually described an exemplar of the word at the top of the page. Attribute descriptions were compiled for each subject in order to provide discrimination among alternative models of word representation. The main independent variables were ratings of necessity, sufficiency, necessity and sufficiency, and importance, as taken from Experiment 1. The main dependent variable was the confidence rating that the description described an exemplar of the target word. Subjects rated their confidence that a given word was, in fact, exemplified by the description appearing below it. For example, they might see the word TIGER at the top of the page, followed by four attributes: "member of the cat family," "four-legged," "carnivorous," and "an animal." Subjects rated on a 1 – 8 scale how likely the list of attributes was to describe a particular tiger.

The alternative representational models tested were a model positing (1) use only of defining (necessary and sufficient) attributes, (2) use of an unweighted sum of attributes, (3) use of a weighted sum of attributes, (4) use of a weighted mean of attributes, (5) use of defining attributes as well as a weighted sum of all attributes, and (6) use of defining attributes as well as a weighted mean of all attributes. Models were fit by linear regression with individual data sets concatenated; that is, there was no averaging across either subjects or items, and thus there was just one observation per data point for a total of 863 data points. Proportions of variance accounted for by each of the six respective models in the confidence-rating data were .36 for (1), .01 for (2), .02 for (3), .11 for (4), .45 for (5), and .38 for (6), concatenated over all word types. Data for individual subjects reflected the pattern for the group. It was concluded that in making decisions about whether sets of attributes represent exemplars of specific words, individuals appear to use defining attributes and a weighted sum of all matching attributes.

The third experiment was designed to verify the results of the second experiment using converging operations. In particular, response latency and response choice were used, and the subjects' task was to choose which of two attributes lists better described a referent of a given word. For example, subjects might see SOFA followed by two lists of attributes: (1) "used for sitting, found in living rooms, slept on, furniture," and (2) "slept on, rectangular in shape, found in bedrooms." The subjects would have to decide whether (1) or (2) was a better exemplar of a sofa. Models were fit to group-average data.

The results again supported the mixed model combining defining attributes with a weighted sum of attributes. For response choices, fits of five of the models described earlier (in terms of proportions of variance accounted for) were .48 for (1), .57 for (3), .46 for (4), .65 for (5), and .57 for (6). Model (2), the unweighted variant of Model (3), was not separately tested. (Because fitting the models to response latencies requires making some processing assumptions, the fits to latencies are presented subsequently.) The data for the three experiments taken as a whole seemed quite strongly to support Model (5), the mixed model in which defining and a weighted sum of attributes are used to refer. This model was then taken as the representational model on the basis of which to test alternative process models.[2]

ALTERNATIVE MODELS OF WORD PROCESSING

Accepting (at least tentatively) a model of word representation in which words possess both defining and characteristic attributes (or, in some cases, only characteristic attributes), we sought to test alternative models of how this attribute information is processed. We compared six basic processing models for the latency task used in Experiment 3, where subjects had to choose which of two attribute lists better described an exemplar of a given target word (SOFA in the previous example).

The models differed from each other in two major respects. The first respect was that of whether subjects were proposed always to test both answer options (exhaustive option processing) or sometimes to test just the first option (self-terminating option processing). In the former case, it was assumed that subjects always check both options in order to make sure that they pick the better of the two; in the latter case, it was assumed that subjects will select one of the options, either the first or the second, if they can eliminate one option after considering only the first (i.e., subjects will choose the first without considering the second if the first is very good or they will choose the second without considering it carefully if the first is very poor). The second respect in which the models differed was that of whether subjects were proposed always to compare the options on the basis of defining attributes and a weighted sum of attributes (exhaustive attribute-information processing), or sometimes to compare the options only on the basis of defining attributes (attribute-information processing with self-termination on defining attributes), or sometimes to compare the options only on the basis of the weighted sums of attributes (attribute-information processing with self-termination on the weighted sums of attributes). Note that the self-termination referred to here is that of the kinds of information used to *compare* answer options. This kind of self-termination does not apply to the encoding of attributes: As specified by the representational model we have ac-

---

[2] The six process models were also tested using the mixed model combining defining attributes and weighted means of attributes, Model (6). In all cases, the combination of defining and weighted sums of attributes fared better than the combination of defining and weighted means of attributes.

cepted, both defining and characteristic attributes as well as their associated
weights are assumed to be encoded for all words.

In sum, then, information processing can be either exhaustive or self-terminating with respect to the answer options considered, and either exhaustive or self-terminating with respect to the kinds of information considered.
In the latter case, self-termination can occur either with respect to the defining attributes or with respect to the weighted sums of attributes. Six models
were generated by crossing the two kinds of option processing with the three
kinds of attribute-information processing.

QUANTIFICATION OF THE WORD-PROCESSING MODELS

Quantification of the processing models is explained by referring to the
following example from Experiment 3: TENT followed by (1) "made of
canvas, supported by poles, portable, waterproof" and (2) "a shelter, used for
camping, made of canvas."

The three models that were self-terminating on option processing contained eight or nine parameters, depending on whether the models were
self-terminating or exhaustive on attribute-information processing. The
parameters and the variables used to estimate them were as follows:

1. *Reading time* was estimated by the total number of words in the two
descriptions. In the example, the total number of words was 16 (excluding
the target word).

2. *Processing time for negations* was estimated by the number of negated
attributes in the descriptions, which was zero for the example.

3. *Comparison of the first description to the target word* was estimated by
the number of attributes in the first description. According to the theory,
each attribute in the first answer option was compared with the encoded
mental representation of the target word. After each comparison, the
weights of matching and mismatching attributes were added to a summed-
weights counter. Mismatching attributes were also checked for necessity,
and if they were necessary this fact was recorded in a defining-attributes
counter. When all attributes had been compared to the word, the set was
checked for sufficiency, and if the set was sufficient this fact was recorded in
the defining-attributes counter. In the example, the comparison variable
would take the value four, the number of attributes in the first description.

4. and 5. Comparison was made of the *summed-weights counter* and the
defining-attributes counter to their respective criteria. After all information
about the first option has been accumulated by Process 3 in a defining-attributes counter and a summed-weights counter, both counters were compared

to separate criteria. If either counter exceeded its criterion, a choice was made and processing terminated. However, if neither counter exceeded its criterion, processing of the second option began. In the example, neither the summed-weights counter nor the defining-attributes counter exceeded its criterion, so the second option was compared to the target word.

6. *Comparison of the second description to the target word* was estimated by the number of attributes in the second description, or by zero. If it was possible to choose on the basis of information gathered from the first answer option only, the value of this second comparison parameter was zero. However, if it was not possible to self-terminate, the second description was compared to the target word's representation, attribute by attribute. Since it is not possible to self-terminate in the example on the basis of defining attributes or on the basis of weighted sums of attributes, this comparison variable would take the value three.

7. *Comparison of options on the basis of defining attributes* was estimated by the difference between the defining-attributes counter for the first answer option and the counter for the second option. According to the theory, comparison time decreased as the difference between the two information counters increased; that is, subjects were faster the more dissimilar the options are. In the example, this difference was in about the middle of the scale, predicting an intermediate comparison time.

8. *Comparison of options on the basis of weighted sums of attributes* was estimated by the difference in summed weights between the two descriptions. As in Parameter 7, comparison time decreased as the difference increased. The difference in summed weights for the example was nearly zero (i.e., the descriptions had nearly identical weighted sums of attributes), predicting a long comparison time.

9. The *justification* parameter was present only in the model that was exhaustive with respect to attribute-information processing. According to this model, the answer options were always compared both with respect to weighted sums of attributes and defining attributes. When the difference in summed weights and the difference in definingness predicted different choices of options, the choice of an option on the basis of definingness (either because the option was sufficient or because the other option contained a mismatching necessary attribute) must be justified. In the example, both the difference in weighted sums of attributes and the difference in definingness predicted that the second option should be chosen. Thus, the justification variable would take the value of zero.

The exhaustive-option-processing models contained five or six parameters, depending on whether the models were self-terminating or exhaustive with respect to attribute-information processing. Four to five of these parameters were the same as those in the self-terminating models: (1) reading time, (2) processing of negations, (3) comparison of options on the basis of defining attributes, (4) comparison of options on the basis of weighted sums of attributes, and (5) justification (but only for the model that was exhaustive with respect to attribute-information processing). The one parameter not in the self-terminating models measured comparison of the two descriptions to the target word's representation. This variable took the value of the total number of attributes in the two answer options, which was seven in the example.

TESTS OF ALTERNATIVE MODELS OF PROCESSING

The six models of information processing just described were pitted against each other in terms of their ability to account for the latency data from Experiment 3. Fits of the six models (expressed in terms of proportions of variance accounted for by the models in the latency data) were

.67 for the model that was self-terminating with respect to scanning of options and assumed that options are compared (when an early choice is not made) on the basis of weighted sums of attributes only if the defining attributes fail to yield a unique solution;

.68 for the model that was self-terminating with respect to scanning of options and assumed that options are compared (when an early choice is not made) on the basis of defining attributes only if the weighted sums of attributes fail to yield a unique solution;

.67 for the model that was self-terminating with respect to scanning of options and assumed that options are always compared (again, when an early choice is not made) with respect to both defining attributes and weighted sums;

.74 for the model that was exhaustive with respect to scanning of options and assumed that options are compared on the basis of weighted sums of attributes only if defining attributes fail to yield a unique solution;

.78 for the model that was exhaustive with respect to scanning of options and assumed that options are compared using defining attributes only if weighted sums fail to yield a unique solution; and

.79 for the model that was exhaustive with respect to scanning of options and assumed that options are always compared with respect to both defining attributes and weighted sums of attributes.

The latter three values of R^2 are higher (and also the corresponding values of root mean square deviation are lower) than the former three values of R^2, despite the need for three fewer parameters in the exhaustive than in the self-terminating models; therefore, it appears quite reasonable to conclude that processing is exhaustive rather than self-terminating with respect to answer options: Subjects always search both answer options. It is less clear whether subjects always compare options on the basis of both defining attributes and weighted sums of attributes. In the absence of clear evidence one way or the other, we have selected as best the model with the highest R^2 (and lowest root mean square deviation), that model in which both kinds of information are always used to compare answer options: Subjects always compare the options with respect to both defining attributes and weighted sums of attributes. In sum, we have selected the process model in which information processing is fully exhaustive both with respect to answer options and with respect to attribute information.

Standardized regression coefficients for the preferred model were .42 for reading time, .37 for processing of negations, .33 for comparison of options to the encoded word, .23 for comparison of options on the basis of defining attributes, .33 for comparison of options on the basis of weighted sums of attributes, and .07 for justification. (Standardized rather than raw regression coefficients are presented here because the various independent variables used to estimate the coefficients were on different scales.) These coefficients seem generally reasonable, and all were significantly different from zero at the .001 level or better except for justification, which was significant at the .05 level.

Preliminary correlations have been computed between overall latency score on the decision task and Vocabulary, Comprehension, and Reading Rate scores from the Nelson-Denny Advanced Reading Test. The simple correlations were somewhat disappointing. The only significant correlation was that between overall latency and reading rate ($r = -.37$). However, the multiple correlation between overall latency on the one hand and both reading rate and reading comprehension on the other was .47, with both rate and comprehension making statistically significant contributions (β for rate = .38 and for comprehension = .30). Thus, reading rate and reading comprehension jointly considered were moderately strongly related to latencies on our task. Vocabulary score did not make a statistically significant incremental contribution to the regression equation.

IMPLICATIONS FOR TEST DESIGN AND ANALYSIS

The theoretical and empirical analysis presented in the preceding part of the chapter has a number of implications for the design and analysis of verbal comprehension tests. Our discussion of these implications is divided into four main parts: goals of testing, test design, test scores, and test validation.

GOALS OF TESTING

Typical goals of psychometric testing of verbal comprehension ability are to assess overall verbal skill (and sometimes separable aspects of it, such as vocabulary and reading comprehension) and to predict future performance in verbal tasks. The kind of componential analysis proposed here (see Sternberg, 1977) permits an additional goal, namely that of understanding real-time verbal comprehension performance in terms of the representation and processing of verbal information. In particular, it is possible to isolate a number of aspects of verbal skill that traditional psychometric analyses have been unable to separate.

TEST DESIGN

The paradigm we have used for assessing real-time verbal comprehension (in Experiment 3 as described earlier) requires the subject to compare the meaning of a target word to each of two descriptions of the word, where the descriptions are posed in terms of attributes. Our next experiment, which was started more recently, is the critical one from the standpoint of the test design we propose. In this new experiment, the subject is asked to compare the meaning of a target word to each of two word options (rather than attribute-list options). The subject's task is to select the option that is more nearly synonymous to the target word. For example, SOFA might be paired with COUCH and CHAIR in a simple item, or MITIGATE might be paired with CHASTEN and ALLEVIATE in a more difficult item. A large number of vocabulary items have been constructed of this form in order to create the proposed verbal comprehension test.

Response measures for the test are response latency and response choice (right or wrong) for each test item.

Several facets need to be manipulated in the construction of test items. We assume the representational and process models selected earlier:

1. *Difficulty of target word.* It is, of course, desirable to have a wide range of target word difficulties. *Sofa,* for example, is an easy target word, whereas *mitigate* is a relatively difficult one. For the purposes of psychometric test properties, difficulty can be measured by word frequency, available norms, and the like. For the purposes of linear modeling, it is necessary to choose words known to differ in the number of defining attributes and the number of characteristic attributes. In our research we have found that some words tend to have more defining attributes than other words (e.g., *violin* has more defining sets of attributes than *tent*). We believe that it is possible to discover similar disparities in the numbers of defining or characteristic attributes in vocabulary items more suitable for psychometric tests.

2. *Closeness of target word meaning to meaning of better option.* It is probably the case that no two words in a language convey exactly the same meaning. In modeling test performance, it is necessary to know just how close the "correct" option is to the target in terms of shared meaning. Our kind of analysis permits going beyond mere ratings of closeness or similar normative data in that meaning comparison is done at the level of word attributes. The two words are compared in terms of number of shared defining attributes, number of unshared defining attributes, and summed weights of all shared and unshared attributes. For example, the word *alleviate* shares the attribute "to lessen" with the word *mitigate*, whereas *chasten* does not. Whether "to lessen" is a necessary attribute (we think it is) or a characteristic attribute with a high weight could be determined by subjective ratings, as in our experiments, or by some more objective means.

3. *Closeness of target word meaning to meaning of poorer option.* The procedure for quantifying this facet is the same as that for quantifying the facet immediately preceding (Item 2), except that the target word is compared to the poorer rather than the better answer option.

In all cases, attribute descriptions of words are gotten by compiling attribute data provided by subjects tested in the manner of Experiment 1, described earlier.

Obviously, these are not the only facets that might be manipulated. The number of answer options, the difficulty of the words constituting the answer options, and even the task (for example, using antonyms as well as synonyms) might be varied further. We hope to bring our theory and technology to a point where we can handle these further complications, but we are not at this point yet.

TEST SCORES

Componential analysis of individual latency data can reveal real-time durations for a number of components, as well as for overall task performance. In particular, it is possible to derive the following kinds of scores:

1. *Global latency.* This is simply a measure of mean response latency per item, and conveys time for verbal processing. For example, the mean response latencies per item for two of the subjects in Experiment 3 were 3.22 and 7.91 seconds.

2. *Global number (or proportion) correct.* This is a measure of extent of vocabulary, analogous to that usually supplied by single psychometric test scores.

3. *Representation identification.* It is possible to use the techniques described earlier to test the alternative representational models we de-

scribed. Normally, it is probably safe to assume that the mixed model with defining and weighted sums of attributes holds, but, if desired, this can be tested against alternative models in individual cases. Facilitated or impeded verbal comprehension performance could be due to form of representation. For example, we have found that vocabulary ability correlates significantly ($r = .40$) with the number of sufficient attributes that one identifies. This correlation indicates that verbal ability may be associated with richer and more articulated representations of word meanings. Another way that representations might be identified is by examining the regression weights obtained from process modeling of individual subjects' data. Thus, for example, one of the subjects in Experiment 3 had weights of .22 for comparison of options on the basis of defining attributes and .28 for comparison of options of the basis of weighted sums of attributes, indicating that this subject weighed each kind of information about equally in making his decisions. This subject could be contrasted to another subject who had weights of .26 for comparison of options on the basis of defining attributes and .10 for comparison of options on the basis of weighted sums of attributes, indicating that she gave over twice as much weight to shared and unshared defining attributes than to weighted sums of shared and unshared attributes.

4. *Strategy identification.* Using the techniques described earlier, it is also possible to test the alternative strategy models of information processing we considered. Again, it is probably safe to assume that most people use the fully exhaustive model, at least at the adult level; but one can test this assumption as needed. To test the exhaustiveness assumption among our subjects, we performed process modeling on individual subjects' data. The best self-terminating option-processing model (attribute-information processing with self-termination on weighted sums of attributes) had higher R^2 than the fully exhaustive model for 9 out of 32 subjects. One of these subjects had an R^2 of .34 under the fully exhaustive model and an R^2 of .37 under the self-terminating model, indicating that she might very well be using a self-terminating option-processing strategy.

5. *Component latencies.* These are latencies for single-component operations, as specified by the information-processing model of performance. It is possible, under the particular model we found to be best (or under the other models as well), to separate latencies for reading time, time for processing negations, time to compare options using defining attributes, time to compare options using weighted sums of attributes, and justification time. As an example, consider the component latencies for one of our subjects: 133 msec per word for reading time, 550 msec for processing each negation, 629 msec for comparing each attribute to the encoded target word, and 2371 msec for justification time. (The component latencies for comparison on the basis of defining and weighted sums of attributes are not very meaningful

because of the arbitrary scales of the variables used to estimate these parameters.) These component latencies make it possible to figure out rather specifically in what aspects of information processing, if any, facilitated or impeded performance occurs.

Taken together, these various kinds of scores yield a wealth of information about verbal comprehension performance, certainly more than is yielded by a single vocabulary test score. To our knowledge, ours represents the first attempt to analyze such performance componentially. Obviously, the diagnostic, predictive, and even training implications of such scores have yet to show their usefulness in actual practice. We are optimistic, though, about the possibilities and believe that the kind of analysis proposed here is definitely worth further exploration.

TEST VALIDATION

The kind of analysis we propose opens totally new possibilities for test validation. We mention what we consider to be the three most important of these: First, with respect to content validity we are prepared to use real vocabulary tests (except, at the present time, for the restriction of the number of answer options to two). It is not necessary to use artificially constructed materials. Second, with respect to predictive validity it is possible to predict (or assess concurrently) criterion scores on the basis of a variegated set of verbal–comprehension measurements. A task that remains before us, as theoreticians and developers, is to discover which aspects of performance are most critical in verbal criterion performances. The use of the kinds of test scores we propose will help us in this task. Third, and most importantly, with respect to construct validity we believe that the proposed procedures provide a linkage between theoretical understanding and practical measurement that has not been possible previously. This kind of linkage has been developed with fluid ability kinds of tasks (e.g., Pellegrino & Glaser, 1980; Sternberg, 1977, 1980, 1981; Whitely, 1976, 1977, 1979), but has not been well developed with crystallized ability kinds of tasks (although work such as Frederiksen's [1980] certainly has provided a step in this direction). We believe that the linkage of verbal comprehension test performance to cognitive theory represents an advance whose time has come.

CONCLUSION

We wish to conclude by noting that although our approach to verbal comprehension is grounded in the cognitive–experimental tradition, it is very much attuned to the needs of individual-differences theorists and practitioners. We believe that developed individual differences in verbal comprehension test performance can be traced to two basic kinds of sources: differences in antecedent experiences and differences in current performance. Differences in antecedent experiences are measured by the kinds of learning from context tasks discussed in our literature review. The idea here is that current vocabulary, in particular, and verbal comprehension skills, in general, can be understood in part in terms of an individual's ability over the course of the life span to have acquired verbal information presented in natural contexts. Differences in current performance are measured by the kinds of procedures described in the middle part of this chapter. Verbal comprehension tests—even seemingly straightforward ones such as synonyms tests—require more than just prior knowledge. They require various kinds of problem solving. In a synonyms test, for example, subjects often have to choose the best of several answer options that may be quite close in meaning to the target word. Sheer knowledge about the target word's meaning may be insufficient to get the correct answer on a given test item. The program of research described here provides a way of disentangling the aspects of problem-solving performance that individuals encounter in verbal comprehension tests. Considered together, knowledge about antecedents of current performance and about modes of current performance themselves seems to us to provide a powerful means to understand why it is that some people are higher verbals than others.

REFERENCES

Anderson, N. H. (1979). Algebraic rules in psychological measurement. *American Scientist, 67*, 555–563.

Cattell, R. B. (1971). *Abilities: Their structure, growth, and action.* Boston: Houghton-Mifflin.

Chi, M. T. H. (1978). Knowledge structures and memory development. In R. S. Siegler (Ed.), *Children's thinking: What develops?.* Hillsdales, NJ: Erlbaum.

Clark, H. H., & Clark, E. V. (1977). *Psychology and language.* New York: Harcourt Brace Jovanovich.

Daalen-Kapteijns, M. M. van, & Elshout-Mohr, M. (1981). The acquistion of word meanings as a cognitive learning process. *Journal of Verbal Learning and Verbal Behavior, 20*, 386–399.

Frederiksen, J. R. (1980). Component skills in reading: Measurement of individual differences through chronometric analysis. In R. E. Snow, P.-A. Federico, & W. E. Montague (Eds.), *Aptitude, learning, and instruction: Cognitive process analyses of aptitude* (Vol. 1). Hillsdale, NJ: Erlbaum.

Frege, G. (1952). On sense and reference. In P. Geach & M. Black (Eds.), *Translations for the philosophical writings of Gottolb Frege.* Oxford: Basil Blackwell & Mott.

Hampton, J. A. (1979). Polymorphous concepts in semantic memory. *Journal of Verbal Learning and Verbal Behavior, 18*, 441–461.

Hunt, E. B. (1978). Mechanics of verbal ability. *Psychological Review, 85,* 109–130.

Hunt, E. B., Frost, N., & Lunneborg, C. E. (1973). Individual differences in cognition: A new approach to intelligence. In G. Bower (Ed.), *Advances in learning and motivation* (Vol. 7). New York: Academic Press.

Hunt, E. B., Lunneborg, C. E., & Lewis, J. (1975). What does it mean to be high verbal? *Cognitive Psychology, 7,* 194–227.

Jackson, M. D., & McClelland, J. L. (1979). Processing determinants of reading speed. *Journal of Experimental Psychology: General, 108,* 151–181.

Jensen, A. R. (1980). *Bias in mental testing.* New York: Free Press.

Katz, J. J. (1972). *Semantic theory.* New York: Harper & Row.

Keating, D. P., & Bobbitt, B. L. (1978). Individual and developmental differences in cognitive-processing components of mental ability. *Child Development, 49,* 155–167.

Keil, F. C. (1981). *Semantic inferences and the acquisition of word meaning.* Unpublished manuscript.

Lansman, M., Donaldson, G., Hunt, E. B., & Yantis, S. (1982). Ability factors and cognitive processes. *Intelligence, 6,* 347–386.

Marshalek, B. (1981). *Trait and process aspects of vocabulary knowledge and verbal ability* (NR 154-376 ONR Tech. Rep. No. 15.) Stanford, CA: School of Education, Stanford University.

Matarazzo, J. D. (1972). *Wechsler's measurement and appraisal of adult intelligence.* Baltimore: Williams & Wilkins.

McNamara, T. P., & Sternberg, R. J. (1983). Mental models of word meaning. *Journal of Verbal Learning and Verbal Behavior, 22,* 449–474.

Pellegrino, J. W., & Glaser, R. (1980). Components of inductive reasoning. In R. E. Snow, P.-A. Federico, & W. Montague (Eds.), *Aptitude, learning, and instruction: Cognitive process analyses of aptitude* (Vol. 1). Hillsdale, NJ: Erlbaum.

Perfetti, C. A., & Lesgold, A. M. (1977). Discourse comprehension and individual differences. In P. Carpenter and M. Just (Eds.), *Cognitive processes in comprehension: 12th Annual Carnegie Symposium on Cognition.* Hillsdale, NJ: Erlbaum.

Posner, M. I., & Mitchell, R. (1967). Chronometric analysis of classification. *Psychological Review, 74,* 392–409.

Rosch, E. (1978). Principles of categorization. In E. Rosch and B. B. Lloyd (Eds.), *Cognition and categorization.* Hillsdale, NJ: Erlbaum.

Russell, B. (1956). On denoting. In R. C. Marsh (Ed.), *Logic and knowledge.* London: George Allen and Unwin.

Schwartz, S. P. (1977). *Naming, necessity, and natural kinds.* Ithaca, NY: Cornell University Press.

Smith, E. E., Shoben, E. J., & Rips, L. J. (1974). Structure and process in semantic memory: A featural model for semantic decision. *Psychological Review, 81,* 214–241.

Sternberg, R. J. (1977). *Intelligence, information processing, and analogical reasoning: The componential analysis of human abilities.* Hillsdale, NJ: Erlbaum.

Sternberg, R. J. (1980). Sketch of a componential subtheory of human intelligence. *Behavioral and Brain Sciences, 3,* 573–584.

Sternberg, R. J. (1981). Intelligence and nonentrenchment. *Journal of Educational Psychology, 73,* 1–16.

Sternberg, R. J., Powell, J. S., & Kaye, D. B. (1982). The nature of verbal comprehension. *Poetics, 11,* 155–187.

Thurstone, L. L. (1938). *Primary mental abilities.* Chicago: University of Chicago Press.

Vernon, P. E. (1971). *The structure of human abilities.* London: Methuen.

Werner, H., & Kaplan, E. (1952). The acquistion of word meanings: A developmental study. *Monographs of the Society for Research in Child Development, 15*(1, Serial No. 51).

Whitely, S. E. (1976). Solving verbal analogies: Some cognitive components of intelligence test items. *Journal of Educational Psychology, 68,* 234–242.

Whitely, S. E. (1977). Information-processing on intelligence test items. Some response components. *Applied Psychological Measurement, 1,* 465–476.

Whitely, S. E. (1979). Latent trait models in the study of intelligence. *Intelligence, 4,* 97–132.

Willis, S., Cornelius, S., Blow, F., & Baltes, P. (1981). *Training research in aging: Attentional processes.* Unpublished manuscript.

Wittgenstein, L. (1953). *Philosophical investigations.* Oxford: Basil Blackwell & Mott.

3

Analyses of Spatial Aptitude and Expertise

James W. Pellegrino
Randall J. Mumaw
Valerie J. Shute

INTRODUCTION

The research discussed in this chapter relates to aptitude analysis and to the analysis of technical skill competence. In both cases, the focus is on the general area of spatial cognition and processing. Spatial ability represents a major individual differences factor (see, e.g., Lohman, 1979; McGee, 1979). However, such abilities are only weakly related to typical academic achievement. There is no major curriculum area that focuses primarily on spatial cognition and processing. Nevertheless, spatial ability measures, like other aptitude and intelligence measures, have served as useful predictors of success in other environments. McGee (1979) identified two major areas where spatial tests have been utilized for prediction. One area is industry and the other involves certain academic settings and vocational–technical training programs. In the job performance area, spatial ability tests have been most useful for predicting success in engineering, drafting, and design. In academic settings and training programs, spatial tests have been most strongly correlated with performance in mechanical drawing, shop courses, art, mechanics, and to some extent mathematics and physics.

Although correlations exist between spatial aptitude measures and job or technical course performance, there is little substantive theoretical basis for explaining and understanding such relationships. Our research on spatial cognition and processing, as well as that of others (e.g., Cooper, 1982) has

Copyright © 1985 by Academic Press, Inc.
All rights of reproduction in any form reserved.
ISBN 0-12-238180-7

been directed at establishing such a base. In the remainder of this chapter we first illustrate some initial attempts to understand the cognitive skills underlying both spatial aptitude and achievement. The next section focuses on efforts to design and use a systematic set of problems to analyze components of processing in a complex spatial aptitude task. The task is a standard index of spatial visualization ability that is predictive of success in technical skills courses such as engineering design and graphics. The following section discusses some initial work that examines dimensions of performance in the engineering design and graphics area. These two focuses are largely disconnected at present, although at the end of the chapter we consider some directions for linking them together.

SPATIAL APTITUDE ANALYSIS

One approach to studying the nature of aptitude is to apply cognitive process theory and methodology to the analysis of performance on tasks found on various aptitude test batteries. This so-called cognitive components approach (Pellegrino & Glaser, 1979) does not presuppose that aptitude is uniquely defined by the circumscribed performances required by tests. Aptitude or ability covers a much wider range of knowledge and skill. However, the cognitive components approach recognizes that various tests have been devised that reliably assess individual differences in cognitive abilities and that these differences are predictive of success and achievement in diverse real-world settings. The question is, then, what are the skills that are being assessed by such instruments and how can the basis for individual variation be understood? The goal is to treat the tasks found on aptitude tests as cognitive tasks (Carroll, 1976) that can be approached and analyzed in the same way that cognitive and developmental psychologists have approached and analyzed other cognitive tasks.

An initial step in a systematic analysis of individual differences in spatial aptitude is identification of the domain of tasks that serve to define it. This involves identifying a core or prototypical set of tasks that frequently occur across many widely used spatial aptitude tests and that have a history of consistent association with the spatial aptitude construct. Such an initial step delineates the task forms that should serve as the target for rational, empirical, and theoretical analysis. A multitask approach is important because an adequate understanding of individual differences in spatial ability cannot be based on an intensive analysis of only a single task with a high loading on the spatial aptitude factor(s). Rather, it is necessary to conduct analyses that consider the various tasks yielding correlated performance, and in so doing specify a set of performances that define the aptitude construct.

A successful analysis of multiple tasks should provide a basis for understanding the patterns of intercorrelations among tasks. More importantly, the analysis of multiple, related tasks should permit the differentiation of general and specific cognitive processes and knowledge. This differentiation can lead to a level of analysis where research can be pursued on the feasibility of process training and transfer.

Spatial aptitude has remained a nebulous psychometric construct even after 70 years of psychometric research. There appears to be little agreement among major studies about the number of distinct spatial abilities that may exist and how best to characterize each one. Lohman (1979) has provided an overview of some of the problems encountered in trying to integrate the major factor-analytic work that has been done on spatial aptitude. First, identical tests appear with different names in different studies, and tests given the same name are often quite different in appearance and cognitive demands. A second problem is that subtle changes in test format and administration can have major effects on the resultant factor structure. A typical change that can produce such an effect is the use of solution time as opposed to number correct as the measure of performance. Finally, perhaps the most important difference relates to procedural variation in factor extraction and rotation.

To correct for some of the problems just described, Lohman (1979) reanalyzed the data from several major studies in an attempt to isolate a common set of spatial factors. The result of these efforts was the delineation of three distinct factors. One factor, labeled *Spatial Orientation,* appeared to involve the ability to imagine how a stimulus or stimulus array would appear from another perspective. Typically, such tasks require the individual to reorient himself or herself relative to the array, as when in a plane or boat that shifts heading relative to some land mass. The other two factors were labeled *Spatial Relations* and *Spatial Visualization.* The spatial relations factor appears to involve the ability to engage rapidly and accurately in mental rotation processes that are necessary for judgments about the identity of a pair of stimuli. Spatial relations tasks can be found in test batteries such as the Primary Mental Abilities test (PMA; Thurstone & Thurstone, 1949). The spatial visualization factor is defined by tests that are relatively unspeeded and complex. Such tasks frequently require a manipulation in which there is movement among the internal parts of the stimulus configuration or the folding and unfolding of flat patterns. Spatial visualization tasks can be found in test batteries such as the Differential Aptitude Test (DAT; Bennett, Seashore, & Wesman, 1974) or as separate tests such as the Minnesota Paper Form Board Test (Likert, 1934; Likert & Quasha, 1970).

The differences between and among spatial relations and visualization tasks seem to reflect two correlated dimensions of performance (Lohman,

1979). One of these is the speed–power dimension. Individual spatial relations problems are solved more rapidly than spatial visualization problems, and the tests themselves are administered in a format emphasizing speed in the former case and both speed and accuracy in the latter case. The second dimension involves stimulus complexity. A gross index of complexity is the number of individual stimulus elements or parts that must be processed. Spatial relations problems, although varying among themselves in complexity, involve less complex stimuli than do spatial visualization problems. In terms of a process analysis of spatial aptitude, the important question is whether individual differences in performance on these various tasks reflect differential contributions of the speed and accuracy of executing specific cognitive processes.

Considerable attention has been given to the analysis of performance on spatial relations tasks (see, e.g., Pellegrino & Kail, 1982). Studies have examined sources of gender, individual, and developmental differences in performance on simple mental rotation problems. These studies have applied a process model originally developed by Cooper and Shepard (1973) for mental rotation tasks. The results are quite consistent in showing that substantial speed differences exist in the encoding and comparison of unfamiliar stimuli and in the execution of a rotation or transformation process that operates on the internal stimulus representation. Adult individual differences exist in all these components of processing and they are mirrored by overall developmental trends. The limited analyses of age changes further suggest that individual differences initially relate to encoding and comparison processes and that the rotation process subsequently becomes an increasingly important source of individual differences. A further potential source of individual differences, one that needs further analysis, involves the strategy for task execution. Systematic individual differences may also exist in the speed and criteria for judging the mismatch between stimuli in different orientations.

The differences in encoding, comparison, and rotation that exist for simple spatial relations tasks are of even greater magnitude in complex spatial relations tasks employing more abstract stimuli. The complexity and abstractness of the stimuli lead to substantial errors on such problems that are also related to individual differences in reference test scores. The particular errors that seem most important for differentiating among individuals involve the processes associated with comparing figures for differences. Latency data for different judgment performance also contribute to predicting individual differences in reference test performance. The data indicate that individuals experience considerable difficulty in establishing the correspondences between common segments of complex stimuli, leading to several iterations through a sequence of processes and often culminating in an incorrect evaluation or guess.

The tasks associated with spatial visualization have received considerably less attention than spatial relations tasks. Relatively little has been done to develop and validate information-processing theories and models for such tasks. There are two major exceptions; these include the early work of Shepard and Feng (1972) and our own recent work (Mumaw, Pellegrino, & Glaser, 1980; Pellegrino, Cantoni, & Solter, 1981). Shepard and Feng (1972) studied performance in a mental paper-folding or surface development task. In the Shepard and Feng study, individuals were presented a representation of a flat, unfolded cube. Two of the surfaces had marked edges and the task was to decide if the marked edges would be adjacent when the pattern was folded to form the cube. The items that were used varied in the number of 90-degree folds required to bring the two marked edges together. Items were also classified by the number of surfaces that had to be carried along with each fold (i.e., the number of surfaces that had to be mentally moved to complete each new fold). Ten different stimulus values were obtained and decision times for items showed a general linear trend consistent with the total number of folds and surfaces that had to be processed to solve a problem. Shepard and Feng were not explicit about a model of performance for this task. Thus, the component processes and their sequencing are not well understood at present and no systematic process analysis of individual differences has been conducted.

ANALYSIS OF A SPATIAL VISUALIZATION TASK

Our analyses of spatial visualization involved performance on the Minnesota Paper Form Board (Likert & Quasha, 1970). Figure 1 illustrates a typical problem from this test. The individual is presented with an array of pieces and five completed figures. The task is to determine which of the five alternative choices is the correct figure that can be constructed from the particular set of pieces. Our analysis of the form board task began with a rational task analysis of the types of problems presented on this test and the dimensions that seem to underly task difficulty and errors. Items on form board tests vary in the number of individual stimulus elements that must be processed, their similarity, and the number of mismatching pieces for incorrect solutions.

From the standpoint of the cognitive processes necessary to solve an item, we hypothesized that the elementary processes included encoding, compari-

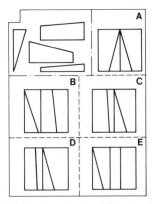

FIGURE 1.   Sample paper form board item.

son, search, rotation, and decision processes. Validation of such assumptions could not be done in the context of the problems present on the actual test. This was a function of the unsystematic nature of the problems themselves. To circumvent this, we developed a variant of this task that emulated the problems and processing required by the psychometric test items. The item type that was created for our studies is shown in Fig. 2. Individual stimulus pairs were constructed consisting of a complete figure and an array of individual pieces. The stimuli were both selected from psychometric tests and constructed so they would permit the evaluation of several models of performance.

Figure 2 also shows a process model for performance on an item of this type. We assume that there is an initial encoding of one of the pieces followed by a search for a potentially corresponding piece. Given the identification of a possible match there is rotation to bring the two stimuli into congruence so that a comparison process can be executed. If the two pieces correspond and all pieces have been examined then a positive response is executed. If all pieces have not been examined then the entire process recycles for examination of another stimulus element. There are three required processes and two optional processes that depend on the nature of the stimulus type. The example problem is one presumably requiring all five processes. The search process is required because the pieces are randomly arranged and have been displaced relative to each other given their position in the completed figure. The rotation process is required because each piece has also been rotated in the picture plane in addition to being spatially displaced. Both rotation and displacement characterize items on psychometric tests. The appropriate general latency equation for such items is also shown in Fig. 2. By varying the number of stimulus elements

Laboratory form board item

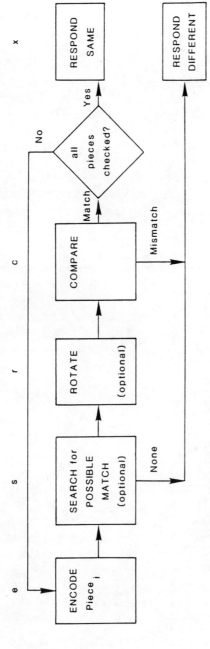

n = total number of pieces

n_i = number of spatially displaced pieces

n_j = number of rotated pieces

$RT = n(e + c) + n_i s + n_j r + x$

FIGURE 2. Laboratory form board item and process model for item solution. $RT = n(e + c) + n_i s + n_j r + x$, where n = total number of pieces, n_i = number of spatially displaced pieces, and n_j = number of rotated pieces.

for a given item we would expect to obtain a monotonically increasing latency function. One would also expect an increasing probability of error.

In order to test the viability of such assumptions and to separate out the different components of processing, several different types of stimuli were designed. These are illustrated in Fig. 3. At the top is the prototypical case just described. The other problem types were designed so that one or more processes are not required for solution. The second stimulus type is one that involves only rotation. This condition should require four of the five processes and may also require a search process. The third stimulus type involves the physical displacement of elements but without any rotation. This condition should only require four of the five processes. The fourth stimulus type involves neither rotation nor displacement of stimulus elements. This condition is designed to assess stimulus element encoding and

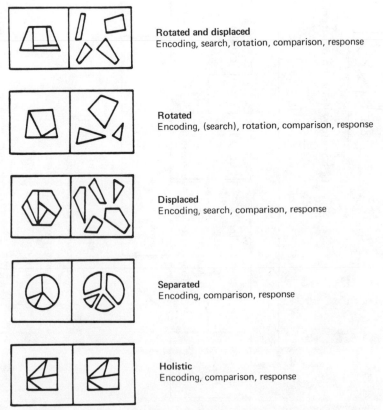

FIGURE 3. Examples of positive match items for experimental conditions differing in process complexity.

comparison. The final stimulus type is a holistic presentation condition that provides a baseline for encoding, comparison, and response. A complementary set of problems was also designed so that a mismatch existed between the completed figure and one or more of the pieces in the array.

These problems have now been used in two studies of individual differences in spatial ability (Mumaw *et al.*, 1980; Pellegrino *et al.*, 1981). The individuals tested were selected to represent varying levels of spatial aptitude as determined by a reference battery that included the Minnesota Paper Form Board Test. Each individual was tested on several hundred of the individual problems that have been illustrated. Before describing some of the results obtained with this task, it is important that we indicate that our experimental task has external validity. When overall accuracy within the experimental task is correlated with scores on the form board reference test, we obtain values approaching the reliability coefficients for the reference test. Of particular concern, however, is the ability to explain what is responsible for such a relationship—that is, the ability to begin to spell out the sources of individual differences in terms of process speed and accuracy.

Figure 4 illustrates general latency performance in our task. As can be seen in the figure, performance in each condition was consistent with a simple additive model and the differences among conditions reflect the contributions of additional processing components. We first focus on the latency results obtained for the positive trials, shown in the left-hand panel of

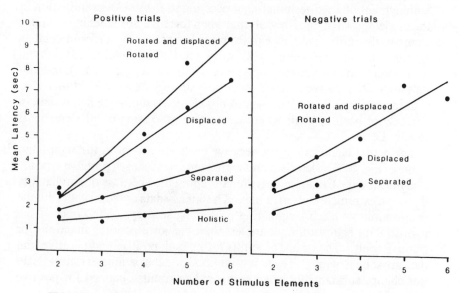

FIGURE 4. Group mean latency data for positive and negative match items.

Fig. 4. The data for the rotated and the rotated and displaced problem types have been combined because they did not differ. The linear functions shown in the figure represent the least-squares regression lines for each of the four problem types. As expected, the condition with the steepest slope was the one requiring search and rotation in addition to encoding, comparison, and response. The next-steepest slope occurred in the condition that required only search in addition to encoding, comparison, and response. The shallowest significant slope occurred in the separated condition. This condition presumably required only encoding, comparison, and response. Finally, the baseline holistic condition showed a basically flat function, as expected.

The adequacy of the model shown earlier and the assumptions about processing for each problem type were tested by simultaneously fitting the data from all conditions. When group mean data were used, the overall fit of the model was quite good and it accounted for over 96% of the variance. The values obtained for each of the individual parameters were plausible and there were no major deviations from the model. Model fitting was also done for each individual subject. Almost all subjects had R values above .90 and only three subjects had poor model fits. Thus, the model was not only representative of the group data but it also provided a good characterization of the performance of each individual.

The latency data for negative trials complement the data for positive trials and permit a test of whether performance in the task is consistent with the employment of a self-terminating processing strategy. An examination of the model shown in Fig. 2 reveals that when there is a mismatching stimulus element, the individual may exit from further processing and immediately execute a negative response. This can occur if no potential match is found during search or if the comparison process indicates a mismatch. If individuals use such a self-terminating processing strategy then the functions relating reaction time to number of stimulus elements should be flatter than in the case of positive trials where exhaustive processing of all elements is required.

The actual latency data for negative trials are shown in the right-hand panel of Fig. 4. The least-squares regression lines for each problem type are also illustrated. Certain points are not represented because of unreliability due to an extremely high error rate. The latency data are consistent with the assumptions of a self-terminating processing strategy. The slopes of the least squares regression lines are less than the corresponding functions for positive trials. The results of jointly fitting both positive and negative trial data are shown herein. The fit is quite good and the parameter estimates do not change substantially when compared to results obtained for positive trials only.

Results of Model Fitting for Positive and Negative Trials ($N = 41$)
    Parameters:
        Encode and compare = 556 msec/element
        Rotate = 299 msec/element
        Search = 689 msec/element
        Preparation – response = 624 msec
        Index reset (negation) = 859 msec
    $R^2 = .94$
    $RMSD = 545$

The error data for both positive and negative trials were also systematic and had considerable importance relative to individual differences. The error data for positive trials are shown in the left-hand section of Fig. 5. As can be seen in the figure, positive trial errors were related to the presence of the rotation component. There was a significant increase in overall errors as a function of the number of times that the rotation process needed to be executed. The other processing components, with the possible exception of search, did not systematically contribute to errors for positive trial types. Individual subjects differed substantially in error rates with an overall range

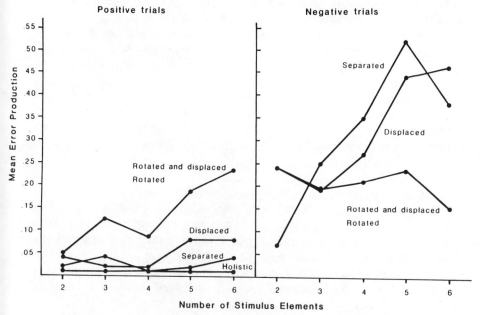

FIGURE 5. Group mean accuracy data for positive and negative match items.

of 0–23% for all positive trial types.   For the problem types involving rotation, the range was 0–43% errors.

Of particular interest is the different patterning of error data for the negative trial types.   The highest error rates were obtained for the conditions that did not require rotation.   This is not to say, however, that the presence of rotation did not lead to errors.   Rather, errors were highest when the ratio of matching to mismatching pieces was high and when processing could proceed rapidly because of the absence of a rotation component.   It appears as if individuals may have processed elements superficially for comparison purposes and thereby failed to detect differences in size and shape for globally corresponding elements.   The individual subject error rates on the negative trials ranged from 5% to 55%.

The error data for the positive and negative trials support the notion of different mechanisms contributing to incorrect final decisions.   In the case of positive trials, errors seem to result from the inability to determine the correspondence between two stimulus elements that must be rotated into actual congruence.   In such cases, either rotation is incorrectly executed or the resultant representation following rotation is imprecise, leading to a rejection of a matching element.   Errors resulting from execution of the rotation process also appear in the negative trials where there is a tendency to accept the match between two similar but nonidentical pieces that are in different orientations.   However, the largest error rates were obtained for pairs of stimulus elements that are oriented the same, have a similar but nonidentical shape, and occur in the context of a larger number of matching pieces.   Such a pattern supports the interpretation that some individuals may be using a global stimulus comparison process that often leads to errors.

With respect to individual differences, there may be two separate aspects of incorrect performance, the encoding and comparison process and the rotation process.   Evidence for such an assumption was provided by the lack of correlation between subject's error rates on positive and on negative trial items.   In two separate studies, the overall correlation across subjects was zero.   However, both error rates were significantly correlated with overall performance on the reference test.

Our analysis of individual differences in spatial visualization ability utilized both latency and accuracy data.   An individual subject's latency data were used to estimate the four basic processing parameters of the general model.   In addition, error rates for both positive and negative trial types were determined for each subject.   The four latency parameters and the two error parameters were then entered into a multiple regression analysis with performance on the Minnesota Paper Form Board Test as the criterion variable.   In our two studies, data have been obtained showing that the combination of both error data and latency parameters accounts for over

60% of the variance in spatial ability as defined by reference test perform-ance. Based on individual subject model fitting and error data we have reached the following conclusions about ability differences. First, skilled individuals make fewer errors on problems involving stimulus rotation or transformation. Second, they are also more accurate in detecting mis-matches between similar stimuli independent of the occurrence of rotation. Third, skilled individuals are faster at searching through an array to find corresponding stimulus elements. Fourth, they are faster in encoding and comparison processes. A general conclusion based on these types of find-ings is that skill in a visualization task such as the form board is related to the speed and quality of stimulus representation processes. A more precise representation of stimulus elements permits more rapid search for a corre-sponding element and a faster and more accurate decision about their iden-tity.

Because ability appears to be associated with several aspects of task per-formance involving both speed of processing and representation, we ex-plored the possibility that subjects also differed in their approach to process-ing different problem types. In particular, we were intrigued by the possibility that some subjects may adopt a very precise analytic mode of processing consistent with the general model shown earlier. Other subjects may be performing the task in a way that represents an analytic or semiana-lytic mode of processing on some item types and a more global, holistic mode of processing on other item types. The particular condition of interest relative to identifying such a mixture of strategies is the separated condi-tion. It is possible to imagine a strategy in which the individual attempts to merge together or fuse the individual stimulus elements into a whole figure, which is then matched against the completed stimulus. Such a strategy should have two consequences. First, the latency function for such items should be relatively flat. Second, on negative separated trials the fusion process may result in forcing all the pieces into a whole, even though one of the elements is incorrect with respect to specific features such as size or angle. The result would be a higher error rate on such items.

The possible existence of such a processing approach was explored by separating the subjects into two groups solely on the basis of their error rates on the separated different item types. The 12 low-error subjects had fewer than 20% errors on these problems. The 18 high-error subjects had consid-erably more than 20% errors on these problems. This partition revealed an interesting pattern of skill differences. As shown in Table 1, the low-error group was primarily composed of high-skill individuals as determined by reference test performance. In contrast, the high-error group was primarily composed of medium- and low-skill individuals.

Of interest is whether these two groups of subjects also show different

TABLE 1
SUBJECT DISTRIBUTION AS A FUNCTION
OF ABILITY LEVEL AND ERROR RATES

Separated item errors	Spatial ability		
	High	Medium	Low
High	1	8	9
Low	9	2	1

latency patterns for the positive trial data.   The left-hand panel of Fig. 6 shows the data for the low-error group.   An important point to note is the fanning of the slopes consistent with the general model of processing, reflecting an analytic-processing approach.   Second, the slope for the separated condition is relatively steep and its value is approximately 600 msec per stimulus element.   The right-hand panel of Fig. 6 shows the data for the high-error group.   There are two important points to notice.   First, the conditions involving rotation show no differentiation from the condition that does not involve rotation.   Second, the slope for the separated condition is shallower, with a value of 375 msec.

We think that these results, when combined with the error data on negative items, support the hypothesis that skill differences are also associated with differences in processing strategy.   The major strategy differences may involve a precise analytic mode of processing versus a less analytic and partly holistic or global processing mode for certain item types.   With respect to the latter, less-skilled subjects show shallow latency functions for separated item types with very high error rates when an incorrect element is embedded in this stimulus format.   They also fail to show evidence of executing a rotation process, with substantially higher error rates on rotation items when an incorrect or mismatching element is in the array.   Our work to date on individual differences in spatial visualization supports the existence of speed and accuracy differences associated with encoding and representational processes.   In addition, it suggests strategy differences reflecting less analytic modes of processing in lower-skill individuals.   Further, validation of such strategy differences requires more precise methods of analysis of the type possible with eye-movement data.

The preceding overview of some of our spatial aptitude research emphasizes that it is possible to construct and validate cognitive process models for performance in complex spatial visualization tasks.   Such models not only provide a good characterization of group performance but they also capture

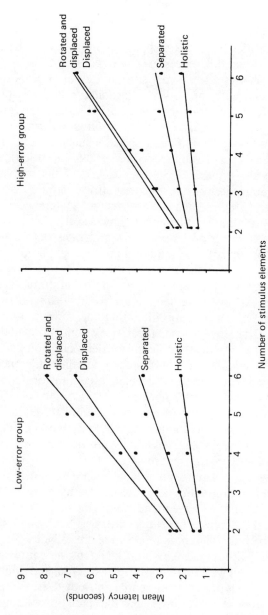

Low-error group

High-error group

Mean latency (seconds)

Number of stimulus elements

FIGURE 6. Positive trial latency data for low- and high-error subjects.

the performance of individual subjects. The problem variants provide a means of determining those aspects of task performance that prove difficult for a given individual.

We can also consider the data on spatial visualization in the context of other data on individual differences in spatial relations to begin to address the issue of what defines general spatial aptitude. It appears that spatial aptitude is associated with the ability to establish sufficiently precise and stable internal representations of unfamiliar visual stimuli that can be subsequently transformed or operated on with a minimal information loss. In spatial relations and visualization tasks, speed of encoding and comparison is significantly related to skill. In more complex tasks, accuracy of encoding and comparison is also significantly related to skill. Thus, individuals who are high in spatial aptitude are faster at representing unfamiliar visual stimuli and what is ultimately represented is more precise. Differences in representation, most likely qualitative differences, may also give rise to other speed differences such as the superior rotation and search rates that are exhibited in various tasks. Problems of representation are most apparent in the more complex tasks that involve the representation and processing of stimuli having several interrelated elements. If we assume that stimulus representation and processing involve a visual short-term or working memory, then skill differences may be a function of coding and capacity within such a memory system. Differences between spatial relations and spatial visualization tasks (factors) may reflect a difference in emphasis on coding versus transformation processes within this system. Another difference between the two factors may involve single versus sequential transformations and the ability to coordinate and monitor the latter.

Our analyses of spatial aptitude are far from complete. Additional tasks within the spatial visualization domain require analysis and modeling. The models we currently have for spatial relations and visualization tasks require refinement, and intensive analyses are needed to determine the underlying bases of the individual differences that have been observed. A systematic analysis of process commonality across tasks also needs to be attempted. Nevertheless, we feel that we have made reasonable progress toward understanding individual differences in spatial aptitude. Such an understanding is essential if individual differences in aptitude are to be useful in creating adaptive instructional environments that facilitate the course of learning and skill acquisition. If we wish to optimize instruction and achievement in the technical skills areas predicted by spatial aptitude tests, then we need to have a better way to assess and understand the spatial-processing skills that individuals bring to the instructional setting, and the impact that these skills can have on the design of instruction and the acquisition of skill.

ENGINEERING DESIGN AND GRAPHICS

The general area of spatial cognition and processing has been largely investigated in isolated laboratory environments. However, spatial ability measures, like other aptitude and intelligence measures, predict success in other environments. As noted earlier, there are two major areas where spatial tests have been utilized for prediction. One area is industry and the other involves certain academic settings and vocational–technical training programs such as engineering design and drafting.

Engineering design and graphics was selected for investigation because it is an area where spatial visualization abilities appear necessary for achieving competence. This is true not only in the correlational literature, but also in individuals' retrospective protocols for performing certain tasks, which will be illustrated subsequently. One major aspect of engineering design courses is training in the production and comprehension of different types of drawings that represent three-dimensional objects. Analyses of course content, examination of texts, and discussions with engineering instructors indicate that emphasis is placed on ability to deal with two major forms of visual representation of a three-dimensional object: isometric and orthographic drawings. An example of each is presented in Fig. 7. An isometric drawing is shown at the left; it is a representation of an object where the viewing angle shows the top-, front-, and right-side views simultaneously. An orthographic drawing generally displays three separate two-dimentional projections representing the same three views, as would be seen by an individual looking directly at each surface. Each orthographic projection also includes information about internal or hidden edges or planes, indicated by the dotted lines. The orthographic drawing at the right of Fig. 7 shows how the isometric drawing on the left would be depicted.

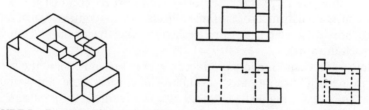

FIGURE 7.   Examples of isometric and orthographic drawings of a three-dimensional object.

COGNITIVE REPRESENTATION OF ENGINEERING DRAWINGS

Two preliminary studies have been conducted that examined issues of representation and comprehension of isometric and orthographic drawings. Because these were initial, probing studies, the questions we sought to answer were relatively simple and were not process oriented. Rather, we focused on trying to understand more about these two different forms of representation and stimulus complexity within and across representations. Initially, an engineering instructor helped us develop a set of stimuli he deemed representative of materials that individuals deal with in such courses. The set of stimuli he created varied considerably but not systematically in complexity, ranging from easy to medium to difficult in ease of processing. Figure 8 contains a representative sample of the orthographic and isometric drawings in the total stimulus set.

The two studies employed similar data collection procedures and analyses. In both cases, a set of drawings was given to individuals who were instructed to do two things. First, they sorted them into groups according to level of object complexity. There were no limitations placed on the number of groups to be formed, yet most of the individuals created four or five groups. Second, they also rank-ordered all objects within and across groups with respect to object complexity. Thus, we could examine the features that contribute to perceived complexity and the groups or clusters that were formed. In the first study, two different subject groups were compared on their ranking and sorting behavior for a set of 48 isometric drawings. The subjects were 29 individuals without any experience in engineering design and graphics courses and 21 students who were at the end of a one-semester course in this area. This provides the basis for a novice–expert contrast. In the second study, a different group of 26 students was tested who were also nearing completion of a one-semester engineering design and graphics course. These subjects performed the ranking and sorting task with two sets of drawings: isometric and orthographic drawings of 42 corresponding objects. Thus, we have the basis for a within-expert contrast for different representational formats of the same objects. In this context, *expert* refers to those individuals who have some explicit training in viewing and constructing such drawings.

Both experts and novices produce interpretable and coherent clusters of the isometrically represented stimuli. The clusters were similar but not always identical. Figure 9 includes a sample of some of the common object clusters formed by both groups. For some clusters, the specific characteristics defining the group can be readily identified and labeled. Multidimensional scaling analysis of the novice and expert sorting data was conducted by

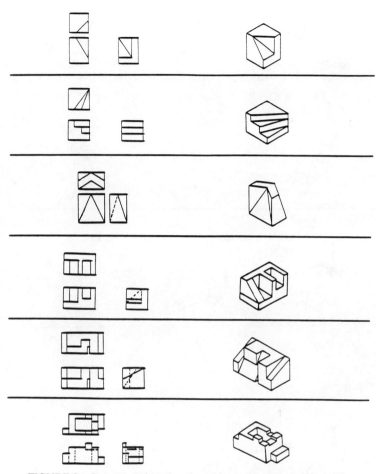

FIGURE 8. Representative stimuli used in sorting and ranking studies.

using INDSCAL. The results of the INDSCAL analysis indicated that both novices and experts were using the same dimensions to sort objects, and the weighting on dimensions was equivalent. This is shown in Table 2, which provides the group weights and a very general characterization of each dimension. The novices and experts also showed general agreement in the average complexity ranking of objects within the entire problem set ($r = .70$). However, they differed in the weighting of certain object features with respect to the evaluation of object complexity. The nature of this difference is systematic. The coordinate values of objects along each of the three dimensions of the INDSCAL analysis were used in multiple regression

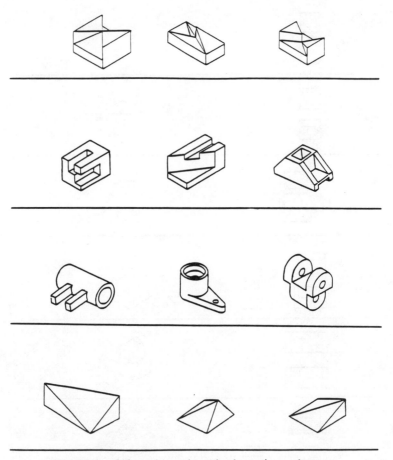

FIGURE 9.   Objects clustered together by novices and experts.

analyses to predict rated object complexity for each subject group. These multiple regression analyses produced different patterns for the two groups, shown in Table 3. The major difference between novices and experts was the relative importance of Dimension 2 in predicting object complexity. This dimension reflects a partition of objects such that those with curved and oblique surfaces are at one extreme and those with simple rectangular and right-angle features are at the other extreme. Objects that have multiple oblique surfaces and those with curved surfaces are systematically rated more complex by the experts than novices. This can be understood by considering that these features of an object are the most problematic in creating an orthographic representation of an isometric drawing. A related

TABLE 2
GROUP WEIGHTS FROM INDSCAL
ANALYSIS OF ISOMETRIC SORTS AND
GENERAL CHARACTERIZATION OF
EACH DIMENSION

	Dimension		
	1[a]	2[b]	3[c]
Novices ($N = 29$)	.61	.50	.38
Experts ($N = 21$)	.54	.53	.37

[a] Number of edges, surfaces, and hidden features.
[b] Right angles (blocklike structures).
[c] Number of oblique surfaces.

factor that the experts appear more sensitive to is the presence of hidden features that would have to be represented in an orthographic drawing. Thus, even though they are dealing with isometric representations, their ranking of the complexity of an object is apparently related to difficulties of representing it orthographically.

The data for experts on both isometric and orthographic representations also produced interesting differences associated with the two different forms of representation. For both forms, there were interpretable and coherent object clusters, but again they were not necessarily identical. An INDSCAL analysis of the sorting data for isometric and orthographic representations revealed a differential weighting pattern for use of the three dimensions. This is illustrated in Table 4, which also includes a characterization of each dimension. A major difference is associated with the dimension that discriminates rectangular versus oblique features of objects.

TABLE 3
MULTIPLE REGRESSION ANALYSIS OF
NOVICES' AND EXPERTS' RANKING
DATA

	Novices		Experts	
Predictor	F	β	F	β
Dimension 1	290.5	.88	61.5	.67
Dimension 2	2.8	.08	34.2	.50
Dimension 3	21.6	.24	4.4	.18
	$R^2 = .89$		$R^2 = .69$	

TABLE 4

DIMENSION WEIGHTS FROM INDSCAL
ANALYSIS OF ISOMETRIC AND
ORTHOGRAPHIC SORTING DATA AND
GENERAL CHARACTERIZATION OF
EACH DIMENSION

	Dimension		
	1[a]	2[b]	3[c]
Isometric	.36	.33	.39
Orthographic	.86	.31	.10

[a] Number of edges, surfaces.
[b] Number of hidden and internal features.
[c] Rectangular versus oblique features.

A subsequent correlational analysis using the INDSCAL dimension coordinates to predict rated complexity within each type of representation confirmed the fact that these dimensions of objects were also differentially salient in judging object complexity. These data are shown in Table 5. Hidden features and oblique surfaces are weighted more highly in the rankings for the isometrically represented stimuli. This suggests that for orthographic drawings, the presence of these features may not be detected because of a failure to integrate or difficulty in integrating all three projections to create a composite mental image of the actual object. The predominant factor for making judgments about objects represented orthographically seems to be the number of surfaces or edges that are illustrated in the three separate views.

Our data analyses suggest several directions for process- and strategy-oriented research. One direction focuses on the process of mapping across different forms of representation. The speed, accuracy, and strategy of determining correspondence between an isometric and orthographic representation should vary with object complexity. Of interest is how specific types of features affect the mapping process. In addition, the orthographic representations are of interest by themselves because there should be systematic differences in the speed and accuracy of constructing composite mental images of objects given the information contained in the individual projections. A related issue involves the processes employed to determine consistency and correspondence of features represented in each of the three separate orthographic views. This seems to involve various spatial comprehension and inference skills.

TABLE 5
MULTIPLE REGRESSION ANALYSIS OF
ISOMETRIC AND ORTHOGRAPHIC
RANKING DATA

	Isometric		Orthographic	
Predictor	F	β	F	β
Dimension 1	29.0	.48	314.6	.90
Dimension 2	11.3	.30	5.8	.12
Dimension 3	36.7	.51	3.4	.09
	$R^2 = .73$		$R^2 = .91$	

STRATEGIES FOR PROCESSING ENGINEERING DRAWINGS

An initial study has been conducted that explores some of the issues discussed (Mumaw, Cooper, & Glaser, 1982). Three forms of representation — isometric drawing (ID), orthographic drawing (OD), and verbal description (V) — were combined to produce three problem types that were used in a problem-solving task. The subject's goal in the task was to determine if the representations shown on two separate slides depicted the same three-dimensional object or were compatible in some way. One problem type was created by pairing orthographic and isometric drawings in the serial order OD–ID. A second problem type was created by pairing a verbal description with an orthographic drawing in the serial order V–OD. For the third problem type (OD), subjects were first shown a slide containing three orthographic projections with one view replaced by an empty frame. The second slide showed a possible third view for that orthographic drawing. The subject had to determine whether the third view given was compatible with the first two views.

Thirty problems were presented for each of the three engineering drawing problem types and given to 28 subjects (14 high spatial aptitude and 14 low spatial aptitude). The subjects were given a maximum of 60, 80, or 100 seconds for the OD–ID, OD, and V–OD tasks, respectively. In addition, each subject responded to questions about solution strategy and problem difficulty after each set of 15 problems. Several other data sources were available for the subjects in this experiment. These included measures of course performance — both an overall course grade and a separate laboratory grade based on drawing assignments — and standardized measures of spatial aptitude. The latter were the spatial subtests of both the Primary

Mental Abilities battery (PMA; Thurstone & Thurstone, 1949) and the Differential Aptitude Test (DAT; Bennett *et al.*, 1974). As noted earlier, the PMA test emphasizes spatial relations ability and the DAT emphasizes spatial visualization. In addition, both verbal and quantitative Scholastic Aptitude Test (SAT) scores were available for all subjects.

The more detailed aspects of performance on the three problem types will be examined, but first it is important to consider the general relationships obtained among aptitude, course grades, and task performance. Correlations were computed between each of the various data sources available for each subject. These results are summarized in Table 6. There are three important groups of correlations that bear consideration. First, the spatial aptitude measures are significantly correlated with both overall course performance and laboratory grades. These data replicate typical findings showing that spatial aptitude predicts performance in engineering design and graphics courses. Of interest is that the correlations are higher for the measure of spatial visualization ability. Second, performance on each of the three engineering drawing problem types is significantly correlated with measures of course performance. These results provide an external validation of the experimental problem types. The differential pattern of correlations across problem types is also of significance and will be discussed subsequently. Third, the correlational data reveal a consistent pattern that addresses the relationship between performance on the engineering drawing tasks and spatial aptitude. First, OD and V – OD task accuracy show significant correlations with both aptitude tests, the OD task at the .05 level and the V – OD task at the .01 level. Accuracy on the OD – ID task, however, is not significantly correlated with either of the aptitude tests. In addition both the OD and the V – OD tasks were significantly correlated with the Quantitative SAT scores of the subjects, but not the Verbal SAT scores. The V – OD task was much more strongly related to spatial and mathematics test scores than to verbal test scores, suggesting that reading and verbal comprehension skills are not as important for this task as are spatial and quantitative reasoning skills.

The experimental procedure provided a rich data base for investigating aspects of problem-solving performance. The subject was allowed to control alternation between the two problem slides until the correct response was determined. Thus, a number of dependent measures were obtained for each trial, including number of alternations between slides, initial viewing time for Slide 1, initial viewing time for Slide 2, total solution time, and accuracy. These data together with retrospective protocols were extremely useful in identifying the solution strategy each subject used for each problem type. Because complex spatial tasks are often susceptible to several solution strategies, both spatial and nonspatial (Lohman, 1979), each subject was

TABLE 6
INTERCORRELATIONS OF SUBJECT PERFORMANCE INDICES

	Course grade	Laboratory grade	Task accuracy		
			OD–ID	OD	V–OD
PMA	.40*	.30	.11	.34	.40
DAT	.58**	.48**	.23	.41*	.54**
Course grade			.40*	.49**	.59**
Laboratory grade			.32	.28	.45*

* $p < .05$. ** $p < .01$.

asked to describe the strategy that had been used. These retrospective protocols provided the first clues to the types of strategy differences that exist between and within subjects. One general difference found in solution strategies can be characterized as the need to construct an isometric representation mentally to mediate problem solving. For instance, a subject may read an entire verbal description and try to imagine the three-dimensional object mentally before viewing the second slide. The need to construct this mediating representation to integrate information may have a large role in determining the spatial requirements of a task. The alternative solution strategy for many subjects was an analytic feature-matching strategy, which requires identifying and comparing local features of the representations. Tasks that are more susceptible to this feature-match strategy may be less related to spatial aptitude because less spatial integration is demanded.

An analysis of the engineering drawing task accuracy data as a function of aptitude and strategy provided data about the spatial demands of each task, which complement conclusions drawn from the correlational analysis. Two levels of both spatial aptitude (high and low) and solution strategy (constructive and analytic) were used to examine task accuracy. The determination of solution strategies was based on specific patterns in the dependent measures and retrospective verbal protocols. As stated earlier, some subjects claimed to construct the isometric representation mentally to mediate problem solution for each of the three problem types. The alternative strategy involved the comparison of local features extracted from the two-dimensional orthographic projections. The number of alternations between slides and the ratio of the time for the first viewing of Slide 1 to total solution time were measures that best indicated a subject's strategy. Subjects who reported a constructive strategy spent a large percentage of their total time on the first viewing of Slide 1. This was assumed to reflect construction time, and they subsequently required few alternations between slides prior to final solution. The analytic or feature-match subjects, on the other hand, had a lower time ratio and used more alternations between slides in order to make several local feature comparisons. The general distinction allowed the classification of most of the 28 subjects for each task. The remaining subjects were either inconsistent in using a certain strategy or used a strategy combining aspects of both construction and feature matching.

For the OD problem type, 24 of the 28 subjects consistently fit one of the two solution strategy patterns. Thirteen subjects were classified as constructive and 11 as analytic. Comparisons of problem-solving accuracy for these two groups and for aptitude groups revealed no main effects. However, when subjects were grouped by both aptitude and strategy, an interaction was obtained whereby low-aptitude subjects using the constructive strategy showed the poorest performance. This pattern was emphasized more strongly and became more interpretable when subject groups were further broken down based on the total time to solution, as shown in Table 7. Subjects who had an average solution time of less than 50 seconds were placed in the fast cells. Those subjects who took longer to solve the items were placed in the slow cells.

There are two important findings to note in Table 7. The first concerns the relationship between aptitude level and strategy selection: 7 of the 11 high-aptitude subjects chose the analytic strategy and 9 of the 13 low-aptitude subjects chose the constructive strategy. This trend is in the opposite direction to what might be expected. The second important result is the occurrence of a significant interaction revealing an incompatibility between aptitude and strategy. Contrasting the performance of the constructive, high-aptitude subjects with the low-aptitude subjects using the same strategy, the constructive, low-aptitude subjects, who worked at the same speed, had an accuracy level that was half that of the constructive, high-aptitude subjects. The constructive, low-aptitude subjects, who took twice as long to solve the problems, however, obtained the same level of performance shown by the constructive, high-aptitude subjects. However, these trends were not found for those subjects using an analytic strategy. The performance of the low-aptitude subjects was identical to the high-aptitude subjects in accuracy and solution time. This pattern of results suggests that there are some limits on the efficiency with which low-aptitude subjects can use the constructive strategy. For these subjects to perform as accurately as the high-aptitude subjects, they must use twice as much time. In addition, when low-aptitude subjects use a strategy that does not seem to depend on mentally constructing an isometric representation, they are able to perform as efficiently as the high spatial aptitude subjects.

The results for the V–OD problems were more straightforward. The analysis of the dependent measures showed that 18 of the 28 subjects consis-

TABLE 7

PERFORMANCE ON OD PROBLEMS AS A
FUNCTION OF APTITUDE AND STRATEGY

		Constructive		Analytic	
		%	N	%	N
High spatial	Slow	—		70	1
	Fast	62	4	55	6
Low spatial	Slow	59	4	—	
	Fast	41	5	56	4

tently fit one of the two strategies. As Table 8 shows, the distribution was quite similar to the OD task data. Five of the nine high-aptitude subjects chose an analytic strategy and six of the nine low-aptitude subjects chose a constructive strategy. The accuracy data also show a pattern similar to the OD task data. The subjects showing the poorest performance were the constructive, low-aptitude subjects. The subjects who performed best were the constructive, high-aptitude subjects. In addition, the accuracy difference between the high- and low-aptitude individuals using the analytic strategy was not substantial. Therefore, like the OD task data, the strategy-by-aptitude interaction, though not significant, was in a direction suggesting that aptitude differences are stronger for the subjects using a constructive strategy. However, unlike the OD task data, total solution time was unimportant and there was a significant main effect due to spatial aptitude. This main effect concurs with the results of the correlational analyses.

The OD–ID task data were the least systematic of the three tasks in two respects. First, solution strategies reported by the subjects were more varied and less consistently used for this task. Only five subjects consistently used a constructive strategy and eight subjects used an analytic strategy. In addi-

TABLE 8

PERFORMANCE ON V–OD PROBLEMS
AS A FUNCTION OF APTITUDE AND
STRATEGY

	Constructive		Analytic	
	%	N	%	N
High spatial	73	4	64	5
Low spatial	54	6	61	3

TABLE 9

PERFORMANCE ON OD–ID PROBLEMS
AS A FUNCTION OF APTITUDE AND
STRATEGY

	Constructive		Analytic	
	%	N	%	N
High spatial	82	3	76	6
Low spatial	77	2	83	5

tion, three subjects used what might be called a reversed strategy. This strategy was very similar to an analytic strategy except that these subjects moved very quickly to the isometric drawing on the second slide and imaged a single projection for comparison with the corresponding projection on Slide 1. Secondly, as Table 9 shows, neither strategy nor spatial aptitude was related to task accuracy. When task accuracy was averaged for the three levels of strategy and two levels of aptitude, no main effects or interactions were found.

These task-specific findings corroborate the results found in the correlational analyses: The V–OD task data show a strong aptitude effect, the OD–ID task data show no aptitude effect, and the OD task data represent a complex interaction in which the effects of aptitude are dependent on the solution strategy a subject chooses. These results, though based on small sample sizes and post hoc determinations of strategy, suggest that the "spatialness" of a task may depend on the need to mediate problem solving with a representation not directly available in the stimuli. The V–OD task seems most dependent on this mediating representation and the OD–ID task seems least dependent on other representations. This interpretation implies that a solution strategy utilizing only information from the two-dimensional representations should not be successful for the OD and V–OD tasks. To accommodate this implication, it may be necessary to recast the analytic and constructive solution strategies in terms of predictive versus facilitative use of an isometric representation. The subject using an analytic strategy may consider parts of the isometric representation to compare single features but never consider the entire object at once. A constructive strategy, on the other hand, may imply that the subject considers the entire isometric representation to make predictions about what will be present on the second slide. In this latter case, the isometric representation is used to predict details of the second representation. In the case of the analytic strategy, the subject only needs to construct the key local parts of the object to facilitate feature comparison.

Another goal of this work is to understand the task domain better, which requires, in part, discovering the characteristics of items that affect the difficulty and/or spatial demands of the task. The preceding analysis suggests that making an item more dependent on mediation through an isometric representation should make the item more spatial. Other data from this experiment also address this question. By isolating OD items on which the constructive strategy group outperformed the analytic group, commonalities were found suggesting manipulations that can increase an item's dependence on mediation. The constructives were more accurate on items in which there was little overlap of local features between Slide 1 and Slide 2. (Figure 10 provides an example.) That is, it is necessary to construct the isometric drawing to determine the compatibility of the three views. Note that the second slide reveals an angled plane that is not shown on Slide 1.

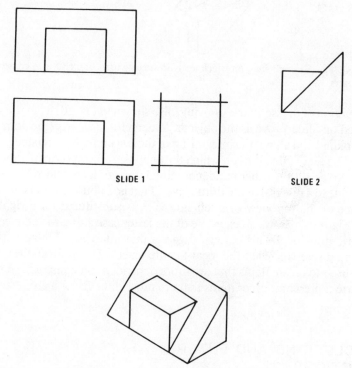

SLIDE 1   SLIDE 2

FIGURE 10. Example item on which constructive strategy users outperformed analytic strategy users.

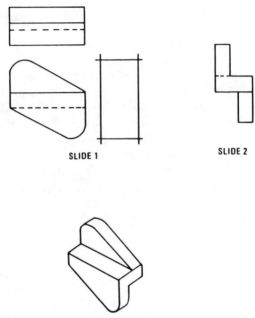

FIGURE 11.   Example item on which analytic strategy users outperformed constructive strategy users.

Construction of the isometric drawing (also shown in Fig. 10) from the views provided on Slide 1 reveals the object's "emergent" property (the dominant angled plane) and allows the integration of these seemingly unrelated projections. The set of OD items on which the analytic subjects outperformed the constructives, on the other hand, contained several items that were incompatible due to a reversal in the third view. That is, a bottom view is shown in the place of the top view or a left-side view is substituted for a right-side view. Figure 11 shows an example of the latter case along with the correct isometric drawing. This pattern suggests that analytics may be better at detecting discrepancies at the local feature level. This information, then, can be used to create items that are more dependent on construction of the isometric representation of items that are more difficult for a given strategy user.

CONCLUSIONS AND FUTURE DIRECTIONS

In the preceding two sections we have provided an overview of efforts to analyze spatial aptitude and competence. Our efforts in this area are only at the initial level of analysis and understanding. In the area of individual differences in spatial aptitude, process-oriented analyses of performance on spatial relations and visualization tasks have taken us beyond the stage of simple test score differences. We are beginning to localize the specific sources of individual differences in reference test scores. Doing so depends on being able to create systematic sets of problems that can be related to a theory or model of task performance. Individuals differ in the speed and accuracy of executing specific mental processes associated with visual – spatial stimuli. An important issue is that they also differ in the strategies they use to solve simple and complex problems. There are both between-individual and within-individual strategy differences. One interesting but very tentative result is that high-spatial individuals appear to be more precise and analytic in solving problems found on aptitude tests and this is also true in solving engineering drawing problems. *Analytic* does not imply use of a nonspatial strategy or process. Rather, it appears to involve a spatial – analytic mode of processing in which spatial detail and precision are maintained and emphasized. This results in greater accuracy on both spatial aptitude tasks and engineering drawing problems. High aptitude individuals also appear capable of integrating complex spatial representations. Thus, they may have at their disposal a variety of processing skills that can be flexibly adapted to the particular demands of a spatial problem.

Our efforts in the area of engineering design and graphics must be viewed as very simplistic attempts to define the task domain. Nevertheless, progress has been made in identifying some of the dimensions of stimulus and task complexity as well as their interactions with spatial aptitude. At the beginning of this chapter we noted that the research on spatial aptitude is largely disconnected from the research on engineering design and graphics. A major concern for the future is linking aptitude research with research on technical skill competence. We believe that a basis for doing so lies in specifying a set of basic spatial information processes. Measures of the speed and power of these processes as well as the strategies for assembling and monitoring them provide a basis for analyzing aptitudes and technical task performance and their relationships. An interesting question is whether deficiencies on specific spatial processes have implications for the acquisition of certain technical skill competencies. As we have shown, aptitude test scores moderately predict performance in a technical skills course. They are, however, insufficient indices of the level of competence that can be achieved. There is also question about the stability of such aptitudes. Some previous research indicates that spatial aptitude scores increase after taking engineering design, mechanical drawing, and drafting courses. It is possible that individuals often have little experience with the type of spatial information processing examined on aptitude tasks. They can, however, gain proficiency in such skills through practice and training. Some of our own very recent research has shown that low spatial ability individuals who participate in several spatial-processing sessions show dramatic increases in performance on standardized aptitude tests (Pellegrino, 1984). Thus, although aptitude may predict achievement it also does not necessarily preclude achievement in the spatial domain. These and other issues can be addressed by continuing to develop and apply a process-oriented approach in the area of spatial cognition.

REFERENCES

Bennett, G. K., Seashore, H. G., & Wesman, A. G. (1974). *Differential aptitude test.* New York: The Pyschological Corporation.
Carroll, J. B. (1976). Psychometric tests as cognitive tasks: A new "structure of intellect." In L. B. Resnick (Ed.), *The nature of intelligence.* Hillsdale, NJ: Erlbaum.
Cooper, L. A. (1982). Strategies for visual comparison and representation: Individual differences. In R. J. Sternberg (Ed.), *Advances in the psychology of human intelligence* (Vol. 1). Hillsdale, NJ: Erlbaum.
Cooper, L. A., & Shepard, R. N. (1973). Chronometric studies of the rotation of mental images. In W. G. Chase (Ed.), *Visual information processing.* New York: Academic Press.
Likert, R. (1934). A multiple-choice revision of the Minnesota Paper Form Board. *Psychological Bulletin, 31,* 674.
Likert, R., & Quasha, W. H. (1970). *Manual for the Revised Minnesota Paper Form Board Test.* New York: The Psychological Corporation.
Lohman, D. F. (1979). *Spatial ability: A review and reanalysis of the correlational literature* (Tech. Rep. No. 8). Stanford, CA: Aptitude Research Project, School of Education, Stanford University.
McGee, M. G. (1979). Human spatial abilities: Psychometric studies and environmental, generic, hormonal, and neurological influences. *Psychological Bulletin, 86*(5), 889–918.
Mumaw, R. J., Cooper, L. A., & Glaser, R. (1982, May). *Individual differences in complex spatial problem solving: Aptitude and strategy effects.* Paper presented at annual meetings of the Midwestern Psychological Association, Minneapolis, MN.
Mumaw, R. J., Pellegrino, J. W., & Glaser, R. (1980, November). *Some puzzling aspects of spatial ability.* Paper presented at annual meetings of Psychonomic Society, St. Louis, MO.
Pellegrino, J. W. (1984, April) *Information processing and intellectual ability.* Paper presented at the annual meetings of the American Educational Research Association, New Orleans, LA.
Pellegrino, J. W., Cantoni, V. J., & Solter, A. (1981, November). *Speed, accuracy and strategy differences in spatial processing.* Paper presented at the annual meetings of the Psychonomic Society, Philadelphia, PA.
Pellegrino, J. W., & Glaser, R. (1979). Cognitive components and correlates in the analysis of individual differences. *Intelligence, 3,* 187–214.
Pellegrino, J. W., & Kail, R. V. (1982). Process analyses of spatial aptitude. In R. J. Sternberg (Ed.), *Advances in the psychology of human intelligence* (Vol. 1). Hillsdale, NJ: Erlbaum.
Shepard, R. N., & Feng, C. (1972). A chronometric study of mental paper folding. *Cognitive Psychology, 3,* 228–243.
Thurstone, L. L., & Thurstone, T. G., (1949). *Manual for the SRA Primary Mental Abilities.* Chicago: Science Research Associates.

4

Theoretically Based Psychometric Measures of Inductive Reasoning*

Earl C. Butterfield
Donn Nielsen
Kenneth L. Tangen
Michael B. Richardson

INTRODUCTION

In principle, it should be possible to derive the items for an intelligence test from a theory of cognition. One reason this has seldom been done is that builders of intelligence tests use items that vary in their difficulty in order to reveal individual differences, but cognitive theory says very little about the population of items to which it applies or about how to vary item difficulty. The first purpose of this chapter is to describe a population of letter series. The second purpose is to describe a theory of inductive reasoning that allows solution of any problem in the population. The third purpose is to show how the theory characterizes the billions of series in the population so that they are a functionally limitless pool for constructing equivalent or individually tailored subtests of intelligence. First the chapter presents a scheme for describing and generating letter series. The next section presents a theory that predicts letter series difficulty. The following section describes several experiments that test the theory. Next, theoretically based procedures for selection and computerized generation of letter series items for standard and

---

* The research herein was supported by U.S.P.H.S. Grants HD-13029 and HD-16241.

77
Copyright © 1985 by Academic Press, Inc.
All rights of reproduction in any form reserved.
ISBN 0-12-238180-7

individually tailored intelligence tests are described. The Appendix presents an algebra for generating series and exploring the characteristics of the letter series population.

We have chosen to work with letter series problems partly because their solution depends on inductive reasoning. Among others, Spearman (1923) and Raven (1938) have both argued that inductive reasoning is central to the concept and testing of intelligence. Virtually all standardized aptitude and intelligence tests include inductive reasoning problems (Pellegrino & Glaser, 1982). Thurstone and Thurstone (1941) began the use of letter series problems to measure intelligence. Our analyses of these problems are extensions of work by Simon and Kotovsky (1963; Kotovsky & Simon, 1973) and by Holzman, Pellegrino, and Glaser (1982; 1983).

DESCRIBING AND GENERATING LETTER SERIES

OVERVIEW OF A SERIES RULE SYSTEM

We begin by explaining how to generate letter series and how to describe the population of problems to which a theory of series solution might apply and from which test items might be drawn. Two considerations may have led prior investigators to neglect these matters. First, there is no apparent limit to the number of taxonomies that could be used to classify letter series, and none is necessarily better than the others. Second, and more important, the nature of letter series is such that no descriptive system can provide a unique characterization of every series (Simon & Kotovsky, 1963). The impossibility of mutually exclusive classification of all series led Simon and Kotovsky to avoid questions about how to generate series. Instead, they built a descriptive language that can be applied to letter series once they are generated, thereby facilitating the study of existing item pools. They used their language to study only the 15 problems included in the Primary Mental Abilities test (Thurstone, 1962). From a scientific point of view, the difficulties with this approach are that the features of these problems that could influence how people solve them are confounded, and the problems do not sample systematically the distribution of those features in the population of problems. From a psychometric point of view, the problem with this approach is that it provides little guidance in how to construct items that might be included on an intelligence test. Holzman *et al.* (1983) generated letter series problems for research purposes, but these authors provided no systematic guidance in how to generate other problems nor any way to judge the extent to which their problems sample the distribution of features in the population of problems.

The work of Simon and Kotovsky and of Holzman *et al.* is nevertheless instructive because it shows that series are frequently composed of subseries, which we call *strings*. The strings are composed of units among which specified relations hold. When the units are letters, the relations include identity (e.g., AAAAA), next (e.g., ABCDE), and back (e.g., ZYXWV), and can be expanded to include double next (e.g., ACEGI), double back (e.g., ZXVTR), and so forth. Their work also shows that the relations among letters on each string and the positioning of strings relative to one another can be expressed in a rule. To generate a problem it is possible to begin with such a rule, select a starting letter for each of its strings, and recursively apply the rule's relations in the order given. Accordingly, it is necessary to decide what kinds of rules to employ before generating a pool of letter series problems.

Simon and Kotovsky (1963) and Holzman *et al.* (1982) expressed their series rules in terms that emphasize mechanisms of a cognitive model more than they emphasize features of series. We use a notational system that emphasizes problem features more than theoretical mechanisms. Although no notational system is entirely atheoretical, our emphasis on problem features allows us to distinguish more clearly between the kinds of problems we pose for people and the mechanisms we think they use to solve the problems. This approach reduces the chances that we will need to revise our notational system as our understanding of mechanisms changes, and it simplifies the answering of questions about the range of problems to which theoretical mechanisms may apply. Table 1 illustrates the rule system we use to notate and to generate letter series.

Rule 1 in Table 1 reads N1 I1 B2 I2. The numbers, which can be viewed as subscripts, indicate only that the rule describes series composed of two strings, the first of which has an N and an I relation and the second of which has a B and an I relation, where N means next one letter up the alphabet, I means identical, and B means back one letter down the alphabet. The illustrative N1 I1 string was created by selecting a C and applying first an N operation, giving the letter D, and then an I operation, giving another D, then an N, giving the letter E, then an I, and so on recursively. The illustrative B2 I2 string was created by starting with a Z and recursively applying back and identity operations. Both of these strings have a period of 2, because only two relations are required to continue each string indefinitely. Finally, the two strings were intermixed in the order specified by the rule, giving the problem DDYYEEXXFFWW. The problem has a period of 4, which is the sum of the periods of the two strings from which it is constructed.

TABLE 1
ILLUSTRATIONS FROM A SYSTEM FOR DESCRIBING AND GENERATING LETTER SERIES

Rule 1

	N1 I1 B2 I2		
String 1	DD EE FF		
String 2:	YY XX WW		
Problem:	DDYYEEXXFFWW		

Rule 2

	N1 B1 N1	=	NI N2 I1
String 1:	CBCDCDEDE	String 1:	C CD DE E
		String 2:	B C D
Problem:	CBCDCDEDE	=	CBCDCDEDE

	N1 B1 N1	=	N1 N2 I1
String 1:	CBCDCDEDE	String 1:	C CD DE E
		String 2:	L M N
Problem:	CBCDCDEDE	≠	CLCDMDENE

Rule 3

	N1-first N1 N1 I2
String 1:	CDE DEF EFG
String 2:	X X X
Problem:	CDEXDEFXEFGX

Rule 4

	N1 N2(+N) I2 I1
String 1:	C CD DE E
String 2:	NN OPP QRSS
Problem:	CNNCDOPPDEQRSSE

Rule 2 in Table 1 shows that different rules can create identical series, which seems to be the chief reason that others have not built a system for generating a large population of series. The second series in Table 1 was created from the rule N1 B1 N1 by starting with the letter B, applying first an N relation, then a B relation, another N, and then beginning again at the start of the rule. That same problem could have been created by the two-string rule N1 N2 I1 if the first string was begun by operating on a B and the second string was begun by operating on an A. The fact that every series generated by one rule can be described equally well by a second rule does not mean that every series generated by the second rule can be described by the first. Thus, whereas every N1 B1 N1 rule can be described as an N1 N2 I1, the reverse is not true. Table 1 shows two problems generated by the rule N1 N2 I1, the first of which can be described as N1 B1 N1 and the second of which cannot.

Because it is impossible for a person to continue a series correctly without forming a mental representation of it (Simon & Kotovsky, 1963), the fact that series generated by one rule can be described equally well by other rules indicates the need for research to find out how people represent series. Also, it is harder to find the regularity in the problem to which both the N1 B1 N1 and N1 N2 I1 rules apply than in the problem to which only N1 N2 I1 applies. It is not true that every series with multiple rules in our system is harder to solve, but it is an interesting question why some are and some are not. The answer has to do with spurious relations, which are considered subsequently.

Rule 3 in Table 1 indicates that sometimes a letter other than the last one on a string can be used by a given relational operation. In the first two rules the letter used was always the last letter on the string, but that is not required. When there is more than one letter per period on a string, the first relation on that string can operate on either the first or last letter in the preceding period. Thus, N1-first indicates that the N relation should be applied to the first letter from the preceding period of String 1 (in this case the letter C), rather than to the last letter on String 1 (in this case the letter E).[1] In the rule system we use, the absence of a first designation following a relation means that the relation is applied to the last letter on the string, as are the two N relations in the third rule and all of the relations in the first and second rules in Table 1.

Rule 4 in Table 1 shows how the rule system notates series composed of strings whose periods change. The (+N) indicates that with every recursive application of the rule an N relation is added to String 2; the example shows how this translates into problems whose period increases. Period length could decrease as well. Moreover, the period of a series may remain constant for several periods and then increase or decrease, even though the periods of its constituent strings vary from the outset. For example, the rule N1(+I) B2 I2 I2 I2(−I) generates problems whose period remains stable at five for five periods of the series, and then increase by one in every successive period: AZZZZ BBYYY CCCXX DDDDX EEEEE FFFFFF (spaces indicate periods of the series). The period of series created by this rule eventually increases because the second string disappears after four recursions through the rule. Every rule containing at least one string with a variable period will

---

[1] Descriptive rules can be written whose first relations on each string operate on letters other than the first or last on that string in the preceding period, but such rules may not allow generation of series. Thus, although I1-second N1 N1 I2 describes the third rule in Table 15, it does not allow generation of the first letter on the first string. Our rule system is designed to allow problem generation. Therefore, it allows only first and last letters to be objects of relational operations, regardless of how many letters there are per period per string. For this same reason, the system excludes rules containing any strings whose letters cannot be generated by a determinant sequence of relational transformations. For example, no string of random or probabilistic letter sequences are included.

produce series whose periods are variable, if the series is continued long enough.

A More Detailed View of the Series Rule System

How many rules does this system generate? Consider rules that use only the I, N, and B relations, for which each relation operates on only the last letter of its string and for which every string has a fixed period P. To generate a letter series from a one-string rule, a single letter from the alphabet, and then successively apply each relation specified by the rule, returning to the start of the rule each time its last relation has been applied. For $P = 3$ alone, there are as many one-string rules as there are combinations, minus three, of the three permissible relations, $3^3 - 3 = 24$ rules. Each such rule can be initialized with any of the 26 letters of the alphabet, giving a population of 624 different one-string series of any given number of letters. To generate a series from any two-string rule, select two letters from the alphabet and use one to initiate each string, recursively applying the relations of the rule to the letters specified by the string numbers. In a two-string problem of $P = 3$, one of the strings will have one of three single relations I, N, or B and one of the strings will have two relations. There are nine combinations and orders of two relations (IN, NI, NB, etc.), so there are $3 \times 9 = 27$ combinations of one- and two-relation strings. For each combination, the single-relation string may fall in any of three positions relative to the two-relation string, so there are $3 \times 27 = 81$ rules with two two strings. There are 26^2 combinations of letters with which to begin each rule, for a total of 54,756 different two-string series of any given number of letters. When $P = 3$ there are 3^3 three-string rules, which is to say there are 27 ways of combining the three relations I, N, and B. For each rule 26^3 starting points can be selected, giving a total of 474,552 different three-string letter series of $P = 3$. Thus, using only the I, N, and B relations, applying each to only the last letter on its string, and excluding series with strings whose period varies, there are 132 rules for generating letter series with $P = 3$. These rules create more than 500,000 series of any given number of letters.

Table 2 shows that as P and the number of permissible relations $\#R$ on a string increase, the number of rules and problems that most of them generate increases rapidly. The top panel of Table 2 shows the number of different ways that $S = 1$ to 6 strings can be assigned to $P = 1$ to 6 within-period positions, given that every letter on every string relates to the immediately preceding letter on that string and every string has a fixed period. Each way of assigning strings to positions is called a string structure; Table 2 shows that there is exactly one structure with one string for each period length. That is,

TABLE 2

NUMBER OF STRING STRUCTURES, RULES, AND SERIES WHEN PERIOD AND
NUMBER OF STRINGS VARY FROM 1 TO 6

Number of strings	Period						Total	Series
	1	2	3	4	5	6		
Number of string structures								
1	1	1	1	1	1	1	—	—
2		1	3	7	15	31	—	—
3			1	6	25	89	—	—
4				1	10	65	—	—
5					1	15	—	—
6						1	—	—
Total	1	2	5	15	52	202	—	—
Number of rules and series given three relations								
1	3	6	24	78	240	726	1,077	28,002
2		9	81	567	3,645	22,599	26,901	18,185,076
3			27	486	6,075	64,881	71,469	1,256,139,144
4				81	2,430	47,385	49,896	2.2801274×10^{10}
5					243	10,935	11,178	1.3281002×10^{11}
6						729	729	2.2519960×10^{11}
Total	3	15	132	1,212	12,633	147,255	161,250	3.8208524×10^{11}
Number of rules given five relations								
	5	47	622	9,372	162,497	3,156,247	3,328,790	

when there is only one string every position within a period, regardless of the period's length, lies on that string. Table 2 also shows that there is exactly one string structure whenever $S = P$. When there are as many strings as positions in a period, the first string always occupies the first position, the second string occupies the second position, and so on. Between the lower limit of one string and the upper limit of P strings (i.e., when $P > S > 1$), the number of structures increases sharply as P increases. For $P = 3$, S can only equal two when $P > S > 1$, and there are three two-string structures for $P = 3$. They are __1__2__2, __1__1__2, and __1__2__1, with the numbers 1 and 2 indicating the positions in each period occupied by the first and second strings respectively. Table 2 shows that there are 7, 15, and 31 two-string structures when $P = 4$, 5, and 6 respectively, and that for $P = 6$ there are 89, 65, and 15, three-, four-, and five-string structures. The bottom row of the top panel in Table 2 gives the total number of string structures for each period length from one to six. The totals increase from 1 for $P = 1$ to 202 for $P = 6$.

The number of string structures, P, and #R combine to give the number of rules. When every string has a fixed period and every letter on a string relates to its immediate predecessor on that string, the number of rules for series of a given P equals $(SS \times R^P) - \#R$, where $SS =$ number of string structures, $\#R =$ number of permissible relations, and $P =$ period length. The term $\#R^P$ is the number of sequences of $\#R$ relations that can occur in P positions. Of these $\#R^P$ sequences, $\#R$ will consist of only one relation, and when a single relation falls on a single string the period of the string is 1. Therefore, to calculate the number of rules when $P > 1$, $\#R$ must be subtracted from the quantity $(SS \times \#R^P)$. When $P = 1$, $\#R$ is not subtracted.

The bottom two rows of Table 2 give the number of rules for $P = 1$ to 6. The next to the bottom row assumes three permissible relations (I, N, B) and the bottom row assumes five (I, N, B, double N, double B). When $\#R = 3$, the number of rules increases across periods from $1 \times 3^1 = 3$ for $P = 1$ to $202 \times 3^6 - 3 = 147,255$ for $P = 6$. When $\#R = 5$ the number of rules increases from 5 for $P = 1$, to 3,156,247 for $P = 6$. Clearly, the number of series rules is very large even when $\#R = 3$, and it increases very rapidly as $\#R$ increases.

The lower panel of Table 2 shows how many rules there are for each combination of $S = 1$ to 6 and $P = 1$ to 6 when $\#R = 3$. Besides showing the distribution of rules across period and number of strings, this breakdown allows calculation of the number of series created by rules whose period varies from 1 to 6. In this panel, the column labeled "Total" is the sum of the rules with $S = 1$ to 6. Thus, there are 1,077 one-string rules from $P = 1$ to 6. To determine how many series are generated by a rule, one solves for the quantity 26^S, which gives the number of combinations of starting letters for the rule. Thus, a one-string rule can be started with any of the 26 letters in the alphabet, a two-string rule can be started with any of $26^2 = 676$ pairs of letters, a three-string rule with $26^3 = 17,576$ trios of letters, and so on. The column labeled "Series" gives the number of series of any given length generated by the total rules given in the "Total" column. Thus, there are $1,077 \times 26 = 28,002$ one-string series with $P = 1$ to 6. For $S = 1$ to 6 and $P = 1$ to 6, there are billions of letter series (approximately 3.8208×10^{11}). And there are many billions more when problems are included in which strings' periods vary within a series, in which a wider range of relations is permitted, and in which relations operate on letters further than one back in the series.[2]

---

[2] Allowing strings' periods to vary increases the number of rules 5^P times, because any of three relations can be added to any relation in a rule, any relation can be subtracted, or no addition or subtraction can occur. Thus, when strings' periods can vary, the number of rules for any given $P = 5^P(SS \times R^P) - R$, where $SS =$ the number of string structures when strings' periods are not allowed to vary (see Table 2). Allowing first letters in the preceding period to be operated on by the first relation on each string also adds many rules. How many is dictated by the number of

The Primary Mental Abilities test covers a very wide range of difficulty with only 15 letter series problems, none of which exceeds $P = 6$ and none of which has any string with a variable period. The easiest of these 15 problems can be solved by average first graders, and the hardest is failed by many highly intelligent adults. From a psychometric viewpoint, longer or variable periods are unnecessary. Within these limits, the rule system we use generates plenty of series from which intelligence subtests might be created.

Creating Equivalent Rules With Fewer Strings

Some series are generated by more than one rule; these are especially interesting because some of them are the easiest and some are the hardest series to solve. We turn now to how to calculate whether two rules are equivalent in the sense that they produce some identical series. The algebra for calculating rule equivalence allows exploration of the letter series problem space, and it is required for a precise definition of spurious relations, which are a major determinant of letter series difficulty. The algebra is also required for theory-guided generation of series by computer, which is described in the last section of this chapter. The algebra is fully explained in the Appendix. Here we describe those aspects required to understand subsequent sections on theory and experimentation.

Within our rule system, equivalence depends on the period and the movement of rules' strings. Whether and how far a string moves can be quantified by giving values to the string's relations. Let $I = 0$, $N = +1$, and $B = -1$. Then, the sum (Σ) of the values of the within-period relations on a string tells how far it moves from period to period. For example,

for BBCCDD, whose rule is N1 I1, $\Sigma = 1 + 0 = +1$
for BCCDDE, whose rule is I1 N1, $\Sigma = 0 + 1 = +1$
for SRSRSR, whose rule is N1 B1, $\Sigma = 1 - 1 = 0$
for RSRSRS, whose rule is B1 N1, $\Sigma = -1 + 1 = 0$
for LLKKJJ, whose rule is B1 I1, $\Sigma = -1 + 0 = -1$
for LKKJJI, whose rule is I1 B1, $\Sigma = 0 - 1 = -1$

---

strings with more than one relation per period. Let *MRSS* stand for the number of multirelation string structures with a given number of multirelation strings per period, and let *MRS* stand for the given number of multirelation strings. Then, because there is always only one string structure per P with no *MRS*, the number of rules per period equals $((1 + \Sigma_{1\,to\,MRS} [2^{MRS} \times MRSS])(5^P \times R^P)) - R$. For example, Table 2 shows that there are 15 *SS* with $P = 4$ when string P is fixed and when only the last letter on its string is used by any relation in the rule. Table 17 shows that 3 of these have $MRS = 2$ and 11 have $MRS = 1$. Therefore, $((1 + [2^1 \times 11] + [2^2 \times 3])(5^4 \times 3^4)) - 3 = 1,771,872$ rules with $P = 4$.

The sums show that N1 I1 and I1 N1 strings both move one letter up the alphabet per period, N1 B1 and B1 N1 produce no movement from period to period, and B1 I1 and I1 B1 move one letter down the alphabet per period.

In order for two rules to be equivalent, they must have the same period and they must contain strings that produce the same movement from period to period, but the strings with equivalent movement must have different periods in the two rules. Consider the one-string rule N1 I1. Its $P = 2$ and its $\Sigma = +1$. Any equivalent rule must have $P = 2$, and it must be composed of strings whose period is not 2, but whose $\Sigma = +1$. Because the minimum period of a string is 1 and the maximum period of any equivalent rule to N1 I1 is 2, any equivalent rule must contain two strings of $P = 1$. Because the movement of these two period-one strings must both be $+1$, the only possible equivalent rule for N1 I1 is N1 N2. Consider the series BBCCDD, which was created by operating on the letter A with the rule N1 I1. This same series results from the rule N1 N2 when both its strings operate on an A. Thus, the rules N1 I1 and N1 N2 are equivalent in that they can produce identical series. In fact, every series created by the N1 I1 rule can also be created by the N1 N2 rule, though the reverse is not true. The N1 I1 rule can operate on only 26 different letters, but the N1 N2 rule can operate on 26^2 pairs of letters. That is, exactly 26 of the 676 problems (of a given length) created by the N1 N2 rule are also created by the N1 I1 rule.

The constraints described in the foregoing paragraph can be applied to any series rule in order to determine whether it has equivalents with either more or fewer strings. For the case of fewer strings, the question is which multistring rules will generate any problems that can be generated by a rule with fewer strings? The Appendix explains how to answer this question.

Creating Equivalent Rules with More Strings

A rule's period limits its number of strings S. Any rule for which $S = P$ has no equivalent with more strings, just as any rule for which $S = 1$ has no equivalent with fewer strings. Any rule for which $P > S > 1$ has at least one string with two or more relations on it. If a rule has a multirelation string that can be divided into more strings (with fewer relations per string), then it has an equivalent rule with more strings. Whether a multirelation string can be divided into more strings depends on its number of relations $\#R$ and their combined movement Σ. When a multirelation string is divided into more strings, every resulting string's movement must equal the movement of the divided string, just as strings can be combined only if they have equal movement. Because the movement of $N = +1$, $I = 0$, and $B = -1$, any multirelation string for which $+1 \geq \Sigma \geq -1$ can be divided into $\#R$ strings. Thus, the multirelation string N1 B1 N1, which has $\Sigma = +1$ and $\#R = 3$, can be divided into three N strings: N1 N2 N3. Put generally, a multirelation string can be divided only if its $\#R \geq 2\Sigma$, but none of its derivative strings can have fewer than Σ relations. Another way of saying this is that Σ of the to-be-divided string is a lower bound on $\#R$ of the strings resulting from the division. Thus, a multirelation string with $\Sigma = +2$ must be divided into strings whose $\#R \geq 2$, which means that a string whose $\Sigma = \pm 2$ is divisible only if its $\#R \geq 4$. These limits stem from the fact that no single permissible relation moves further than ± 1 letter along the alphabet.

Application of the ideas in the foregoing paragraph allows ready determination of whether a rule has any equivalents with more strings. If a rule has equivalents with more strings, deriving those equivalents is similar to deriving equivalents with fewer strings, explained fully in the Appendix.

Whereas it is seldom true that series created by a rule with more strings can be described by equivalent rules with fewer strings (see preceding subsection, "Creating Equivalent Rules with Fewer Strings," and the Appendix), the reverse is always true. Every series generated by a rule that has an equivalent with more strings is described by that equivalent because the letters created by the rule with fewer strings necessarily lie within ± 1 of letters on their greater number of equivalent strings in every period of the series. We turn now to series in which the same letters lie on different strings but only in some periods of the series. Such series are said to contain spurious relations.

Series with Spurious Identity Relations

More precisely, a letter series is said to contain spurious relations if it contains duplicate letters that are *not* related to one another by identity relations that lie on the same string in *any* of the equivalent rules that describe the series. Conversely, a series is said to contain no spurious identities if each set of duplicated letters in the series is related by identity relations to a single string by any of the equivalent rules for the series. It is easiest to judge the presence of spurious relations for series generated by a rule with no equivalents. The following pairs of series were generated by the indicated rules, none of which has any equivalent.

1. N1 B2   A Z B Y C X
               A D B C C B
2. N1 B2 I3   B M X C L X D K X
               J N L K M L L L L
3. B1 B1 I2   T S G R Q G P O G
               H G E F E E D C E

The lower series in each pair contains spurious relations, the upper series does not. Notice that the lower series are markedy more difficult to solve. The upper series in Pair 1 contains no identical letters, so it could not possibly contain spurious identity relations. The upper series in Pair 2 contains three X's, but they all lie on the same string, which is also true of the three G's in the upper series of Pair 3. None of these identical letters results from spurious relations, because they are all related by identities that lie on a single string. The lower series in Pair 1 contains two B's that lie on different strings, as do its two C's. These four letters form two spurious relations, one for the B's and one for the C's. The lower series in Pair 2 contains five L's, three of which lie on String I3. Were it not for the other two L's, one of which lies on N1 and one of which lies on B2, there would be no spurious relations in this series. As it is, the five L's enter into seven spurious relations, one between strings N1 and B2, three between N1 and I3, and three between B2 and I3. The lower series in Pair 3 has four E's, which enter into three spurious relations between B1 B1 and I2. The Appendix explains how to calculate spurious identities for rules that do have equivalents.

Most one-string rules and all rules with $S > 1$ will produce some series with spurious relations. The number of such series is determined by the number of strings in the rule and the number of different letters on each string. The number of different letters on a string is determined by the number of recursions through the rule that produced it, its movement along the alphabet, and the relative positioning of identity relations on the string. Thus, three recursions through an N string produce three letters and four recursions produce four letters (ABC versus ABCD). Three recursions through a rule with an NI string give three different letters on that string, but three recursions for an IN string give four letters (AABBCC versus ABBCCD). Three recursions through an NB string produce two letters, and four recursions through an I string produce one letter (ABABAB versus JJJJ). The more moving strings a rule has and the more recursions used to generate its 26^S series, the more spurious identities its series will have and, within the limit described subsequently, the more series it will produce with any spurious relations.

Table 3 gives the number of series with spurious relations produced by any two- or three-string rule with different numbers of letters on the series' strings. The upper portion of Table 3 concerns series produced from two-string rules.[3] It shows the number of series with any spurious relations produced by any two-string rule when the number of different letters on one

---

[3] The number of series with spurious identities produced by any two-string rule equals $26(L1 + L2 - 1)$, where L1 and L2 are the number of letters on the first and second strings, respectively.

TABLE 3

NUMBER OF SERIES WITH ANY SPURIOUS IDENTITIES PRODUCED BY
ANY TWO- OR THREE-STRING RULE, GIVEN THE NUMBER OF
LETTERS ON THOSE STRINGS

	Two strings							
Smaller String	Larger string							
	2	3	4	5	6	7	8	9
1	52	78	104	130	156	182	208	234
2	78	104	130	156	182	208	234	260
3		130	156	182	208	234	260	286
4			182	208	234	260	286	312
5				234	260	286	312	338
6					286	312	338	364
7						338	364	390
8							390	416
9								442

		Three strings							
Middle string	Smallest string	Largest string							
		2	3	4	5	6	7	8	9
1	1	1924	2470	2964	3406	3796	4134	4420	4654
2	1	2470	2964	3406	3796	4134	4420	4654	4836
	2	3614	4056	4446	4784	5070	5304	5486	5616
3	1		3406	3796	4134	4420	4654	4836	4966
	2		4446	4784	5070	5304	5486	5616	5694
	3		5434	5720	5954	6136	6266	6344	6370
4	1			4134	4420	4654	4836	4966	5044
	2			5070	5304	5486	5616	5694	5720
	3			5954	6136	6266	6344	6370	6344
	4			6786	6916	6994	7020	6994	6916
5	1				4654	4836	4966	5044	5070
	2				5486	5616	5694	5720	5694
	3				6266	6344	6370	6344	6266
	4				6994	7020	6994	6916	6786
	5				7670	7644	7566	7436	7254

string ranges from 2 to 9 and the number of different letters on the other string ranges from 1 to 9. Using three recursions, the rules N1 B2 and B1 N2 I2 I1 I1 will each produce 676 series with three letters on each of their strings, and Table 3 shows that 130 of these 676 for each rule will contain some spurious relations. The lower portion of Table 3 shows the number of series that result from any three-string rule whose number of letters per longest string ranges from 2 to 9 and whose other two strings have from 1 to 5 letters.[4]   Using four recursions, the rule I1 N1 N1 B2 I3 will produce 17,576 series with eight letters on String 1, four letters on String 2, and one letter on String 3.   Table 3 shows that 4,966 of the 17,576 series produced by this rule will contain some spurious relations.

As Table 3 suggests, the number of series with spurious relations increases rapidly as the number of strings in the series increases.   There are many more series with spurious relations for three-string rules than for two-string rules.   For rules with two strings, the number of series with spurious relations increases directly with the number of letters on the two strings.   For rules with three strings, the number of series with spurious relations varies curvilinearly with the number of letters on the strings.   For example, when the two shorter strings have four letters, the number of series with spurious relations increases as the longer string increases in length from four to seven letters, but the number of series with spurious relations decreases as the number of letters on the longer string goes from seven to nine letters (see Table 3 for this and other examples).   This curvilinear relationship happens for all series generated from rules with more than two strings, and it results from the fact that a series is classified as having spurious relations as soon as any of its two strings share a letter.   As any of three strings becomes longer, the odds that it will share a letter with either of two other strings increase; as soon as it shares a letter with either of the two others, sharing a letter with the third becomes irrelevant to the question of whether the series has any spurious relations.

THE LETTER SERIES PROBLEM SPACE

The foregoing facts about letter series allow systematic exploration of the letter series problem space.   The Appendix to this chapter contains such an exploration for series with $P = 3$.   When $P = 3$ and the permissible relations are I, N, and B, there are 132 rules whose strings have a fixed period and whose relations operate on the last letter on their string.   If every one of these rules produced only series with no equivalent descriptions, there would be a total of 529,932 unique series with $P = 3$.   Only 30 of the 130 rules produce no series with equivalent descriptions.   Six of these have one string, 18 have two strings, and six have three strings.   Together, these rules produce 117,780 unique series.   A group of 18 three-string rules produces series that

---

[4] The number of series with spurious identities produced by any three-string rule equals $26(L1 + L2 - 1) + 26((26 - L1 - L2 + 1)(L1 + L2 + 2(L3 - 1)) + 1 + \ldots + L3 - 1)$, where $L1, L2, L3$ are the numbers of letters on the three strings ranked from highest to lowest.

are described by one of 42 two-string rules. Therefore, $42 \times 26^2 = 28,392$ of the $18 \times 26^3 = 318,368$ series produced by these 18 three-string rules have both a two string and a three-string description, and 287,976 have only a three-string description. The remaining three three-string rules produce series that are described by one or more of 21 two-string and 18 one-string rules. Of the series generated by these three-string rules, 364 have five descriptions, 52 have four descriptions, 52 have three descriptions, 12,948 have two descriptions, and 39,312 have one description. Even though 102 of the 132 rules with $P = 3$ produce series with equivalent descriptions, over 90% of the series (445,068/486,876) produced by the 132 rules can be described by only one rule, and the number of series that the 132 rules would produce if there were no equivalences among them is reduced by only 8%.

The Appendix also shows how many of the series produced by each rule contain spurious relations. Of the 445,068 series with only one description, 96,512 contain spurious relations. Of the 41,340 series with two descriptions, 5,928 contain spurious relations. All 52 of the series with three descriptions contain spurious relations, as do all 52 with four descriptions. Of the 354 with five descriptions, 104 produce series with spurious relations. Thus, 102,648 of the 486,876 series with $P = 3$ contain at least one spurious relation.

Letter series with $P = 3$ are representative of the population of letter series in all important respects. For $P = 3$, only 2.4% (11,804/486,876) of the series generated by all rules are composed entirely of nonmoving strings, and this fraction drops precipitously as P increases. Most letter series have moving strings. A distinct minority (21% when $P = 3$) of letter series contain spurious relations, and this remains true even when P and S become quite large. About 9% of series with $P = 3$ can be described by more than one rule, and the equivalent descriptions for any series are known. Most equivalent descriptions have more than one string, and a distinct majority of series (91% when $P = 3$) can be described by only one rule.

LETTER SERIES FROM THE PRIMARY MENTAL ABILITIES TEST

The chief job of any theory of letter series solution is to model how people represent and continue the billions of series in the population. Before turning to models of how people do these things, we consider the question of how representative the letter series included on intelligence tests are of the population of series problems. We do this by examining the 15 series included in the Primary Mental Abilities Test. Table 4 lists these 15 problems, gives the rule for each that is simplest in the sense that it has the smallest number of strings and the largest number of I relations with which the

TABLE 4
PROPERTIES OF THE 15 LETTER SERIES ON THE PRIMARY MENTAL ABILITIES TEST

Series	Simplest rule	2P letters	Number of other rules	Moving strings	Spurious relations
1. CDCDCD	N1 B1	Yes	1	No	No
2. AAABBBCCCD	N1 I1 I1	Yes	4	Yes	No
3. ATBATAATBAT	I1 I2 N3 I1 I2 B3	No	1	No	No
4. ABMCDMEFM	N1 N1 I2	Yes	0	Yes	No
5. DEFGEFGHFGHI	N1-first N1 N1 N1	Yes	4	Yes	Yes
6. QXAPXBQY	N1 I2 B3 B1 I2 N3	No	3	No	No
7. ADUACUAEUABUAF	I1 N2 I3 I1 B4 I3	Yes	0	Yes	No
8. MABMBCMCD	I1 I2 N2	Yes	1	Yes	No
9. URTUSTUTTU	N1 N2 B1	Yes	1	Yes	Yes
10. ABYABXABW	B1 N1 B2	Yes	1	Yes	No
11. RSCDSTDE	I1 N1 I2 N2	Yes	3	Yes	No
12. NPAOQPRA	N1 N2 I3	Yes	0	Yes	Yes
13. WXAXYBYZCZADB	I1 N1 N2	Yes	1	Yes	Yes
14. JKQRKLRSLMST	I1 N1 I2 N2	Yes	3	Yes	No
15. PONONMNMLMLK	N1 B1 B1	Yes	4	Yes	Yes

problem can be represented in our system, indicates whether the series has at least $2P$ letters, lists how many equivalents there are to the simplest rule that describes the series, and notes whether the series has any moving strings and any spurious relations. Notice first that $2P$ letters is the minimum number required to specify unambiguously any rule that might have generated a series, and 2 of the 15 series in Table 4 (Numbers 3 and 6) have fewer than $2P$ letters. This undoubtedly makes them more difficult than they would be if they had at least $2P$ letters. Fully 90% (12 of 15) of the series have equivalent descriptions, which is a considerable overestimate of the 9% population rate of series with multiple descriptions. Of the 15 problems, 20% have no moving strings, which is also a considerable overestimate of the population rate of 2.4% with no moving strings. Five of 15 or 33% of the problems have spurious relations, which is a modest overestimate of the population rate of 21%. Of the 15 problems, 20% have one-string rules, which is a huge overestimate of the population rate of 0.1%.

From a test constructor's point of view, it does not matter at all if a set of items represents the descriptive properties of the population of items from which it is drawn. What matters is whether the sampled items represent the distribution of difficulty of such items for the population of people to whom a test is to be administered, and that the items yield reliable scores with usefully high validities. Accordingly, the nonrepresentativeness of the problems on the Primary Mental Abilities Test may be precisely what is required for a measure of general intelligence. Only a good theory of series difficulty could say otherwise. From a cognitive researcher's viewpoint, it matters a great deal whether a set of problems is representative of the attributes of the population of items. The chief question that has been asked by researchers who have studied letter series is how people solve them. In the absence of this information, the only way to insure solid exposure to all of the possible ways people solve them is to sample items so that they represent all known attributes of the population of problems and so that no one attribute is so overrepresented that it might distort the investigator's view of the importance of particular processes. The items on the Primary Mental Abilities Test are not a satisfactorily representative sample for discovering how people solve letter series, even though they might be an excellent sample for assessing intelligence as it is reflected in the solution of inductive reasoning problems.

TWO THEORIES OF LETTER SERIES CONTINUATION

Simon and Kotovsky (1963; Kotovsky & Simon, 1973) developed the only published theory that predicts the relative difficulty of letter series. Tests of the theory have been reported by Holzman *et al.* (1982; 1983). We turn now to a description of this theory and to an extension of it that we have developed.

Simon and Kotovsky (1963) assumed that people know three things about letters in the alphabet: They know when two letters are identical, they know which letter follows any letter in the alphabet, and they know which letter precedes any letter. Simon and Kotovsky proposed that people use this information when they represent a letter series and when they continue a series. During representation, they presumably use the information to induce which letters go on a string. Simon and Kotovsky proposed, that having assigned letters to a string, people use the information on that string to calculate a problem's period. Then they use the period and the represented string to guide their induction of which letters go on other strings. Having assigned all letters to a string, people supposedly form a rule describing the series. The rule is formed of what Simon and Kotovsky called memory lists.

A memory list is a psychological counterpart to what we mean by a string that moves up or down the alphabet from one period to the next of a series. Thus, for the problem RJFRKERLD, whose rule in our notational system is I1 N2 B3, Simon and Kotovsky would say a person forms two memory lists, one for the N2 and one for the B3 string. In our terms these are moving strings, whereas I1 is a nonmoving or identity string. According to Simon and Kotovsky, people represent nonmoving strings as the letters on the strings, without forming a memory list. Holtzman *et al.* (1982) subscribed to Simon and Kotovsky's theory, so according to all these investigators representation is the formation of a rule by inductive processes that include noting alphabetic relations, period discovery, and assembly of memory lists into a rule. The properties of these rules are described in Simon and Kotovsky (1963).

One implication of this account is that period length, or something about its computation, should be related to representational difficulty, and therefore to the accuracy with which people solve series. Contrary to this implication, period length is not related to the accuracy with which people solve letter series (Holzman *et al.*, 1982; Simon & Kotovsky, 1963; and Experiment 3, described subsequently). Another implication is that spurious identity relations should interfere with the assignment of letters to memory lists, thereby making series with spurious identities especially difficult, which they are (Simon & Kotovsky, 1963; Experiment 5 and 6, described subsequently).

We turn now to Simon and Kotovsky's account of series continuation, as opposed to series representation. Put briefly, people are said to continue a series by applying the same operations they use to induce its representation. The application of the operations is said to be guided by the rule formed during representation. The chief source of difficulty during continuation is said to be the number of memory lists that must be employed. The number of memory lists that must be used for an entire period of the problem has been shown to predict the difficulty of letter series problems (Kotovsky & Simon, 1973) and number series and number analogy problems (Holzman *et al.*, 1982; 1983). Series with no moving strings require no memory lists for their representation, and are especially easy to solve.

At the conceptual level, Simon and Kotovsky's approach distinguishes representation from continuation, but at the level of predictor variables it does not. The failure of period length to predict accuracy removed what seemed the most viable measure of representational difficulty. Holzman *et al.* have tried to remedy this by providing a measure of the method that a person might use to discover a problem's period. We will show subsequently that this measure lumps together many problems that differ widely in their difficulty after the effects of number of memory lists are allowed for, which suggests that it is not a satisfactory index of representational processes. Because both of these unsuccessful derivations of representational measures used the P of series, we have developed an explanation of how people represent letter series that does not depend on P.

Our explanation is consistent with facts reported by Simon and Kotovsky and with the findings of our exploration of the series problem space (in the section "Describing and Generating Letter Series"). The first fact is that problems composed entirely of nonmoving strings are extremely easy to continue. Presumably, strings composed entirely of identical letters are also easy to represent. The second fact is that problems with spurious identities across strings are extremely difficult to continue, even when they make relatively few memory demands. Presumably, such problems are especially difficult to represent. Taken together, these two facts show that identities can either markedly simplify or markedly complicate series representation, depending on whether the identities are on the same or different strings. In other words, identities play a critical role in the representation of series. The third and fourth facts were revealed by our exploration of the series problem space. Few series are composed entirely of nonmoving strings, and few have any spurious relations. We show in the following section, "Experimental Tests of Theories of Letter Series Continuation," that there is wide variation in difficulty among the series with moving strings but no spurious relations.

We began our explanation of series difficulty by assuming that series composed entirely of identity strings could be represented perceptually, without inducing any properties of their string structures. This is the reverse of the assumption made by Simon and Kotovsky that it requires no working memory to continue series composed entirely of identity strings. Our assumption is that if memory is not required to continue a series, perception is sufficient to represent it.

Next, we assumed that the representation of problems with spurious relations required deep and full knowledge of the ways in which letters can enter into strings to form series. Accordingly, we focused on problems with moving strings but without spurious relations. Our question was, what sorts of knowledge would allow people to represent such problems? Put another way, the question was, what sorts of problem features would simplify the induction of rules to represent such problems, which are the bulk of all letter series?

We were led by this question and the evidence that period length does not influence series difficulty to suspect that the nature of the moving strings in a series is important to its representation. This possibility, along with the notion that identical letters play a central role during representation, led to the idea that the functional units of moving strings may be either individual letters or groups of identical letters. It seemed especially likely to us that identical letters would be represented as a unit of a moving string if they were adjacent to one another. It also seemed likely that units composed of groups of different identical letters would be represented as falling on the same moving string if each group (i.e., unit) contained the same number of identical letters. In other words, we hypothesized that the representation of moving strings is influenced by two orthogonal features, the adjacency or nonadjacency of groups of identical letters on a string and the equality or inequality in number of identical letters among the groups. According to this hypothesis, the easiest moving string to represent would be composed of units that have the same number of adjacent identical letters, and the hardest moving string to represent would be composed of units with different numbers of nonadjacent identical letters. Strings composed of units with unequal numbers of adjacent letters or equal numbers of nonadjacent letters would be intermediate in their representational difficulty. As a first approximation, we hypothesized that nonadjacency (as opposed to adjacency) of letters within units would pose greater representational difficulty than inequality (as opposed to equality) among units in number of letters. This gave us the following predicted rank order of representational ease: Adjacent and Equal; Adjacent and Unequal; Nonadjacent and Equal; and Nonadjacent and Unequal.

In order to make our hypotheses about single moving strings apply to multistring series, we assumed that the difficulty of representing a series was determined by its most difficult-to-represent string. So if two series contained a moving string composed of adjacent and equal units, but one contained a second such string and the other contained a second moving string of nonadjacent and equal units, the latter would be predicted more difficult to represent. Having come this far in our thinking about representation, we had a predicted difficulty ordering with five levels. The easiest level consisted of series composed entirely of nonmoving strings, and the next four levels, described in the foregoing paragraph, consisted of series with moving strings, but without spurious relations. What we lacked was an account of any psychological processes that would produce such an ordering and a way to predict the effects of spurious relations.

To consider psychological processes, we assumed that series representation is guided by simple experientially based knowledge, namely, that identical things form a class, that when looking for things that go together one should start with things that are near one another, and that a good beginning strategy for relating nonidentical things is to look for abstract similarities among them, such as how many there are of each. Concatenating these bits of knowledge gave the first five levels of the six-level hierarchy of knowledge shown in Table 5, to which we shall return shortly.

Our chief uncertainty about how people resolve the representational difficulty presented by spurious relations was whether they use the knowledge that would allow them to represent nonmoving strings when there are no spurious relations in a series or whether they use a more abstract conception of string structure. It seemed to us that this choice could ultimately be decided empirically. If as people resolve the difficulties that are presented

TABLE 5
LEVELS OF KNOWLEDGE FOR REPRESENTING THE STRINGS OF
LETTER SERIES AND SAMPLE SERIES THAT REQUIRE EACH LEVEL FOR
THEIR REPRESENTATION

---

1. Identical letters form strings.

        1. O E I O E I O E I   2. K K T K K T K K T

2. Equal numbers of adjacent identical letters form units that can be related by a moving relation.

        1. E E U F F U G G U   2. V V V W W W X X X

3. Unequal numbers of adjacent identical letters form units that can be related by a moving relation.

        1. V V W W W X X X Y   2. S T T U V V W X X

4. Equal numbers of nonadjacent identical letters form units that can be related by a moving relation.

        1. M X M N X N O X O   2. R R B R Q Q C Q P P D P

5. Unequal numbers of nonadjacent identical letters form units that can be related by a moving relation.

        1. A B J B C J C D J   2. A F A B B G B C C C H C

6. A series is continuable only when all strings in its rule connect the same relative positions within and across periods.

        1. I H G H G F G F E   2. Q N P O M N M L L

---

by spurious relations they use the same knowledge they use to represent moving strings, then the difficulty of series with spurious relations should vary with the nature of the moving strings in the series. On the other hand, if more abstract knowledge is required to represent series with spurious relations, the nature of the strings from which the series are constructed should not influence the difficulty of solving the series. Because our choice would eventually be tested we opted arbitrarily for the idea that representing spurious series required more abstract knowledge, and we placed our hypothesis about the nature of that knowledge at the sixth level of the knowledge hierarchy, which we postulated as the guide to people's efforts to represent letter series.

Table 5 shows the knowledge hierarchy that we hypothesize underlies the representational efforts of people who are effective solvers of letter series problems. The table includes examples of problems that can be represented completely with the knowledge of each level when it is used in combination with knowledge of lower levels. That is, our theory asserts that people who understand the knowledge at any particular level also understand the knowledge at lower levels, and they use the knowledge from the bottom of the hierarchy up whenever they are faced with a series problem. In addition to being a set of predictions about the relative difficulty of series with different features, the hierarchy is the theory's way of predicting the order in which representational knowledge is acquired and the order in which it is used by any individual faced with any series problem. In order to translate our theory of representation into a predictor of series difficulty, we simply assign to a series the ordinal value of the knowledge level required to represent it. Thus, series composed entirely of nonmoving strings are given Knowledge = 1 and series with spurious relations are given Knowledge = 6 as predictors of their representational difficulty.

We mentioned earlier that Holzman *et al.* (1982) have proposed an index of representational difficulty, which they refer to as a method of period discovery (MPD). They postulate two such methods, one called adjacent and one called nonadjacent. Series that yield to the adjacent method are predicted to be easier to solve. The adjacent method works with all series that in our system require Knowledge = 3, with a majority that require Knowledge = 2, and with a minority of problems that require Knowledge = 1, 4, 5, or 6. The nonadjacent method works with no problems falling at Knowledge = 3, with a minority that fall at Knowledge = 2, and with the majority of problems falling at Knowledge = 1, 4, 5, or 6. Thus, even though there is a marked difference in the rationale for their index and our knowledge hierarchy, the two give correlated predictions about series difficulty.

In summary, our theory is that people represent series by identifying letters with strings and that the chief source of difficulty in this identification is the nature of the moving strings to be identified. The result of representation is a relational rule, like those described in the section "Describing and Generating Letter Series." Period length plays no role in representation. However, once a person has completely represented a problem by assigning every letter to a string, the period of the problem is transparent because it equals the number of relations required to specify fully all of the strings in the series. A problem's period is the number of relations in the rule representing the problem. In other words, period is an epiphenomenon of representing a problem, not a guide to its representation, even though period is indispensable when characterizing the population of series problems.

Having hypothesized an alternative view of the sources of difficulty in representing letter series, we asked ourselves about the processes required to continue or extrapolate the series. It seemed to us that Simon and Kotovsky and others were correct in suggesting that factors influencing memory load determine the difficulty of extrapolation. However, it also seemed that a more process-oriented explanation of memory load could be achieved. In other words, we strove to identify processes that might explain the predictive value of Simon and Kotovsky's number of memory lists, which Holzman *et al.* (1982) called memory place keepers. It seems to us that there are two such processes, which are best appreciated by considering what a person must do to continue a series after representing it by inducing its string structure. First, the person must locate the appropriate letters from which to generate each letter needed to continue the series. We assume that this is done by working backwards through the letters of the problem, and that this work is under the control of the person's representation of the series' string structure. Second, having found a required letter by working backwards, a person must create the letter required for continuation by performing the relational transformation specified in his or her representation of the series' string structure.

What we mean by working backwards through a problem is illustrated by the following four series

$$N1\ I1\ I1 \quad B\ B\ B \quad C\ C\ C \quad D\ D\ D$$
$$B1\ N2\ I2 \quad K\ R\ R \quad J\ S\ S \quad I\ T\ T$$
$$B1\ B2\ I1 \quad M\ F\ M \quad L\ E\ L \quad K\ D\ K$$
$$N1\ B2\ I3 \quad A\ H\ P \quad B\ G\ P \quad C\ F\ P$$

In order to facilitate the illustration, the series are shown with breaks at their period boundaries. Simon and Kotovsky used as their index of continuation difficulty the number of memory lists in the series rule, regardless of the number of letters a person is required to generate as a response to the series problem. Similarly, we use as one of our indices the number of letters a person must work backward in order to find all of the letters to continue a problem for an entire period, regardless of the number of letters called for as a response. Consider the last three letters of the first series. In order to generate those three, a person needs to move backward from the first D to the last C. We call every letter moved back a count; we would say this problem has a count of 1 because a person only needs to work back one letter to reach the sole letter needed to perform the only relational transformation required to create the three D's. The next problem requires more counts. In order to generate the I in the last period of the second problem, the person must move back to the J in the preceding period. Even though there are two S's between the J and the I, we count them as one letter because they form a single unit. So locating the J needed to generate the I requires two counts, one for the two S's and one for the J. To locate the S required to generate the two T's also requires a count of two, one for one I and one for the last S, so the second series has a count value of 4. In the third series, locating the L to generate the first K requires a count of 1, locating the E to generate the D requires a count of 3, and locating the first K to generate the second requires a count of 2, for a total of 6. In the fourth series, the C and F both require counts of 3, but the P requires no counts because it is located on a nonmoving string, which requires no memory operations for its continuation.

One need not examine a series in order to determine its count value. That can be done from its rule. For any rule

$$\text{Counts} = \#MS(P - \#AIR)$$

where $\#MS$ = the number of moving strings in the rule and $\#AIR$ = the number of identity relations that are immediately adjacent to the preceding relation on their string (i.e., adjacent identity relations). Thus, because the rule N1 I1 I1 has one moving string, $P = 3$, and two adjacent identity relations, its Count = $1(3 - 2) = 1$. Similarly, for the rule B1 B2 I1, Counts = $2(3 - 0) = 6$. Note that because $\#MS$ equals what Simon and Kotovsky meant by number of memory lists, the equation for Counts defines the relationship between the two theories of letter series continuation. Moreover, the formula for Counts shows that there are conditions under which P might correlate with series difficulty, even though in our account it is not a determinant of series solution. If across a sample of problems the number of moving strings or the number of adjacent identities are constant, then P is perfectly correlated with Counts. Therefore, if one did not view Counts as a constituent of series continuation and if one did not sample widely from the problem space, it would be possible to conclude that P is a primary determinant of accuracy.

The chief difference between our theory and that of Simon and Kotovsky with respect to the role of moving relations is that we weight N and B relations according to their difficulty. Simon and Kotovsky make no distinctions among the relations, though they have noted their differential difficulty (Simon & Kotovsky, 1963).

We turn now to the second process that might explain why Simon and Kotovsky's number of memory lists is a reliable predictor of series difficulty. By reference to relational transformations, we meant earlier to convey that the number of moving relations that must be applied to generate P letters of a series is an index of the difficulty of continuing that series. We assume that performing a back relation is harder than performing a next relation, and that performing an identity relation places no burden on memory. These assumptions are realized by giving each I relation on each moving string in a rule a value of 0, each N relation on each moving string a value of 1, and each B relation a value of 2. Then the sums of the values of the relations on all moving strings is the relational value of the series, called Relations. Thus, for the rule N1 I1 I1 Relations = 1, for I1 B2 N3 Relations = 3, and for N1 B1 B2 B3 Relations = 4, because the nonmoving N1 B1 string contributes nothing to Relations.

In conclusion, we have described two related theories of the processes required to solve letter series problems. The theories are related in the sense that they both incorporate the distinction between processes used to represent series and processes used to translate those representations into continuation responses. Moreover, both theories assume that people know when letters are identical, that they know which letter follows and which precedes each letter in the alphabet, and that they use this knowledge both when representing and when continuing series. Concerning representational processes, the theories differ with respect to the role they assign to period discovery. Simon and Kotovsky and others have assumed that period discovery is central to representation, and we assume that it is an epiphenomenon of string discovery. At the level of predictor variables, the differences are that Simon and Kotovsky's theory suggests that P and methods of extracting P are indices of representational difficulty, while our theory suggests that the level of knowledge required to discover the most difficult to represent string in a series is the index of representational difficulty. Our knowledge hierarchy contains a level designed to account for the great difficulty of series with spurious relations, but Simon and Kotovsky proposed no way to account for the difficulty of this significant minority of series problems. Concerning processes for continuing a series, the two theories are more closely related. Simon and Kotovsky's theory yields one predictor of continuation difficulty, namely, the number of memory lists required to represent a series. Our theory contains two processes designed to explain why their predictor works and to improve upon it. One process is designed to reflect the difficulty of locating letters required to continue a series, and the predictor associated with it is Counts $= \#MS(P - \#AIR)$. A second process has to do with the difficulty of transforming the found letters into desired letters, and the predictor associated with it is the sum of the relational values on all moving strings in a series rule, when $I = 0$, $N = 1$, and $B = 2$. We turn now to experimental tests of the theories.

EXPERIMENTAL TESTS OF THEORIES OF LETTER SERIES CONTINUATION

PREDICTIONS

If the premises of our theory are valid and if the work of others leading up to it is reliable, then we should find that our predictors Knowledge, Counts, and Relations, Simon and Kotovksy's predictor Number of Memory Lists, and Holzman et al.'s (1983) predictor MPD are each related to series continuation difficulty when the others are uncontrolled. The P of the series and Number of Memory Lists should not be related to series difficulty when Counts and Relations are controlled, and MPD should be unrelated to series difficulty when Knowledge is controlled. Knowledge, Counts, and Relations should each be related to difficulty when all of the other predictors are controlled. These predictions should hold throughout the population of letter series problems.

The following experiments evaluate these expectations. Moreover, the experiments test two uncertainties in our derivation of predictors. Both of these uncertainties have to do with our hierarchy of representational knowledge. Even though the two factors of Adjacency of identical letters within units of moving strings and Equality of numbers of letters among units are orthogonal features of series, we assumed when we built our knowledge hierarchy that they combine to produce a monotonic ordering of difficulty. This assumption was based on the hypothesis that nonadjacency should produce a greater increase in difficulty than inequality. This hypothesis is testable, and if incorrect would call for a change (e.g., from a hierarchy of knowledge to a two-dimensional knowledge space). When faced with the choice of whether to hypothesize that spurious relations are resolved by application of the same knowledge that allows representation of any moving string or to hypothesize a more abstract level of knowledge, we chose more abstract knowledge. This choice is testable, and if incorrect would call for a change (e.g., dropping the highest level of the knowledge hierarchy and addition of a separate predictor to capture the difficulty of series with spurious relations).

EXPERIMENT 1: DIFFICULTY OF PERIOD 3 LETTER SERIES

Since there seemed no practical way in a single experiment to sample representatively from all series problems, we used as the first test of our theory only problems with $P = 3$ whose strings had a fixed period and whose relations operated on the last letter on their spring. Because there are only 132 rules (see Appendix) for creating such series, we could use all the rules and test later for generality of the theory across different values of P, variations in the period of strings, and relations' reference letters.

Subjects

The subjects were 95 normal public school children distributed about equally across the five primary grades 2–6.

Procedures

The 132 rules with $P = 3$ were divided into two pools of 80 rules. Each pool contained 52 unique rules and 28 rules that were shared by the other pool. The purpose of sharing was to insure that both pools represented the entire range of the three predictors generated by the theory and, for the benefit of the second-grade subjects, to include all 16 of the predicted easiest problems in both pools. Each pool was made to contain the same distribution of predictor values and an equal number of rules with backward-moving and next-moving strings. Otherwise, the rules were assigned randomly to pools. For each rule in each pool of 80 rules, two nine-letter series were generated by selecting two starting points for each string of each rule. Starting points were selected randomly from the 26 letters of the alphabet, except that no spurious relations were allowed in any problem generated from a multistring rule, no words were allowed in any problem, and no moving string was allowed to cross the Z-to-A boundary. For each pool of 80 rules the two different problems were assigned randomly to two protocols, giving four test forms, two for each pool of rules. Within each form, the 80 series were ordered randomly and then each form was divided into halves. Within forms, halves were counterbalanced.

Each letter series was followed by three underlined spaces, in which subjects were told to record the next three letters of the series. Testing was done in groups of approximately 12 children. Test forms were distributed randomly, so that for the entire sample of 95 children, 46 received test forms representing one pool of 80 rules and 49 children received forms representing the other pool. Two testing sessions of approximately 40 minutes were used. The first 40 items in each form were completed during the first testing session, and the second 40 were completed during the second session.

The following instructions appeared on the first page of each test form, and were read aloud by the experimenter at the beginning of the first testing session:

    Your job is to write the correct letters in the blanks.
1. Read the row of letters below.
    A Z A Z A Z _____ _____ _____
    The next letters for this problem would be A Z A.
    Write the letters in the blanks.
    Now read the next row of letters and decide what the next letters should be.
    Write the letters in the blanks.
2. D F X D F X D F X _____ _____ _____
    You should have written the letters D F X.
    Now read the rows of letters below and fill in each blank with a letter.
3. M M M N N N O O O _____ _____ _____
4. Z Z Y Y X X _____ _____ _____
5. Z Z A Y Y B X X C _____ _____ _____
    Wait until you are told what your answers should have been.

Now work the following problems for practice.
Write the correct letter in each blank.
6. D E E F G G H I I _____ _____ _____
7. H A A G B B F C C _____ _____ _____
8. F S G T H U _____ _____ _____
9. Q P Q P Q P _____ _____ _____
Wait until you are told the correct answers before doing problems on
the following pages.

Dependent Variable

The dependent variable was the percentage of children for each rule in
each pool of 80 who gave the three letters that continued each series correctly. Thus, the dependent variable combined data from two different
starting points for each rule, across two different orders of series, and from
two counterbalancings of halves of the different orders. Preliminary analyses showed that none of these factors contributed any systematic variance to
the dependent variable.

Predictor Variables

The predictor variables were Knowledge *(KN)*, Counts *(CNT)*, Relations
(REL), and Number of Memory Lists *(#ML)* for each problem, calculated as
described in the section "Two Theories of Letter Series Continuation."
Method of Period Discovery *(MPD)* was not included as a predictor because
period did not vary in this experiment.

Results

The protocol of 80 rules given to 46 children was called Form I and the
protocol given to 49 children was called Form II. The dependent variable
was called %R+, meaning the percentage of children who responded correctly to problems of each rule in either form.

Because Forms I and II represented the same values of the predictors, they
should have been equally difficult, even though 58 of their 80 rules were
different. For Form I, the mean percentage of correct responses per problem was 54.7, with a standard deviation of 23.8. For Form II the mean was
58.4, with a standard deviation of 22.3. The difference between the two
forms does not approach statistical significance.

Table 6 shows that all four predictors were correlated significantly ($p <$
.001) and substantially with %R+ for both Forms I and II. All intercorrela-

TABLE 6

CORRELATION COEFFICIENTS (r AND R) AND STANDARDIZED
REGRESSION WEIGHTS OF THE PREDICTORS KNOWLEDGE (KN),
COUNTS (CNT), RELATIONS (REL), AND NUMBER OF MEMORY LISTS
($\#ML$) FOR SERIES CONTINUATION ACCURACY (%R+) ON TWO
FORMS CONTAINING 80 LETTER SERIES WITH $P = 3$

	Form I				Form II			
	%R+	KN	CNT	REL	%R+	KN	CNT	REL
Zero-order coefficients (r)								
KN	−.642**				−.668**			
CNT	−.793**	.298*			−.853**	.387*		
REL	−.830**	.410**	.745**		−.852**	.447**	.819**	
#ML	−.739**	.321*	.951**	.755**	−.860**	.545**	.908**	.860**
Multiple coefficients (R)								
KN + CNT + REL + #ML			.951**				956**	
Standardized regression weights								
KN			−.375**				−.362**	
CNT			−.565**				−.447**	
REL			−.440**				−.388**	
#ML			.275				.106	

* $p < .01$; ** $p < .001$, all two-tailed.

tions of the four predictors were significant ($p < .05$), but CNT, REL, and $\#ML$ correlated more strongly with one another than with KN. Table 6 also summarizes the results of linear multiple regression analyses done separately for Forms I and II using KN, CNT, REL, and $\#ML$ as predictors for %R+. For both forms the partial regression weights for KN, CNT, and REL were significant ($p < .001$), and across forms the weights for KN, CNT, and REL differed by less than one standard error of measurement from the means of their weights. The partial regression weight for $\#ML$ was not significant for either form. The multiple correlations were .951 and .956 for Forms I and II, respectively.

The results of Experiment 1 provide preliminary support for several conclusions. During letter series solution, induction amounts to the assigning of letters to strings and depends on knowledge that allows the indentification of strings' units and relationships among units. Once the string structure of a series has been induced, success at continuing it depends on memory processes, as Simon and Kotovsky suggested. These memory processes are better conceived as locating needed letters and transforming them into desired letters than as the number of memory lists to be used.

EXPERIMENT 2: DIFFICULTY OF PERIOD 3 NUMBER SERIES

Experiment 1 clarified why #*ML* accounts in part for difficulty differences among letter series. Holzman *et al.* (1982) showed that #*ML* also accounts in part for difficulty differences among number series. Experiment 2 allows us to ask whether our theory provides similar clarification of the relationship between #*ML* and number series difficulty. It also allows a preliminary view of whether our hypothesis about representation applies to number series as well as to letter series. Moreover, because we used the same rules to generate number series that we used in Experiment 1 to generate letter series we can examine the relative difficulty of number and letter series.

Subjects

The subjects were 107 normal public school children distributed about equally across the five primary grades 2–6.

Procedures

The procedures were identical to those of Experiment 1, except that only the 80 rules from Form II were employed and the items in the series were double-digit numbers rather than letters. The numbers used to start the string(s) in a series varied from 10 to 97 in steps of three so that the starting points for strings could be 10, 13, 16, 19 . . . 97.

Results

As in Experiment 1, the dependent variable was the percentage of children correctly answering the series representing each of 80 rules. Table 7 shows that the number series were easier than letter series with the same rules. Column 1 of Table 7 shows that the mean and standard deviation of %$R+$ for number series were 71.8 and 13.1. The corresponding values for letter series in Form II of Experiment 1 were 58.4 and 22.3 (second column of Table 7). To determine whether our theory would clarify the source of this differential difficulty, as well as to test the applicability of the theory to number series, a linear multiple regression analysis was performed on the number data. The predictors *KN, CNT, REL,* and #*ML* were correlated with %$R+$. Table 7 summarizes the results of this analysis and allows comparison of the results for numbers with the comparable results for letters from Form II of Experiment 1.

The column "Number Series, All Grades" in Table 7, under "Correlation Coefficients," shows that all four predictors correlated significantly ($p <$ .001) with accuracy for number series, as they did for letter series. Together, they yielded a multiple correlation for numbers of .881, which though sub-

TABLE 7

PERCENTAGE CORRECT, CORRELATION COEFFICIENTS
(r AND R), AND STANDARDIZED REGRESSION WEIGHTS
OF FOUR PREDICTORS: KNOWLEDGE (KN),
COUNTS (CNT), RELATIONS (REL), AND
NUMBER OF MEMORY LISTS ($\#ML$) FOR NUMBER AND
LETTER SERIES

	Number series, all grades	Letter series	Number series, mean match
Percentage correct			
M	71.8	58.4	58.9
SD	13.1	22.3	16.6
Correlation coefficients (r)			
KN	−.651***	−.668***	−.645***
CNT	−.737***	−.853***	−.781***
REL	−.670***	−.852***	−.721***
#ML	−.667***	−.860***	−.734***
Multiple coefficients (R)			
KN + CNT + REL + #ML	.881***	.956***	.889***
Standardized regression weights			
KN	−.575***	−.362***	−.484***
CNT	−1.02***	−.447***	−.840***
REL	−.271*	−.388***	−.260*
#ML	.814***	.106	.532**

* $p < .05$; ** $p < .01$; *** $p < .001$, all two-tailed.

stantial and significant ($p < .001$) is lower than the comparable correlation of .956 for letters. Because numbers were easier than letters, we entertained the possibility that the smaller multiple correlation for numbers was due to scale attenuation. To check on this possibility, a multiple regression analysis was done for %R+ calculated for a group of subjects ($n = 54$) chosen from the lower grades of the numbers experiment so as to match the mean accuracy of the subjects who received letters in Experiment 1. For these matched subjects, the multiple correlation of the four predictors and numbers accuracy was nearly identical to that for the whole group of numbers subjects (.889 versus .881), and it was still lower than for the letters group ($R = .956$). We conclude that scale attenuation does not account for the lower multiple correlations for number series.

Table 7 also shows the partial regression weights for each of the four predictors. As in Experiment 1, KN, CNT, and REL all contributed significantly to the prediction of %R+. As each of the three predictors increased, accuracy decreased. The standardized regression weights for KN and CNT

were insignificantly larger and the standardized weight for *REL* was insignificantly smaller for both analyses of the numbers data than for the comparable analysis of Form II letters in Experiment 1. Thus, the data provide no indication of why number series are easier than letter series.

Unlike the results for letters, *#ML* contributed significantly to the prediction of number series difficulty. However, the direction of the relationship is not as predicted by Simon and Kotovsky, even though the direction of the zero-order correlation was as predicted. The zero-order correlation of *#ML* and *%R+* was negative (the more memory lists the less recall), but the partial regression weight was positive (the more memory lists the greater recall). Removing the variance associated with *KN, CNT,* and *REL* did not simply reduce the contribution of *#ML* to insignificance, it reversed the relationship. This reversal is probably due to multicolinearity of the predictor variables in this experiment. Whether or not this is the correct inference, it is apparent that the predictors *CNT* and *REL* provide a better account than *#ML* of the difficulty of number series, just as they provide a clarification of the difficulty of letter series.

The data from Experiment 2 provide further support for the conclusions that series problems are represented by assigning stimulus units to strings and that the difficulty of making these assignments is determined by the adjacency of the constituents of the units and the equality of the constituents across units. The data also provide further support for the hypothesis that there are two memory components to series continuation, the location of needed letters and the transformation of them into desired letters.

It should be noted that Experiment 2 does not begin to exhaust the relational operations that are used with numbers. Therefore, while the results with numbers are encouraging for our theory, the theory would need to be elaborated before it could provide an account that applied generally to number series. The elaboration would need at least to specify the relative difficulty of a wider range of transformations, such as division, exponentiation, or multiplication. As it stands, the only relational transformations specified by the theory are addition and subtraction by one.

EXPERIMENT 3: AN EXAMINATION OF THE EFFECTS OF PERIOD WITH OTHER FACTORS CONTROLLED

Simon and Kotovsky (1963) used the 15 series from the Primary Mental Abilities test to examine the effects of period on series difficulty. They found that period does not influence difficulty. In view of the centrality of *P* to their account of series representation, and in view of the fact that since their pioneering work we have learned how to vary *P* while controlling factors that do influence series difficulty, another study of the effects of *P* seemed necessary. For Experiment 3, we created 20 series at each value of $P = 3$ to 6, we controlled Holzman *et al.*'s (1982) predictor Method of Period Discovery, and we varied KN, CNT, REL, and $\#ML$ orthogonally with P. The questions were whether P and $\#ML$ predicted series difficulty when the other factors were controlled.

In addition to varying P of the problems, we varied the order of problems so as to provide an additional test of the importance of period. Some subjects received randomly ordered problems. Other subjects received problems blocked with respect to P. If calculating P contributes to the difficulty of solving letter series, then the randomized order of problems should be more difficult or the relation of P to difficulty should be larger, because for every problem there should be uncertainty about P. For blocked problems, on the other hand, P should become apparent after a few problems of the same P, thereby simplifying the problems or reducing the relation between P and $\%R+$.

Subjects

The subjects were 229 normal public school children distributed about equally across the five primary grades 2–6. Approximately one-third of the children received the condition in which P varied randomly across problems, and the remaining two-thirds were assigned about equally to one of four conditions in which P was blocked across problems.

Procedures

Two pools of 80 rules were formed from two sets of 20 rules at each of four periods ($P = 3$, 4, 5, and 6). For each period in each pool, rules were selected so that the distributions of $\#ML$ were identical. For each period in each pool, there were four rules with $KN = 1$, $CNT = 0$, and $REL = 0$. The remaining 16 rules of each period in each pool had $KN = 2$ and four of these 16 met one of the following four sets of constraints on CNT and REL:

    (1) $1 \leq CNT \leq 2$; $1 \leq REL \leq 2$; $3 \leq CNT + REL \leq 5$
    (2) $2 \leq CNT \leq 5$; $2 \leq REL \leq 4$; $6 \leq CNT + REL \leq 8$
    (3) $5 \leq CNT \leq 9$; $1 \leq REL \leq 6$; $9 \leq CNT + REL \leq 11$
    (4) $6 \leq CNT \leq 12$; $1 \leq REL \leq 6$; $12 \leq CNT + REL \leq 15$

As a consequence of these contraints on rule selection, there was substantial variability in CNT, REL, and $\#ML$ and there was minimal variation in KN; all of these predictors correlated with one another, but none of them correlated with P. It was also true that the period of all problems could be discovered by Holzman *et al.*'s adjacent method of period discovery.

Two sets of problems were generated from each pool of 80 rules. Each problem contained $3P$ letters (e.g., 12 letters for problems with $P = 4$). Starting points were selected randomly from the 26 letters of the alphabet, except that no spurious relations or words were allowed in any problem, and no moving string was allowed to cross the Z-to-A boundary. Each set of 80 problems formed a separate protocol. Within each protocol, five orders of items were formed. In the random order, the 80 problems were randomized irrespective of period, and the random order was divided into halves of 40 problems, which were counterbalanced. For the four blocked orders, problems were randomized within period. Then, the periods were arranged in four orders: 3546, 4635, 5463, and 6354, which will be referred to as Orders 3, 4, 5, and 6, respectively.

Each letter series was followed by two answer spaces in which subjects were told to record the next two letters of the series. Testing was done in groups of approximately 20 children. Test forms were distributed randomly, so that for the entire sample of 229 children, 78 received the random condition, and 41, 35, 38, and 37 children received the blocked condition in which the first period length was 3, 4, 5, and 6 respectively. Two testing sessions of approximately 50 minutes were used. The first 40 items in each form were completed during the first testing session, and the second 40 were completed during the second session. Instructions were like those used in Experiment 1.

Predictor Variables

The predictor variables were KN (1 or 2), CNT (0–12), REL (0–6), and $\#ML$ (0–3).

Results

The percentages correct per problem were 60.5, 71.0, 69.9, 64.2, and 62.9 for the random order and Orders 3, 4, 5, and 6, respectively. The corresponding standard deviations for the five order conditions were 17.0, 17.1, 16.7, 15.8, and 16.1 correct. None of the five means differed ($p < .05$) from any other, and there were no significant order effects.

The five order conditions were analyzed separately to provide independent replications of the effects of the five predictors. For each condition, a correlation was calculated between each predictor and $\%R+$. The five correlations for P hovered around zero (.004, .119, .017, $-.024$, $-.023$), and did not approach statistical significance. For KN, the five correlations were $-.720$, $-.563$, $-.667$, $-.698$, $-.696$, each of which is significant at $p < .001$. For CNT, REL, and $\#ML$ the five correlations (see Table 8) were also significant at $p < .001$. Clearly, when KN, CNT, REL, and $\#ML$ are controlled, variation in P from 3 to 6 has no influence on difficulty, but each of the other predictors taken alone has a strong influence.

TABLE 8

Correlation Coefficients (r and R) and Standardized Regression Weights of Period (P), Knowledge (KN), Counts (CNT), Relations (REL), and Number of Memory Lists ($\#ML$) with Series Continuation Accuracy (%$R+$) for Five Orders of Series Ranging in P from 3 to 6

	Order of series				
	Random	3546	4635	5463	6354
Correlation coefficients (r)					
P	.004	.119	.017	−.024	−.023
KN	−.720***	−.563***	−.667***	−.698***	−.696***
CNT	−.769***	−.769***	−.720***	−.762***	−.793***
REL	−.798***	−.753***	−.749***	−.738***	−.788***
$\#ML$	−.792***	−.732***	−.728***	−.747***	−.773***
Multiple coefficients (R)					
$KN + CNT + REL + \#ML$	.849***	.798***	.794***	.828***	.855***
Standardized regression weights					
KN	−.330***	−.172	−.323**	−.423***	−.370***
CNT	−.241	−.814**	−.372	−.795**	−.789**
REL	−.325*	−.333*	−.349*	−.126	−.272
$\#ML$	−.049	.460	.156	.411	.474

* $p < .05$; ** $p < .01$; *** $p < .001$, all two-tailed.

The protocol for this experiment forced correlations among KN, REL, and CNT by allowing variation of CNT and REL within only one of the two levels of KN and allowing no variation of KN within any level of CNT or REL. Although this was desirable for studying the effects of P, it militated against finding independent contributions of these three predictors. This is shown by multiple regressions of KN, CNT, REL, and $\#ML$ with %$R+$ for each of the five order conditions (see Table 13). In each of the five analyses, the regression weight for two of the three predictors KN, CNT, and REL were significant ($p < .05$), but in none of the analyses were all three significant. For KN the regression weights were significant in four of the five analyses, and for CNT and REL the regression weights were significant in three of the five analyses. This relative unreliability should be attributed to the forced pattern of covariation among predictors for the present experiment, not to their lack of validity. As in Experiment 1, $\#ML$ failed to contribute significantly to the multiple prediction of letter series difficulty.

Figure 1 shows the findings graphically. In the left-hand panel of the figure are the mean percentage of correct responses for each period, combined across orders but separated for children from each of the five grade levels. No effect of period can be seen at any grade level. Also, there is a

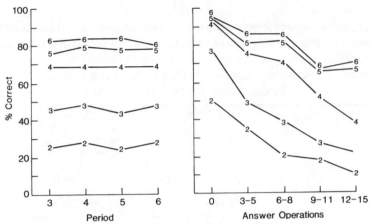

FIGURE 1. Meanpercent correct continuation of letter series for children in grades 2 to 6 plotted against period and against answer operation (CNT and REL).

clear developmental trend: Older children performed more accurately than younger children. The right-hand panel of the figure shows the relationship to %R+ of the combined Answer Operations variable $(CNT + REL)$. For each grade, accuracy falls off as the sum of CNT and REL increases.

We conclude that within the range of $P = 3$ to 6, period length and #ML do not relate to accuracy when KN, CNT, and REL are held constant. The effects of CNT and REL are general across values of P.

EXPERIMENT 4: INDIVIDUAL DIFFERENCES IN REPRESENTATIONAL AND MEMORY PROCESSES THAT INFLUENCE SERIES DIFFICULTY

The results of the foregoing experiments indicate that KN, CNT, and REL influence series difficulty independently of one another and independently of P and #ML. They indicate as well that P and #ML do not influence series difficulty when KN, CNT, and REL are controlled. The first purpose of the present experiment was to determine whether individual differences among people, as well as differences among problems, can be characterized in terms of our measures of representational (KN) and memory (CNT and REL) processes. The second purpose was to determine whether Holzman *et al.*'s predictor, Method of Period Discovery (MPD), influences series difficulty independently of KN.

To simplify Experiment 4, CNT and REL were not treated as separate dimensions of the problem set. Rather, a composite index of memory operations was formed by adding *CNT* and *REL,* and problems were created so they varied on this composite index and *KN.* This allowed us to minimize the correlation between *KN* and both *REL* and *CNT,* and at the same time it simplified the classification of subjects for the purpose of studying individual differences. Moreover, we were still able to examine separately the extent to which *CNT* and *REL* predicted problem difficulty.

Subjects

The subjects were 129 normal children distributed across the elementary grades 2–6 as follows: $n = 19$, 12, 25, 30, and 43. The unequal numbers across grades stemmed jointly from differential availability of children of different ages and from the length of the protocol. Because of its length, fewer younger than older children completed the protocol. The percentages of children completing the protocol were 56, 50, 83, 86, and 94 for grades 2–6 respectively.

Procedures

Two pools of 16 sets of six rules were used to create four test forms of 96 letter series. One set in each pool consisted of six rules with $KN = 1$ and $OP = 0$, where $OP = CNT + REL$. Except for the rules in this set, *KN* and *OP* were varied orthogonally in each pool of rules. In each pool there were three sets of six rules for each value of $KN = 2$ to 6. At each *KN* value, the three sets represented the ranges of $OP = 3–4$, $6–7$, and $9–11$, with the same constraints on *CNT* and *REL* used in Experiment 3.

Within pools, each of the 96 rules was used to generate two series, following the same restrictions used in previous experiments. The two problems were assigned randomly to different test forms, and the 96 problems in each of the four resulting forms were ordered randomly. Four blank spaces followed each problem. Subjects were told to record the next four letters of each series, as in Experiment 1. Subjects were tested in groups of about 20 each, and test forms were randomized across subjects. Two 50-minute testing sessions were used.

Results for Problems

Our first analyses were similar to those of earlier experiments, except that MPD was also used as a predictor. That is, the five predictors were *KN,* *CNT, REL, #ML,* and *MPD,* and the criterion variable was percentage of children answering correctly the problems representing each rule. Preliminary analyses showed that two pools of 96 rules gave identical results, so the data were combined by summing the number of correct responses for 96

TABLE 9

CORRELATION COEFFICIENTS AND STANDARDIZED
REGRESSION WEIGHTS OF KNOWLEDGE (*KN*) COUNTS
(*CNT*), RELATIONS (*REL*), NUMBER OF MEMORY LISTS
(*#ML*), AND METHOD OF PERIOD DISCOVERY (*MPD*)
WITH SERIES CONTINUATION ACCURACY
(*%R+*) FOR 96 LETTER SERIES

	%R+	KN	CNT	REL	#ML	Regression weight
KN	−.686***					−.534***
CNT	−.658***	.259*				−.541***
REL	−.554***	.239*	.599***			−.222**
#ML	−.477***	.101	.834***	.666***		.178
MPD	−.425***	.674***	.151	.017	−.077	.034

* $p < .05$; ** $p < .01$; *** $p < .001$, all two-tailed.

pairs of rules with identical predictors. Table 9 gives the results for the multiple regression analysis of the combined data.

All five predictors correlated significantly ($p < .001$) with %R+, but only *KN, CNT,* and *REL* contributed to the multiple correlation ($R = .863$). With *KN, CNT,* and *REL* controlled, neither *#ML* nor *MPD* were related to %R+. A nonlinear dummy variable regression yielded $R = .94$, which is appreciably higher than R for the linear regression. Inspection suggested that the greater R for the nonlinear analysis resulted from two features of the data. First, problems at *KN* = 6 differed in their difficulty according to the *KN* level of strings from which they were created. Second, problems classed at *KN* = 3 and *KN* = 4 differed less in difficulty than they had in earlier experiments. In earlier experiments, problems at these levels of *KN* were not equated on *CNT* and *REL*, as they were in the present experiment.

Results for Individuals

Any individual who passes problems requiring given levels of *KN* and *OP* (*CNT* + *REL*) should pass problems requiring the same or lower levels of *KN* and *OP*. Conversely, any person who fails problems requiring given levels should fail problems requiring higher levels of *KN* and *OP*. We tested these predictions first by calculating conditional probabilities between success and failure at each combination of levels of representational knowledge and answering operations and success above and below the levels of those combinations.

Subjects answered 16 groups of 6 problems. Each group of problems had

TABLE 10

CONDITIONAL PROBABILITIES OF PASSING
FOR SUBJECTS WHO PASSED AND SUBJECTS
WHO FAILED PROBLEMS WITH EACH OF
16 COMBINATIONS OF REPRESENTATIONAL
KNOWLEDGE (KN) AND MEMORY
OPERATIONS (OP)

			KN			
OP	1	2	3	4	5	6

Conditional probability of passing equal or lower combinations

0		[a]				
3–4		.99	.98	.87	.97	.90
6–7		.96	.93	.90	.96	.97
9–11		.98	.93	.90	.93	.96

Conditional probability of passing higher combinations

0	.01					
3–4		.02	.10	.01	.13	.09
6–7		.05	.09	.01	.12	.14
9–11		.11	.12	.05	.07	[b]

[a] No lower combination with which to evaluate subjects who passed.

[b] No higher combination with which to evaluate subjects who failed.

a different combination of KN and OP. To judge whether a subject had succeeded on any of these 16 groups of problems, we used a criterion of 4 of 6 problems correct. In this way, we found that the probability of passing the 1/0 (KN/OP) combination was 96/129 = .76. That is, 96 of 129 subjects passed at least 4 of 6 problems requiring $KN = 1$ and $OP = 0$. Similarly, the probability of passing the 6/9 to 11 combination was 13/129 = .10. Our theory's assumption about order of acquisition of knowledge leads to the prediction that the 13 subjects who passed at least 4 of 6 of the 6/9 to 11 problems would pass 4 out of 6 of the problems in each of the other 15 combinations of KN and OP, because each other combination has an equal or lower requirement for both representational knowledge and answering operations. In other words, the conditional probability should be very high of passing any of the 15 groups of problems with knowledge requirements equal to or lower than 6/9 to 11, given that the combination 6/9 to 11 was passed. The lower right entry ($KN = 6$, $OP = 9$ to 11) of the top section of Table 10 shows that the conditional probability of passing any other combination was .96 for subjects who passed 6/9 to 11. The 31 subjects who failed the 1/0 combination should fail all of the other combinations because the other combinations all have higher KN and OP requirements. The upper left entry ($KN = 1$, $OP = 0$) in the lower panel of Table 10 shows that the conditional probability of passing any of the combinations above 1/0 was .01 for those subjects who failed 1/0. The remainder of the entries in the top portion of Table 10 show the conditional probabilities of passing problems with lower requirements for those subjects who passed any given combination of requirements. Thus, the entry opposite $OP = 6$ to 7 and under $KN = 3$ shows the mean probability with which the subjects who passed the problems in 3/6 to 7 passed the problems with KN/OP combinations of 1/0, 2/3 to 4, 3/3 to 4, and 2/6 to 7. The entries in the lower portion of Table 10 show the conditional probabilities of passing problems with higher requirements for those subjects who failed any combination of requirements. Thus, the entry for $KN = 3$, $OP = 6$ to 7 shows the mean probability with which those subjects who failed problems with the 3/3 to 4 combination passed problems with KN/OP combinations of 4/3 to 4, 4/6 to 7, 4/9 to 11, 5/3 to 4, 5/6 to 7, 5/9 to 11, 6/3 to 4, 6/6 to 7, 6/9 to 11, 2/9 to 11, and 3/9 to 11. All of the probabilities in the upper panel should be high, and all of the probabilities in the lower panel should be low. Table 10 confirms these predictions, indicating that our theory applies to differences among people as well as to differences among problems.

To allow further tests of the model's applicability to individuals, we classified each subject two ways. Table 11 illustrates the classifications, called Max and Min. For three different subjects, the table shows percentages correct for each of the 16 combinations of KN and OP, the Max and Min scores, and the number of discrepant combinations for each score. Each subject's percentages correct for each KN/OP combination are arranged so that entries in the same column have the same value of KN and entries in the same row have the same values of OP. KN increases across columns from left to right, and OP increases across rows from top to bottom. A subject's Max score for KN is simply the KN level of the right-most column in which any entry exceeds 66% correct. A subject's Max score for OP is simply the OP range of the lowest row in which any entry exceeds 66%. Thus, the Max scores for the three subjects in Table 11 are 4, 6, and 6 for KN and 9 to 11, 9 to 11, and 6 to 7 for OP. For the Max score, discrepant KN/OP combinations (cells) are ones at or below either the KN or OP Max that have fewer than 66% correct. Thus, the first subject has no discrepant cells, the second subject has one discrepant cell, and the third subject has three discrepant cells. For the Max score, discrepant cells are indicated by a single asterisk. The Min score is the combination of KN and OP levels that minimizes the number of discrepant cells. When there are no discrepant cells for the Max score,

TABLE 11

PERCENTAGES CORRECT FOR THREE SUBJECTS WITH
DIFFERENT MAX AND MIN SCORES

				KN			
OP	1	2	3	4	5	6	
Subject 1							
0	100						
3–4		100	67	100	50	33	Max = 4/9 to 11, discrepancies = 0
6–7		67	83	100	33	33	Min = 4/9 to 11, discrepancies = 0
9–11		67	100	67	16	16	
Subject 2							
0	100						
3–4		100	83	100	67	100	Max = 6/9 to 11, discrepancies = 1
6–7		100	100	100	100	83	Min = 6/9 to 11, discrepancies = 1
9–11		100	100	100	83	50[b]	
Subject 3							
0	100						
3–4		100	67	100	50[a]	83[b]	Max = 6/6 to 7, discrepancies = 5
6–7		83[b]	50[a]	50[a]	0[a]	33[a]	Min = 4/3 to 4, discrepancies = 2
9–11		33	33	33	16	0	

[a] Discrepant by Max.
[b] Discrepant by Min.

Min = Max, as for Subject 1 in Table 11. When there are discrepant cells for the Max score, Min may or may not equal Max. For Subject 2 in Table 11, Min = Max even though there is a discrepant cell for the Max score. The reason is that lowering either KN or OP for this subject increased the number of discrepant cells. Thus, if his KN level was set at 5 rather than 6, he would have two discrepant cells rather than only one. For the third subject, Min ≠ Max because lowering his KN score from 6 to 4 and his OP score from 6–7 to 3–4 reduced his discrepancies from five to two. For the Min score, discrepant cells are indicated by two asterisks.

For subjects who pass only cells at or below a given KN/OP combination and fail all cells above a given combination, which is what our theory predicts, the Min and Max schemes yielded identical scores on KN and OP. To the extent that subjects pass different representational levels at different answering levels and different answering levels at different representational levels, the Min and Max systems yield different scores. Therefore, the extent of agreement between the Max and Min scoring systems is an index of the extent to which subjects behave according to the theory. All 129 subjects were classified with both the Min and Max systems. For 87 of the subjects the Min and Max classifications gave the same KN and OP scores. Including these 87 subjects, 98 of the 129 subjects were classified at the same level of KN, and 108 were classified at the same level of OP by the Min and Max systems. The modal and median differences between the Min and Max classifications were zero for both KN and OP. The mean differences in classification were .45 for KN and .69 for OP. The correlation between the KN classifications for Min and Max was .931 ($p < .001$). The correlation between the OP classifications for Min and Max was .941 ($p < .001$). Both the Min and Max scores predicted subject's total scores ($S+$) for the 96 problems with great accuracy. For Min, KN correlated .943 with total $S+$, OP correlated .934, and the multiple correlation of KN and OP with $S+$ was .963. For Max, KN correlated .932 with total $S+$, OP correlated .927, and the multiple of KN and OP with $S+$ was .944. We concluded that the two schemes agree substantially in their classifications of subjects, providing support for the hypothesis that the theory allows characterization of individual subjects. Moreover, the extent of the agreement allows the inference that the two scores are interchangeable, so we used only the Min scores in subsequent analyses.

Assuming no error of measurement, a subject who behaved as predicted by the theory would fail the criterion (four out of six problems) for all of the 16 combinations of KN and OP that lie above his or her Min classification on either KN or OP. Also, assuming no error of measurement, a subject who behaved as predicted would pass the criterion (four out of six problems) for all of the 16 combinations of KN and OP that lie at or below his classification on both KN and OP. In other words, except for errors of measurement, there should be no discrepant cells from a subject's Min classification. Of the 129 subjects, 67 subjects had zero Min discrepancies, 27 had one discrepancy, 22 had two, 8 had three, and 5 had four.

We used Min scores to answer two additional questions about individual differences. The first question was whether children at higher grades secured higher KN and OP scores than children at younger grades. According to the theory, scores for both Min KN and Min OP should increase with grade. The median Min KN scores for children from the second through the sixth grades were 0, 1, 3, 4, and 5, respectively. The median Min OP scores by grade were 0, 0, 4, 7, and 11. Expressed together as KN/OP scores, the medians were 0/0, 1/0, 3/4, 4/7, and 5/11. We concluded that both representational and answering knowledge increase with age, and that the theory does allow a description of the development of knowledge required to solve series completion problems. The second question was whether knowledge about representation and knowledge about answering covary within people. Across problems KN and OP correlated .217, but across people Min KN and OP scores correlated .898 ($p < .001$). We concluded that growth in representational and answering knowledge go hand in hand, even though the two contribute independently to the difficulty of a series problem.

EXPERIMENT 5: ORTHOGONAL VARIATION OF SPURIOUS RELATIONS AND REPRESENTATIONAL KNOWLEDGE REQUIREMENTS OF LETTER SERIES

Experiment 3 used no series with spurious relations. The only series in Experiments 1 and 2 with spurious relations resulted from one-string rules whose multistring equivalents would earn them a KN of 4 or 5. Thus, only Experiment 4 used series with spurious relations among strings from relatively low levels of KN. Inspection of the data from Experiment 4 suggested that the knowledge level of the strings influences the difficulty of series with spurious relations. The first purpose of Experiment 4 was to test the reliability of this possibility. If reliable, this finding would require elimination of KN level 6 from our representational hierarchy.

Experiment 4 is also the only one in which KN levels 2 through 5 were equated on memory operations $(CNT + REL)$. Examination of data from these levels suggested that nonadjacency of letters within units adds no more difficulty than inequality of letters among units. The second purpose of Experiment 5 was to check the reliability of this possibility. If reliable, it would call for a reconceptualization of the knowledge hierarchy.

Whereas Experiments 1–4 were designed for regression analysis, Experiment 5 was designed for an analysis of variance. Three factors were crossed within subjects. The factors were Spurious Identities (None versus Some), Memory Operations (High versus Low), and Knowledge Requirement (2, 3, 4, or 5). Spurious Identities and Knowledge Requirement were the factors of primary interest. If our original decisions about the knowledge hierarchy were correct, then Experiment 5 should show equal difficulty differences between the four KN levels for problems without spurious identities and there should be no differences among problems with spurious identities as a function of $KN = 2$ to 5. All problems with spurious identities should be more difficult than all problems without spurious identities. These predictions should hold for series with both high- and low-memory operations. In other words, in Experiment 5 there should be a significant main effect for Memory Operations and a significant interaction of Knowledge Requirement and Spurious Identities.

Subjects

The subjects were 15 normal elementary school children from grades 4 to 6.

Procedures

Twenty-four rules with $P = 3$ or 4 were selected so that there were six at each KN level 2 to 5. At each level of KN, three rules had low (3–5) and three rules had high (9–12) values of *OP*. Each rule was used to generate two problems, one with no spurious identities across strings and one with from four to six spurious identities. The problems were ordered randomly and the thirds of the ordering were counterbalanced to form three protocols.

The data were collected in two group testing sessions of approximately 40 minutes' duration. Children were required to provide five-letter responses. The instructions were similar to those used in Experiment 1.

Results

The dependent variable was the number of correct continuation responses per condition. Scores could range from 0 to 3. The data were analyzed with a $2 \times 2 \times 4$ within-subjects analysis of variance. Each of the three main effects were significant ($p < .005$), Operations and Spurious Identities (*SI*) interacted ($p < .05$), and none of the other interactions approached significance. The mean correct for $KN = 2$ to 5 were 1.84, 1.43, 1.28, and .90, respectively. Simple effects were evaluated with t tests, which revealed that $1.84 > 1.43 = 1.28 > .90$. That is, KN levels 3 and 4 did not differ from one another, but $KN = 2$ was easier than all other levels and $KN = 5$ was harder than all other levels. This pattern of significant ($p < .05$) differences held for each of the four combinations of Spurious/Nonspurious and High/Low Operations.

The chief focus of Experiment 5 was on the effects of KN and *SI*. The pattern of simple effects for KN and the failure of KN to interact with *SI* require a reconceptualization of representational knowledge. Instead of a single hierarchy, knowledge required to identify series' string structures should be represented in theory as two dimensions. One dimension concerns the knowledge that a string's units can be formed of either adjacent or nonadjacent identical letters. The other dimension concerns the knowledge that units falling on the same string can be composed of the same or of different numbers of letters. Beyond these two dimensions, the theory needs to account for the effects of spurious identities. Experiment 6 concerns how this should be done.

The memory operations dimension was included in Experiment 5 in order to determine whether the effects of representational knowledge and its interaction with spurious identities were comparable for problems with different *CNT* and *REL*. The data show that the effects of these variables are comparable for both Low and High Operations. That is, neither the $KN \times$ Operations nor the $KN \times SI \times$ Operations interactions were significant. However, the results were not entirely as expected. Although the main effects of Spurious Identities and Operations were significant, t tests of the simple effects of their interaction showed that problems without spurious identities were easier only for Low Operations (1.97 versus 1.35). At High Operations there was no significant difference for Nonspurious and Spurious problems (.88 versus .99). High Operations were harder than Low Operations for both Nonspurious (1.97 versus .88) and Spurious (1.35 versus .99) series.

The pattern of simple effects for the $SI \times$ Operations interaction could be due to scale attenuation. Both high operations and spurious identities make series problems more difficult. The data show that series with both spurious identities and high operations were answered correctly less than 25% of the time. Therefore, it is possible that the two factors interacted because these problems were too difficult for the children employed as subjects. If older subjects were used, the result might be two main effects rather than an interaction. Until this possibility is studied, no theoretical conclusion can be drawn from the interaction of SI and Operations.

EXPERIMENT 6: THE EFFECTS OF NUMBER OF SPURIOUS IDENTITIES

Because Experiment 5 indicated the desirability of considering the presence of spurious relations as a separate predictor, we performed Experiment 6 to determine whether the number of spurious identities influences difficulty. Kotovsky and Simon (1973) concluded from data on the accuracy with which people complete the 15-letter series on the Primary Mental Abilities Test that the presence of spurious relations makes a series more difficult to continue, but those series do not allow examination of the number of spurious relations. We selected nine rules of $P = 3$, all of which require $KN = 2$ when no spurious relations are present and none of which has any equivalent rule. Each of the nine rules was used to generate three problems with no spurious relations and three problems with spurious identities. The question was whether the number of spurious identities increases difficulty of series with identical rules.

Subjects

The subjects were 20 normal sixth-grade children from a public elementary school classroom.

Procedures

Each of nine rules ($P = 3$) was used to generate three nine-letter series with no spurious relations, where spurious means any I relation among letters on different strings. With the exceptions that no spurious identities were allowed and no string was allowed to cross the Z-to-A boundary, the starting points for the strings in the nonspurious problems were selected randomly. Each of the nine rules was also used to generate three nine-letter series with spurious relations. For each rule, one spurious problem was created with an adjacent spurious identity in the first three of a series' nine letters, one with an adjacent spurious identity in the second three letters, and one in the third three letters. This constraint on the location of adjacent identities combined with differences among the nine rules to create variation among the series in number of spurious identities. The 54 series thus created were randomly arranged in a protocol with three answer spaces for each series.

The 20 sixth-grade subjects were instructed to provide the three letters that correctly continued each series. Subjects were tested in groups of 10 for one session of approximately 30 minutes' duration, using instructions like those employed in Experiment 1.

Dependent Variable

The dependent variable was the percentage of subjects who correctly continued each series for three letters.

Predictor Variables

Three predictor variables were used. KN was calculated as in foregoing experiments. Accordingly, each nonspurious problem had $KN = 2$ and each spurious problem had $KN = 6$. The number of letters entering into a spurious identity, SI, was calculated for each spurious series. Series without spurious identities were given $SI = 0$. The third predictor, OP, was the sum of CNT and REL for each rule. OP scores varied from rule to rule, but were the same for spurious and nonspurious series of the same rule.

Results

Preliminary analyses showed that the location of adjacent spurious identities had no influence on accuracy, so the data were collapsed across this variable. The problems without spurious relations were answered correctly at a higher percentage (67.4%) than problems with spurious relations (51.0%). Before testing the significance of this difference, we analyzed the 27 problems with spurious relations ($KN = 6$) to see if number of spurious relations mattered. For these 27 problems, we performed a multiple regression analysis in which the predictors were OP and SI. Both variables contributed significantly to percent correct responding, as indicated by the fact that both regression weights were significant ($p < .01$). Therefore, to assess the effects of the presence or absence of spurious relations, we pooled the problems with and without spurious relations and performed a multiple regression analysis using *KN, OP,* and *SI* as predictors. All three variables correlated significantly with %*R*+, and the regression weight of each was significant ($p < .05$). The use of *OP* as a predictor amounts to covarying the effects of *CNT* and *REL* from those of *KN* and *SI,* which were the factors of primary interest in the experiment. The significance of the regression weight for *KN* indicates that the presence of spurious relations does increase the difficulty of letter series. The significance of the regression weight for *SI* indicates that as the number of spurious identities increased, the subjects' accuracy decreased. The multiple correlation of the three predictors with %*R*+ for all 54 problems was .845 ($p < .001$).

FIVE CONCLUSIONS

Taken together, the foregoing six experiments allow five inferences.

1. Simon and Kotovsky's predictor variable #*ML* is best viewed as a composite measure of two memory processes, the location of letters needed to continue a series and the transformation of those letters into desired letters.

The predictor #*ML* was examined in four experiments with letter series. In all four, the zero-order correlation between #*ML* and series difficulty was significant and in the expected direction. The more memory lists, the greater the difficulty of letter series. In all four of these experiments, #*ML* failed to contribute significantly to the multiple prediction of series difficulty. The pattern of correlations among #*ML, CNT,* and *REL* indicates that the variance in difficulty associated with #*ML* is accounted for completely by *CNT* and *REL.* In the fifth experiment, which used number series, the zero-order correlation between #*ML* and %*R*+ was negative, as it was in the four experiments with letter series. But in a multiple regression analysis, #*ML* contributed positively to series difficulty. When the variance associated with *KN, CNT,* and *REL* was removed from the contribution of #*ML* to the prediction of number series difficulty, problems with more memory lists were easier to solve. This finding requires repliction, but even if replicated it would not qualify the conclusion that #*ML* contributes nothing to the prediction of letter series difficulty.

2. Holzman *et al.*'s (1983) predictor *MPD* (method of period discovery) is best viewed as a correlate of knowledge required to represent strings of a series.

Experiment 3 showed that the period of letter series contributes nothing to their difficulty. Experiment 4 showed a significant zero-order correlation between *MPD* and series difficulty, but *MPD* did not contribute significantly to the multiple prediction of difficulty. The pattern of relations among the predictors indicates that the variance in difficulty accounted for by *MPD* is explained completely by *KN*.

3. Series composed entirely of nonmoving strings are represented perceptually without reference to knowledge about the structure of strings.

Experiments 1, 2, 3, and 4 all showed that series composed entirely of nonmoving strings are the easiest to solve. Experiment 4 showed that young children who fail all problems with any moving strings may nevertheless solve all series with no moving strings.

4. The representation of series containing any moving string is guided by knowledge about the role of adjacency or nonadjaceny in defining strings' units and the role of equality or inequality among units in defining their string membership. This is true whether or not the series has spurious relations. The presence of spurious relations makes application of knowledge about units and string membership more difficult, perhaps because units and spurious relations are both defined by the presence of duplicated letters.

By varying *CNT* and *REL* orthogonally with *KN* in the range of 2 to 5, and by including a greater variety of moving strings at *KN* = 6, Experiment 4 suggested that we were wrong in two aspects of our initial hypothesis about representational knowledge. First, nonadjacency of letters in units did not contribute more difficulty than inequality in number of letters among units. Second, more abstract knowledge is not required to represent series with spurious relations. Experiment 5 provided independent corroboration of the pertinent findings of Experiment 4. Experiment 6 showed that the effects of spurious relations are predicted better by the number of spurious identities than by the presence of any spurious relations.

5. Very nearly perfect prediction of letter series difficulty would be provided by five variables: *CNT, REL,* Adjacency, Equality, and Spurious Identities.

By Spurious Identities (*SI*), we mean the number of letters shared among strings. By Adjacency, we mean a variable whose values range from 0 to 2: Series with no moving strings receive a 0, series with moving strings whose units are composed entirely of adjacent letters receive a 1, and series with any moving string whose units are composed of nonadjacent letters receive a 2. By Equality, we mean another variable whose values range from 0 to 2: Series with no moving strings receive a 0, series with moving strings, each of which is composed of units of the same number of letters, receive a 1, and series with any moving string whose units have different numbers of letters receive a 2. *CNT* and *REL* are defined as they have been throughout this chapter. With these definitions, every problem composed entirely of nonmoving strings would receive a 0 on all five predictors. Any problem with at least one moving string would necessarily earn a score greater than zero on all predictors except *SI*.

. None of the foregoing experiments directly support this entire conclusion, but taken together they indicate that it is a reasonable inference. Experiment 5 showed that if Adjacency and Equality were substituted for *KN* in multiple regression analyses, a greater proportion of variance in series difficulty would be accounted for. Experiments 1, 2, 3, and 4 indicated that when *KN* is used in combination with *CNT* and *REL,* very high multiple correlations result. Experiments 5 and 6 indicated that if *SI* was used instead of *KN* = 6, a greater proportion of variance in series difficulty would be predicted. Because there was little unaccounted variance in Experiment 4 when *KN, CNT,* and *REL* were used as predictors, very nearly perfect prediction of series difficulty would have resulted if the five foregoing predictors had been used.

The greatest uncertainty about Conclusion 5 stems from the fact that none of the experiments reported here used any series composed of strings with variable periods or whose reference letters were not the last letter on the string. A recently completed investigation in our laboratory indicates that these predictors account for practically all of the variance in difficulty of such series.

We turn now to the question of how our model can guide the selection of letter series for the construction of intelligence subtests.

TWO THEORETICALLY DERIVED PSYCHOMETRIC MEASURES OF INDUCTIVE REASONING

The experiments described in the preceding section of this chapter show that it is possible to predict with substantial accuracy the relative difficulty of letter series problems. Moreover, using the information presented in the second section, "Describing and Generating Letter Series," it is possible to generate problems that will fall at any particular level of predicted difficulty. Because a chief characteristic of items on intelligence tests is that they are graded by difficulty, it should be possible to generate letter series subtests of intelligence from the theory described in the third and fourth sections using the item generating principles described in the second section. It remains to be seen whether scores on such theoretically based subtests would relate to scores on other measures of intelligence, as they must to be taken as valid measures of intelligence.

Experiment 7: Prediction of Difficulty of 15-Letter Series from the Primary Mental Abilities Test

An economical way of estimating whether scores on series problems generated theoretically will relate to other measures of intelligence is to determine whether the theory predicts the difficulty of letter series known to produce scores that do relate to other measures of intelligence. The 15-letter series included on the Primary Mental Abilities Test produce scores that relate to other measures of intelligence. Moreover, Simon and Kotovsky (1963) have reported the numbers of two separate groups of subjects who correctly answered each of these 15 problems. To determine whether the theory developed in the preceding accounts well for the difficulty of these 15 problems, we used the two sets of data reported by Simon and Kotovsky and a third set that we collected.

Subjects

The subjects were 30 normal third-grade and 47 sixth-grade children.

Procedure

The 15 problems from the Primary Mental Abilities Test were administered to groups of approximately 15 children, using instructions like those for the foregoing experiments. The children were instructed to provide three-letter continuation responses.

Predictor Variables

The three predictor variables were *KN, CNT,* and *REL* calculated as described previously.

Dependent Variables

One dependent variable was the percentage of children who gave three correct letters for each of the 15 problems. Two other dependent variables were the percentage of 67 high school students and the percentage of 12 adults tested by Simon and Kotovsky (1963) who gave correct one-letter responses for each of the 15 problems.

Results

Table 12 summarizes the results of Experiment 7. The mean percentage correct of the 77 elementary school students per problem was 45.5. The standard deviation of 29% reflects the fact that percentage correct ranged

TABLE 12

Mean and Standard Deviation Percentage
Correct and Correlation Coefficients of
Percentages Correct for Knowledge (KN),
Counts (CNT), and Relations (REL) with Three
Groups of Subjects on the 15 Letter Series
from the Test of Primary Mental Abilities

	Percentage correct three-letter responses by 77 elementary students[a]	Percentage correct one-letter responses by 67 high school students[b]	Percentage correct one-letter responses by 12 adults[b]
Percentage correct			
M	45.5	70.8	61.7
SD	29.0	15.5	26.5
Correlation coefficients (r)			
KN	−.746*	−.548*	−.723*
CNT	−.741*	−.751*	−.601*
REL	−.720*	−.698*	−.579*
Multiple coefficients (R)			
KN + CNT + REL	.944*	.884*	.896*

* $p < .001$, one-tailed.
[a] Experiment 7.
[b] Data from Simon & Kotovsky (1963).

from 95% to 13% across the 15 problems. All three of the predictors correlated significantly ($p < .001$) with percentage correct, as can be seen under "Correlation Coefficients" (Table 12). The multiple correlation of KN, CNT, and REL with %R+ was .944, which corresponds to 89% of the variance among the 15 problems. Table 12 also summarizes the results of analysis of the data from 67 high school students (Simon & Kotovsky, 1963). Although the high school students were more accurate overall (70.8% versus 45.5%) than the elementary students of Experiment 7, the same pattern of relations held between the three predictors and the high school students' percentages correct. All three predictors correlated significantly ($p < .001$) with percentage correct, and they combined to yield a multiple correlation of .884. Table 12 also summarizes the results of analysis of data from 12 adults (Simon & Kotovsky, 1963). Again, KN, CNT, and REL each correlated significantly ($p < .001$) with %R+. The predictors combined to yield a multiple correlation of .896 with %R+. We infer that letter series generated to differ on KN, CNT, and REL so as to produce a predicted ordering of difficulty will yield scores that correlate across individuals with other measures of intelligence.

EXPERIMENT 8: ONE-LETTER VERSUS THREE-LETTER CONTINUATION RESPONSES

The similarly high multiple correlations across the three data sets analyzed in Experiment 7 suggest that letter series are equally difficult no matter how many letters subjects are required to give as continuation responses. The irrelevance of the number of response letters is also suggested by the similarly large correlations of the various predictors across Experiments 1–6. Like Simon and Kotovsky (1963), we built our theory on the assumption that the number of letters required does not influence the difficulty of continuing a series. Nevertheless, it seemed prudent to perform a direct test of this assumption before deriving a psychometric measure of inductive reasoning from our theory.

Subjects

The subjects were 24 sixth-grade children assigned randomly to groups of 8 and 16 children.

Procedure

Twenty-four rules were selected from the 132 rules studied in Experiment 1. The rules were selected to vary as widely as possible in difficulty. Each rule was used to generate two problems, with the same restrictions that were used in Experiment 1 about spurious relations and words. The resulting 48 problems were presented in random order to one subject at a time, using a CRT display. Eight subjects were required to give one-letter responses, and 16 subjects were required to give three-letter responses. All subjects responded by typing letters on a keyboard arranged in alphabetic (A to Z) order, not in typewriter keyboard order. The experiment began with practice finding and typing individual letters from the alphabet. The speed of locating individual letters was timed, and was subsequently found to be unrelated to accuracy for either the one-letter or three-letter conditions.

Dependent Variables

The dependent variable was the percentage of problems of each rule that each group answered correctly. Thus, there were 24 scores each for the one-letter and for the three-letter conditions.

Results

The mean error rate for the one-letter condition was 25.4% and for the three-letter condition 22.7%. This difference did not approach statistical significance ($t < 1.0$). Success rates for the 24 rules ranged from 20% to 100% and correlated .867 ($p < .001$) across the one-letter and three-letter conditions. We concluded that the number of letters that subjects are required to generate does not influence the difficulty of letter series continuation.

TWO SUBTESTS OF INTELLIGENCE

Experiments 1–6 suggest that five predictors provide the most complete account of letter series difficulty. Nevertheless, creating a set of letter series ordered by their predicted difficulty is straightforward. It can be done several ways. We suggest two here.

One approach is to let representational and memory requirements covary so that more difficult-to-represent problems require more memory operations. Here is an ordering by representational requirement, from easiest to hardest.

No moving strings (1)

Most difficult moving string has equal-sized units of identical adjacent letters (2)

Most difficult moving string has equal-sized units of nonadjacent identical letters (4)

Most difficult moving string has unequal-sized units of nonadjacent identical letters (5)

Spurious identities are present in problems whose most difficult moving string has unequal-sized units of nonadjacent identical letters (5)

The numbers in parthetheses are the *KN* values of the problems described. $KN = 3$ is omitted because it does not differ in difficulty from $KN = 4$. All series with spurious identities are created from series with $KN = 5$.

Table 13 shows the foregoing ordering expanded by the addition within representational levels of problems that vary in their memory requirements, and at the highest representational level in the number of spurious identities in the series. Moreover, the number of memory operations covaries with representational difficulty. Three illustrative rules and a series generated by each are given for each of the 11 levels of the difficulty ordering. Series representing 1 rule from each level or any group of 11 other rules with the

TABLE 13

PROBLEMS FOR PROPOSED SUBTEST OF INTELLIGENCE CONTAINING 11
DIFFICULTY LEVELS OF LETTER SERIES MADE BY COVARYING
REPRESENTATIONAL REQUIREMENTS AND MEMORY OPERATIONS

Difficulty level	*KN*	*CNT*	*REL*	*SI*	Rules	Series
1.	1	0	0	0	B1 N1	KLKLKL
					I1 I1 I2	RRGRRGRRG
					I1 I2 I3 I4	CMWUCMWUCMWU
2.	2	1	1	0	N1 I1	AABBCC
					N1 I1 I1	HHHIIIJJJ
					N1 I1 I1 I1	NNNNOOOOPPPP
3.	2	2	2	0	B1 I2	TDSDRD
					I1 B2 I1	QKQQJQQIQ
					B1 I1 I2	UUATTASSA
4.	2	4	2	0	N1 N2	EOFPGQ
					N1 N1 I2 I3	GHCXIJCXKLCX
					B1 I2 I3 I4	MTRWLTRWKTRW
5.	4	6	2	0	N1 N2 I1	VCVWDWXEX
					B1 I2 N3 B3 I1 I3	HYBAHAGYBAGAFYBAFA
					N1 I1 N2 I1	OOKOPPLPQQMQ
6.	4	6	3	0	B1 N2 I1	INIHOHGPG
					N1 B2 I2 I1	FZZFGYYGHXXH
					N1 I1 B2 I1	LLDLMMCMNNBN
7.	4	8	3	0	N1 B2 I1 I2	JHJHKGKGLFLF
					N1 N2 I1 N2	CSCTDUDVEWEX
					N1 B2 I3 I1	RFYRSEYSTDYT
8.	5	8	4	0	I1 B1 I2 B2	VUMLUTLKTSKJ
					N1 B2 I1 N1	AQABCPCDEOEF
					B1 I2 I1 B1	SCSRQCQPOCON
9.	5	8	6	0	B1 I1 I2 B2 B2	RRJIHQQHGFPPFED
					N1 I1 N1 B2 B2	AABPOCCDNMEEFLK
					I1 B1 B1 B2	ZYXGXWVFVUTE
10.	5	12	6	2	I1 B2 B1 B3	LIKSKHJRJGIQ
					I1 B1 B1 I2 N2 N2	VUTJKLTSRLMNRQPNOP
					B1 I1 I2 B2 B3	FFLKJEEJIHDDHGF
11.	5	16	8	8	I1 B2 B3 B1 B4	KLMJYJKLIXIJKHW
					B1 I2 N2 N2 B3 B4	DCDEKMCEFGJLBGHIIK
					B1 I2 B2 B3 I4 B5 I6	PNMXSROOMLWSQONLKVSPO

same *KN, CNT, REL,* and *SI* values should produce large individual differences in number of series answered correctly, and the scores earned by
individuals should correlate with scores on other measures of intelligence.
The difficulty range of the 11 levels is such that any group of 11 series
representing them should constitute a subtest suitable for all ages from six
years through adulthood.

TABLE 14

PROBLEMS FOR PROPOSED SUBTEST OF INTELLIGENCE CONTAINING
11 DIFFICULTY LEVELS OF LETTER SERIES MADE BY VARYING
MEMORY OPERATIONS AND SPURIOUS IDENTITIES

Difficulty level	CNT	REL	SI	Rules	Series
1.	1	1	0	N1 I1	DDEEFF
				N1 I1 I1	RRRSSSTTT
				N1 I1 I1 I1	IIIIJJJJKKKK
2.	1	2	0	B1 I1	QQPPOO
				B1 I1 I1	IIIHHHGGG
				B1 I1 I1 I1	ZZZZYYYYXXXX
3.	2	2	0	B1 I2	DRCRBR
				B1 I1 I2	UUXTTXSSX
				B1 I2 I2	FVVEVVDVV
4.	3	2	0	B1 I2 I3	WIFVIFUIF
				N1 N1 I2	DELFGLHIL
				B1 B2 N1	XTYXSYXRY
5.	4	3	0	N1 B2	GNHMIL
				B1 I1 N2 I2	GGHHFFIIEEJJ
				N1 I1 I1 B2	RRRISSSHTTTG
6.	6	3	0	B1 I2 N3	ZMAYMBXMC
				N1 N2 N1	EAFGBHICJ
				B1 N2 I3	QSKPTKOUK
7.	8	4	0	N1 N1 B2 I3	QROHSTNHUVMH
				N1 N2 N1 N2	GNHOIPJQKRLS
				B1 N2 B2 B3	LOMUKOMTJOMS
8.	10	4	0	N1 N1 I2 N2 N2	FGORSHIOTUJKOVW
				B1 I2 I3 B4 I5	FHJULEHJTLDHJSL
				B1 N2 B3 N2 N3	XBJCKWDJEKVFJGK
9.	12	5	0	B1 N2 I3 B4	WBJQVCJPUDJO
				N1 I1 B2 B3 I4	CCSNADDRMAEEQLA
				B1 I1 N2 I3 B4 I4	FFKRIIEELRHHDDMRGG
10.	16	5	4	N1 N2 B3 N4	AELIBFKJCGJK
				B1 N2 N3 I3 N4	URMMGITSNNHSTOOI
				B1 I1 I1 N2 N3 N4	YYYGKUXXXHLVWWWIMW
11.	18	6	10	N1 N1 B2 I3 I4 B5	EFRERKGHQERJIJPERI
				N1 B2 B2 N3 B4 N4	BMLFFGCKJGFGDIHHFG
				N1 B2 N1 I3 N1 N4	CKDGEMFJGGHNIIJGKO

Table 14 shows another group of letter series rules derived from our theory so that they are ordered by their difficulty. All rules in this ordering lie at $KN = 2$. The rules vary in their memory requirements and in the number of spurious identities they contain. Because these rules do not vary in their representational requirements, scores from a group of series derived from these rules might produce a different pattern of relationships with scores from other measures of intelligence than scores from series derived from the rules in Table 13. Nevertheless, the rules in Table 14 or other rules with the same *KN, CNT, REL,* and *SI* values generate series that, when administered to a group of people, should yield percentage correct scores that correlate with scores on other measures of intelligence.

COMPUTERIZED SERIES GENERATION AND TEST ADMINISTRATION

The construction and administration of letter series problems could be computerized easily. A very simple approach would be to store a set of rules, like those in Tables 13 and 14, and to program the computer to create letter series from the rules. This approach requires programming the selection of rules, the generation of series, and the scoring of responses. The selection of rules could be random or serial by predicted difficulty or contingent on the correctness of an individual's responses. For generating series, the chief programming requirements would be to prevent the occurrence of spurious identities when they are not called for and to generate the proper number when they are called for. Most of the rules in Tables 13 and 14 contain strings whose Σs are unequal, and the only test for spurious identities required by any of these rules is whether different strings share letters. If they do when they should not, the starting point of one offending string can be simply changed so that it is further from the starting point of the other offending string. If they do not when they should the starting point of any string can be simply changed so that it equals some letter in another string, and then starting points can be adjusted until the desired number of spurious identities is obtained. Simple adjustment of starting points will also work for rules with strings having the same Σ but no spurious identities. However, when spurious identities are required and the rule has two or more strings with the same Σ, the algebra for calculating equivalent rules (see Appendix) must also be programmed and used. Generating the answer for any series requires only more recursion through the rule than is required to generate the series itself.

A more complex but nevertheless feasible approach would be to store the characteristics of the rules to be generated and to let the computer do rule generation as well as series generation. The stored characteristics should include all of the following factors that the test constructor intends to vary across rules: *ADJ, EQU, CNT, REL,* and *SI. ADJ* and *EQU* equal adjacency and equality as defined in the section "Two Theoretically Derived Psychometric Measures of Inductive Reasoning." *CNT, REL,* and *SI* equal counts, relations, and spurious identities as used throughout this chapter. Any number of approaches could be used for rule generation, but we recommend starting with *REL* and using it to choose a provisional set of moving relations. For example, if *REL* = 4, four N's, two B's, or two N's and one B could be selected. We recommend next considering *CNT* and using a variant of the formula *CNT* = #*MS*(*P* − #*AIR*) to select a provisional number of moving strings. Because the number of adjacent identity relations will be under the control of the program and adds no difficulty to any series problem, the variant #Strings = *CNT*/#*MS* can be used. Notice that #*MS* may not exceed the number of relations chosen in the first step, but that a different number of relations can generally be selected to satisfy the requirement that #Strings, #*MS*, and *CNT* must all be integers. After provisional moving relations and a provisional number of moving strings are selected, we recommend using *ADJ* and *EQU* to define the nature of the moving strings further. A useful principle in this regard is that no string whose units are equal can have an I relation before any moving relation, but any string whose units are unequal must have an I before one or more of the moving relations on that string. Another useful principle is that any string whose units are composed of adjacent identical letters must have at least one I relation immediately after a moving relation on its string, but any string with nonadjacent letters must have a relation from another string between the moving relation and the I relation. After each of the rule's moving strings are defined, we suggest using *ADJ, EQU,* and *CNT* to determine how to interweave the moving strings and how many nonmoving strings to add. The variables *ADJ* and *EQU* are relevant to interweaving strings and to the addition of I relations to the moving strings, whereas *CNT* is relevant to how many nonmoving strings should be added. Finally, we recommend use of the algebra for finding equivalent rules to determine whether any identical letters on different strings are spurious.

Either of the foregoing approaches to computerizing the generation of letter series problems would substantially simplify the construction of letter series subtests of intelligence. This would be true whether the subtest is of the standard variety or is created on the spot for individually tailored testing.

SUMMARY

In the second section we described a rule system for generating letter series and in the Appendix an algebra that allows exploration of the series problem space and computerized creation of rules. In the next section, we described two related theories of the processes underlying letter series solution. One theory is by Simon and Kotovsky (1963) and the other is described for the first time in this chapter. Though related, the theories generate different variables to predict the relative difficulty of letter series problems. We then reported six experiments that test the differential validity of the two theories. The experiments indicate that a revised version of the theory first described in the previous section predicts the relative difficulty of letter series with great accuracy. Next, we described two sets of letter series problems derived from the revised theory. Either of these sets of problems should serve as valid psychometric measures of the aspects of intelligence having to do with inductive reasoning. We concluded with a sketch of some procedures for a computer program that would allow the creation of many more sets of psychometrically useful letter series problems.

APPENDIX

This appendix describes an algebra for calculating equivalent letter series rules with fewer strings, equivalent rules with more strings, and number of spurious relations. This algebra allows computerized generation of letter series problems and exploration of the series problem space. The appendix concludes with such an exploration for series with $P = 3$.

CREATING EQUIVALENT RULES WITH FEWER STRINGS

Within our rule system, equivalence depends on the period and the movement of rules' strings. Let the relations $I = 0$, $N = +1$, and $B = -1$. Then, the sum (Σ) of the values of the within-period relations on a string tells how far it moves from period to period. In order for two rules to be equivalent, they must have the same period and they must contain strings that produce the same movement from period to period, but the strings with equivalent movement must have different periods in the two rules. Here are five multistring rules, followed by the sums of each of their strings (i.e., $\Sigma 1$ = sum of the values of the relations on the first string).

(1)	N1 N1 B2	$\Sigma 1 = +2, \Sigma 2 = -1$
(2)	I1 N2 I2 B3	$\Sigma 1 = 0, \Sigma 2 = +1, \Sigma 3 = -1$
(3)	I1 B2 N2	$\Sigma 1 = \Sigma 2 = 0$
(4)	N1 B2 N3	$\Sigma 1 = \Sigma 3 = +1, \Sigma 2 = -1$
(5)	B1 N1 I2 B3 I3 B4	$\Sigma 1 = \Sigma 2 = 0, \Sigma 3 = \Sigma 4 = -1$

Rules 1 and 2 have no equivalents with fewer strings because the sums of the relations on their strings are unequal. To achieve fewer strings strings must be combined, and only strings with identical sums can be combined. Table 15 shows all of the sequences of 1, 2, 3, and 4 I, N, or B relations that sum to

TABLE 15
SEQUENCES OF 1, 2, 3, AND 4 I, N, OR B RELATIONS WHOSE SUMS (Σ) RANGE FROM -4 TO $+4$

			Number of Relations (#R)	
Σ	1	2	3	4
$+4$				NNNN
$+3$		NNN		INNN, NINN, NNIN, NNNI
$+2$		NN	INN, NIN, NNI	NNNB, NNII, NINI, NNBN
				NIIN, INNI, NBNN, IINN
				ININ, BNNN
$+1$	N	IN	IIN, NNB	NNBI, BNNI, NINB, INNB
		NI	INI, NBN	NIII, IINI, NBNI, BNIN
			NII, BNN	NIBN, INBN, INII, IIIN
				NBIN, NNIB, BINN, IBNN
0	I	I	III, INB, NIB, NBI	INBI, IBNI, INIB, BIIN
		NB	IBN, BIN, BNI	IIII, NNBB, BBNN, NIBI
		BN		BINI, NIIB, IINB, NBNB
				BNBN, BNII, NBII, IBIN
				IIBN, NBBN, BNNB
-1	B	IB	IIB, BBN	BNBI, BBNI, BBIN, IBNB
		BI	IBI, BNB	BIII, IIBI, NBBI, BNIB
			BII, NBB	BIBN, INBB, IBII, IIIB
				NBIB, NIBB, BINB, IBBN
-2		BB	IBB, BIB, BBI	BBBN, BBII, BIBI, BBNB
				BIIB, IBBI, BNBB, IIBB
				IBIB, NBBB
-3			BBB	IBBB, BIBB, BBIB, BBBI
-4				BBBB

values ranging from -4 to $+4$. Any number of strings composed of sequences having the same Σ can be combined with one another.

The process of combining strings creates a new string with the same Σ as the combined strings, but the new string has a different sequence of relations from the combined strings. The structure of the new string and the sequence of relations on it can be deduced from the structure and Σ of the combined strings. Consider Rule 3. It has the two-string structure __1__2__2. When its two strings are combined, its equivalent rules have the structure __1__1__1. Rule 4 has the three-string structure __1__2__3. When its first and third strings are combined, it has the two-string equivalent structure __1__2__1. Rule 5 has the four-string structure __1__1__2__3__3__4. When its strings are combined, its equivalent rules have the two-string structure __1__1__1__2__2__2. Whenever, as in Rules 3 and 5, there are adjacent relations on any combined strings, some of the relations on the new reduced string structure are given directly by relations on the combined strings. In Rule 3, the N and I relations are adjacent on String 2. In Rule 5, the B and N relations on String 1 and the B and I relations on String 3 are adjacent.

Any relation that succeeds and is adjacent to another relation on a string will occur in its analogous position in the structure created by combining that string with another. Thus, the N2 relation of Rule 3 will become an N1 relation in the third position of the one-string equivalent(s) of Rule 3. Similarly, the N1 and I3 relations of Rule 5 will become N1 in the second position and I2 in the fifth position of the two-string equivalent(s) of Rule 5. In other words, some relations in an equivalent rule are known from the original rule; they can be called RK. Table 16 shows the RK for the reduced equivalents of Rules 3 and 5, and it indicates the unknown relations with question marks. These unknowns are called $R?$.

An equivalent rule's $R?$ can be derived from its RK and the Σ of the strings from which it is derived. The Σ of a string created by combination must equal the Σ of each of the combined strings. Therefore, $\Sigma R?$ on an equivalent string must equal the Σ of either of the combined strings minus the ΣRK on the equivalent string. Each of the two combined strings in Rule 3 has $\Sigma = 0$. $RK = +1$ on the one-string equivalent of these strings. Therefore, the Σ of the two $R?$ on this string must be -1, because $\Sigma R? = \Sigma - \Sigma RK$. Table 15 shows that there are two sequences of two relations with $\Sigma = -1$: IB and BI. It follows that there are two one-string equivalents of Rule 3: I1 B1 N1 and B1 I1 N1. In Rule 5, String 1 can be combined with String 2, and String 3 can be combined with String 4. Table 16 shows that the RK of these combinations are an N in the second position and an I in the fifth position of the equivalents to Rule 5. The N has an $RK = +1$, and the string it falls on has $\Sigma = 0$. Therefore, the two $R?$ on its string must have $\Sigma R? = -1$, because $\Sigma R? = \Sigma - \Sigma RK$, and there are two one-string equivalents of the first two strings in Rule 5: I1 N1 B1 and B1 N1 I1. Strings 3 and 4 of Rule 5 have $\Sigma = -1$, and the I on their one equivalent string has $\Sigma RK = 0$, so their equivalent string's $\Sigma R? = -1 - 0 = -1$. Therefore, the two one-string equivalents of Strings 3 and 4 in Rule 5 are I2 I2 B2 and B2 I2 I2. Table 16 shows that combining the two equivalent strings gives four two-string rules that generate some of the same series as Rule 5.

When there are no adjacent relations on the strings being combined, there is no RK on their equivalent string(s). When this is true, as it is for Rule 4, $\Sigma R? = \Sigma$ of each of the combined strings, and the relations on the equivalent string are given directly by Table 15. $\Sigma 1 = \Sigma 3 = +1$ for Rule 4. Table 15 gives two two-relation strings with $\Sigma = +1$: IN and NI. Therefore, there are two two-string equivalents for Rule 4: I1 B2 N1 and N1 B2 N1.

The number of series generated by a rule is determined by the number of

TABLE 16
Calculations for Combining a Rule's Strings to Yield Equivalent Rules with Fewer Strings

Rule 3

	I1 B2 N2	$\Sigma 1 = \Sigma 2 = 0$
Equivalent structure	__1__1__1	
Unknown from known relations	_?_1_?_1_N1	$\Sigma RK = 1$
		$\Sigma R? = \Sigma - \Sigma RK = 0 - 1 = -1$
Equivalent rules	I1 B1 N1	
	B1 I1 N1	

Rule 5

	B1 N1 I2 B3 I3 B4	$\Sigma 1$ and $2 = 0$
Equivalent structure	__1__1__1__2__2__2	
Unknown from known relations	_?_1_N1_?_1_?_2_I2_?_2	$\Sigma RK = 1$
		$\Sigma R1? = \Sigma 1 - \Sigma RK1 = 0 - (-1) = +1$
		$\Sigma R2? = \Sigma 3 - \Sigma RK2 = -1 - 0 = -1$
Equivalent rules	I1 N1 B1 I2 I2 B2	
	I1 N1 B1 B2 I2 I2	
	B1 N1 I1 I2 I2 B2	
	B1 N1 I1 B2 I2 I2	

strings in the rule, and equals the quantity 26^S, where S = number of strings in the rule. Only the series generated by the equivalent rule with the fewest strings are described by all of a set of equivalent rules. Thus, if a three-string rule has a one-string equivalent, only 26 of 17,576 series generated by the three-string rule can be described by the one-string rule as well.

Whether a series can be described by an equivalent rule with fewer strings depends on the particular letters used to generate the series from a rule with more strings. For a particular series to be described by two equivalent rules, letters on the strings defined by the rule with the greater number of strings must be equidistant in their alphabetic order from one another throughout the series and the equal distance must be ± 1 letter in the alphabet. Here are two series generated by the two-string rule N1 N2 B3:

ARLBSKCTJ
QRLRSKSTJ

Rules I1 N1 B2 and N1 I1 B3 are both equivalents for N1 N2 B3. Whether either of these is a valid description of either of the foregoing series can be calculated by determining the alphabetic distances between the letters on the N1 and N2 strings. The B3 string can be ignored because its Σ precludes it from being combined with either of the other strings. In the first series, the letters on N1 and N2 are equidistant from one another in the alphabet throughout the series, but that distance is $> \pm 1$. Therefore, neither of the two-string equivalents applies to the first series. In the second series, the letters on the two strings are equidistant within ± 1 letter, and the nature of the differences shows that I1 N1 B2 is a valid description of the second series, whereas N1 I1 B2 is not. In practice, it is not necessary to examine an entire series to determine whether it is described by equivalent rules. It is only necessary to look at the first two periods of the problem. If the alphabetic difference between letters on different strings is the same and if the letters lie within ± 1 of each other in the first two periods, then the series can be described by two equivalent rules.

CREATING EQUIVALENT RULES WITH MORE STRINGS

If a rule has a multirelation string that can be divided into more strings, then it has an equivalent rule with more strings. Whether a multirelationstring can be divided depends on its number of relations #R and their combined movement Σ. A multirelation string whose $\#R \geq 2\Sigma$ can be divided, but none of its derivative strings can have fewer than Σ relations. Deriving equivalent rules with more strings is similar to deriving equivalents with fewer strings. The main difference stems from the fact that the string structures of equivalents with more strings are not given directly by the original rule, as they are in the case of equivalents with fewer strings. Table 17 lists all of the possible structures with a greater number of strings that can be derived from any multirelation string with $\#R = 2$, 3, or 4. The chief work in determining equivalent rules with a greater number of strings is to select all of the workable structures from the possible structures for the rule being derived. We concern ourselves here only with strings having four or fewer relations. The following procedures generalize perfectly to strings with greater numbers of relations.

Here are five rules with multirelation strings and the Σ and #R for each string in each rule:

(6)	N1 N1 I1 B2	$\Sigma 1 = 2, \#R1 = 3$
		$\Sigma 2 = -1, \#R2 = 1$
(7)	N1 B1	$\Sigma 1 = 0, \#R1 = 2$
(8)	B1 N1 N2 N2	$\Sigma 1 = 0, \#R1 = 2$
		$\Sigma 2 = +2, \#R2 = 2$
(9)	B1 N1 N1	$\Sigma 1 = +1, \#R1 = 3$
(10)	B1 N2 I1 N2 N1 N2 B2	$\Sigma 1 = 0, \#R1 = 3$
		$\Sigma 2 = 2, \#R1 = 4$

TABLE 17
ONE-STRING STRUCTURES WITH 2, 3, OR 4 RELATIONS AND THEIR POTENTIALLY EQUIVALENT MULTISTRING STRUCTURES

	Number of Relations (#R)		
	2	3	4
One-string structure	__1 __1	__1 __1 __1	__1 __1 __1 __1
Equivalent structures	__1 __2	__1 __1 __2	__1 __2 __2 __2
		__1 __2 __1	__1 __1 __2 __2
		__1 __2 __2	__1 __2 __1 __2
		__1 __2 __3	__1 __2 __2 __1
			__1 __1 __1 __2
			__1 __1 __2 __1
			__1 __2 __1 __1
			__1 __1 __2 __3
			__1 __2 __1 __3
			__1 __2 __3 __1
			__1 __2 __2 __3
			__1 __2 __3 __2
			__1 __2 __3 __3
			__1 __2 __3 __4

Rule 6 has no equivalent because neither string can be divided. String 1 cannot be divided because its $\#R < 2\Sigma$ (i.e., $3 < [2 \times 2]$), and String 2 has only one relation. Rule 7 can be divided because its $\#R > 2\Sigma$ (i.e., $2 > [2 \times 0]$). Although String 2 of Rule 8 cannot be divided ($\#R < 2\Sigma$), its String 1 can be, so Rule 8 has at least one equivalent with more strings. Rules 9 and 10 both have equivalents with more strings.

Table 17 shows that there is only one alternative string structure for Rule 7: __1 __2. Because the Σ of both of the strings in this structure must equal the Σ of Rule 7, the only possible equivalent for Rule 7 is I1 I2. String 1 of Rule 8 has the same $\#R$ and Σ as Rule 7, so the equivalent for that string is I1 I2, just as the equivalent for Rule 7 is I1 I2. Accordingly, the only equivalent to Rule 8 is I1 I2 N3 N3.

Table 17 shows four possible alternative structures for Rule 9. Structure __1 __2 __3 must be an equivalent, because every divisible string for which $+1 \geq \Sigma \geq -1$ can be divided into its $\#R$ strings. Because for Rule 9, $\Sigma = +1$, its three-string equivalent is N1 N2 N3. The three other structures with $\Sigma = 1$ (see Table 17) each have two strings. To determine which of them are equivalents for Rule 9, first the known relations in each structure should be found. Table 18 shows those known relations RK, which were derived by the same principle used when figuring RK for equivalent rules with fewer

TABLE 18
CALCULATIONS FOR DIVIDING A RULE'S STRINGS TO YIELD EQUIVALENT RULES WITH MORE STRINGS

Rule 7	N1 B1	$\Sigma = 0, \#R = 2$
Possible structure	___1 ___2	
Equivalent rule	I1 I2	$\Sigma1 = \Sigma2 = 0, \#R1 = \#R2 = 1$
Rule 8	B1 N1 N2 N2	$\Sigma1 = 0, \#R1 = 2$
		$\Sigma2 = 2, \#R2 = 2$
Possible structure	___1 ___2 ___3 ___3	
Equivalent rule	I1 I2 N3 N3	$\Sigma1 = \Sigma2 = 0, \#R1 = \#R2 = 1$
		$\Sigma3 = 2, \#R3 = 2$
Rule 9	B1 N1 N1	$\Sigma = +1, \#R = 3$
Possible structure	___1 ___2 ___3	
Equivalent rule	N1 N2 N3	$\Sigma1 = \Sigma2 = \Sigma3 = +1 = N$
		$\#R1 = \#R2 = \#R3 = 1$
Possible structure	___1 ___1 ___2	
Unknown from known relations	?1 N1 ?2	$\Sigma RK1 = +1$
		$\Sigma?1 = \Sigma1 - \Sigma RK1 = 0 = I$
		$R?2 = \Sigma1 = +1 = N$
Equivalent rule	I1 N1 N2	$\Sigma1 = \Sigma2 = +1$
		$\#R1 = 2, \#R2 = 1$
Possible structure	___1 ___2 ___2	
Unknown from known relations	?1 ?2 N2	$\Sigma R?1 = \Sigma1 = +1 = N$
		$\Sigma RK2 = +1$
		$\Sigma R?2 = \Sigma1 - \Sigma RK2 = 0 = I$
Equivalent rule	N1 I2 N2	$\Sigma1 = \Sigma2 = +1$
		$\#R1 = 1, \#R2 = 2$
Possible structure	___1 ___2 ___1	
Unknown from known relations	B1 ?2 ?1	$\Sigma RK1 = -1$
		$\Sigma R?1 = \Sigma - RK1 = +2$
		$R?1/\#R?1 > +1 = NPR^{a}$
Equivalent rule	None	
Rule 10	B1 N2 I1 N2 N1 N2 B2	
Equivalent rules	I1 N2 I3 N4 I5 N4 N2	
	I1 N2 B3 N4 N3 N4 N2	
	B1 N2 I3 N4 N1 N4 N2	

[a] NPR, no permissible relation.

strings. That is, succeeding adjacent relations in the structure with more strings are the same as the analogous relations in the structure with fewer strings. Thus, in the first two-string structure, the second relation on String 1 must be an N, giving ?1 N1 ?2. In the second two-string structure the second relation on string 2 must be an N, giving ?1 ?2 N2. According to Table 18, the first relation on String 1 in the third two-string structure is a B, giving B1 ?2 ?1. The reason it is the first relation on String 1 instead of the second is that the second is not both adjacent and successive to the first, but the first is both successive and adjacent to the second; this can be appreciated by writing the structure twice, just as one would use a rule (at least) twice in generating a series: __1__2__1__1__2__1.

In order to determine which of the three two-string structures allow equivalents for Rule 9, R? for each string in each structure is calculated. Table 18 shows that for structure ?1 N1 ?2, the known relations for String 1 have a movement value of $+1$ (i.e., $RK1 = +1$). Accordingly, the unknown relation on String 1 has a value of 0 and is therefore an I (i.e., $R?1 = \Sigma - RK1 = 1 - 1 = 0$). There are no RK on string 2, so $R?2 = \Sigma = 0$, yielding an I. Entering the derived relations into the structure __1__1__2 gives the rule I1 N1 N2 as an equivalent to B1 N1 N1. Similar calculations (see Table 18) show that N1 I2 N2 is also an equivalent for Rule 9. The last possible structure, __1__2__1, does not yield an equivalent. Table 18 shows that the first string in this structure has $RK1 = -1$ and that $R?1 = \Sigma - RK1 = +1 - (-1) = +2$. Because there is only one unknown relation on String 1 and because no single relation has a value of $+2$, there is no permissible relation (NPR) with which to complete String 1 in the structure __1__2__1. Therefore, there is no __1__2__1 equivalent to B1 N1 N1. The test for whether a string can be constructed from the permissible relations (I, N, and B) is to calculate the ratio of the movement value of a string's unknown relations to its number of unknown relations ($R?/\#R?$). If this ratio assumes any value from -1 to $+1$, a string can be constructed from the permissible relations, but if $+1 \le R?/\#R \le -1$, then there are no permissible relations with which to construct a string. The violation of this restriction is shown for Rule 9 in Table 18 by the notation $R?1/\#R?1 > +1 =$ NPR, which is verified by substitution, $+2/1 > +1$. In summary, of the four possible string structures from which equivalents might be constructed for the rule B1 N1 N1, three yield valid equivalents: __1__2__3, __1__1__2, and __1__2__2. Their corresponding rules are N1 N2 N3, I1 N1 N2, and N1 I2 N2. The fourth possible structure, __1__2__1, yields no valid equivalent, because its first string would violate the constraint $+1 \le R?/\#R \le -1$.

Rule 10 has two strings that are complexly intertwined. String 1 is similar to Rule 9, except that all four of the string structures to which it might be converted yield equivalent structures. String 2 has $\#R = 4$ and $\Sigma = 2$. Table 17 shows that there are 14 possible equivalent structures for a string with four relations. All but three of these are eliminated as possibilities for String 2 of Rule 10 by the fact that its $\Sigma = 2$. A minimum of two relations is required to add up to $\Sigma = 2$. Of the 14 possible structures for String 2 of Rule 10, only three have two relations on each string (see Table 17). The three are __1__1__2__2, __1__2__1__2, and __1__2__2__1. The structure __1__1__2__2 yields no equivalent, because $R?1/\#R1 > +1$. The structure __1__2__1__2 yields no equivalent, because $R?2/\#R2 > +1$. Structure __1__2__2__1 yields the equivalent N1 N2 N2 N1 because

$R?1 = R?2 = +1 = N$. Because String 1 of Rule 10 has four equivalents and String 2 has one equivalent, there are $4 \times 1 = 4$ equivalents for the rule B1 N2 I1 N2 N1 N2 B2. Table 18 shows the four correct rules, which were constructed by substitution into the original string structure of Rule 10. That is, position for position, each equivalent structure for String 1 and the equivalent structure for String 2 were substituted for the original two strings, and the new structures' strings were renumbered according to the occurrence of their first relation (see Table 18).

SERIES WITH SPURIOUS IDENTITY RELATIONS

Even though a series has spurious relations only if none of its valid rules relates all instances of a particular duplicated letter to a single string with identity relations, it is not necessary to determine all equivalent rules for a series to decide if it has spurious relations. Instead, one can judge from the equivalent with the fewest strings. There is always exactly one such rule because two rules with the same number of uncombinable strings can never describe a single series.

The series AAFFBBEECCDD is described by the four rules N1 N2 B3 B4, N1 N2 B3 I3, N1 I1 B2 B3, and N1 I1 B2 B2. Because N1 I1 B2 I2 has fewer strings, it is used to judge whether the series has spurious relations. As for all series, the criteria are whether the strings share any letters and whether any moving string (i.e., a string whose $\Sigma \neq 0$) has both N and B relations. If different strings share any letters or if any moving string has both N and B relations, the series has spurious relations. Table 19 shows the foregoing series broken into strings according to its two-string rule. The values in the far right column of Table 19 show that the series has the potential for spurious relations in that there are many duplicated letters in the series. String 1 and String 2 both have three pairs of duplicated letters, but none of the letters is shared across strings, so by the first criterion there are no spurious relations in this series. The column headed Σ shows that both strings move, but neither string has both an N and a B relation. Consequently, by the second criterion this series has no spurious relations. It should be noted that a moving string cannot have both N and B relations unless its $\#R \geq 3$ and its $\Sigma \leq \#R - 2$. Accordingly, for any series described by a rule in which every string has $\#R < 3$, only the criterion of shared letters need be applied to determine whether the series contains spurious relations.

The series AAGFBBEDCCCB is described by the two rules N1 N2 B3 B3 and N1 I1 B2 B2. Because N1 I1 B2 B2 has fewer strings, it is used to judge whether the series has spurious relations. Since no string has $\#R \geq 3$, the question about spurious relations is answered by examining for shared let-

TABLE 19
MOVEMENT (Σ), NUMBER OF RELATIONS (#R), DUPLICATED LETTERS,
SHARED LETTERS, AND SPURIOUS RELATIONS FOR EACH STRING OF SERIES
WITH FOUR DIFFERENT RULES

Rule	Series strings	Σ	#R	Duplicated letters	Shared letters	Spurious relations
N1 I1	AA BB CC	+1	2	6	0	0^a
B2 I2	FF EE DD	−1	2	6	0	0^a
						0^b
N1 I1	AA BB CC	+1	2	6	2	0^a
B2 B2	GF ED CB	−1	2	0	1	0^a
						2^b
N1 I1 N1	DDE FFG HHI	+2	3	6	0	0^a
N1	M N O	+1	3	6	0	0^a
B2 B2 N2	KJK JIJ IHI	−1	3	8	0	2^a
						0^b
I1 N1 B1	A B A A B A A B A	0	3	9	9	0^a
N2 B2 B2	E D C D C B C B A	−1	3	7	3	2^a
						12^b

^{a} Within string.
^{b} Across strings.

ters.   The two strings share the letter C: There are two C's in the first string and one in the second string.   Accordingly, this series has two spurious relations (see Table 19).

The series DDEFFGHHI is described by the rule N1 I1 N1, which has no equivalents.   No series with only a one-string rule can share letters across strings; therefore, the only test for spurious relations for this series is whether it has both N and B relations, which it does not.   All of its duplicated identical letters are related to its single string by identity relations, so it has no spurious relations.   This can be seen as well in the fact that its $\Sigma > \#R - 2$ (see Table 19).

The series MKJKNJIJOIHI has several equivalent rules, but the one with the fewest strings is N1 B2 B2 N2.   Table 19 shows that its two strings share no letters, but String 2 has $\#R = 3$ and $\Sigma = -1$.   Because $\Sigma = \#R - 2$ it could have both N and B relations, and it does.   Therefore, it has spurious relations.   Table 19 indicates that it has two spurious relations.   When spurious relations arise because of N and B relations on the same moving string, that string is converted to the multistring equivalent that minimizes the number of duplicated letters on different strings and maximizes the number of duplicated letters that are related by identity relations.   Then, the number of spurious relations is equal to the sum of the products of the

TABLE 20

ALL LETTER SERIES RULES WITH $P = 3$

Row number		
1	I1 N2 B3	(17,576/3,406)
2	I1 B2 N3	(17,576/3,406)
3	N1 I2 B3	(17,576/3,406)
4	N1 B2 I3	(17,576/3,406)
5	B1 I2 N3	(17,576/3,406)
6	B1 N2 I3	(17,576/3,406)
7	N1 N1 I2	(676/156)
8	N1 I2 N1	(676/156)
9	I1 N2 N2	(676/156)
10	B1 B1 I2	(676/156)
11	B1 I2 B1	(676/156)
12	I1 B2 B2	(676/156)
13	N1 N1 N2	(676/208)
14	N1 N2 N1	(676/208)
15	N1 N2 N2	(676/208)
16	N1 N1 B2	(676/208)
17	N1 B2 N1	(676/208)
18	B1 N2 N2	(676/208)
19	B1 B1 N2	(676/208)
20	B1 N2 B1	(676/208)
21	N1 B2 B2	(676/208)
22	B1 B1 B2	(676/208)
23	B1 B2 B1	(676/208)
24	B1 B2 B2	(676/208)
25	I1 N1 N1	(26/0)
26	N1 I1 N1	(26/0)
27	N1 N1 I1	(26/0)
28	I1 B1 B1	(26/0)
29	B1 I1 B1	(26/0)
30	B1 B1 I1	(26/0)
31	N1 N2 I3	(16,224/3,224) :	I1 N1 I2 (676/78)

#										
33	I1 N2 N3	(16,224/3,224) :	I1 I2 N2	(676/104)	I1 N2 I2	(676/78)				
34	B1 B2 I3	(16,224/3,224) :	I1 B1 I2	(676/104)	B1 I1 I2	(676/78)				
35	B1 I2 B3	(16,224/3,224) :	I1 I2 B1	(676/104)	B1 I2 I1	(676/78)				
36	I1 B2 B3	(16,224/3,224) :	I1 I2 B2	(676/104)	I1 B2 I2	(676/78)				
37	N1 N2 B3	(16,224/5,148) :	N1 I1 B2	(676/156)	N1 I1 B2	(676/130)				
38	N1 B2 N3	(16,224/5,148) :	N1 B2 I1	(676/156)	N1 B2 I1	(676/130)				
39	B1 N2 N3	(16,224/5,148) :	B1 I2 N2	(676/156)	B1 N1 I2	(676/130)				
40	B1 B2 N3	(16,224/5,148) :	I1 B1 N2	(676/156)	B1 I1 N2	(676/130)				
41	B1 N2 B3	(16,224/5,148) :	I1 N2 B1	(676/156)	I1 N2 B1	(676/130)				
42	N1 B2 B3	(16,224/5,148) :	N1 I2 B2	(676/156)	N1 I1 B2	(676/130)				
43	I1 I2 N3	(15,548/2,184) :	I1 I1 N2	(676/78)	I1 I1 N2	(676/104)	B1 N1 N2	(676/104)	B1 N1 N2	(676/104)
44	I1 N2 I3	(15,548/2,184) :	I1 N2 I1	(676/78)	I1 N2 I1	(676/104)	B1 N2 N1	(676/104)	B1 N2 N1	(676/104)
45	N1 I2 I3	(15,548/2,184) :	N1 I2 I2	(676/78)	N1 I2 I2	(676/104)	N1 B2 N2	(676/104)	N1 B2 N2	(676/104)
46	I1 I2 B3	(15,548/2,184) :	I1 I1 B2	(676/78)	I1 I1 B2	(676/104)	B1 N1 B2	(676/104)	B1 N1 B2	(676/104)
47	I1 B2 I3	(15,548/2,184) :	I1 B2 I1	(676/78)	I1 B2 I1	(676/104)	B1 B2 N1	(676/104)	B1 B2 N1	(676/104)
48	B1 I2 I3	(15,548/2,184) :	B1 I2 I2	(676/78)	B1 I2 I2	(676/104)	B1 N2 N2	(676/104)	B1 N2 N2	(676/104)
49	I1 I2 I3	(11,804/0)	I1 I1 I2	(624/0) :	I1 I1 I2	(26/0)	N1 I1 B1	(26/0)	B1 I1 N1	(26/0)
50			I1 I2 I1	(624/0) :	I1 I2 I1	(26/0)	N1 B1 I1	(26/0)	B1 N1 I1	(26/0)
51			I1 I2 I2	(624/0) :	I1 I2 I2		I1 B1 I1		I1 B1 N1	
52			N1 B1 I2	(624/0) :	N1 B1 I2		N1 I1 I1		I1 N1 I1	
53			N1 I2 B1	(624/0) :	N1 I2 B1		N1 I1 I1		I1 N1 I1	
54			I1 N2 B2	(624/0) :	I1 N2 B2		I1 N1 I1		I1 N1 I1	
55			B1 N1 I2	(624/0) :	B1 N1 I2		B1 N1 I1		I1 N1 I1	
56			B1 I2 N1	(624/0) :	B1 I2 N1		I1 B1 I1		I1 N1 I1	
57			I1 B2 N2	(624/0) :	I1 B2 N2		I1 B1 I1		B1 I1 N1	
58	N1 N2 N3	(13,754/4,654)	I1 N1 N2	(598/104) :	I1 N1 N2	(26/0)	N1 N1 B1	(26/26)	B1 N1 N1	(26/26)
59			N1 N2 I1	(624/130) :	N1 N2 I1		N1 I1 I1	(26/0)	N1 I1 I1	
60			N1 N2 I2	(624/130) :	N1 N2 I2		N1 I1 I1	(26/0)	N1 I1 I1	
61			N1 I1 N2	(598/104) :	N1 I1 N2	(26/0)	I1 B1 N1		B1 N1 N1	
62			I1 N2 N1	(598/104) :	I1 N2 N1		N1 B1 N1	(26/26)	B1 N1 N1	
63			N1 I2 N2	(598/104) :	N1 I2 N2		N1 B1 N1	(26/0)	B1 N1 N1	
64	B1 B2 B3	(13,754/4,654)	I1 B1 B2	(598/104) :	I1 B1 B2	(26/0)	B1 B1 N1	(26/26)	N1 B1 B1	(26/26)
65			B1 B2 I1	(624/130) :	B1 B2 I1		B1 I1 I1	(26/0)	B1 I1 I1	
66			B1 B2 I2	(624/130) :	B1 B2 I2		B1 I1 I1	(26/0)	B1 I1 I1	
67			B1 I1 B2	(624/130) :	B1 I1 B2	(26/0)	B1 I1 I1		B1 I1 I1	
68			I1 B2 B1	(598/104) :	I1 B2 B1		B1 N1 B1	(26/26)	N1 B1 B1	
69			B1 I2 B2	(598/104) :	B1 I2 B2		B1 N1 B1	(26/0)	N1 B1 B1	

number of identical letters shared between all pairs of strings of that multistring equivalent.

The series AEBDACADBCABACBBAA was generated by the rule I1 N2 N1 B2 B1 B2, and it has no equivalent rule with fewer strings. Table 19 shows that its two strings share 12 letters, and that these 12 letters account for 12 spurious identities $[(6 \times 1) + (3 \times 2)]$. Moreover, String 2 has both N and B relations and seven duplicated letters, resulting in two more spurious relations. String 1 has nine duplicated letters, but its $\Sigma = 0$, so none of these letters results in spurious relations. This is so because any multirelation string whose $\Sigma = 0$ has an equivalent rule with more strings that results in all duplicated letters being related to their own string by identity relations.

In summary, to determine whether a series has spurious relations, first its letters are separated into strings according to the rule that has the smallest number of strings. If the separate strings share any letters, the series has spurious relations. Then all strings whose $\#R \geq 3$ are examined. If any such string has both N and B relations, which it can only if $\Sigma \leq \#R - 2$, then the series has spurious relations. The number of spurious relations is the sum of the products of the number of identical letters shared by all possible pairs of strings, determined after any string with both N and B relations has been divided into a larger number of strings to minimize the number of shared letters on different strings.

RELATIONSHIPS AMONG LETTER SERIES RULES WITH $P = 3$

When $P = 3$ and the permissible relations are I, N and B, there are 132 rules whose strings have a fixed period and whose relations operate on the last letter on their string. All 132 of these rules are listed in Table 20. Rules that share a row are equivalent in that they produce some series that can be described by at least one other rule in that row. Notice that most of the one-string rules in Rows 49 through 69 are listed in more than one row. The pattern of multiple listings of one-string rules indicates how many series have more than two descriptions. Thus, a rule like N1 I1 B1, which is listed three times, produces 26 series that can be described by it, by each of the three two-string rules in whose row it is listed, and by the three-string rule I1 I2 I3. Tracing out the pattern of multiple listings shows that the 42 rules in Rows 49 through 69 apply to 364 series with five descriptions, 52 with four descriptions, 52 series with three descriptions, 12,948 series with two descriptions, and 39,312 series with one description. There are two numbers in parentheses following each rule. (The one-string rules that occur in more than one row have numbers after their first occurrence only.) The first of these numbers is the number of series that are produced by the preceding rule and are not described by another rule with the same or a smaller number of strings, so the total number of different series produced by the rules in any row can be obtained by summing the first numbers in the parentheses on that row. The second number in each set of parentheses is the number of series that are produced by the preceding rule and are not described by another rule with the same or a smaller number of strings, but do contain spurious relations when created by three recursions through the rule. Thus, the first rule, I1 N2 B2, generates 17,576 series for any given number of recursions through the rule; when those series are generted by three recursions, 3,406 of them contain at least one spurious relation.

REFERENCES

Holzman, T. G., Pellegrino, J. W., & Glaser, R. (1982). Cognitive dimensions of numerical rule induction. *Journal of Educational Psychology, 74,* 360–373.

Holzman, T. G., Pellegrino, J. W., & Glaser, R. (1983). Cognitive variables in series completion. *Journal of Educational Psychology, 75,* 603–618.

Kotovsky, K., & Simon, H. A. (1973). Empirical tests of a theory of human acquisition of concepts for sequential patterns. *Cognitive Psychology, 4,* 399–424.

Pellegrino, J. W., & Glaser, R. (1982). Analyzing aptitudes for learning: Inductive reasoning. In R. Glaser (Ed.), *Advances in instructional psychology* (Vol. 2). Hillsdale, NJ: Erlbaum.

Raven, J. C. (1938). *Progressive matrices: A perceptual test of intelligence* (individual form). London: Lewis.

Simon, H. A., & Kotovsky, K. (1963). Human acquisition of concepts for sequential patterns. *Psychological Review, 70,* 534–546.

Spearman, C. (1923). *The nature of intelligence and the principles of cognition.* London: Macmillan.

Thurstone, L. L., & Thurstone, T. G. (1941). *Factorial studies of intelligence.* Chicago: University of Chicago Press.

Thurstone, T. G. (1962). *Primary mental abilities.* Chicago: Science Research Associates.

5

Cognitive Analyses of Tests: Implications for Redesign*

Richard E. Snow
Penelope L. Peterson

INTRODUCTION

Since the early 1960s, two streams of work in psychology have been building toward a substantial revision of the theory and method of educational and differential psychological research. One of these streams—called here the cognitive information-processing (CIP) approach—has shown how cognitive tasks and tests can be analyzed to reach an improved understanding of the mental process and content structures that underlie complex performance. A new kind of cognitive instructional psychology has grown up on

* A portion of this chapter was presented at the Symposium on New Developments in Assessment—Contributions from Western Countries, International Congress of Applied Psychology, Edinburgh, Scotland, July 1982. Other portions were presented by the second author at the American Educational Research Association, New York, March 1982, under the title *Contributions from Aptitude–Treatment Interaction Research to Test Design,* and by the first author at the American Educational Research Association Convention, Montreal, Canada, April 1983, under the title *Tests as Vehicles between Laboratory and Field.* Work on the chapter was supported partly by the Wisconsin Center for Education Research through National Institute of Education Grant No. NIE-G-81-0009, and partly by the Personnel and Training Research Programs, Office of Naval Research through Contract No. N00014-79-C-0171. The views and conclusions contained in this chapter are those of the authors and should not be interpreted as necessarily representing the official policies, either expressed or implied, of the National Institute of Education, the Office of Naval Research, or the U.S. Government. Some of the work of the first author on this chapter was also supported by a James McKeen Cattell Fund Award, for which he is extremely grateful.

Copyright © 1985 by Academic Press, Inc.
All rights of reproduction in any form reserved.
ISBN 0-12-238180-7

this approach (see, e.g., Klahr, 1976; Resnick, 1981; Snow, Federico, & Montague, 1980b). A parallel cognitive differential psychology seems also close to fruition (see, e.g., Resnick, 1976; Snow, Federico, & Montague, 1980a; Sternberg, 1977). The other stream—called here the aptitude-treatment interaction (ATI) approach—has shown how experimental treatment situations can be manipulated to influence aptitude-outcome relations, and how the evaluation of such relations can be used to suggest adaptive and thus improved instructional assignments based on individual differences among learners (see, e.g., Cronbach & Snow, 1977; Snow, 1977; Snow & Peterson, 1980).

It has been suggested elsewhere that a combination of the CIP and ATI approaches provides the best means of reaching "a process theory of individual differences in learning—one that explains aptitude and achievement in common psychological process terms and accounts for the effects of specified instructional conditions on these processes" (Snow, 1980a, p. 40). It is suggested here that the redesign of aptitude and achievement assessment instruments, based on an alliance of CIP and ATI thinking and analyses, will be an integral part of work toward that goal. Such assessment instruments can be made to serve as vehicles of communication between laboratory and field, connecting the controlled experimental observations of the laboratory with the correlational networks observed in the study of "nature's" experiments, particularly in the field of education. Beyond its contribution to theory development, such instrument redesign can be expected to lead to practical improvements in diagnostic assessment for a variety of test uses.

The purpose of this chapter is to elaborate this argument, using various example findings from past research as implications for test redesign and redevelopment. First, two simple examples are given to show how ATI and CIP results convert into faceted diagnostic tests. Then, other recent developments in CIP and ATI research are briefly surveyed. Methodological problems and prospects needing further research are noted in passing, but are not given detailed consideration.

BASIC EXAMPLES

THE GAVURIN STUDY

The first simple example comes from a small study by Gavurin (1967); for detailed discussion see Snow, 1978b. Gavurin used an anagrams test as a measure of verbal reasoning ability. Anagrams are common words presented with their letters scrambled into more or less random order; each item in the test presents one such word. The examinee's task is to rearrange the letters to recognize and report the correct stimulus word. Errors or solution times provide the score. Anagrams tests are usually found to correlate highly with other verbal comprehension (e.g., vocabulary) and reasoning (e.g., letter series) tests. But Gavurin was interested in the degree to which some sort of spatial processing ability might be involved in such reasoning. Therefore, he randomly assigned examinees to one of two administration conditions. In one, the examinees solved anagram items with the letters presented on movable tiles that could be rearranged manually. In the other condition the tiles were taped together, forcing the examinees to rearrange the letters mentally, as in the conventional printed test. A paper form board test of spatial ability was then shown to correlate .54 with anagram performance in the mental condition but $-.18$ in the manual condition. The result suggests that the spatial ability test represents individual differences in some cognitive process involved in mental (i.e. internal) anagram solution but not involved when examinees can try out alternative letter rearrangements manually (i.e., externally). More generally, the implication from this and other studies is that spatial reasoning is sometimes useful in verbal problem solving, and there is evidence suggesting that the converse is also true (see Kyllonen, Lohman, & Snow, 1984). The often noted positive correlation between conventional printed verbal and spatial reasoning tests has been taken as evidence for G (the general intelligence or general ability factor) for complementary relations between major primary ability factors, or for both.

This simple, between-person experiment is an ATI study because it uses an experimental treatment contrast to manipulate the relation between a criterion task performance (i.e., anagram solution) and an external aptitude construct (i.e., spatial ability). We converted Gavurin's data to the raw regression analysis shown in Fig. 1(a), because ATI thinking must always be based on raw regressions or on regressions standardized on the total population, not on correlations. The latter are standardized within groups or treatments and thus will reflect ATI effects accurately only when group or treatment variances are equal — a rare event. (See Cronbach & Snow, 1977, for detailed discussion of this and related points).

In ATI theory, individual differences come into play upon situational demand. In this case, the situation has been engineered to demand spatial ability under one condition and not under another. Note that the regression slopes intersect, suggesting that mental performance is superior to manual performance for high spatial ability examinees and inferior for low spatial ability examinees. Thus, if such a result is replicable, the difference between mental and manual anagram performance, on a reaction time scale, becomes an alternate measure of spatial ability. This also supports a CIP hypothesis; mental rearrangement of stimulus configurations may be a component cognitive process common to anagram and paper form board tasks.

Thus something is learned about an information-processing aspect of both spatial ability and verbal reasoning test performance.

The Gavurin study could easily be converted into a within-person, faceted cognitive test simply by providing two separately timed forms, one for each condition. Blocks of items or trials might also be added to counterbalance performance order for the two experimental conditions. The within-person comparison provides two independent (cell) scores or a single contrast (cell difference) score that should correlate with other spatial ability tests just as Gavurin's scores did. This conversion of a between-person experiment to a within-person faceted test does raise other methodological questions, of course. Although there are strong methodological arguments favoring the design and use of such experiments as tests (Calfee, 1976; Calfee & Hedges, 1980), it is also the case that within-person experiments can produce treacherous confoundings and artificial effects (see Poulton, 1979). However, conventional tests as typically designed and administered may suffer from the same unwanted within-person effects as do within-person experiments. At least, faceted test designs allow the systematic study of such effects.

Obviously, such a test can also be made multifaceted by crossing other experimental treatment contrasts of interest with this one. There are many CIP experiments, to be touched on briefly later, that suggest facets relevant to process analyses of verbal and spatial ability. Each such facet would be designed to bring out the effects of one or more component processes, just as the mental versus manual contrast was designed to isolate a mental rearrangement component in the Gavurin study. Potentially, such contrasts can be sharpened through continuing research with the test design to tease out important diagnostic assessments of particular information-processing skills and strategies, as well as strengths and weaknesses, that are now confounded in the total scores of conventionally designed tests.

THE SCHMITT–CROCKER STUDY

A second introductory example is provided by the Schmitt and Crocker (1981) study of the interaction of individual differences in test anxiety with alternative item formats in a multiple-choice achievement test. Here, a conventional test-anxiety measure provided the external variable. For the achievement test, examinees were randomly divided among two format conditions. In one, examinees were directed to read the question stem, then generate their own responses and write these in a space provided before turning to the next page to read the alternative multiple-choice responses presented for that item, and only then record their choice. In the other condition, the same items were presented in a traditional multiple-choice format, with stem and choices adjacent on the same page. Schmitt and

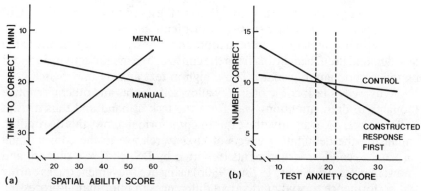

FIGURE 1. ATI effects in two studies: (a) Regression analysis based on data from Gavurin (1967) and (b) Regression analysis reported by Schmitt and Crocker (1981).

Crocker reported the regression analysis reproduced in Fig. 1(b). The vertical dashed lines in the figure indicate the regions of significance determined by the Johnson–Neyman–Potthoff technique (see Cronbach & Snow, 1977). Outside the central region marked by the dashed verticals the regression lines can be considered significantly separate, so persons with aptitude scores outside this region can be expected to perform differentially in the two treatments. The technique thus helps to determine the importance of a given ATI effect. The extension of the technique to apply to within-person experiments, however, has not been studied methodologically, to our knowledge.

It is clear that students low in test anxiety did particularly well when asked to generate answers before responding to the choice alternatives. However, students high on text anxiety did worse with this treatment and better with the traditional multiple-choice format. The authors noted that for 51% of the students in the sample — those average or below average in level of test anxiety — there seemed to be real value in constructing an answer before facing the confusions presented by the multiple-choice foils. But for about 24% of the sample — those showing a high level of test anxiety — this strategy was not only ineffective but actually destructive relative to the conventional control condition.

The Schmitt–Crocker study is an ATI study of the same design as the Gavurin experiment. Again, examinees showing individual differences in some relevant aptitude (in this case test anxiety rather than spatial ability) are differentially well or poorly served by alternative testing conditions. And again, the differences between performance under the two conditions provides an alternative metric for test anxiety (in this case on a number-correct rather than a time scale).

The finding also connects with CIP hypotheses in two ways. First, CIP analyses of test anxiety have suggested an attentional interpretation. Examinees low in test anxiety may attend more consciously and consistently to the task demand itself, benefitting from the constructive mental activity induced by the experimental format. Those high in text anxiety may be self-conscious as well as task-conscious; they allow self-doubts and other disruptive thoughts to draw attention away from the task at hand and thus disrupt performance. Apparently, the experimental format allows this disruption, enhancing the debilitating effects of anxiety relative to the conventional format. Second, in experiments (reported by Bethell-Fox, Lohman, and Snow, in press, and Snow, 1978a, 1980b) using eye movement tracks during test performance to study individual differences in information-processing strategies, the most effective strategy for multiple-choice items appeared to be one in which examinees construct a possible solution from stem analysis before inspecting the response alternatives to find a match. This constructive-matching strategy was prevalent among higher-ability examinees in the Snow project studies; it would be promoted by the experimental format used by Schmitt and Crocker. A less effective strategy found in Snow's project, called a response-elimination or feature-comparison strategy because it involved much rapid eye movement between stem and alternatives rather than constructive stem analysis, would be impossible in Schmitt and Crocker's experimental format. But it might be more effective for less able or more anxious students under conventional testing conditions because it maintains attention on the concrete features of the task and avoids the intrusion of self-conscious or irrelevant thoughts.

Just as with Gavurin's experiment, the Schmitt–Crocker design could be converted into a faceted, within-person experiment and administered as a test with two, perhaps counterbalanced, parts. Also, just as with Gavurin's test, other facets could be crossed with the constructive response versus conventional format contrast to tease out further distinctions. Some older research on test anxiety has suggested what one such additional facet might be. In a study by Smith and Rockett (1958), students taking a multiple-choice test were allowed to write their notes and comments on the test booklet as they went along. The notes were not scored for correctness or incorrectness; only the multiple-choice responses were scored. It was found that highly test-anxious students did better when given an opportunity to write on the examination than when not given such an opportunity. This finding is particularly interesting in view of the fact that in most standardized testing situations students are not allowed to write on the test booklets, and presumably did not do so in the conventional format used by Schmitt and Crocker. Crossing this note-taking versus no-note-taking facet with the constructive versus conventional format facet might drive the regression slopes pictured in Fig. 1(b) still further apart and obtain a testing condition — conventional format with note taking allowed — that would show no performance decrement and perhaps even a facilitative effect for highly test-anxious examinees.

RECENT ADVANCES

Much modern research in cognitive psychology seeks improved descriptions of the content and process structures involved in complex cognitive performance. There are now CIP theories of intelligence, of learning, of reading, and of various kinds of complex problem solving. Many of these bear directly also on the analysis of formal instruction, of achievement following such instruction, and of ATI among alternative instructional conditions.

Much of this research is based on within-person laboratory experiments designed to isolate measures of component processes in a CIP model of the task at hand. Potentially, each such experiment could become a multifaceted test administrable in the context of field research as well as in the laboratory. It is in this sense that tests can become vehicles of communication between laboratory and field. Possible cognitive mechanisms can be isolated in laboratory experiments that, when converted into transportable tests, can be evaluated as to their relevance in the analysis of real-world cognitive behavior in the context of instructional ATI studies. In turn, assessments obtained with these measures can show important complications that must be built into subsequent laboratory research. We now look at some of the current categories and issues in CIP and ATI research to see how this sort of test design might work.

Sternberg (1982) has provided a concise survey of current cognitive psychology as it relates to ability test development. He identified four categories of research that bear on an information-processing analysis of individual differences, calling these the cognitive correlates, cognitive components, cognitive contents, and cognitive-training approaches. We have elaborated to produce Fig. 2 as a schematic summary of Sternberg's and our own ideas. The figure depicts several important implications for the purposes of this discussion.

A CONTINUUM OF TEST COMPLEXITY

First, there appears to be a continuum of increasing cognitive complexity, shown as a horizontal arrow at the top of the figure, along which most mental tests can be arrayed. Correlational evidence exists to support the hypothesis

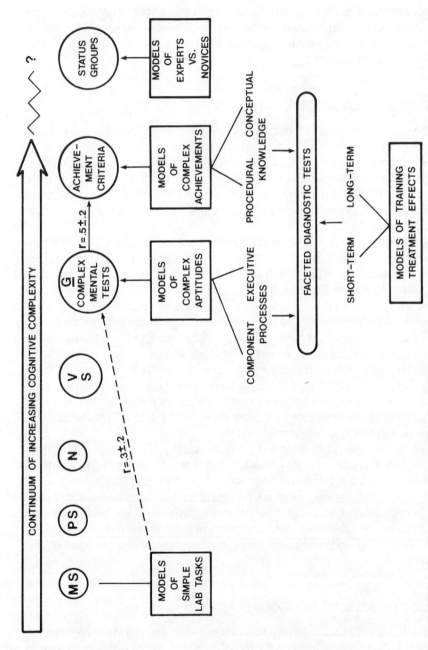

FIGURE 2. A schematization of cognitive psychological models and distinctions in relation to present and future cognitive tests.

that this continuum corresponds to increasing correlation with a general intelligence or general ability factor (G), to the vertical dimension in hierarchical factor models, and to the simplex dimension in Guttman's radex model of cognitive tests (see Marshalek, Lohman, & Snow, 1983; Snow, Kyllonen, & Marshalek, 1984.) In other words, relatively simple tests that appear to involve few component processing steps show low correlations with G; as mental tests appear to require more component-processing steps, or more complex organization and adaptation of such steps, correlation of the tests with G is found to be higher. In Fig. 2, some conventional ability factors are identified in circles placed along the continuum to suggest this. Relatively simple memory span (MS), perceptual speed (PS), and numerical ability (N) measures on the left show low correlation with G; more complex verbal (V) and spatial (S) comprehension and reasoning measures show somewhat higher correlation with G and appear more to the right along the continuum; and still more complex measures of reasoning and problem solving are indicated at G in the large centered circle.

THE COGNITIVE CORRELATES APPROACH

What Sternberg (1982) called the cognitive correlates approach obtains parameter measures from CIP models of simple laboratory tasks (usually paradigmatic tasks from earlier cognitive psychology; in the box below the MS and PS circles in Fig. 2) and then correlates these with complex ability test scores. The paradigmatic laboratory tasks often appear to be measures of fairly simple memory and perceptual speed processes. As shown, their correlations with G usually are modest ($r = .3 \pm .2$). Thus, even though many of these paradigmatic tasks can be and have been converted into faceted tests for group administration (see Rose, 1980), work with these tasks in applied settings is of interest only in some special cases; it is, after all, the complex tests that predict most of the real-world performance criteria of interest, as suggested by the higher correlation ($r = .5 \pm .2$) connecting the complex measures of G and the achievement criteria in the figure.

THE COGNITIVE COMPONENTS APPROACH

The so-called cognitive components approach, in contrast, pursues CIP models of the complex ability tests directly (in the box beneath the G circle in Fig. 2). Sternberg's research (1977, 1979, 1981) led the way in developing this approach, but many others such as Pellegrino and Glaser (1980), Whitely (1976), and Snow (1980b, 1981) have been pursuing it. So, for example, a model for a multiple-choice geometric analogies test might contain independent parameters representing component processes such as *en-*

coding each term in the analogy, *inferring* the relationship between the A and B terms, *applying* this relationship to the C term, *testing* the idealized answer against the presented alternatives, and so on. The experiments used to provide measures of these component parameters all could be rendered as multifaceted tests, though because precise reaction-time measures are usually crucial in these models such tests would need to be computerized.

In new research on spatial ability following this approach (Kyllonen, 1983; Kyllonen *et al.*, 1984; Lohman, 1979a, 1979b) it has become clear that many spatial items can be solved by logical reasoning and do not require spatial strategies. Thus, spatial items can be made more or less difficult for high-spatial persons compared to high-logical–analytical persons by varying the degree to which spatial strategies are needed to solve the items. Also, spatial strategies can sometimes be used to solve items on logical–analytic reasoning tests. Building on this work as well as on experiments such as Gavurin's (1967), it now seems possible to construct a faceted test that will distinguish fluid–analytic and spatial visualization abilities at a component process level. Although much focused research and development is still needed for success here, this has been a nearly impossible problem for research using conventional tests.

There is another problem for further research on such test designs, however, because more recent findings have suggested that there are also executive processes involved in strategy shifting within complex mental tests, in addition to individual differences in the component parameters (see Bethell-Fox *et al.*, in press; Kyllonen, Woltz, & Lohman, 1981). Nonetheless, as the experimental conditions that display these executive process differences are better understood, test facets can be designed to capture them. In one study, for example (Swiney, 1983), a contrast between blocks of items chosen to be similar in various aspects of item difficulty and blocks of mixed items in which item difficulty varied widely suggested that mixed items yield higher correlations with G. Perhaps, then, executive flexibility and adaptiveness to processing demands can be distinguished in such contrast scores. These preliminary results are quite promising, though there are various complications still to be studied. The familiarity versus novelty distinction in test content (see Snow, 1981) also appears to be a promising avenue for isolating some kinds of executive processes. The aim of all this work, in short, is to build models of complex test performance that distinguish various component and executive processes in faceted diagnostic tests, as suggested by the flow of Fig. 2.

It is important to note that the evaluation of component and executive process measures in such research involves within-person ATI analyses. Hypotheses that suggest that selected component process parameters should relate to external measures involving the same process, while other parameters should not, are in effect predicting that certain experimental treatment contrasts will manipulate the relations between performance measures in one or more cells within the experiment to one or more performance measures external to it. Such analyses within faceted test designs may also permit the extension of generalizability theory (see Cronbach, Gleser, Nanda, & Rajaratnam, 1972) beyond the analysis of error variation to the analysis of several kinds of covariations in such designs, including ATI effects. A unified theory of test reliability and validity might thus be envisioned.

THE COGNITIVE CONTENTS APPROACH

Further to the right beyond G on the complexity continuum in Fig. 2 are the real-world cognitive performances—the criteria that complex cognitive tests are designed to predict: the achievement criteria. Models of these achievements are the goals of the cognitive contents approach. Research by Greeno (1978, 1980), Pellegrino and Glaser (1980), Resnick (1981), and many others is leading to models of achievement that will help to explain the differences between more and less able learners. This work should lead in turn to faceted tests of differences in knowledge organization and to distinctions between procedural and conceptual knowledge acquisition. Such achievement tests would be parallel in form to the faceted process diagnostic tests emanating from the cognitive components approach.

Good examples of faceted achievement tests used to assess some of the qualitative structural differences resulting from different kinds of instruction may be found in the work of Egan and Greeno (1973), Greeno and Mayer (1975), Mayer, Stiehl, and Greeno (1975), and Yalow (1980). For example, Egan and Greeno (1973) used a faceted posttest with a 2×3 design. The first facet was problem context. The problems were either word problems or problems with symbols. The second facet was problem type and involved the extent of transformation necessary before a formula could be applied. Problems were either familiar, transformed, or constructed to be unsolvable by direct application of a rule learned. Egan and Greeno found significant ATI between aptitude and type of problem, and they were able to draw conclusions about qualitative cognitive structural effects of instruction well beyond the typical amount-learned interpretations. We note here again that the analysis of such tests as measures of outcome from instruction must also be conducted within an ATI framework. In effect, these studies posit aptitude $\times$ instructional treatment $\times$ achievement test facet interactions. When both aptitude and achievement outcome measures are rendered as multifaceted experimental designs, however, the generalized regression analyses advocated by Cronbach and Snow (1977) for ATI work may become overburdened; the number of terms to be estimated in such complex equations quickly exceeds conventional statistical limits. As more multi-faceted tests are built, there will be increasing need for careful study of alternative or supplementary methods of analysis.

EXPERT – NOVICE COMPARISONS

Still further out to the right on the complexity continuum, presumably, is the research contrasting experts and novices and other such status groups in such problem-solving areas as chess, physics, mathematics, and radiology. Sternberg (1982) included this work in the cognitive contents category, but we distinguish it in Fig. 2. Although this work should lead to CIP models of expert performance and thus to faceted diagnostic tests also, the models and their test design implications remain rather much of a question mark at present. For the purposes of educational research, especially, the expert – novice comparisons may not be centrally important. The cognitive knowledge and process characteristics that correlate with a status group difference of this sort may provide little explanation of how learners get into those status groups. The most important status comparison for the purposes of diagnostic testing in education seems to be that between more and less able learners, all of whom are novices.

DIRECT TRAINING

Sternberg's (1982) fourth category, and our fifth, is the new research on direct training of information-processing skills and strategies. The training approach may produce important advances in our understanding of individual differences in ability and achievement, especially as it concentrates on cognitive components, executive processes, procedural knowledge, and conceptual knowledge (and probably not as it concerns parameters of simple tasks or expert – novice differences). There have already been some successes with cognitive training, for example in the work of Belmont, Butterfield, and Ferretti (1982) and of Campione, Brown, and Ferrara (1982). And training research can help theory building and test design whether or not a particular process or knowledge component turns out to be trainable. Although it would be extremely important to learn how to train particular component or executive processes, even components shown to be nontrainable provide implications for testing.

One old idea in this regard that could open a whole new realm for test development and validation research comes from Vygotsky (1978). He proposed that tests should be readministered, with coaching, as many times as it took to reach maximum performance. Using the final trials as the test score would increase predictive validity, he thought. To our knowledge, this hypothesis has never been investigated. Conventional tests have almost never been constructed or analyzed in parts or blocks designed to detect learning or practice effects within the test. It is the case, however, that short tests are often found to be highly valid, and some ATI studies have even found Part 1 of an ability test interacting with instructional treatment contrasts when Part 2 of the same test did not (e.g., Koran, McDonald, & Snow, 1971). One hypothesis suggests that early trials or blocks of items may be the most valid in some situations, if executive processes (adaptive flexibility or strategy assembly and transfer processes) are the aspects of test performance that are crucial in predicting achievement criteria under some instructional treatments. On the other hand, there are conditions where it is reasonable to hypothesize that performance must be stabilized or tuned over practice *before* valid measures can be derived. Some ATI research has suggested that, for instructional work, "superficial individual differences that result from inadequate understanding of the task or from failure to hit upon an effective strategy should be systematically eliminated" by tuning the student (Cronbach & Snow, 1977, p. 131). Such tuning may greatly alter aptitude – treatment – outcome relationships.

The implication for this discussion is that mental tests, including new faceted tests based on cognitive component analyses or cognitive content analyses, should be designed also to produce learning curves over blocks of items. Inserted in this sequence might be training treatments designed to alter component skills or executive strategies. It is possible that these learning sample tests, by offering measures reflecting different points along a learning curve or adaptation continuum, might turn out to provide both the best diagnoses and the best predictions, especially in analyses of instruction.

There is a further point to the training approach. A training study by Kyllonen *et al.* (1984) combined faceted test construction with alternative strategy training treatments in an analysis of performance on a spatial ability test (Paper Folding). The results clearly showed that strategy training influenced performance differentially as a function of examinee aptitude profile, an ATI effect that also appeared on a transfer test (Surface Development). It was also clear that aptitude × strategy training × item characteristics interactions existed. What made an item difficult, then, depended significantly on both the aptitude profile of examinees and their strategy training experience. It appeared again that strategy shifting and related executivelike adaptations often occurred across items within the task, with the apparent aim of adapting to varying aspects of item difficulty. Mental test items thus cannot easily be categorized into homogeneous groups for the purpose of building CIP models. A combination of CIP and ATI analysis, however, can be expected to sharpen our understanding of what processing strategies might pair with what types of items for what kinds of persons to yield diagnostic distinctions. Again, the implication is that faceted tests can include specific training treatments to help diagnose process differences. Other strategy training research by Mathews, Hunt, and Mac-Leod (1980) and Sternberg and Weil (1980) also supports this possibility.

OTHER FEATURES OF TEST DESIGN
TO BE INVESTIGATED

A host of other features of test design, including administration, scoring, and interpretation conditions, can and should be investigated using ATI and CIP methods. As just one example, consider the design of test directions. These are in effect miniature instructional treatments. As such, they are subject to many of the same ATI effects that have been found in the study of larger instructional treatments. It can be expected that, as test directions place heavier information-processing demands on the examinee, use elaborate or unusual explanations, or encourage examinee initiative or self-direction, they will be likely to cause test performance to be more highly associated with G differences among examinees. As the test directions reduce the information-processing demands on the examinee, using simplified demonstrations and redundancy to substitute for complex verbiage, they will be likely to reduce the dependance of test performance on G (see Snow, 1977). Also, as test directions become ego involving, ATI effects related to examinee differences in test anxiety can be expected (Cronbach & Snow, 1977). In short, the conditions of testing can be designed to increase or reduce the involvement of such examinee characteristics in the performance of interest. Many existing tests pay no attention to these sources of confounding. Test redesigns should do so.

A final series of points relates much of the preceding to the problem of redesigning tests to avoid various kinds of bias associated with differences between genders or among major ethnic, cultural, or socioeconomic groups. We use gender differences as the example here, but it should be clear that the point applies as well to other group comparisons. Again, a combination of CIP and ATI approaches helps address this problem.

First, in the study of selection bias, ATI methodology is the approach of choice. The basic statistics of ATI research and of selection bias research are virtually identical, except that in the latter case the focus is on group-differentiated rather than treatment-differentiated regressions. Significant interaction implies that the test – criterion relationship functions differently in the two gender groups. Within a test gender × item interaction can be similarly examined. In the evaluation of CIP models, also, interactions with gender imply the existence of some kind of gender-linked process difference.

A prime suspect in the face of such findings is some kind of content or process bias. In some achievement tests, differences in frequency of male and female referents have been found and these have been associated with performance differences at least at some grade levels; females have shown better performance on items with female referents than on items with male referents (Donlon, Ekstrom, & Lockheed, 1979; Tittle, McCarthy, & Steckler, 1974). Donlon (1973, 1982) has made the same point in analyses of the geometry versus algebra emphasis in some mathematics tests, and Marshall (no date) has shown male – female differences in distractor choices even where total scores do not differ by gender. Redesigning tests to balance male – female referents or obvious school subject matter differentials is simple enough, but a more subtle issue will still remain and it requires CIP – ATI analysis.

If a particular strategic process is used in test performance by a higher (or lower) proportion of females than males, then to that extent the test may be measuring different cognitive functions in those proportions; this can be reflected as an average male – female difference in total or item scores or in the correlation of the test with other measures. If, as is suspected, for example, a higher proportion of females use verbal – analytic reasoning and a higher proportion of males use some kind of spatial process in reasoning when a test allows either strategy (as many figural or spatial ability tests do), then a complex pattern of interactions with gender may occur. Tests aimed at diagnosing strengths and weaknesses in these sorts of reasoning can be confounded as a result unless they are carefully redesigned with such gender-linked propensities in mind. The solution to such problems lies not in ignoring them and not in deleting test items that show gender differentials. It is rather, again, in faceted test design. The aim should be to build into the test design contrasts that clearly distinguish the two (or more) kinds of strategic processes that can be used. Then each individual person, male or female, can be diagnosed in terms of relative strength in each kind of cognitive processing. The average group differences arising from this source then become irrelevant.

CONCLUSION

Various cognitive ability and achievement constructs have been measured by cognitive tests, and there is a long tradition of psychometric theory and technological development on which such tests are based. There is also a great deal of correlational evidence about the interrelationships among cognitive tests and between them and various real-world performance criteria. But only with the advent of ATI research has it been recognized that experimental conditions can be manipulated to influence test–test or test–criterion relationships with the aim of understanding something of the nature of the constructs the tests are presumably measuring. And it has only been with the advent of CIP research that it has been possible to build and test detailed, substantive process and content models of these constructs. Although ATI and CIP approaches can be, and for the most part have been, used independently, they seem particularly suitable for use in combination; CIP analysis can be used to suggest the internal task manipulations that should isolate key process and content differences in cognitive constructs, and ATI analysis can be used to evaluate these task manipulations with respect to external measures of the constructs. Together they provide a powerful means of developing and testing causal, not just correlational, hypotheses about the constructs underlying cognitive tests. And together they suggest the redesign of conventional tests as multifaceted cognitive tasks that provide sharper diagnostic distinctions among the performance characteristics of interest while controlling out personal characteristics that confound such diagnoses.

REFERENCES

Belmont, J. M., Butterfield, E. C., & Ferretti, R. (1982). To secure transfer of training, instruct self-management skills. In D. K. Detterman and R. J. Sternberg (Eds.). *How and how much can intelligence be increased?* Norwood, NJ: Ablex.

Bethell-Fox, C. E., Lohman, D. F., & Snow, R. E. (1983). *Adaptive reasoning: Componential and eye movement analysis of geometric analogy performance. Intelligence*, in press.

Calfee, R. C. (1976). Sources of dependency on cognitive processes. In D. Klahr (Ed.), *Cognition and instruction.* Hillsdale, NJ: Erlbaum.

Calfee, R. C., & Hedges, L. V. (1980). Independent process analyses of aptitude-treatment interactions. In R. E. Snow, P. A. Federico, & W. E. Montague (Eds.), *Aptitude, learning, and instruction: Vol. 1. Cognitive process analyses of aptitude.* Hillsdale, NJ: Erlbaum.

Campione, J. C., Brown, A. L., & Ferrara, R. (1982). Mental retardation and intelligence. In R. J. Sternberg (Ed.). *Handbook of human intelligence.* New York: Cambridge University Press.

Cronbach, L. J., Gleser, G. C., Nanda, H., & Rajaratnam, N. (1972). *The dependability of behavioral measurements: Theory of generalizability for scores and profiles.* New York: Wiley.

Cronbach, L. J., & Snow, R. E. (1977). *Aptitudes and instructional methods: A handbook for research on interactions.* New York: Irvington.

Donlon, T. F., (1973). *Content factors in sex differences on test questions* (RN-73-28). Princeton, NJ: Educational Testing Service.

Donlon, T. F., (1982, January). *Issues in the construction and use of tests in studies of sex differences in mathematics.* Paper presented at the annual meeting of the American Association for the Advancement of Science, Washington, DC.

Donlon, T. F., Ekstrom, R. B., & Lockheed, M. E. (1979). The consequences of sex bias in the content of major achievement test batteries. *Measurement and Evaluation in Guidance, 11,* 202–216.

Egan, D. E., & Greeno, J. G. (1973). Acquiring cognitive structure by discovery and rule learning. *Journal of Educational Psychology, 64,* 85–97.

Gavurin, E. I. (1967). Anagram solving and spatial aptitude. *Journal of Psychology, 65,* 65–68.

Greeno, J. G. (1978). A study of problem solving. In R. Glaser (Ed.), *Advances in instructional psychology* (Vol. 1). Hillsdale, NJ: Erlbaum.

Greeno, J. G. (1980). Some examples of cognitive task analysis with instructional implications. In R. E. Snow, P. A. Federico, & W. E. Montague (Eds.), *Aptitude, learning, and instruction: Vol. 2. Cognitive process analyses of learning and problem solving.* Hillsdale, NJ: Erlbaum.

Greeno, J. G. & Mayer, R. E. (1975). *Structural and quantitative interaction among aptitudes and instructional treatments.* Unpublished paper, University of Michigan, Ann Arbor, MI.

Klahr, D. (Ed.). (1976). *Cognition and instruction.* Hillsdale, NJ: Erlbaum.

Koran, M. L., McDonald, F., & Snow, R. E. (1971). Teacher aptitude and observational learning of a teaching skill. *Journal of Educational Psychology, 62,* 219–228.

Kyllonen, P. C. (1983). *An information processing model of spatial ability.* Unpublished doctoral dissertation, Stanford University, Stanford, CA.

Kyllonen, P. C., Lohman, D. F., & Snow, R. E. (1984). Effects of task facets and strategy training on spatial task performance. *Journal of Educational Psychology, 76,* 130–145.

Kyllonen, P. C., Woltz D. J., & Lohman, D. F. (1981). *Models of strategy and strategy shifting in spatial visualization performance* (Tech. Rep. No. 17). Stanford, CA: Aptitude Research Project, School of Education, Stanford University.

Lohman, D. F. (1979a). *Spatial ability: A review and reanalysis of the correlational literature* (Tech. Rep. No. 8). Stanford, CA: Aptitude Research Project, School of Education, Stanford University.

Lohman, D. F. (1979b). *Spatial ability: Individual differences in speed and level* (Tech. Rep. No. 9). Stanford, CA: Stanford University, School of Education, Aptitude Research Project.

Marshalek, B., Lohman, D. F., & Snow, R. E. (1983). The complexity continuum in the radex and hierarchical models of intelligence. *Intelligence, 7,* 107–128.

Marshall, S. P. (no date). *Sex differences in mathematics errors: An analysis of distractor choices.* Unpublished manuscript, University of California, Santa Barbara.

Mathews, N. N., Hunt, E. B., & MacLeod, C. M. (1980). Strategy choice and strategy training in sentence-picture verification. *Journal of Verbal Learning and Verbal Behavior, 19,* 531–548.

Mayer, R. E., Stiehl, C. C., & Greeno, J. G. (1975). Acquisition of understanding and skill in relation to subjects' preparation and meaningfulness of instruction. *Journal of Educational Psychology, 67,* 331–350.

Pellegrino, J. W., & Glaser, R. (1980). Components of inductive reasoning. In R. E. Snow, P. A. Federico, & W. Montague (Eds.), *Aptitude, learning, and instruction: Vol. 1. Cognitive process analyses of aptitude.* Hillsdale, NJ: Erlbaum.

Poulton, E. C. (1979). Models for bias in judging sensory magnitude. *Psychological Bulletin, 86,* 777–803.

Resnick, L. B. (Ed.) (1976). *The nature of intelligence.* Hillsdale, NJ: Erlbaum.

Resnick, L. B. (1981). Instructional psychology. *Annual Review of Psychology, 32,* 659–704.

Rose, A. M. (1980). Information-processing abilities. In R. E. Snow, P. A. Federico, & W. E. Montague (Eds.), *Aptitude, learning, and instruction: Vol. 1. Cognitive process analyses of aptitude.* Hillsdale, NJ: Erlbaum.

Schmitt, A. P., & Crocker, L. (1981, April). *Improving examinee performance on multiple-*

choice tests. Paper presented at the annual meeting of the American Educational Research Association, Los Angeles.

Smith, W. F., & Rockett, F. C. (1958). Test performance as a function of anxiety, instructor, and instructions. *Journal of Educational Research, 52,* 138–141.

Snow, R. E. (1977). Learning and individual differences. In L. S. Shulman (Ed.), *Review of Research in Education 4.* Itasca, IL: Peacock.

Snow, R. E. (1978a). Eye fixation and strategy analyses of individual differences in cognitive aptitudes. In A. M. Lesgold, J. W. Pellegrino, S. D. Fokkema, & R. Glaser (Eds.), *Cognitive psychology and instruction.* New York: Plenum Press.

Snow, R. E. (1978b). Theory and method for research on aptitude processes. *Intelligence, 2,* 225–278.

Snow, R. E. (1980a). Aptitude and achievement. In W. B. Schrader (Ed.), *New directions for testing and measurement No. 5.* San Francisco: Jossey-Bass.

Snow, R. E. (1980b). Aptitude processes. In R. E. Snow, P. A. Federico, & W. E. Montague (Eds.), *Aptitude, learning, and instruction: Vol. 1. Cognitive process analyses of aptitude.* Hillsdale, NJ: Erlbaum.

Snow, R. E. (1981). Toward a theory of aptitude for learning I. Fluid and crystallized abilities and their correlates. In M. Friedman, J. P. Das, & N. O'Connor (Eds.), *Intelligence and learning.* New York: Plenum Press.

Snow, R. E., Federico, P. A., & Montague, W. E. (Eds.) (1980a). *Aptitude, learning, and instruction: Vol. 1. Cognitive process analyses of aptitude.* Hillsdale, NJ: Erlbaum.

Snow, R. E., Federico, P. A., & Montague, W. E. (Eds.) (1980b). *Aptitude, learning, and instruction: Vol. 2. Cognitive process analyses of learning and problem-solving.* Hillsdale, NJ: Erlbaum.

Snow, R. E., Kyllonen, P. C., & Marshalek, B. (1984). The topography of ability and learning correlations. In R. J. Sternberg (Ed.), *Advances in the psychology of human intelligence* (Vol. 2). Hillsdale, NJ: Erlbaum.

Snow, R. E., & Peterson, P. L. (1980). Recognizing differences in student aptitudes. *New Directions for Teaching and Learning: Learning, Cognition and College Teaching, 2,* 1–24.

Sternberg, R. J. (1977). *Intelligence, information processing and analogical reasoning: The componential analysis of human abilities.* Hillsdale, NJ: Erlbaum.

Sternberg, R. J. (1979). The nature of mental abilities. *American Psychologist, 34,* 214–230.

Sternberg, R. J. (1981). Toward a unified componential theory of human intelligence: I, fluid abilities. In M. Friedman, J. P. Das, & N. O'Connor (Eds.), *Intelligence and learning.* New York: Plenum Press.

Sternberg, R. J. (1982, April). *What cognitive psychology can (and cannot) do for test development.* Paper presented at the First Buros-Nebraska Symposium on Measurement and Testing, Lincoln, NE.

Sternberg, R. J., & Weil, E. M. (1980). An aptitude × strategy interaction in linear syllogistic reasoning. *Journal of Educational Psychology, 72,* 226–239.

Swiney, J. F., Jr. (1983). *A study of executive processes in intelligence.* Unpublished doctoral dissertation, Stanford University, Stanford, CA.

Tittle, C. K., McCarthy, K., & Steckler, J. F. (1974). *Women and educational testing: A selected review of the research literature and testing practices.* Princeton, NJ: Educational Testing Service.

Vygotsky, L. (1978). *Mind in society.* Cambridge, MA: Harvard University Press.

Whitely, S. E. (1976). Solving verbal analogies: Some cognitive components of intelligence test items. *Journal of Educational Psychology, 68,* 234–242.

Yalow, E. (1980). *Individual differences in learning from verbal and figural materials* (Tech. Rep. No. 12). Stanford, CA: Aptitude Research Project, School of Education, Stanford University.

III

Latent Trait Models for Test Design

6

The Assessment of Learning
Effects with Linear Logistic Test
Models

Hans Spada
Barry McGaw

INTRODUCTION

After many years of development and application, the logistic models originating in the basic models of Rasch (1960) have become widely accepted as valuable tools in test construction and test analysis (Andersen, 1980; Wright & Stone, 1979). Estimation procedures have been improved (Gustafsson, 1980); old test statistics have been criticized (Stelzl, 1979) and alternatives developed (Rost, 1982; Wollenberg, 1982); technical questions have been successfully answered (Fischer, 1981); and members of the growing family of logistic models have been recommended for a variety of purposes (Andrich, 1982; Kubinger, 1979; Nährer, 1980a; Whitely, 1980; Whitely & Schneider, 1981).[1]

In the early 1970s in Vienna, considerable progress was made in the use of the simple dichotomous and the polychotomous Rasch models, and with extensions such as the linear logistic test model and linear logistic models with relaxed assumptions. This work, however, was largely ignored in English-speaking countries. Fischer (1978), the leader of the Viennese group, provided a review in English of this earlier work done in German. Since the middle of the 1970s, research elsewhere increasingly has also sought generalizations of the Rasch models.

---

[1] S. E. Whitely is now S. Embretson.

Copyright © 1985 by Academic Press, Inc.
All rights of reproduction in any form reserved.
ISBN 0-12-238180-7

A major current concern in educational and psychological measurement is the cognitive processes involved in answering test items (see Spada & Reimann, 1982). This is reflected in diagnostic analyses of such processes from the perspectives of particular psychological theories of cognition and in attempts to measure changes in individual cognitive structures over time.

In this chapter we attempt to consider issues of test construction and psychological theorizing simultaneously. The linear logistic test model is discussed in some detail to show how one might go beyond the estimation of person abilities and item difficulties and changes in them over time. Other logistic latent trait models for measuring learning gains are also discussed. These use different assumptions about interactions among persons, items, and time to account for different learning effects. Applications of the psychometric models are illustrated with empirical studies, which, though already published, are not all readily accessible to English-speaking readers. Finally, discrepancies between the assumptions of the psychometric models and aspects of psychological theories of learning, thinking, and development are examined.

THE LINEAR LOGISTIC TEST MODEL

THE FORM OF THE MODEL

The linear logistic test model (LLTM) is an extension of Rasch's (1960) simple test model in which the performance of an individual v on a test item i is accounted for solely in terms of the individual's ability θ_v and the item's difficulty σ_i. The probability of the person responding correctly to the item is given by

$$p(+|v, i) = \frac{\exp(\theta_v - \sigma_i)}{1 + \exp(\theta_v - \sigma_i)}. \tag{1}$$

The LLTM provides for a decomposition of the item difficulties of the simple Rasch model into linear combinations of more elementary components as

$$\sigma_i = \sum_{j=1}^{m} q_{ij}\eta_j + c, \tag{2}$$

where the η_j $(j = 1, 2, \ldots, m)$ are parameters for the elementary components, q_{ij} the hypothetical frequencies with which each component j influences the solution of each item i, and c is a scaling constant arbitrarily fixing the origin of the scale. The elementary components can be, for example, cognitive operations (characterized by their difficulties) required for solution of an item or instructional conditions (characterized by their efficacy) experienced by the individual before attempting solution of the item.

Estimates of the elementary parameters η_j can be derived if the frequency matrix $Q = \| q_{ij} \|$ is specified in advance by hypothesis, if this matrix has rank m, and if some other more technical conditions are met (Fischer, 1982). In the first use of the LLTM, Scheiblechner (1972) estimated item difficulties σ_i from the simple Rasch model and obtained multiple regression estimates of the elementary parameters from these item parameter estimates and the matrix of hypothetical frequencies Q. Fischer (1973, 1974) and Fischer and Formann (1972) developed a conditional maximum likelihood (CML) procedure for the direct estimation of the elementary parameters. (See Thissen, 1982, for a marginal maximum likelihood [MML] method.) The estimation of the parameters η_j is therefore, sample free in the same sense as the item parameter estimation of the Rasch model.

Goodness of fit of the LLTM to experimental data has been tested in a number of ways. Conditional likelihood ratio (CLR) tests (see Andersen, 1973) have been used to compare parameter estimates derived from different subsamples of persons taking the test and, in the case of the elementary parameters, also from different subsamples of test items. The marginal linear condition, defined by Equation 2, has been tested by graphic methods and CLR tests through comparison of estimates of the item parameters σ_i obtained directly from the simple Rasch model with others obtained indirectly by calculation from estimates of the elementary parameters η_j obtained from the LLTM with the hypothetical frequencies q_{ij}. The most stringent testing of the marginal constraint has involved a demanding validation. Nährer (1977, 1980b) used estimates of the η_j and a hypothesized Q matrix to calculate item difficulties for newly devised items and then compared these results with estimates obtained from the performances of a fresh sample of individuals on the new items.

ACCOUNTING FOR TASK PERFORMANCE

In a study of the development of the concept of proportion (Spada, 1976b; Spada & Kluwe, 1980), with balance scale problems of the type employed by Inhelder and Piaget (1958), the LLTM was used to relate test performance to ability to perform particular cognitive operations. From the Piagetian literature and from observations of children solving balance scale problems, the eight separate cognitive operations shown in Table 1 were defined.

Twenty-four tasks requiring the use of various combinations of the cognitive operations in Table 1 were developed. Two of these tasks are shown in Figure 1. Task 1 is hypothesised to require for solution use of Operations 1 and 3 once each. This psychological structure of the task is represented in

TABLE 1

COGNITIVE OPERATIONS HYPOTHESIZED AS RELEVANT FOR THE
SOLUTION OF BALANCE SCALE PROBLEMS

Number	Cognitive operation
1.	Attention to and deductions from differences in weights.
2.	Attention to and deductions from differences in lengths of lever arms.
3.	Compensation for a change in a weight or the length of a lever arm by a change in the same modality on the other side.
4.	Compensation for a change by a change in the other modality on the other side.
5.	Compensation for a change by a change in the other modality on the same side.
6.	Additional consideration of the factor of change required to produce equilibrium.
7.	Additional deduction from the law of levers declaring that, for equilibrium, the product of weight and length of lever arm must be the same on both sides.
8.	Compensation for an inequality in one modality by a reciprocal inequality in the other modality on the same side.

the task structure matrix Q by the row vector $\mathbf{q}_1 = (10100000)$. For Task 2, the psychological structure is represented by the vector $\mathbf{q}_2 = (10010000)$.

In this use of the LLTM, development in the ability to solve proportional tasks is assumed to be purely quantitative. Qualitative changes are not modeled. For all individuals (at least in the 11–16-year age range studied) it is assumed that the task structure, represented by Q, remains constant and that the difficulties η_j of the cognitive operations are invariant. Individual development, producing an increased capacity to perform the cognitive operations and seen in improved solution of the tasks, is reflected in higher estimates of ability θ_v.

With data from 949 German secondary school students on the 24 paper and pencil tasks, Spada (1976b) was able to test the adequacy of this model. The goodness of fit of the simple Rasch model, without the additional constraint of the LLTM given in Equation 2, was tested with the usual conditional likelihood ratio tests (Andersen, 1973). Estimates of the task difficulties from different subsamples of the students were similar, although in some cases, because of the large sample size, the differences among them were found to be statistically significant. The goodness of fit of the linear marginal condition, expressed in the task structure matrix Q, was tested by comparing direct estimates of the task difficulties σ_i obtained using the simple Rasch model with indirect estimates of them computed from LLTM estimates of the difficulties η_j of the cognitive operations. Although a graphic comparison revealed these two sets of estimates of the task difficulties to be similar, a conditional likelihood ratio test of the linear marginal condition of the LLTM showed the differences to be statistically significant.

Task 1: Combination of Operations 1,3

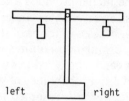   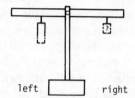

The drawing shows a balance
scale with weights hung in a
way that produces equilibrium

Now the weight on the left hand side
of the bar is increased. In order to
keep the bar in equilibrium, the weight
on the right side of the bar must
                     stay the same ☐
                     be decreased ☐
                     be increased ☐
                     I do not know ☐

Task 2: Combination of Operations 1,4

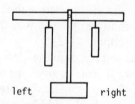   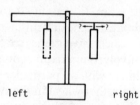

The drawing shows a balance
scale with weights hung in
a way that produces equilibrium

Now the weight on the left hand side
of the bar is decreased. In order to
keep the bar in equilibrium the weight
on the right hand side of the bar must

                     stay in the same
                     position   ☐
                     be hung further inwards ☐
                     be hung further outwards ☐
                     I do not know   ☐

FIGURE 1.   Examples of balance scale problems.   (Adapted from Spada, 1976b.)

The estimates of the difficulties of the cognitive operations were $\eta_2 - \eta_1 =$ 0.4, $\eta_3 = 0.6$, $\eta_8 = 0.6$, $\eta_5 = 1.2$, $\eta_4 = 1.4$, $\eta_7 = 1.4$, and $\eta_6 = 1.6$. (The structures of the tasks used did not allow the separate estimation of Parameters 1 and 2, only an estimate of their difference.)

These analyses showed that, although the model provided a fairly good account of the data, at least some of the task structure hypotheses were not valid and/or that the formulation of the hypotheses in terms of the LLTM was, to some extent, inappropriate. This formulation requires the strong assumption that developmental differences can be modeled in quantitative terms and reflected in different estimates of θ_v. Probabilities of success on tasks are allowed to vary but the task structures are presumed to be constant. Specific hypotheses about developmental changes in solution strategies could be incorporated in the model as alterations in the task structure matrix for subsamples of the subjects. If such changes in the operations used to solve tasks do occur, but are unrecognized, they serve only to invalidate the application of the LLTM (see Spada & May, 1982).

ACCOUNTING FOR LEARNING DURING TESTING

In the study of balance scale problems, no allowance is made in the model for learning while working through the tasks. In another study (Spada, 1977), task responses on a single testing were analyzed in a way that produced a single estimate of ability θ_v for each person completing the tasks but changing estimates of the difficulties of the cognitive operations as they were practiced over successive items (see Scheiblechner, 1972).

The tasks involved interconnecting wheels and required the identification of the direction in which a particular wheel would rotate, given the direction of rotation of another wheel in the system. Some problems involved open rotation mechanisms in which rotation of one wheel could be transmitted through the system to produce rotation in the designated wheel. Other problems involved closed rotation systems, in some of which movement was impossible. Two such systems are illustrated in Figure 2. The hypotheses about the psychological structure of tasks of this type were expressed in a solution algorithm and in the corresponding set of six operations shown in Table 2. The structure of Task 1 in Figure 2 is represented in the task structure matrix Q by the row vector $\mathbf{q}_1 = (111100)$ and that of Task 2 by $\mathbf{q}_2 = (021111)$.

Task difficulty is thus related, as before, by the linear marginal condition in Equation 2 to the difficulty of more elementary operations. In this case, however, the model was elaborated to accommodate improvement in performance with practice on successive tasks. The frequency of practice is

Task 1: An Open Rotation Mechanism
    Requiring Operations 1, 2, 3, 4.

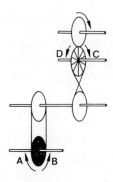

In which direction does the
wheel with spokes rotate?

in direction C □
in direction D □
I don't know □

In which direction does the
black wheel rotate?

in direction A □
in direction B □
I don't know □

Task 2: A Closed Rotation Mechanism
    Requiring Operations 2 (twice), 3, 4, 5, 6.

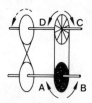

If you try to rotate the white
wheel in the given direction,
the wheel with spokes

rotates in direction C □
rotates in direction D □
doesn't rotate at all,
because a movement is
impossible with this
form of transmission. □
I don't know □

If you try to rotate the white
wheel in the given direction,
the black wheel

rotates in direction A □
rotates in direction B □
doesn't rotate at all,
because a movement is
impossible with this
form of transmission □
I don't know □

FIGURE 2. Examples of wheel rotation problems. (Adapted from Spada, 1977.)

TABLE 2
COGNITIVE OPERATIONS HYPOTHESIZED AS RELEVANT FOR THE
SOLUTION OF PROBLEMS CONCERNED WITH THE ROTATION OF
INTERCONNECTED WHEELS

Number	Operation
1.	Two wheels touching at their peripheries rotate in opposite directions.
2.	Two wheels fixed on a common axle rotate in the same direction.
3.	Two wheels linked by a simple transmission belt rotate in the same direction.
4.	Two wheels linked by a crossed transmission belt rotate in opposite direction.
5.	To examine whether movement is possible, each specific part of the transmission has to be analyzed.
6.	If different parts of the system would produce competing rotations in the same wheel, no movement is possible.

determined from the hypothetical task structure. The number of times operation j is practiced prior to its recurrence in task i is

$$h_{ij} = \sum_{u=1}^{i-1} q_{uj}, \tag{3}$$

where q_{uj} is the frequency with which operation j is needed to solve task u. The difficulty of operation j without practice is defined as η_j and the maximum reduction in difficulty through practice as β_j $(0 < \beta_j < \eta_j)$. The difficulty of operation j, when encountered in task i, is then defined as

$$\eta_{ij} = \eta_j - h_{ij}^* \beta_j, \tag{4}$$

where

$$h_{ij}^* = h_{ij} b / (1 + h_{ij} b)$$

with b a weighting factor $(b > 0)$ determining how fast h_{ij} approaches 1 and thus how fast $h_{ij}^* \beta_j$ approaches the upper limit of the practice effect. In defining the marginal condition Equation 5, the η_{ij} of Equation 4 is substituted for the η_j of Equation 2 to give

$$\sigma_i = \sum_{j=1}^{m} q_{ij} \eta_{ij} + c$$
$$= \sum_{j=1}^{m} (q_{ij} \eta_j - q_{ij} h_{ij}^* \beta_j) + c. \tag{5}$$

The frequencies h_{ij} are defined as indicated by Equation 3 and the weight b must similarly be fixed by hypothesis before application of the model for the η_j and β_j of Equation 4 to be estimable. A preliminary study showed $b = .2$

TABLE 3

TASK STRUCTURE MATRIX Q FOR THE ESTIMATION
OF OPERATION DIFFICULTIES (η_j) AND MAXIMUM
LEARNING EFFECTS (β_j) WHILE COMPLETING A TEST

Item number	Coefficients for η_j q_{ij}						Coefficients for β_j $q_{ij}h_{ij}^*$					
	1	2	3	4	5	6	1	2	3	4	5	6
1.	1	1	0	0	0	0	0	0	0	0	0	0
2.	1	0	1	1	0	0	.17	0	0	0	0	0
3.	1	1	1	1	0	0	.29	.17	.17	.17	0	0
4.	0	2	1	1	1	1	0	.58	.29	.29	0	0
5.	1	1	2	1	1	1	.38	.44	.76	.38	.17	.17
$\vdots$												

produced the best fit. When an operation has been practiced once before, $h_{ij}^* = .17$; when twice, $h_{ij}^* = .29$; when three times, $h_{ij}^* = .38$, and so on (see Table 3). The definition of h_{ij} implies that the learning increments are successively smaller. With the elaboration of the marginal linear condition introduced by Equation 4, the task structure matrix is extended to accommodate the β as well as the η.

With data from 1199 German secondary school students solving wheel rotation tasks like those in Figure 2, Spada (1977) was able to test the adequacy of this model. Initial tests of the simple Rasch model showed some significant variations in task difficulty estimates σ_i obtained from different subsamples of the students. These differences were not substantial, however, their statistical significance being due to the large sample size. Using the LLTM, the estimates of η_j and β_j shown in Table 4 were obtained. The actual pattern of tasks used did not allow separation of the parameters for Operations 5 and 6. Because the initial difficulties of Operations 2 and 3 were so low, maximum reductions in difficulty were not estimated.

The goodness of fit of the linear marginal condition, expressed in the task structure matrix Q and the modification introduced by Equation 4, was tested by comparing simple Rasch estimates of the σ_i with estimates computed from the LLTM estimates of the η_j and β_j. A graphical comparison revealed the estimates to be similar but a conditional likelihood ratio test showed the differences to be significant. Comparisons of estimates of the η_j and β_j obtained from different subsamples of students or from different subsets of items, however, showed consistency of estimates for all but Operation 4. Nährer (1977) used estimates of operation difficulties and the hypothesized Q matrix from an earlier study by Spada, Fischer, and Heyner

TABLE 4

ESTIMATES OF DIFFICULTIES OF
OPERATIONS REQUIRED FOR SOLUTION
OF WHEEL ROTATION PROBLEMS
AND ESTIMATES OF MAXIMUM
LEARNING EFFECTS

Operation	Difficulty without practice	Maximum gain with practice	Difficulty after practice
3	.2	—	.2
2	.2	—	.2
4	.6	.3	.3
1	2.3	2.1	.2
5, 6	2.8	1.9	.9

(1973) to predict the difficulties of newly constructed wheel rotation problems. These predictions closely paralleled empirical estimates obtained when the items were given to new samples of students.

In this application of the LLTM, learning within a test is modeled as a decrease in the difficulties of cognitive operations required to solve tasks (operation-specific learning). It could not be similarly modeled directly in terms of item difficulties because the items themselves cannot sensibly be repeated within a test. Each learning effect β_j is assumed to be constant for all individuals, due only to repeated opportunities to use the operation and uninfluenced by whether particular attempts to use it are successful or not. The model allows no possibility of response-contingent effects. Furthermore, this application of the model does not allow the possibility of the mode of solution altering as a consequence of learning. Such changes in the operations used for task solution (algorithmic learning) could be included if they were hypothetically formulated.

Although no individual differences in learning rates are provided for, individual differences in abilities to perform the tasks are, of course, reflected in different ability estimates θ_v.

CONTRIBUTION TO TEST DEVELOPMENT

Although the restrictiveness of the assumptions of the LLTM places limits on its capacity to model psychological explanations of test performance, it does have some important advantages in test development. The major one is that it obliges the test developer to have a clear view of the structure of the test.

The decomposition of tasks into component operations offers a systematic view of test items that can facilitate item development. It discourages the use of more or less arbitrary collections of trial items to be sieved through a classical or latent-trait net on the basis of the performance on them of a preliminary sample of individuals. Nährer's (1977) success in predicting the difficulty of new items is eloquent testimony to the usefulness of item development on the basis of a validated analysis of the component operations involved in item solution. Having in mind these possibilities of applying the LLTM, Hornke and Habon (1982) stated that the trend to combine results of cognitive psychology and the tools of probabilistic latent trait theory is a first step to "intentional item writing and thus constructing tests with desirable properties known in advance" (p. 2). Present strategies for item writing and analysis are criticized as offering only post hoc justification for the selection of the final test items. A good example of the alternative rational item construction is the development of a new reasoning test similar to Raven's Progressive Matrices by Formann and Pinswanger (1979). The items of the new test were developed by systematically combining a small number of elementary components and thus defining a universe of test items. An analysis of subsamples of these items showed them to be unidimensional in the sense of the Rasch model. In addition, the difficulties of the items were predicted fairly well from LLTM estimates of the difficulties of the elementary components (Hornke & Habon, 1982; Nährer, 1980a).

The application of the LLTM in constructing items with predictable complexity (row vectors q_1) and difficulty (parameters σ_i) offers a new and interesting way to define and guarantee construct validity of a test. If the test constructor is able to trace the difficulty of the items back to cognitive operations required for their solution, the question of what the test measures can be answered, at least in part, before the correlation with any criterion variable is computed.

Item construction according to theoretical principles is also of relevance for content validity. Content validity can be achieved if the test consists of a representative sample from a domain of items within which all the items can be constructed objectively by means of specified construction rules (Klauer, 1978). The LLTM can facilitate the derivation of such construction rules.

For tailored testing, Fischer and Pendl (1980) recommended use of the LLTM for systematic construction of items with predictable difficulty for use in the bank of items. Several applications of the LLTM have indicated, however, that learning of the components occurs as a result of practice while completing a test. The difficulty of an item thus is not fixed but depends on the item's position in the test. Use of such items in tailored testing is, therefore, at least questionable (see Fischer, 1982).

At least two further critical remarks seem necessary to avoid too optimistic a picture of the possibilities of using the LLTM to construct better tests. One is that use of the LLTM is restricted to tests for which elementary and stable components of items can be identified and then successfully combined in the construction of new items. The literature shows that this is more likely for reasoning tests than, for example, for personality tests and more likely for school tests in subject areas like mathematics and physics than for those in areas like history and sociology. The second critical remark is that the way in which item solution processes and effects of practice are modeled by the LLTM is at variance with several aspects of relevant contemporary psychological theories. More is said on this second point later.

AMBIGUITY OF PARAMETERS FOR ABILITY, TASKS, AND OPERATIONS

Despite the value of the LLTM's analysis of task performance in terms of performance on elementary operations, there are some difficulties in interpreting the parameters of the model. The decomposition of the item difficulties is, of course, quite precisely defined in Equation 2 but its psychological interpretation is not equally clear.

The probability of individual v completing operation j correctly is given by the simple Rasch model as

$$p(+|v, j) = \frac{\exp(\theta_v - \eta_j)}{1 + \exp(\theta_v - \eta_j)}. \tag{6}$$

If the probability of person v solving a task correctly depended on the probability of the correct use of all the component operations, the task probability would be simply the product of the operation probabilities, assuming independence of the operations. This, however, is not the task probability estimated by the LLTM since, in general,

$$p(+|v, i) = \frac{\exp\left\{\theta_v - \sum_{j=1}^{m} q_{ij}\eta_j + c\right\}}{1 + \exp\left\{\theta_v - \sum_{j=1}^{m} q_{ij}\eta_j + c\right\}}$$

$$\neq \prod_{j=1}^{m} \left\{\frac{\exp(\theta_v - \eta_j)}{1 + \exp(\theta_v - \eta_j)}\right\}^{q_{ij}}$$

$$= \prod_{j=1}^{m} \{p(+|v, j)\}^{q_{ij}}. \tag{7}$$

The representation of the item parameters σ_i as linear combinations of the number and difficulty of hypothesized component operations offers statistical advantages in estimation and significance testing but does not allow the relation between success probabilities for items and component operations that the formulation in Equations 1 and 6 seems to invite.

The inequality in Equation 7 also raises problems for the interpretation of the person parameters θ_v obtained from the simple Rasch model and the LLTM. The probability of success of persons on tasks may be estimated in the standard fashion of the simple Rasch model, Equation 1, but cannot be decomposed into similar probabilistic formulations of success in the use of operations. Nevertheless, task performance can be understood in terms of the ability to solve tasks in a domain defined by task construction principles based on the more elementary operations.

FOUR LOGISTIC MODELS OF LEARNING BETWEEN TESTS

THE FORM OF THE MODELS

The cases considered so far show how the persons-by-items data matrix obtained from a single testing can be used to estimate the person parameters θ_v and the item parameters σ_i of the simple Rasch model and the elementary component parameters η_j of the LLTM. No allowance is made for an interaction between persons and items that would produce different relative item difficulties for different persons. Such an interaction might be caused by different preexperimental learning histories of the persons or by differences in learning effects while completing the test. Test items are said to be homogeneous if this interaction can be ignored.

If data are gathered on more than one occasion, some of the restrictive assumptions required in applying the simple Rasch model and the LLTM to data from a single testing can be dropped. If a sample of n persons ($v = 1, \ldots, n$) is tested by means of k items ($i = 1, \ldots, k$) on s occasions ($t = 1, \ldots, s$), then the nks data points can be arranged in the form of a data cube. The assumption that the same items are given on the successive testing occasions makes the presentation easier but is not necessary for many of the following arguments.

Four logistic test models to assess learning effects between test applications are shown in Table 5. A general logistic test model, Equation 8 (given in Table 5), for the probability of person v responding correctly to item i given on occasion t provides a starting point for the derivation of these four models, which reflect different types of learning effects. The general model in Equation 8 is tautological because the number of parameters λ_{vit} equals the number of data points. This model, in principle, allows for a learning gain that is different for different persons on different items on different testing

TABLE 5
FOUR LOGISTIC TEST MODELS FOR ASSESSING LEARNING EFFECTS
BETWEEN TEST APPLICATIONS

General form:

$$p(+|v, i, t) = \frac{\exp(\lambda_{vit})}{1 + \exp(\lambda_{vit})},$$ (8)

where λ_{vit} is the parameter reflecting the ability of person v to solve item i in the test on occasion t.
Restrictions on parameters:
  Model I: Global learning effects

$$\lambda_{vit} = \theta_v - \sigma_i + \delta_t,$$ (9)

where θ_v is the person ability parameter, σ_i is the item difficulty parameter, and δ_t is the global learning effect parameter (with $\delta_1 = 0$).
  Model II: Person-specific learning effects

$$\lambda_{vit} = -\sigma_i + \delta_{vt},$$ (10)

where δ_{vt} is the person-specific learning effect parameter.
  Model III: Item-specific learning effects

$$\lambda_{vit} = \theta_v - \sigma_{it},$$ (11)

where σ_{it} is the item-specific learning effect parameter.
  Model IV: Global learning effects with heterogeneous item sample

$$\lambda_{vit} = \theta_{vi} + \delta_t,$$ (12)

where σ_{vi} is the person-by-item interaction parameter.

---

occasions. To obtain models that are practicable, restrictions on the λ_{vit} have to be imposed. Rost and Spada (1983) have given a detailed account of the eight resulting logistic test models, discussing parameter estimation and interpretation, tests of fit of the models, and the psychological plausibility of the assumptions. The presentation in this chapter is confined to those four models that are of most practical relevance.

The formal structure of these models is not new. Scheiblechner (1971) discussed models of this type in the context of sociometric analysis. His data cube consisted of the choices made by n persons among k choice alternatives, with each alternative chosen or not by each person with respect to each of s separate choice criteria. He proved the existence of conditional inference for models of this type, thus establishing that these logistic models allow for specific objective comparisons in the sense of the Rasch model. The models are, therefore, characterized by the same advantageous properties as the Rasch model, namely sample-free parameter estimation and CLR—in a few cases likelihood ratio (LR)—tests for evaluating the goodness of fit.

ACCOUNTING FOR DIFFERENT LEARNING EFFECTS

In Model I in Table 5, the restriction imposed on the λ_{vit} is given by Equation 9. Learning is assumed to be constant for all persons and all items, with the parameter δ_t characterizing a *global learning* effect between test occasions 1 and t. In this very restrictive model no allowance is made for any interaction between persons and items, between persons and time of testing, or between items and time. Any such interaction would invalidate the model. If the model does fit the data, global effects of treatments given between the tests can be estimated sample-free with regard to persons and items. Model I can be understood as an example of the so-called multifactorial model first discussed by Micko (1970).

In Model II, the restrictive assumption that learning gain is the same for all the persons and the items under study is discarded. The restriction in this model, given by Equation 10 in Table 5, introduces a parameter δ_{vt} for the person-by-time interaction. It provides for an assessment of *person-specific learning effects*. It assumes that all the learning effects can be reflected in these parameters characterizing individually different learning gains. The restrictive assumptions of the model are that there is no change from test to test in the relative item difficulties and that the usual homogeneity assumption of no person-by-item interactions is valid. This is the model to measure person-specific changes over time if they are not accompanied by a change in the item difficulty parameters.

Model III makes it possible to assess *item-specific learning*. An item-by-time interaction parameter σ_{it} is introduced in the restriction given by Equation 11 (in Table 5) to quantify a learning gain that is different from item to item. The model is valid if all learning effects can be traced back to changes in the relative difficulties of the items between test occasions under the side condition that these changes are constant for all persons. Changes in relative item difficulties from test to test that are different from person to person would introduce a second-order interaction and invalidate Model III, leading back to the tautological general model of Equation 8. Model III is useful if, between a pretest and a posttest, a treatment has different effects on different items but no person-specific learning effects.

Model IV accommodates cases in which items are not homogeneous with respect to persons by introducing a person-by-item interaction parameter θ_{vi} in Equation 12 (in Table 5). To provide for a *heterogeneous item sample,* however, Model IV adds the restrictive assumption of *global learning,* estimated as δ_t, which was required in Model I. Model IV is the basis of the linear logistic test model with relaxed assumptions (LLRA) developed by Fischer (1972, 1976, 1982). By dropping the usual assumption of unidimensionality, Model IV copes with situations in which learning effects are assessed by means of items measuring different abilities.

The additional four models which Rost and Spada (1983) have described provide even more flexibility for the assessment of learning effects. These models include two or all three of the interaction parameters θ_{vi}, σ_{it}, and δ_{vt} but the increased flexibility in modeling learning is paid for in problems in parameter estimation and interpretation and in problems in testing the fit of the models.

Parameter estimation is straightforward for Models I–IV. For the sake of simplicity, the procedures are described for the case of only two test occasions, t_1 = pretest and t_2 = posttest. The data cube is n (persons) by k (items) by 2 (test occasions). For Model II, the cube is rearranged into a matrix with $2n$ rows and k columns. With the simple Rasch model, $2n$ person parameters θ_{vt} and k item parameters σ_i can be estimated, treating the matrix as though two separate samples of n persons had taken the k item test rather the one sample taking it twice. For Model III, the cube is rearranged into a matrix with n rows and $2k$ columns. With the simple Rasch model, n person parameters θ_v and $2k$ item parameters σ_{it} can be estimated, treating the matrix as though a sample of n persons had taken two separate samples of k items.

The parameters in Model I can be estimated using the LLTM. Equation 11 of Model III is analogous to Equation 1 for the simple Rasch model. The analogue of Equation 2 for the linear decomposition of the item parameters is

$$-\sigma_{it} = -\sigma_i + \delta_t \tag{13}$$

given k item parameters and one time parameter (since $\delta_1 = 0$) instead of the $2k$ interaction parameters σ_{it}. The Q matrix giving the relationships defined by Equation 13 is given in Table 6.

Fischer (1972, 1976, 1982) discussed estimation procedures for the LLRA based on Model IV.

Because different interaction parameters are included in the different models, the number of parameters to be estimated varies substantially. For a case with 1000 persons measured on 20 items as both pretest and posttest there are 40,000 data points. There would be 1000 person parameters θ_v, 20 item parameters σ_i, 2 global learning effect parameters δ_t, 2000 person-specific learning parameters δ_{vt}, 20 item-specific learning parameters σ_{it}, and 20,000 person-by-item interaction parameters θ_{vi}. (In using the LLRA based on Model IV the main interest is in the learning parameters δ_t. Estimation of the person by item interaction parameters θ_{vi} is, in general, neither possible nor necessary.)

A general approach to testing the fit of any one of these models is to analyze the validity of the assumptions by which it differs from the other models. For example, Model I can be tested by analyzing whether the

TABLE 6

TASK STRUCTURE MATRIX Q FOR
ESTIMATION OF ITEM DIFFICULTIES (σ_i)
AND GLOBAL LEARNING EFFECT (δ_2)
FOR A PRETEST–POSTTEST DESIGN

Test	Item number	Coefficients for σ_i					Coefficient for Posttest (δ_2) Pretest: $\delta_1 = 0$
		1	2 $\cdots$	i	$\cdots$	k	
Pretest	1	1	0	0		0	0
	2	0	1	0		0	0
	$\vdots$						
	i	0	0	1		0	0
	$\vdots$						
	k	0	0	0		1	0
Posttest	1	1	0	0		0	1
	2	0	1	0		0	1
	$\vdots$						
	i	0	0	1		0	1
	$\vdots$						
	k	0	0	0		1	1

learning effects are global (Model I) and not person-specific (Model II) or item-specific (Model III). Both graphic and CLR tests can be used for comparisons of the σ_{it} estimated by direct use of the simple Rasch model with Model III to the σ_{it} obtained using Equation 13 and the estimates of σ_i and δ_t obtained by use of the LLTM with Model I. Similar testing of δ_{vt} estimates from Models I and II can be undertaken. The usual tests for the simple Rasch model — comparisons of the parameter estimates obtained from different subsamples of persons and items — are also applicable.

ASSESSING DIFFERENT TREATMENT EFFECTS

The LLTM can be used to decompose the item difficulty parameters, σ_i of Models I and II and σ_{it} of Model III, into linear combinations of parameters for elementary operations. It can also be used to decompose the global learning parameters δ_t of Model I into parameters for treatment conditions experienced by different subgroups of individuals before particular test occasions.

To illustrate, consider a simple experimental design in which two groups receive different types of instruction and a control group receives no relevant instruction. Of interest is the effect of each of the instructional methods on the improvement of some ability of the students. This ability is assessed with samples of items from a homogeneous item domain given before and after instruction. The learning effects are assumed to be global in the sense that the learning gain is constant for all items and all students receiving the same treatment.

To estimate the effects of the two experimental instructional methods, a linear marginal condition can be defined for the LLTM as

$$\delta_{t(v)} = \sum_{a=1}^{2} q_{t(v)a} \eta_a + \tau_t, \tag{14}$$

where $\delta_{t(v)}$ is the global learning effect for the instructional method given between pretest and posttest to the subsample of students containing student v, η_a is the global learning effect for the instructional method given between pretest and posttest, $q_{t(v)a}$ is 1 if the instructional method a is used with student v and 0 if not, and τ_t is a global trend parameter between pretest and posttest independent of treatment.

The manner in which the Q matrix of the LLTM is set up for this simple example is shown in Table 7. Application of this model provides estimates of treatment effects η_1 and η_2 for the two instructional methods and a trend effect τ common to treatment and control conditions, as well as estimates of person abilities θ_v and item difficulties σ_i.

Sample-free estimates of these treatment effect and trend parameters can be obtained even in the absence of random sampling, that is, without approximately equal ability distributions in the different samples of students. Using the LLTM, the significance of the effects and of the difference between them can be tested statistically by means of CLR tests. These tests do not rely upon the variance of the ability parameters; they are conditional tests, in which the ability parameters do not even enter. The use of the LLTM in this context has the additional advantage that it is not necessary to give the same test on the different occasions. Provided that some items are repeated, the other test items can be selected in such a way that their difficulty is adapted to the achievement level of the students at the time the test is given. If the item difficulties can be traced back to operation difficulties, completely different item samples can be used. In more sophisticated applications of the LLTM, by redefining $q_{t(v)a}$, not only the type of treatment but also the dose of treatment can be taken into account.

Application of the LLRA on the basis of Model IV is similar to that of the LLTM with Model I. The main difference is in the assumption of homogeneity. Model I requires it; Model IV does not (Fischer, 1976).

TABLE 7

MATRIX Q FOR ESTIMATION OF ITEM
DIFFICULTIES (σ_i), GLOBAL TREATMENT EFFECTS
(η_a), AND TREND (τ_2) FOR A
PRETEST–POSTTEST DESIGN

Samples of students	Tests	Items	Coefficients for						
			σ_i				η_a		
			1	2 $\cdots$	k	1	2	τ_2
Treatment 1	Pretest								
		1	1	0	0	0	0	0
		2	0	1	0	0	0	0
		$\vdots$						
		k	0	0	1	0	0	0
	Posttest								
		1	1	0	0	1	0	1
		2	0	1	0	1	0	1
		$\vdots$						
		k	0	0	1	1	0	1
Treatment 2	Pretest								
		1	1	0	0	0	0	0
		2	0	1	0	0	0	0
		$\vdots$						
		k	0	0	1	0	0	0
	Posttest								
		1	1	0	0	0	1	1
		2	0	1	0	0	1	1
		$\vdots$						
		k	0	0	1	0	1	1
Control	Pretest								
		1	1	0	0	0	0	0
		2	0	1	0	0	0	0
		$\vdots$						
		k	0	0	1	0	0	0
	Posttest								
		1	1	0	0	0	0	1
		2	0	1	0	0	0	1
		$\vdots$						
		k	0	0	1	0	0	1

Applications to Educational Measurement

Spada (1973) used Model I to estimate global learning parameters δ_t. Data were obtained from 40 persons on 4 successive days with four parallel tests. No relevant instruction occurred between testing. The learning effects were solely the consequence of practice while trying to solve items. The estimated learning effects were: Day 1, $\delta_1 = 0.0$; Day 2, $\delta_2 = 0.6$; Day 3, $\delta_3 = 1.3$; and Day 4, $\delta_4 = 2.1$. The estimates reflect a substantial learning gain. A person with a probability of success of .50 on an item on Day 1 would have a probability of success of .90 on a parallel item on Day 4. In this study, the additional capacity of the LLTM to decompose items into operations was not used. The fit of Model I was shown to be relatively good. It was tested by contrasting Model I with Models II and III and by comparison of estimates from low and high scorers. By means of studies of this type it is possible to assess and correct for the often misleading effect of test practice on the outcome of further test occasions.

Rost (1977) used the person-specific learning parameters δ_{vt} to estimate individual differences in learning rates. All persons received common instruction between pretest and posttest. Each person's δ_{vt} was taken as an index of ability to learn (see Guthke, 1976). Rost (1977) undertook detailed tests of goodness of fit with a variety of the logistic test models. None of Models I–IV fitted his data well, the best fit being obtained with a model that included two interaction parameters, a person-specific learning effect δ_{vt} and an item-specific learning effect σ_{it}.

Spada, Hoffmann, and Lucht-Wraage (1977) used an extension of Model I of the type given as Equation 14 in a curriculum evaluation. The extension was more elaborate in using a larger number of treatments, in using more than two test occasions, and in taking into account different amounts of treatment. Four independent elements of the curriculum were identified and 16 separate instructional conditions were established to include all combinations of them, ranging from a control condition with none included to one which included all four instructional elements. A Rasch scaled situation test was developed to assess seven variables corresponding with the objectives of the curriculum (Spada & Lucht-Wraage, 1980) and the LLTM was used to estimate the effectiveness of each instructional condition a on each variable r as the parameter η_{ar}. In order to use Model I, it was assumed that learning was global and not person-specific, depending only on the type and amount of instruction.

Model IV has been applied by Fischer and his colleagues, in the form of the linear logistic model with relaxed assumptions, in various ways (see Fischer, 1978, 1982).

LEARNING AND THE VALIDITY OF LOGISTIC TEST MODELS

In the preceding parts of this chapter we have presented both theoretical arguments and empirical results to justify the use of (linear) logistic test models. Promising techniques have been recommended for explaining the difficulty of items, for using this knowledge to develop better tests, and for assessing treatment effects in terms of changes in person abilities and item difficulties. We have also referred to problems due to the restrictiveness of the assumptions of the models. Assuming the same solution algorithm to be used by all persons excludes the possibility of different persons solving an item correctly in different ways. Assuming all changes to be quantitative excludes the possibility of modeling qualitative developmental changes. Assuming local stochastic independence of item responses excludes response contingent learning effects while completing a test.

In our concluding discussion we analyze these deficiencies of the models further. We consider

1. cases in which the simple Rasch model and the LLTM are not applicable because the nature of learning before testing, during testing, or between tests invalidates the models; and
2. respects in which all the logistic test models discussed fail to conform to important psychological theories of learning and development.

In discussing Item 1, we argue from within the framework of logistic modeling. In discussing Item 2, we evaluate the models from an external perspective.

CASES FOR WHICH THE SIMPLE RASCH MODEL AND THE LLTM ARE INAPPLICABLE

For learning while taking a test, the simple Rasch model is applicable only if global learning or item-specific learning occurs, with constant gains for all persons. Person-specific learning falsifies the model. The same is true for applications of the LLTM that decompose item-specific learning into changes in the difficulties of elementary cognitive operations.

If learning between test applications is global or person-specific, the simple Rasch model fits the data. In case of item-specific learning, with constant gain for the subjects, application of the Rasch model is also possible if the change in item difficulties is taken into account in an appropriate form and tested against the possibility of an item-by-person interaction that would invalidate the model.

Differences in the prior learning histories of individuals, however, can invalidate the models. These histories normally differ from person to person and are unknown. Provided they produce only preexperimental global or person-specific learning effects, there is a good chance that the simple Rasch model and the LLTM would fit the data. If the learning has item-specific effects, the person-specific learning histories will cause the relative difficulties of items to be different for different persons. These item-by-person interactions will invalidate the simple Rasch model and the LLTM.

The LLTM is a powerful tool with which data can be arranged to detect deviations from the assumptions of the simple Rasch model and the LLTM itself. One strategy is to group items according to their cognitive structures and to estimate person parameters from the different subsets of items. Lindström (personal communication, 1980), for example, has shown that even the rotation system tasks may yield data that violate assumptions of the Rasch model. Using subsets of items that required the use of cognitive operations as different as possible, he found statistically significant differences between the person parameter estimates, indicating person-by-item interactions.

PSYCHOLOGICAL THEORIES OF LEARNING AND PSYCHOMETRIC METHODS FOR MEASURING CHANGE: SIDES OF DIFFERENT COINS?

The simple Rasch model, the LLTM, and the four logistic test models for measuring change are all inapplicable if the data reflect second-order interactions among persons, items, and time. If the effects of learning or development are different for different persons for different items for different times in the learning or development sequence, these models are invalidated. Nearly all psychological models of development (e.g., the theory of Piaget), of human learning (e.g., theories based on semantic networks by Dörner, 1976, and Norman & Rumelhart, 1975), and of problem solving (e.g., the production systems models of Newell & Simon, 1972; models combining the technology of semantic networks and production systems such as that of Greeno, 1978), however, postulate such differences in learning and developmental effects. Cognitive processes are represented in such a way that a restructuring of components is assumed.

A study by Spada, Reimann, and Häusler (1983) illustrates the problem. In this study, the constructive process of hypothesis development was analyzed in children and adolescents. The subjects' task was to learn as much as possible about the laws of relevance to a certain area of physics by choosing simulated experiments from this field, by explaining the choices, by predicting the outcomes of the experiments, by obtaining the corresponding experimental results, and by processing all of this with the aim of further developing hypotheses about the phenomena. The resulting structured sequences of information search and processing were analyzed with a special process-scoring system. The results of the investigation suggest that the individual knowledge structures differ and so cannot be assessed by means of (linear) logistic test models.

The more differentiated the picture of the psychological base of a particular behavior, the more doubtful is it that logistic test models will fit. In fact, most relevant psychological theories postulate cognitive changes due to learning and development, which would result in test data reflecting interactions that cannot be handled by logistic models. Lüer (1980) argued that "we have to set aside the idea that thought is a product of a psychical apparatus that deals with a limited number of variables functioning similarly in every situation" (p. 38).

The alternative, however, is not clear. Information-processing theories offer no sufficiently developed methodology for assessing individual changes in memory structure or in solution algorithms. Consequently, many strategies and techniques for evaluating instruction and learning are unsatisfactory with regard to both the demands of psychological theorizing and the psychometric requirements for measuring change. The LLTM and the four logistic test models for measuring change are an attempt to bridge the gap between the trends to take psychological theorizing and educational theorizing truly seriously. At present it is not clear whether this and other attempts (see Sternberg & McNamara, Chapter 2 in this volume) will be successful or whether psychological theories of learning and development and psychometric methods for measuring change will remain sides of different coins. Nevertheless, it is possible to argue in the meantime that the measurement of item-specific and person-specific learning effects with logistic test models is a useful step toward a formalization of a structural learning process.

REFERENCES

Andersen, E. B. (1973). A goodness of fit test for the Rasch model. *Psychometrika, 38,* 123–140.

Andersen, E. B. (1980). *Discrete statistical models with social science applications.* Amsterdam: North-Holland.

Andrich, D. (1982). Using latent trait measurement models to analyze attitudinal data: A synthesis of viewpoints. In D. Spearritt (Ed.), *The improvement of measurement in education and psychology* (pp. 89–126). Melbourne: Australian Council for Educational Research.

Dörner, D. (1976). *Problemlösen als Informationsverarbeitung.* Stuttgart: Kohlhammer.

Fischer, G. H. (1972). A measurement model for the effect of mass media. *Acta Psychologica, 36,* 207–220.

Fischer, G. H. (1973). The linear logistic test model as an instrument in educational research. *Acta Psychologica, 37,* 359–374.

Fischer, G. H. (1974). *Einführung in die Theorie psychologischer Tests.* Bern: Huber.

Fischer, G. H. (1976). Some probabilistic models for measuring change. In D. N. M. de Gruijter & L. J. T. van der Kamp (Eds.), *Advances in psychological and educational measurement* (pp. 97–110). New York: Wiley.

Fischer, G. H. (1978). Probabilistic test models and their applications. *German Journal of Psychology, 2,* 298–319.

Fischer, G. H. (1981). On the existence and uniqueness of maximum-likelihood estimates in the Rasch model. *Psychometrika, 46,* 59–77.

Fischer, G. H. (1982). *Logistic latent trait models with linear constraints: Formal results and typical applications* (Research Bulletin No. 24). Vienna: Institute for Psychology, University of Vienna.

Fischer, G. H., & Formann, A. K. (1972). *An algorithm and a FORTRAN program for estimating the item parameters of the linear logistic test model* (Research Bulletin No. 11). Vienna: Institute for Psychology, University of Vienna.

Fischer, G. H., & Pendl, P. (1980). Individualized testing on the basis of the dichotomous Rasch model. In L. J. T. van der Kamp, W. F. Langerak, & D. N. M. de Gruijter (Eds.), *Psychometrics for educational debates* (pp. 171–188). New York: Wiley.

Formann, A. K., & Pinswanger, K. (1979). *Wiener Matrizen-Test.* Weinheim: Beltz.

Greeno, J. G. (1978). A study of problem solving. In R. Glaser (Ed.), *Advances in instructional psychology (Vol. 1)* (pp. 13–75). Hillsdale, NJ: Erlbaum.

Gustafsson, J. E. (1980). A solution of the conditional estimation problem for long tests in the Rasch model for dichotomous items. *Educational and Psychological Measurement, 40,* 377–385.

Guthke, J. (1976). Entwicklungsstand und Probleme der Lernfähigkeitsdiagnostik. Teil II. *Zeitschrift für Psychologie, 184,* 215–239.

Hornke, L. F., & Habon, M. W. (1982). *Rationale Konstruktion von Testaufgaben* (Projekt: Computerunterstütztes adaptives Testen). Forschungsbericht Universität Düsseldorf.

Inhelder, B., & Piaget, J. (1958). *The growth of logical thinking from childhood to adolescence.* New York: Basic Books.

Klauer, K. J. (1978). Kontentvalidität. In K. J. Klauer (Ed.), *Handbuch der Pädagogischen Diagnostik (Vol. 1)* pp. 225–256. Düsseldorf: Schwann.

Kubinger, K. (1979). Das Problemlöseverhalten bei der statistischen Auswertung psychologischer Experimente. Ein Beispiel hochschuldidaktischer Forschung. *Zeitschrift für Experimentelle und Angewandte Psychologie, 26,* 467–495.

Lüer, G. (1980). Mathematical and psychometric models of cognitive development from the viewpoint of information processing theories. In R. Kluwe & H. Spada (Eds.), *Developmental models of thinking* (pp. 33–41). New York: Academic Press.

Micko, H. C. (1970). Eine Verallgemeinerung des Messmodells von Rasch mit einer Anwendung auf die Psychophysik der Reaktionen. *Psychologische Beiträge, 12,* 4–22.

Nährer, W. (1977). *Modellkontrollen bei der Anwendung des linearen logistischen Testmodells in der Psychologie.* Unpublished doctoral dissertation, University of Vienna.

Nährer, W. (1980a). Zur Analyse von Matrizenaufgaben mit dem linearen logistischen Testmodell. *Zeitschrift für Experimentelle und Angewandte Psychologie, 27,* 553–564.

Nährer, W. (1980b). Modellkontrollen bei der Anwendung des linearen logistischen Testmodells. *Diagnostica, 26,* 112–118.

Newell, A., & Simon, H. (1972). *Human problem solving.* Englewood Cliffs, NJ: Prentice-Hall.

Norman, D., & Rumelhart, D. (Eds.) (1975). *Explorations in cognition.* Reading, MA: W. H. Freeman.

Rasch, G. (1960). *Probabilistic models for some intelligence and attainment tests.* Copenhagen: Pedagogiske Institut.

Rost, J. (1977). *Diagnostik des Lernzuwachses: Ein Beitrag zur Theorie und Methodik von Lerntests* (IPN-Arbeitsbericht 26). Kiel: IPN, University of Kiel.

Rost, J. (1982). An unconditional likelihood ratio for testing item homogeneity in the Rasch model. *Education Research and Perspectives, 9,* 7–17.

Rost, J., & Spada, H. (1983). Die Quantifizierung von Lerneffeckten anhand von Testdaten. *Zeitschrift fur Differentielle und Diagnostische Psychologie, 4,* 29–49.

Scheiblechner, H. (1971). The separation of individual and system influences on behavior in social contexts. *Acta Psychologica, 35,* 442–460.

Scheiblechner, H. (1972). Das Lernen und Lösen komplexer Denkaufgaben. *Zeitschrift für Experimentelle und Angewandte Psychologie, 19,* 476–506.

Spada, H. (1973). Die Analyse kognitiver Lerneffekte mit stichprobenunabhängigen Verfahren. In K. Frey & Lang (Eds.), *Kognitionspsychologie und naturwissenschaftlicher Unterricht* (pp. 94–131). Bern: Huber.

Spada, H. (1976a). Measurement as an element of curricular evaluation. *Studies in Educational Evaluation, 2,* 85–102.

Spada, H. (1976b). *Modelle des Denkens und Lernens.* Bern: Huber.

Spada, H. (1977). Logistic models of learning and thought. In H. Spada & W. F. Kempf (Eds.), *Structural models of thinking and learning* (pp. 227–262). Bern: Huber.

Spada, H., Fischer, G., & Heyner, W. (1973). Die Analyse von Denkoperationen und Lernprozessen bei der Lösung von Problemstellungen aus der Mechanik mittels des linearen logistischen Modells. In H. Spada, P. Häussler, & W. Heyner (Eds.), *Denkoperationen und Lernprozesse als Grundlage fur lernerorientierten Unterricht: Versuchsplanung und erste Ergebnisse* (IPN-Arbeitsbericht 5) (pp. 219–293). Kiel: IPN, University of Kiel.

Spada, H., Hoffmann, L., & Lucht-Wraage, H. (1977). Student attitudes towards nuclear power plants: A classroom experiment in the field of environmental psychology. *Studies in Educational Evaluation, 3,* 109–128.

Spada, H., & Kluwe, R. (1980). Two models of intellectual development and their reference to the theory of Piaget. In R. Kluwe & H. Spada (Eds.), *Developmental model of thinking* (pp. 1–32). New York: Academic Press.

Spada, H., & Lucht-Wraage, H. (1980). A pencil and paper test to assess attitudes: An analysis of reactions to open-end items based on the model of Rasch. In L. van der Kamp, W. F. Langerak, & D. N. M. de Gruijter (Eds.), *Psychometrics for educational debates* (pp. 277–289). New York: Wiley.

Spada, H., & May, R. (1982). The linear logistic test model and its application in educational research. In D. Spearritt (Ed.), *The improvement of measurement in education and psychology* (pp. 67–84). Melbourne: Australian Council for Educational Research.

Spada, H., & Reimann, P. (1982). Educational measurement. *German Journal of Psychology, 6,* 286–305.

Spada, H., Reimann, P., & Häusler, B. (1983). Hypothesenerarbeitung und Wissensaufbau beim Schüler. In L. Kötter & H. Mandl (Eds.), *Kognitive Prozesse und Unterricht: Jahrbuch für Empirische Erziehungswissenschaft* (pp. 139–167). Düsseldorf: Schwann.

Stelzl, I. (1979). Ist der Modelltest des Rasch-Modells geeignet, Homogenitätshypothesen zu prüfen? Ein Bericht über Simulationsstudien mit inhomogen Daten. *Zeitschrift für Experimentelle und Angewandte Psychologie, 26,* 652–672.

Thissen, D. (1982). Marginal maximum likelihood estimation for the one-parameter logistic model. *Psychometrika, 47,* 175–186.

Whitely, S. E. (1980). Multicomponent latent trait models for ability tests. *Psychometrika, 45,* 479–494.

Whitely, S. E., & Schneider, L. M. (1981). Information structure for geometric analogies: A test theory approach. *Applied Psychological Measurement, 5,* 383–397.

Wollenberg, A. L. van den (1982). Two new test statistics for the Rasch model. *Psychometrika, 47,* 123–140.

Wright, B. D., & Stone, M. H. (1979). *Best test design.* Chicago: MESA.

7

Multicomponent Latent Trait
Models for Test Design

Susan E. Embretson (Whitely)

INTRODUCTION

This chapter presents several component latent trait models (CLTM) that can be used for test design. These CLTM are psychometric models that provide estimates of the cognitive demands in each item and specify the relationship of cognitive demands to the cognitive abilities that are reflected in item solving. Thus, the item parameters of CLTM can be used to design tests that measure specified aspects of individual differences.

Component latent trait models are also useful for hypothesis testing about the cognitive processes that are involved in task responses. That is, modeling the cognitive components in intelligence test items, such as reported in the chapters by Sternberg and McNamara (Chapter 2 in this volume) and by Pellegrino, Mumaw, and Cantoni (Chapter 3 in this volume), can be conducted in the context of a psychometric model. The psychometric model context has the incidental advantage of providing item and person parameters for each postulated cognitive variable in the model.

The chapter contains four main sections. First, a conceptual model for test design is presented. The model shows the relationship of the cognitive features of the items to construct validity. The next section presents several component latent trait models that can be used for test design. The models include the multicomponent latent trait model (MLTM; Whitely,[1] 1980b), the general component latent trait model (GLTM; Embretson, in press a) and a new MLTM for items that can be solved by alternative processing

---

[1] S. E. Whitely is now S. E. Embretson.

Copyright © 1985 by Academic Press, Inc.
All rights of reproduction in any form reserved.
ISBN 0-12-238180-7

strategies. The following section shows how item parameters from the various CLTMs can be used to design tests to measure specified individual differences. The last section presents an overview and a summary.

TEST DESIGN AND CONSTRUCT VALIDITY

It is useful to conceptualize construct validation research as concerning two separate issues, construct representation and nomothetic span (see Embretson, 1983, for an extended discussion). Construct representation refers to the processes, strategies, and knowledge stores that are involved in item responses. Construct representation is studied by task decomposition methods, such as presented by the various chapters on cognitive component analysis in this book (i.e., Sternberg & McNamara, Chapter 2; Pellegrino *et al.*, Chapter 3; Butterfield, Nielsen, Tangen, & Richardson, Chapter 4). Construct representation is understood when the various components, metacomponents, strategies, and knowledge stores that are involved in solving psychometric items are explicated.

Nomothetic span, in contrast, concerns the utility of the test as a measure of individual differences. It is supported by elaborating the pattern, magnitude, and frequency of relationships of the test score with other measures of individual differences, such as criterion scores, group membership, or scores on other tests.

Establishing the nomothetic span of a test through correlational research is standard practice in test development. However, the relationship between construct representation and nomothetic span is crucial to the construct validity of the test and to test design. Specifically, it is important to determine how individual differences in performing the underlying cognitive variables influence the test's variance and its covariances with other measures.

It is important to note that the cognitive variables that are identified by construct representation research *may or may not* be sources of individual differences in the test score. The cognitive variables are not necessarily sources of individual differences in the test scores because they may not vary systematically over individuals or they may be too highly correlated with other cognitive variables to contribute uniquely to test variance.

The relationship of construct representation to nomothetic span is elaborated by correlational research in which measures of individual differences in the underlying cognitive variables, test scores, and external measures are obtained. The ability measured by the test score is postulated to be an intervening variable (MacCorquodale & Meehl, 1948) that summarizes the influences of the cognitive variables on individual differences in test scores

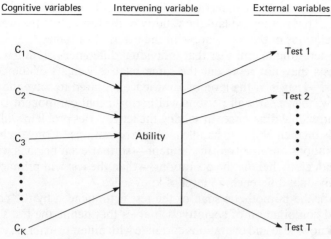

FIGURE 1.   Ability as an intervening variable.

and the predictive validity of the test.   Figure 1 shows a conceptual model of the relationship of the underlying cognitive constructs to ability and the nomothetic span of the test.

According to the definition of an intervening variable, ability is merely an inductive summary.   That is, ability is completely explained by the weighted combination of the underlying cognitive variables, which, in turn, account for the predictive validity of the test.   Thus, ability is merely a convenient referent for a particular combination of cognitive variables with a certain pattern of nomothetic span.

For example, the letter series task has been studied as a measure of inductive reasoning ability (Thurstone & Thurstone, 1941).   Butterfield *et al.*'s chapter in this volume (Chapter 4) exemplifies construct representation research on the task.   Two major cognitive variables were identified in the task: level of knowledge and number of operations.   These variables, in turn, can be sources of individual differences in solving the letter series task.   That is, persons may vary in the level of knowledge that they can apply to the task and in their ability to perform multiple operations.   Individual differences in solving a particular set of letter series problems is a weighted combination of individual differences on the two cognitive variables.   Thus, the reasoning ability measured by the test scores (usually number correct) is an inductive summary of the particular weighting of the underlying variables for a given letter series test.

Figure 1 also shows the nomothetic span of the test.   That is, ability is related to other measures of individual differences.   However, because ability is merely an inductive summary, a weighted combination of measures of the cognitive variables can replace ability to describe the nomothetic span of the test. That is, they explain the validity of the test in that they reproduce the correlations of the test score with the external variables.

It is interesting to consider that individual differences on different letter series tests may not represent the same relative weights of the cognitive variables. That is, if the level of knowledge required to solve the items is quite low, then nearly all persons will perform that component correctly. Thus, individual differences in solving the letter series problem will depend primarily on their ability to handle multiple operations. Conversely, if very few operations are involved in the item—so that even persons with little ability can easily handle the operations—then the test will primarily measure individual differences in level of knowledge.

In turn, the nomothetic span of the test is influenced by the particular weighted combination of cognitive variables that define the test score. If level of knowledge and operations correlate with different external variables, then the nomothetic span of the test depends on which cognitive variable has primary influence. For example, the letter series test that measures primarily individual differences in handling multiple operations will probably relate to individual differences in situations that place heavy demands on active memory processes. Level of knowledge, on the other hand, may relate more to achievement levels.

In general, then, the construct validity of the test depends on the relative influence of underlying cognitive variables on the individual differences in item solving. Tests with different relative weights of the cognitive variables will have different nomothetic spans. Although a more detailed consideration of research methods for nomothetic span is beyond the scope of this chapter, the relationship of construct representation and nomothetic span can be tested in structural equation models (see Embretson, 1983, for examples).

On first glance, this conceptualization of construct validity seems to suggest few generalities in ability measurement because subsets of the same item type may measure very different aspects of individual differences. Factor-analytic research, in fact, supports this conclusion, because the same item type can load on quite different factors when measured from different tests. Whitely (1973) presented examples from French's (1951) summary of factor studies of ability.

However, the flexible impact of the cognitive variables on the test score is precisely what permits test design. That is, items can be selected or constructed to measure *specified* aspects of individual differences if the relative impact of the various underlying variables on item solving is known. Construct representation research in the context of CLTM can yield item parameters that describe the cognitive demands of the item, which, in turn, can be used to manipulate or select items.

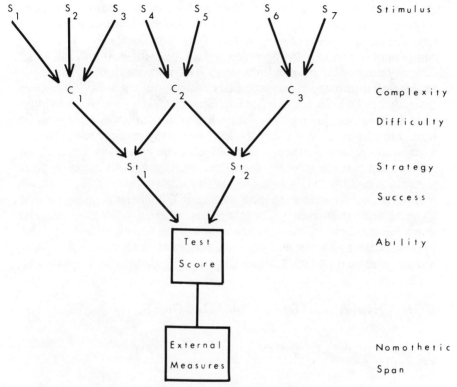

FIGURE 2.   Relationship of cognitive variables to test score.

Figure 2 presents a conceptualization of the various levels of cognitive variables that may influence test scores. Many of the sources of individual differences in information processing were contained in Sternberg's (1977) outline of componential theory. However, the major focus of Fig. 2 is the test score. The various sources of individual differences are considered important only if they influence item-solving accuracy.

A major assumption for the model in Fig. 2 is that the correct information outcome from several component processes (e.g., C_1) is required to solve the item. For example, consider the following verbal analogy item:

Blacksmith : Horse : : Cobbler : ?
(1) Man (2) Shoe (3) Saddle (4) Nail (5) Mare

According to various theories of analogical reasoning (Pellegrino & Glaser, 1980; Sternberg, 1977; Whitely & Barnes, 1979), solving the analogy requires the person to encode correctly the meaning of the words, to infer a relationship between the related pair in the stem (i.e., Blacksmith : Horse), to link the relationship to the unmatched term (Cobbler), and so forth.

The stimulus content of the item (e.g., S_1) influences the difficulty of the component processes. In the preceding analogy, for example, encoding difficulty can be controlled by vocabulary level of the words or by basing the analogy on a primary versus secondary meaning of the word. Inference difficulty can be influenced by the relational distance of the words in long-term memory and linking the relationship to the unmatched term can be made difficult by using word pairs that have many possible relationships. These influences are further elaborated later in an example.

Some items may be solved by more than one strategy. A strategy involves a distinct combination of components that can be executed to solve the item. Figure 2 shows that components C_1 and C_2 form strategy St_1 and that C_2 and C_3 form strategy St_2. The total item may be solved by either strategy, given that the decision is made to execute it. The combination weights for the stimuli, components, and strategies determine the nature of the ability that is measured by the test score and, hence, the nomothetic span of the test.

COMPONENT LATENT TRAIT MODELS

MULTICOMPONENT COMPONENT LATENT TRAIT MODELS

Basic Model

Multicomponent latent trait models (MLTMs) measure the cognitive demands of items by linking a psychometric model to a mathematical model that operationalizes the constructs of an information-processing theory. These MLTMs are process–product models. That is, it is assumed that solving the item requires the correct information outcome from several processing components. The MLTM is particularly applicable to complex intelligence test items, such as verbal analogies, syllogisms, verbal analogies, series completions, pratical judgment items, and mathematical reasoning items. Two kinds of data are required for the models: (1) responses to the standard psychometric item and (2) responses to a series of subtasks that represent an exhaustive set of information-processing components.

To estimate the cognitive demands in an item set, a theory of the underlying processes must be explicitly postulated and the theory must provide a good fit to the data. Consider the verbal classification item presented in Table 1. Two global components have been supported for this item type, Rule Construction and Response Evaluation (Whitely, 1981; Whitely & Schneider, 1980). The subtasks define two component processes that must

TABLE 1
Verbal Classification Item

Total Item	Keats	Byron	Wordsworth
	(a) Pope (b) Houseman (c) Spenser (d) Kipling (e) Shelley		
Rule Construction	Keats	Byron	Wordsworth
	Rule	?	
Response Evaluation	Keats	Byron	Wordsworth
	(a) Pope (b) Houseman (c) Spenser (d) Kipling (e) Shelley		
	Rule: Romantic poets		

be executed correctly for item solution. Thus, the probability of solving the item depends on the probability of solving the components. Whitely and Schneider (1980) postulated that the component probabilities combined multiplicatively. The components for verbal classification items are sequentially dependent because the outcome to the first component is prerequisite to executing the second component successfully. However, if the rule is supplied for the Response Evaluation component, as in the subtask on Table 2, then the two component processes may be assessed independently.

Table 2 shows the frequencies of the eight possible response patterns to the total item and the two subtasks that were obtained from a sample of 70 college undergraduates on 45 verbal classification items. In this study, the standard psychometric item was presented first. The subtasks were presented several weeks later to minimize memory effects. For each item eight response patterns, defined by the standard task and the two subtasks, were possible, as shown on Table 2. For example, the pattern 110 means that the two components were executed correctly but that the total item was not.

The relationship of the component process products to the total item, as postulated by Whitely and Schneider (1980), can be expressed by the following mathematical model:

$$P(X_{ijT} = 1) = (a - g)\prod_k P(X_{ijk} = 1) + g. \tag{1}$$

That is, the probability that the total item is solved $P(X_{ijT} = 1)$ is the product of the subtask probabilities $P(X_{ijk} = 1)$. A further refinement of the model is the inclusion of the constants a and g, which are postulated to represent executive processing and guessing, respectively. The constant a is the probability that the component information is applied to the total task given that correct outcomes have been obtained. The constant g is the probability that the correct outcome is obtained given that at least one component is incorrect.

The probability of each of the eight possible outcomes to the components and total item can also obtained by a mathematical model. Table 2 shows

TABLE 2
FREQUENCIES AND CONDITIONAL
PROBABILITIES FOR JOINT RESPONSE
PATTERNS ON VERBAL CLASSIFICATIONS

C_1	C_2	T	f	$P(x_T = 1\|\underline{x}_k)$	Model
1	1	1	1313	.82	$aP_{X_1}P_{X_2}$
1	1	0	281	.18	$(1-a)P_{X_1}P_{X_2}$
0	1	1	414	.58	$gQ_{X_1}P_{X_2}$
0	1	0	296	.42	$(1-g)Q_{X_1}P_{X_2}$
1	0	1	118	.27	$gP_{X_1}Q_{X_2}$
1	0	0	315	.73	$(1-g)P_{X_1}Q_{X_2}$
0	0	1	80	.19	$gQ_{X_1}Q_{X_2}$
0	0	0	333	.81	$(1-g)Q_{X_1}Q_{X_2}$

these probabilities. The formula that gives these probabilities is the following:

$$P(X_k, X_T) = \left[\prod_k P_{X_k}^{X_k} Q_{X_k}^{1-X_k}\right][a^{X_T}(1-a)^{1-X_T}]\prod_k^{X_k}$$

$$\times [g^{X_T}(1-g)^{(1-X_T)}]\left(1 - \prod_k P_{X_k}^{X_k}Q_{X_k}^{1-X_k}\right). \qquad (2)$$

It can be shown that the sum of the response patterns where $X_T = 1$ is equal to Equation 1.

It should be noted that MLTM is an individual response model. That is, a probability is given for each person to each item. To apply the prediction to individual persons who differ systematically in their success on the total item and subtasks, a psychometric model is needed. The psychometric model not only controls for person differences in predicting the individual response probabilities, but it also yields estimates of subject differences in the processing components.

The Rasch latent trait model may be applied to give the probability $P(X_{ijk} = 1)$ that person j passes component subtask k on item i as follows:

$$P(X_{ijT} = 1) = \frac{e^{\theta_{jk}-\xi_{ik}}}{1 + e^{\theta_{jk}-\xi_{ik}}}, \qquad (3)$$

where θ_{jk} = ability of person j on component k and ξ_{ik} = difficulty of item i on component k. Thus, the probability that person j solves component k on item i depends on his or her ability and the component's difficulty in the item.

The MLTM combines Equation 1 and Equation 3 to give the probability

$P(X_{ijT} = 1)$ that person j passes total item i as follows from the components:

$$P(X_{ijT} = 1) = (a - g) \prod_k \frac{e^{\theta_{jk} - \xi_{ik}}}{1 + e^{\theta_{jk} - \xi_{ik}}} + g. \qquad (4)$$

The item difficulties and person abilities have a compensatory relationship within each component. That is, they are additive in determining response probabilities. The measurement scales for the person and item parameters are similar to z scores. For example, consider a verbal classification item that has high difficulty ($\xi_{i1} = 3.28$) on the Rule Construction component. A person with above-average ability ($\theta_{j1} = 1.50$) has the following chance of passing the component, as shown by applying Equation 3:

$$P(X_{ijk} = 1) = \frac{e^{1.50 - 3.28}}{1 + e^{1.50 - 3.28}} = .15.$$

If the item is very easy on the Response Evaluation component ($\xi_{i2} = -3.00$) and the person has slightly below-average ability on this component ($\theta_{j2} = -.50$), then it can be shown by Equation 3 that the probability of the component is .92.

If the a and g parameters are .82 and .39, respectively, then the probability that this person solves the total item is given as follows by MLTM:

$$P(X_{ijT} = 1) = (.82 - .39)(.15)(.92) + .39 = .45.$$

Notice that the relationship between the components is noncompensatory. The person's high probability on Response Evaluation does not compensate for the low probability on Rule Construction. The model assumes that all information outcomes are required for solution. Thus, if one outcome has a low probability, the item has a low probability of being solved.

Alternative mathematical models can be postulated in MLTM to evaluate the quality of the component decomposition. Actually, MLTM is a family of models that vary by the mathematical models that relate the subtasks to the total item. Equation 2 gives the likelihood of each response pattern, given the model. If the likelihoods are summed over person and items, maximum likelihood estimators for the model parameters can be derived (see Embretson, in press a). The maximum likelihoods can be used for testing hypotheses about the components in the total item. Because -2 times the log likelihood of the data is distributed as χ^2, under certain conditions alternative models can be compared.

To give an example, Whitely and Schneider (1980) tested four alternative models for verbal classification items that varied in the inclusion of a third event (i.e., Event Recovery) and in the inclusion of the a and g parameters to represent executive functioning and guessing. The third component was found to contribute only slightly, but the *a* and *g* parameters had strong contributions to goodness of fit.

It should be noted that converging operations from laboratory research, especially response-time studies, are also needed to support a component decomposition. For example, Sternberg (1979) has obtained support for somewhat similar components on verbal classifications.

MLTM for Multiple Strategies

The basic model assumes that only one combination of components leads to item solution. However, modern cognitive theory of problem solving emphasizes the role of multiple strategies. Furthermore, several studies have found that intelligence test items often involve more than one strategy (e.g., Sternberg & Weil, 1981). Thus, an MLTM in which the mathematical model reflects alternative strategies is needed to provide an adequate explanation of many item types.

Mathematical models of strategies can be developed by (1) defining which components form the strategy and (2) specifying an order for strategy execution. It is useful to map component event sequences on an information-processing path diagram to explicate these relations.

An example is the verbal analogy item presented on Table 3. Several studies have suggested that analogies can be solved by an associational process (Achenbach, 1970; Gentile, Kessler, & Gentile, 1969), rather than by a rule-oriented process as exemplified earlier for verbal classification items.

Table 3 shows some subtasks that define two global Rule-Oriented components, Rule Construction and Response Evaluation, and an Association component. The Rule Construction subtask involves specifying the rule that the correct completion to the analogy must fulfill, whereas the Response Evaluation component involves selecting an alternative to fulfill a given rule. The Association component involves choosing the response alternative that is mostly highly associated to the unmatched term (i.e., Dog).

TABLE 3
Subtask Set

Total Item	Cat : Tiger : : Dog: _____
	(a) Lion (b) Wolf (c) Bark (d) Puppy (e) Horse
Association subtask	Dog
	(a) Lion (b) Wolf (c) Bark (d) Puppy (e) Horse
Rule Construction	Cat : Tiger : : Dog: _____
	Rule _____ ?
Response Evaluation	Cat : Tiger : : Dog: _____
	(a) Lion (b) Wolf (c) Bark (d) Puppy (e) Horse
	Rule: A large or wild canine

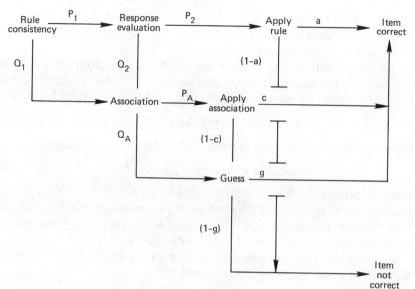

FIGURE 3.   An information-processing path diagram for verbal analogies.

Figure 3 shows an information-processing path diagram of the two strategies. The diagram not only explicates the theory of the strategies, but also is useful for developing mathematical models for MLTM.

The diagram shows the various paths that lead to item solution from the two strategies. The Rule-Oriented strategy involves the component events on the path across the top of the diagram. On the arrows are symbols that represent the probability that the event is executed correctly. The last event is a decision-making process for applying the rule to the item, designated by *a*. Thus, the probability that the item is solved by the Rule-Oriented strategy is given as follows:

$$P(X_T = 1|\text{Rule}) = aP_1 P_2. \tag{5}$$

That is, the probability of solving the item by the rule strategy is the product of the probabilities of the Rule Construction and Response Evaluation components times the application probability.

Figure 3 also shows that the Association strategy consists of a single component and its application probability. However, Fig. 3 shows that Association is postulated to be attempted only if one or both components of the Rule-Oriented strategy fail. The sequential dependency of association on failing the Rule-Oriented strategy in verbal analogies was suggested by data from other studies (e.g., Heller, 1979).

The probability that the item is solved by association is obtained by tracing two paths. The first path results after failure of the Rule Construction component. The outcome to the Response Evaluation component is not relevant to this path because it is postulated to be sequentially dependent on obtaining the correct outcome to the rule construction.

The second path in Fig. 3 for Association is traced from solving Rule Construction but failing Response Evaluation. Thus, the probability that the item is solved by association is the sum of the two paths, as follows:

$$P(X_T = 1|\text{Assoc}) = cQ_1 P_A + cP_1 Q_2 P_A.$$

Rearranging and simplifying the terms gives the following equation:

$$P(X_T = 1|\text{Assoc}) = cP_A(1 - P_1 P_2). \tag{6}$$

Thus, the probability that the item is solved by the Association strategy is the effectiveness of the Association strategy cP_A times the probability that the Rule-Oriented strategy is failed. Thus, the order of execution for the Association strategy is clearly shown by the relation in Fig. 3.

The probability that the task is solved by guessing is given by two separate paths, $Q_1 Q_2 g$ and $P_1 Q_2 g$, which sum as follows:

$$P(X_T = 1|\text{Guess}) = gQ_1 Q_2 Q_A + gP_1 Q_2 Q_A.$$

It can be shown that this sum equals the probability of g times the probability that no other information is available, as follows:

$$P(X_T = 1|\text{Guess}) = g(1 - P_1 P_2)(1 - P_A). \tag{7}$$

The probability that the item is solved is given by the sum of the two strategies and guessing, as follows:

$$P(X_T = 1) = P(X_T = 1|\text{Rule}) + P(X_T = 1|\text{Assoc}) + P(X_T = 1|\text{Guess}). \tag{8}$$

Another way to examine strategies in MLTM is by the sample space for the response patterns. Table 4 presents the sample space for the joint outcomes to the three subtasks—Rule Construction, C_1; Response Evaluation, C_2; and Association, C_A;—and the Total Item, T. Thus, all possible outcomes to the components and items appear on Table 4. Also given on Table 4 is the probability of each outcome, in terms of the probabilities of the components and metacomponents. It can be shown that the sum of the outcomes for a given strategy yields the same probability as the paths in Fig. 3. For example, a successful association strategy is given by three joint outcomes on Table 3, 0111, 1011, and 0011. In these three outcomes at least one component of the Rule Strategy is failed and the Association component is passed. It can be shown by simple algebra that the sum of the probabilities given on Table 4 equal the probabilities on the information-processing path diagram.

The MLTM for strategies incorporates a psychometric model into each component outcome, in this case Rule Construction, Response Evaluation,

TABLE 4
PROBABILITY SPACE FOR AN
ALTERNATIVE STRATEGY MODEL[a]

C_1	C_2	C_A	T		Probability		
1	1	1	1	a	P_1	P_2	P_A
1	1	1	0	$(1-a)$	P_1	P_2	P_A
1	1	0	1	a	P_1	P_2	Q_A
1	1	0	0	$(1-a)$	P_1	P_2	Q_A
0	1	1	1	c	Q_1	P_2	P_A
0	1	1	0	$(1-c)$	Q_1	P_2	P_A
1	0	1	1	c	P_1	Q_2	P_A
1	0	1	0	$(1-c)$	P_1	Q_2	P_A
0	0	1	1	c	Q_1	Q_2	P_A
0	0	1	0	$(1-c)$	Q_1	Q_2	P_A
1	0	0	1	g	P_1	Q_2	Q_A
1	0	0	0	$(1-g)$	P_1	Q_2	Q_A
0	1	0	1	g	Q_1	P_2	Q_A
0	1	0	0	$(1-g)$	Q_1	P_2	Q_A
0	0	0	1	g	Q_1	Q_2	Q_A
0	0	0	0	$(1-g)$	Q_1	Q_2	Q_A

[a] Where C_1, C_2, C_A = outcome on component 1, 2, Association respectively; P_1, P_2, P_A = probability given for person; on item i for the component latent-trait model; T = outcome for Total Item; a = conditional probability of rule application; c = conditional probability of applying association; g = conditional probability of guessing.

and Association. Equation 3 shows the psychometric model. Thus, for example, P_A is given as follows:

$$P(X_A = 1) = \frac{e^{\theta_{jA} - \xi_{iA}}}{1 + e^{\theta_{jA} - \xi_{iA}}}.$$

Thus, the full MLTM combines the mathematical model of Equation 8 with the component response models, as in Equation 3. The difficulty of the item on each component within each strategy and the corresponding person abilities are thus estimated in the model.

An important implication of the model is that item-solving success can be predicted for a person on each strategy that can be applied to an item. Like other latent trait models, the predictions are given for each person by item encounter. To give an example, Embretson (in press b) estimated parameters for the model in Fig. 3 and obtained estimates of .76, .27, and .42 for a, c, and g, respectively. Suppose a certain verbal analogy item had component difficulties of 0.00, 1.00, and −2.50 for Rule Construction, Response Evaluation, and Association, respectively. For a person with abilities of 1.00, 1.00 and 0.00, respectively, for the three components, it can be shown that the psychometric model for the components (i.e., Equation 3) would give the probabilities of .73, .50, and .92, respectively, for correctly executing the three components.

The component probabilities are combined by MLTM mathematical model to give strategy predictions. The probability that the person solves the item by the Rule-Oriented strategy is given by applying Equation 5 to the relevant component probabilities from the psychometric model and the a parameter, as follows:

$$P(X_T = 1 | \text{Rule}) = (.76)(.73)(.50) = .28.$$

The probability that the person solves the item by the Association strategy is given by Equation 6, as follows:

$$P(X_T = 1 | \text{Assoc}) = (.27)(.92)(1 - (.73)(.50)) = .16.$$

The guessing probability is given by Equation 7 as follows:

$$P(X_T = 1 | \text{Guess}) = (.42)(1 - (.73)(.50))(1 - .92) = .02.$$

Thus, the probability that the person solves the item is the sum of these three probabilities, as given by Equation 8:

$$P(X_T = 1) = .28 + .16 + .02 = .46.$$

These estimates show that the person has the highest probability of solving the item by the Rule-Oriented strategy but that Association is a possible alternative, because the item is quite likely to be solved by the strategy (due to a very low difficulty on Association) if it is applied.

If average abilities are assumed, it is also possible to assess the best strategy for an item. This will be shown more completely in the section on test design.

In Embretson's (in press b) application of MLTM for strategies on verbal analogy items, several alternative models were tested for goodness of fit. The results indicated that while the Association strategy had some impact on performance, another alternative strategy, Response Elimination, was more important. Thus, the results suggested the need to include alternative strategies when assessing the cognitive demands of items.

GENERAL COMPONENT LATENT TRAIT MODEL

The general component latent trait model (GLTM) links the component responses in MLTM to the stimuli in the item subtask. This feature is particularly useful for test construction because the items can be developed to have a given difficulty level on a component by manipulating the stimuli according to the GLTM.

Suppose that component difficulty ξ_{ik} is influenced by m complexity factors in the item subtask stimuli q_{imk}. A linear model of the difficulty of the item on the component could be constructed as follows:

$$\xi_{ik} = \sum_m \eta_{mk} q_{ikm} + a_k, \tag{9}$$

where q_{ikm} = complexity of factor m in component k on item i, η_{mk} = weight of factor m in component k difficulty, and a_k = a normalization constant. If a good account of component difficulty is obtained by Equation 9, then the stimulus factors can replace component item difficulty in an MLTM.

The GLTM actually contains two mathematical models: (1) The components are modeled by the stimulus complexity factors and (2) the total item is modeled by the difficulty of the components. Thus, Equation 9 is combined with Equation 4 to give GLTM, as follows:

$$P(X_{ijT} = 1) = (a - g) \prod_k \frac{e^{\theta_{jk} - \left(\sum_m q_{imk}\eta_{mk} + a_k\right)}}{1 + e^{\theta_{jk} - \left(\sum_m q_{ikm}\eta_{mk} + a_k\right)}} + g.$$

The GLTM is general because it contains as special cases MLTM (i.e., when the complexity model equals the component difficulties) and the linear logistic latent-trait model (LLTM) (Fischer, 1973). The LLTM is considered more fully in this book in the chapter by Spada and McGaw (Chapter 6).

Like LLTM, GLTM assumes that the various complexity factors combine additively to determine component (item) difficulty. It is assumed that the different complexity factors do not require qualitatively different abilities to process. Only one ability factor, θ_{jk}, is postulated for persons on each component.

COMPONENT LATENT TRAIT MODELS IN TEST DESIGN

The conceptual model presented in Fig. 2 suggests that test design can be implemented in at least three levels by (1) controlling component difficulty by a manipulation of the stimuli, (2) selecting items according to component difficulty, and (3) selecting items according to the strategies that can be applied effectively. The ways that component latent trait models can be used for test design in each of the three areas are considered in the following.

Manipulating Stimulus Content

Controlling the components that are involved in a task by manipulating stimulus content is standard practice in experimental cognitive psychology

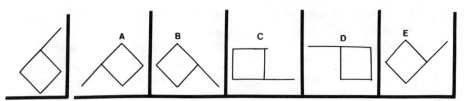

FIGURE 4.   A figure rotation item.

but not in test development.   Consider, for example, the figure rotation task as presented in Figure 4.   Thurstone and Thurstone (1941) included figure rotations to measure spatial ability on the tests of Primary Mental Abilities (PMA).   The task is to discriminate rotations from reflections of a target (on the left in the figure).   Although Thurstone and Thurstone (1941) no doubt had an implicit theory of the task that guided their item development, the rationale for the stimulus content was not made explicit and most certainly item selection was not based on a well-supported theory of the task.   Although the items may meet a psychometric criterion of high intercorrelations, just what aspect of spatial performance is involved in solving items on the PMA is not clear.

In contrast, experimental cognitive research on the task carefully controls stimulus content to determine what processes are involved in item solving. Shephard and Metzler (1971), for example, developed a set of rotation stimuli to test a model of cognitive processing.   The type of stimulus and the angle of rotation was carefully controlled, according to theory, so that each item fulfilled a given specification.   Furthermore, these specifications can predict item difficulty.

To give another example, deductive reasoning is often measured by a test of syllogisms (e.g., Thurstone & Thurstone, 1941).   As with the rotation task, the theoretical rationale for item inclusion is unclear.   In contrast, the premises of syllogisms have been systematically manipulated to control task difficulty in many theoretical studies (Revlis, 1975; Sells, 1936).

These studies suggest that the content of items can be controlled according to an explicit rationale to determine the processes that are involved in task solution.   Of course, if the items are to measure individual differences psychometric criteria also must be met.

For some item types, such as figure rotations and abstract syllogisms, the stimulus properties can be scored by an inspection of the content (e.g., angle of rotation and premise type, respectively, for the two examples).   Other item types, particularly those with word stimuli, may require data that has been obtained from a relevant sample.   Several sources of these already exist.   For example, word usage frequencies are available in Kucera and Francis (1967) and several qualities, such as meaningfulness and imagery potential, are available in Toglia and Battig (1978).

To show how component difficulty can be controlled by stimulus content, consider again the example of a verbal analogy that is presented on Table 3. The Rule Construction component is obviously fairly complex because it is influenced by several aspects of the item stem. According to various theories of analogical reasoning (Pellegrino & Glaser, 1980; Sternberg, 1977; Whitely & Barnes, 1979), solving the item requires the correct inference to the word pair (Cat:Tiger) to be linked to the unmatched term (Dog). Whitely and Curtright (1980) investigated several aspects of the stem stimuli that, according to various theories, should influence the inference process. Three variables that influenced Rule Construction were (1) relational span, the number of relationships that can be inferred to the related pair; (2) inference saliency, the probability that the correct inference is educed without the unmatched term; and (3) syntactic complexity, the match of word order in the related pair to the basic syntactic structure of the inference (e.g., Cat:Tiger requires a reversal of terms for the inference "Tiger is a Cat").

Whitely and Curtright (1980) provided data on these three variables for a large bank of verbal analogy items. Relational span and inference saliency were the means obtained from a study that presented the related pairs alone and asked subjects to list all inferences that could form the basis of an analogy. Syntactic complexity was scored by two raters from an inspection of the items.

These three variables can be used to control the difficulty of the Rule Construction component in an item if the GLTM weights are known, according to Equation 9. To illustrate, the following model of the Rule Construction component difficulty ξ_{i2} was obtained from the Whitely and Curtright item bank sample:

$$\xi_{i1} = .49q_{i11} - 1.92q_{i12} - .40q_{i13} + .99,$$

where q_{i11} = relational span, q_{i12} = inference saliency, and q_{i13} = syntactic complexity. Moderately good reproduction difficulty was obtained from the three variables ($R = .54$, $p < .01$).

The implications for test design should be obvious. If the test developer has the relevant stimulus data, then Rule Construction can be made difficult by selecting word pairs with high relational span or low inference saliency. Or word order can be reversed to increase syntactic complexity. The impact of these features on component difficulty can be estimated by the equation just given.

It should be noted that by no means are the three variables shown in this example a complete account of rule construction difficulty. Clearly, variables such as encoding difficulty and the difficulty of linking the inference to the unmatched term need to be included.

Although the GLTM does not require that the stimulus factors be orthogonal to estimate the weights, orthogonality is highly desirable to assure that the various features can be manipulated independently and have the effects on component difficulty that are indicated by the GLTM equation. In the current example, relational span and inference saliency correlate .25 in the data given. Because these stimulus features have not been controlled in item sets, their correlation probably varies over item sets. Like multiple regression, predictor correlations influence the GLTM weights. Thus, estimates of independent effects can be obtained reliably only from orthogonal predictor sets. On the other hand, syntactic complexity met the orthogonality criterion because it was virtually uncorrelated with the other two variables.

It should be noted that at least two assumptions underlie the application of GLTM to control component difficulty. First, the variables must have separable effects on performance. Although it is possible to add interaction terms in GLTM, just as in multiple regression, these terms may not fully describe the interdependencies. A particular combination of the stimulus features could, possibly, define a different processing algorithm. Second, the variables must define difficulty on the same psychological continuum. That is, items must have the same relative difficulties for all subjects, as only one ability parameter is given for each component in GLTM. If the variables define different cognitive demands within the component, then persons may vary in their ability to process the different stimulus features.

Selecting Component Difficulties

If the MLTM item parameters are known, then the component processing ability that is measured by item solving can be controlled by selecting items on the component parameters. Consider the verbal classification item presented in Table 3. The Rule Construction and Response Evaluation components define independent sources of difficulty.

It should be noted that the correlation between component difficulties is arbitrary. The correlation arises by happenstance or by the test developer's implicit theory of what makes a good item. For example, perhaps the test developer believes that only one source of difficulty should occur for each item. Thus, the correlation would be negative.

Figure 5 shows a plot of the component difficulties of 45 verbal classification items. As can be seen from Fig. 5, the difficulties were not highly correlated ($r = .16$) in the item set. Thus, it is possible to select items that are difficult on different components.

Consider Item 20, which has a Rule Construction difficulty of -4.78 and a Response Evaluation difficulty of 0.20. For a person with average abilities on both components (i.e., $\theta_{jk} = 0.00$), the MLTM model gives the following

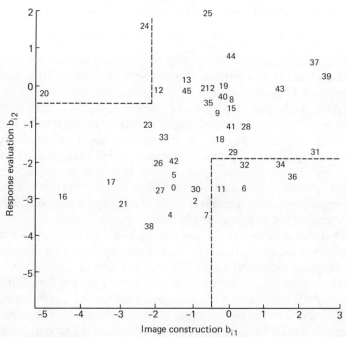

FIGURE 5. Plot of component difficulties for verbal classifications. The item numbers are given on the plot.

prediction (assuming that $a = 1.00$ and $g = .25$):

$$P(X_{ijT}) = 1) = (1 - .25)\left[\frac{e^{0.00-(-4.78)}}{1 + e^{0.00-(-4.78)}}\right]\left[\frac{e^{0.00-.20}}{1 + e^{0.00-.20}}\right] + .25$$

$$= (1 - .25)(.99)(.45) + .25 = .58.$$

Now, although the person has only average ability to solve Rule Construction, a very high probability ($p = .99$) is obtained for executing this component correctly. However, the person still has only an average probability of solving the item because the item demands some ability on Response Evaluation. Even if a person had ability substantially below average on Rule Construction, $\theta_{j2} = -2.00$, the probability of solving this component would still be very high (i.e., $p = .94$). Thus, Item 20 (and Item 24), if selected, would measure Response Evaluation ability but not Rule Construction ability.

In contrast, consider Item 6, which has difficulties of .40 and -2.75, respectively, on Rule Construction and Response Evaluation. Applying MLTM as before for a person with average ability (0.00) on both components gives the following probabilities for solving the total item:

$$P(X_{ijT} = 1) = (1 - .25)(.40)(.94) + .25 = .53.$$

Notice that an average probability of solving the item is given, but that in this item the probability of Response Evaluation is very high. Thus, failure on the item stems from the person's Rule Construction ability.

Test developers, perhaps, have understood component selection intuitively in their practices. For example, if verbal reasoning is to be measured by verbal analogy items, such as on the Cognitive Abilities Test, the vocabulary level is kept easy. On the other hand, verbal analogies can measure vocabulary. The Scholastic Aptitude Test analogies are characterized by low usage frequencies. An advantage of MLTM, however, is not only that this process of item development is made explicit and objective, but that the design variables are linked to psychological theory.

Figure 6 shows more clearly how the relative difficulties of two components influence the ability that is measured and shows how the measurement of one component depends on the difficulty of a second component. In Fig. 6, the probability of solving an item is regressed on the first component ability for items with various response potentials on the second component $(\theta_{j2} - \xi_{i2})$. Notice that the response potential for the second depends on both persons and items, because it is the exponent of the second component in the MLTM.

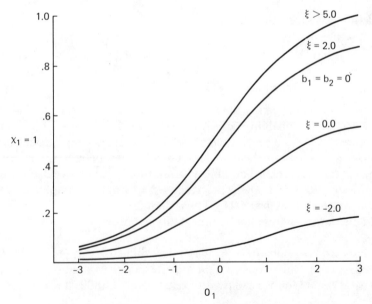

FIGURE 6.   Regression of total item probability on component ability.

It can be seen in Fig. 6 that an item regresses most strongly on the first component ability when the response potential on the second component is very high. Stated another way, if the second component is well within the person's ability range, then item performance will measure ability on the first component. However, if the response potential on the second component is low, Fig. 6 shows that item solving depends only slightly on the first component ability.

As noted in the section of this chapter on test design, the component abilities that are reflected in item solving possibly can influence the nomothetic span of the test. This possibility was supported, in fact, for the verbal classication example is presented earlier, because Whitely (1980a) found that Rule Construction and Response Evaluation ability in verbal classification items correlate differently with the various content areas of educational achievement.

Selecting Strategy Difficulty

Many item types can be solved by more than one strategy. This may or may not be desirable with respect to the intended goals of measurement. Different strategies involve different combinations of component abilities, as well as a decision to operationalize the strategy.

For example, if analogical reasoning ability is conceptualized as reflecting the ability to induce and apply rules, then only the Rule-Oriented strategy should be effective in solving items. That is, if applied, the Association strategy or any other strategy should have a very low probability of leading to item solution. On the other hand, analogical reasoning ability could be conceptualized as the ability to apply any one of several strategies to bear on the problem. If so, then items that can be solved by more than one strategy are needed.

The MLTM for multiple strategies can provide estimates that can be used to select items by the availability of two or more strategies. If ability is fixed to the population mean (0.00) and the application probabilities are fixed to 1.00 then the availability of the Rule-Oriented strategy $(P(X_{ijT} = 1)|\text{Rule}))$ and the Association strategy $(P(X_{ijT} = 1)|\text{Assoc}))$ can be assessed for each item.

Figure 7 shows the availability of the Rule-Oriented versus the Association strategies for some verbal analogy items. The dotted line shows equal probabilities for the two strategies. If only the Rule-Oriented strategy is desired, then items below the line would be selected. However, if items with multiple strategies are desired, then the items above the line, which can also be solved by Association, should be selected. To measure multiple strategies, the Association strategy must be more effective than the Rule-Oriented strategy because, as indicated earlier, Association is attempted only if the Rule-Oriented strategy fails.

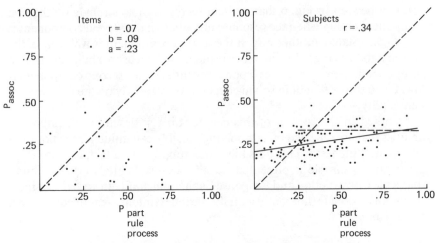

FIGURE 7.   Strategy availability probabilities for verbal analogies.

CONCLUSION

The purpose of this chapter has been to show how component latent trait models can be used for test design. The chapter began by presenting a conceptual model for test design that related three levels of cognitive variables — stimulus features, components, and strategies — to the test score. The test developer may seek to control any or all three levels of cognitive variables when designing tests.

Three component latent trait models were presented. The models can be implemented at different levels of controlling the cognitive variables to determine the aspects of ability that are measured by item solving accuracy. The general component latent trait model (GLTM) can be used to control component difficulty from the stimulus features of items. The multicomponent latent trait model (MLTM) can be used to select items on component difficulty. The multicomponent latent trait model for strategies can be used to select items by the strategies that can lead to item solution.

The chapter should not be regarded as a complete account of test design by component latent trait models. Only an overview of the several component latent trait models was presented, with one example each for application. However, it is hoped that the reader will be able to generalize to other item types and problems.

In conclusion, it should be noted that the component latent trait models presented here require subtask response data. Test developers typically do not have such data available, so implementing the models requires additional research on the items. The increased potential for test design, however, may well be worth the extra research. It also should be noted that subtask data may become more prevalent in testing as a result of computerized adaptive testing. Computerized adaptive testing can estimate ability by administering fewer items to each person, thus giving time for other tasks. Furthermore, the interactive format of computerized testing makes subtasks quite feasible. Thus, component latent trait models may have wider applicability in future testing.

REFERENCES

Achenbach, T. M. (1970). The children's association responding test: A possible alternative to group IQ tests. *Journal of Educational Psychology, 5,* 340–348.

Embretson, S. E. (1983). Construct validity: Construct representation versus nomothetic span. *Psychological Bulletin, 93,* 179–197.

Embretson, S. E. (1984). A general latent trait model for response processes. *Psychometrika, 49,* 175–186.

Embretson, S. E. (in press). Intelligence and its measurement: Extending contemporary theory to existing tests. In R. J. Sternberg (Ed.), *Advances in the psychology of human intelligence,* Volume 3. Hillsdale, NJ: Erlbaum.

Fischer, G. H., (1973). The linear logistic test model as an instrument in education research. *Acta Psychologica, 37,* 359–374.

French, J. W. (1951). The description of aptitude and achievement tests in terms of rotated factors. *Psychometric Monographs, 5.*

Gentile, J., Kessler, K., & Gentile, K. (1969). Process of solving analogies items. *Journal of Educational Psychology, 60,* 494–502.

Heller, J. (1979). *Cognitive processing in verbal analogy solutions.* Unpublished doctoral dissertation, University of Pittsburgh, Pittsburgh, PA.

Kucera, H., & Francis, W. N. (1967). *Computational analysis of present-day American English.* Providence, RI: Brown University Press.

MacCorquodale, K., & Meehl, P. E. (1948). On a distinction between hypothetical constructs and intervening variables. *Psychological Review, 55,* 95–107.

Pellegrino, J. W., & Glaser, R. (1980). Components of inductive reasoning. In R. E. Snow, P. A. Federico, & W. E. Montague (Eds.), *Aptitude, learning and instruction: Cognitive process analyses.* Hillsdale, NJ: Erlbaum.

Revlis, R. (1975). Two models of syllogistic reasoning: Feature selection and converstion. *Journal of Verbal Learning and Verbal Behavior, 14,* 180–195.

Sells, S. B. (1936). The atmosphere effect: An experimental study of reasoning. *Archives of Psychology, 200.*

Shephard, R. N., & Metzler, J. (1971). Mental rotation of three-dimensional objects. *Science, 171,* 701–703.

Sternberg, R. J. (1977). Component processes in analogical reasoning. *Psychological Review, 31,* 356–378.

Sternberg, R. J. (1979). The nature of mental abilities. *American Psychologist, 34,* 214–230.

Sternberg, R. J., & Weil, E. M. (1981). An aptitude-strategy interaction in linear syllogistic reasoning. *Journal of Educational Psychology, 72,* 226–239.

Thurstone, L. L., & Thurstone, T. C., (1941). Factorial studies of intelligence, *Psychometric Monographs, 2.*

218   SUSAN E. EMBRETSON (WHITELY)

Toglia, M. P., & Battig, W. F. (1978). *Handbook of semantic word norms.* Hillsdale, NJ: Erlbaum.
Whitely, S. E. (1973). *Types of relationships in reasoning by analogy.* Unpublished doctoral dissertation, University of Minnesota, Minneapolis.
Whitely, S. E. (1980a). Modeling aptitude test validity from cognitive components. *Journal of Educational Psychology, 72,* 750–769.
Whitely, S. E. (1980b). Multicomponent latent trait models for ability tests. *Psychometrika, 45,* 479–494.
Whitely, S. E. (1981). Measuring aptitude processes with multicomponent latent trait models. *Journal of Educational Measurement, 18,* 67–84.
Whitely, S. E., & Barnes, G. M. (1979). The implications of processing event sequences for theories of analogical reasoning. *Memory and Cognition, 7,* 323–331.
Whitely, S. E., & Curtright, C. A. (1980, July). *Performance and stimulus complexity norms for verbal analogy test items* (Tech. Rep. NIE-80-4 for National Institute of Education). Lawrence: University of Kansas. July, 1980.
Whitely, S. E., & Schneider, L. (1980, April). *Process outcome models for verbal aptitude* (Tech. Rep. NIE-80-1 for National Institute of Education). Lawrence: University of Kansas.

8

Psychometric Models for Speed-Test Construction: The Linear Exponential Model

Hartmann Scheiblechner

SPEED IN PSYCHOLOGICAL RESEARCH

THEORETICAL RELEVANCE FOR COGNITION AND INFORMATION PROCESSING

Hunt and associates (Hunt, Frost, & Lunneborg, 1973) argued that intelligence tests should be firmly based on a dynamic theory of the thought process; there have been no objections to this argument. In contrast, traditional psychometry has developed an atheoretical pragmatic technology. The general laws and models of cognitive psychology have been neglected in favor of established individual differences in mental functioning.

Only recently the test design movement has revived the interest in whether dynamic thought processes can be used as a base for test construction. If so, then time and speed automatically become major variables that aid the identification of the hardware components (e.g., buffers, memory stores), their organization, and the software programs (e.g., encoding, recoding, retrieval, transfer, transformation) by linking them in a cognitive information-processing model (e.g., Hunt's distributed memory model). Posner's matching task (Posner & Boies, 1971), Sternberg's (1970) memory-scanning task, and the work of many others provide illustrative examples for the use of time for identifying models of mental functioning. On the other hand, ideally, psychometric tests should be derived from the dynamic thought

Copyright © 1985 by Academic Press, Inc.
All rights of reproduction in any form reserved.
ISBN 0-12-238180-7

model to measure directly the parameters of the hardware components and programs involved in different types of intellectual performance.

The Posner name versus physical identity paradigm (Posner & Boies 1971; Posner, Boies, Eichelman, & Taylor, 1969) requires that the subject identify two printed letters as being the same or different in accordance with their exact physical identity (e.g., *A* is the same as *A*) in the physical identity condition or in accordance with their name, regardless of type case (e.g., *A* is the same as *a*) in the name identity condition. The difference of approximately 70 milliseconds in reaction times is interpreted as the added time required to retrieve the name associated with each character and therefore as evidence for an additional processing stage and memory store operating in a symbol identification task.

In Sternberg's (1970) memory-scanning paradigm the subject is shown from one to five characters, displayed simultaneously for 3 seconds. Following this a probe character is shown. The subjects' task is to indicate whether or not the probe was a member of the original set of characters. Reaction time typically increases linearly with the number of items in the memory set. The slope of this function is interpreted as the average increase in reaction time (about 20 milliseconds) with an increase of one item in the memory set size. The slope is interpreted as a measure of the rate at which one can access information in short-term memory (STM).

The Clark and Chase (1972) simple sentence and picture comparison task, the Bolland Sunday + Tuesday task (cited in Hunt, Lunneborg, & Lewis, 1975), the Stroop Color-Word Interference Test, and many others provide examples for the identification of coding, scanning, comparison, semantic interference, and processes (verbal versus imaginal) involved in cognitive information processing by means of reaction times. The Clark and Chase task illustrates the well-known, but often repressed, equivalence principle. That is, equivalent overall performances can be achieved by radically different strategies. Furthermore, the Clark and Chase task illustrates the analytic principle that differing strategies can be discriminated by breaking up overall time followed by detailed, separate analysis of partial reaction times; that is, encoding or sentence comprehension can be distinguished from decision or picture verification time (Hunt, 1978). In the last section of this chapter, it is argued that the strategy by which the subject reproduces list elements from STM (or intermediate term memory [ITM] in Hunt's terms) in a free recall experiment can only be investigated by consideration of the pattern of reaction times (interresponse times) and not by a mere count of correct reproductions.

Hunt (1973; Hunt *et al.*, 1978) demonstrated quite convincingly that such mechanistic, psychophysical symbol manipulation processes as measured by the tasks mentioned earlier play an important role in complex reasoning and in mental processes as assessed by traditional psychometric, especially verbal, tests. Some processes occur automatically and some require additional resources for their execution (i.e., controlled processes). The controlled processes are especially likely to constitute limiting factors of mental performance. High-verbal subjects have been shown to manipulate information in STM (or ITM) more rapidly than low verbals, to make a more rapid conversion from physical representation to a conceptual meaning (e.g., to recognize a word as a word or a letter as a letter), to be able to hold more information in STM, and to retain better the presentation order of information.

These results indicate a relationship between active memory processes and production systems. Active memory (also called current information processing [CIP]) is the work space within which information manipulation takes place. A production is a symbolic transformation rule together with an action device. The speed and reliability of mechanistic active memory processes limit the feasibility of using complex production systems.

Such results indicate the possibility of measuring intelligence by a person's information-processing capacity. These specific measures could be more telling in studies of the biological control of cognition (e.g., studies of retardation etiologies and therapeutic actions) than generalized intelligence test measures.

Last, but not least, the advancement of computer-aided instruction and computer-directed assessment gives increasing importance to the careful timing of exposure of learning and test materials. This technology makes the measurement of response latency feasible for routine testing.

PSYCHOMETRIC AND APPLIED CONSIDERATIONS

In the following sections, the linear exponential model (LEM; Scheiblechner, 1979), including some new developments relevant for practical applications (proven in Appendixes I and II), is explained. Then, a new distribution-free generalization of LEM, the monotone probabilistic additive conjoint measurement structure (MPAM) is presented. Both models are applicable to psychometric speed test data, but ideally psychophysical tasks such as Posner's or Sternberg's paradigm, referred to earlier, should be analyzed and tested by the same formal structures as well.

It is generally accepted that by the observation of continuous variables such as reaction times, more information can be gained than by qualitative observations. However, the appropriate psychometric models for data analysis are less well known and reaction times pose additional problems. In the present section the following issues are discussed with special reference to LEM: (1) the summation of reaction times, (2) group testing and the speed versus power procedure of experimental assessment, (3) false (and missing) reactions and the speed – accuracy trade-off problem, (4) individual model fitting versus psychometric models with individual parameters, and (5) the use of strong versus weaker ordinal models.

For practitioners and applied psychometricians, the analysis of reaction times is by far most convenient if they simply can add them over items, persons, or presentations. In this way a representative, meaningful measure is obtained, although the items or presentations may differ in difficulty and the persons may vary in performance. The alternative is to assess and keep track of every single reaction of each individual separately. The reasonableness and optimality of the summation procedure (the measurement of a single total working time instead of many separate reactions included) involves, however, the statistical concept of sufficiency, which in turn implies a model of the exponential family type. The sufficiency means that by the summation no information is lost (relative to the information present in the single reactions), and if the sum is intended to preserve full information then the model must be of the exponential family type. The LEM is the simplest formal structure that grants the optimality of summation and yet allows for a full quantitative analysis of the data in terms of individual, item, and experimental condition parameters.

A major concern for the practitioner (of decreasing importance with the advancement of computer-directed testing) is the feasibility of group testing, which in the case of reaction times is linked with the speed versus power procedure of experimental assessment. If a psychometric test is presented with a fixed time limit and the number of correct responses per subject is counted, this is the speed condition of test administration. If time for work on the test is unlimited and the total time needed to complete the whole test is measured per subject, this is the power condition of experimental assessment. Group testing usually required the speed condition for test presentation, where the time limit should be chosen such that at most two or three subjects per group complete the whole test within the limited time.

Now the problem of comparison of the two experimental measures, number of items solved versus total time needed, arises. The LEM not only gives an efficient and simple estimator of the person parameter for the speed condition and thus allows for group testing, but the estimator is equivalent to the power condition (as shown in Appendix II). Thus the two experimental procedures become completely comparable. This implies that (1) the experimental conditions for test administration can be chosen from a widely varying range and (2) the time limit (and/or the set of experimental tasks) can be adapted specifically to the group of testees at hand or the psychological question under consideration, and yet comparable measures are ensured. The common scale of comparison is neither the raw score (number of items solved) nor the total time needed but the person's standing on a unidimensional (latent) scale of ability or performance.

A further point is the problem of wrong (or missing) responses, a tedious and complicated matter for the psychometrician but fascinating to the cognitive psychologist as a speed–accuracy trade-off. The LEM is derived under the assumption (definition) that all responses are correct or, more precisely, that wrong responses do not terminate the latency. In all cases, the latency is defined as ending only with a correct response. Therefore, LEM should only be applied if the percentage of errors is low, perhaps around 3%.

However, LEM does give a limited hindsight response to the problem of errors or speed–accuracy trade-off. In the speed condition, the raw score is simply reduced by the (small) number of errors. This amounts to the fiction that all the time lost for errors occurred at the item following the last correct response of the subject and forms part of the time where he or she tried in vain to find the next correct response. This fiction is formally perfectly correct if the item with the last correct response and the item where the error occurred have the same difficulty. It is a reasonable approximation to the extent that the number of errors and the differences in item difficulties are small. In the power condition, subjects with errors are treated as if they were tested in the speed condition with their total time needed as time limit and their raw score defined by the total number of test items minus the number of errors.

Both scoring algorithms derive from the lack-of-memory assumption for the exponential distribution and from the result proven in Appendix II that in the speed condition the ineffectual time following the last correct response can simply be ignored for person parameter estimation. The lack of memory assumption means that if a latency is interrupted at an arbitrary point in time (under the condition that it has not ended before) and started again, the remaining latency is distributed the same as the latency from the beginning. Both procedures for the treatment of errors could be replaced by more elaborate and precise estimations (they tend to disadvantage the subjects with errors somewhat) but it is important for a latency model to be robust against a small number of errors and to provide simple and close approximations.

Why should the cognitive psychologist, interested in general laws and not in individual differences, care about psychometric models? First, taking reaction times as in Posner's or Sternberg's paradigm is largely meaningful only to the extent that it is ensured that all subjects actually use the strategy and follow the model assumed by the experimenter. If the psychological processes actually differ essentially from the model, then it is helpful at least to ensure that the processes are alike for all subjects.

Second, although the cognitive models predominantly are fitted individually (not to speak about the very questionable group mean fitting), large parts of the inference rest on the inter- and intraindividual comparison of the resulting parameters across and within subjects and experimental conditions. That is, although not primarily designed to be measures of individual differences they are used as if they were individual measures.

Third, from a formal, statistical point of view, observing reactions of the same subject over repeated, usually varying presentations and experimental conditions presents just the same problem as collecting data from a set of items and individuals. That is, the problem of nuisance parameters is the same in both areas.

Fourth (but related to the second and third points), psychometric models such as LEM provide the statistical rationale for the common summation, averaging, or fitting procedures of individual cognitive models. In short, individual differences are present and play equally important parts even if the researcher is only interested in general laws. The individual differences problem and the problem of general laws cannot be separated. It is important for general laws to show that they are general (i.e., valid for all subjects). Elaborate psychometric models can be applied to psychophysical data and treat the problem of generality or concordance of mental processes of different subjects under the heading of model control (test of fit for the model). For example, in the Clark and Chase simple sentence and picture comparison task (where the subject establishes the truth of the sentence " − not above + " with respect to the picture ±) the sentence can be converted into an internal imaginal representation and compared with the mental representation of the picture. This strategy is preferred by high-spatial subjects (Hunt, 1978). Or the picture can be converted into an internal symbolic (verbal) representation and compared with the internal representation of the sentence. This strategy is preferred by high-verbal subjects. A psychometric analysis of reaction times may well detect the presence of two different types of reactions (processes) and subjects.

Finally, parametric models as LEM are notoriously strong models; otherwise they could not have the elegant properties previously mentioned. That is, they make very strong assumptions. Given a large enough sample and crucially relevant test of the fit (tailored to the substantial process under investigation) it is certain that they eventually will turn out not to be literally valid even if they give a quite precise representation of data. Therefore it is wise to consider weaker (ordinal or qualitative) models that retain the gist and essential (though perhaps less elegant) qualities of the strong models but avoid statistically strong and psychologically less important assumptions. The MPAM is the distribution-free ordinal analogue of LEM, retaining the additive structure and probabilistic character of LEM as well as the ordinal information of the dependent variable. However, it does not require the exponential assumption.

THE MODEL

THE MODEL FOR A SINGLE-LATENCY DISTRIBUTION

Imagine a subject trying to solve a typical speed test item, such as a simple arithmetic task. The subject knows and is able to perform the correct response; the only problem is finding it in memory and executing it as quickly as possible. Suppose the brain produces an unobservable rapid sequence of trial responses or flow of associations, some of them correct, some not. Some or all of the trial responses are selected and tested for appropriateness. If the trial response fits the task it is executed (see Figure 1). If the flow of trial responses runs with constant speed and contains a constant fraction of appropriate answers (independent of time), the proba-

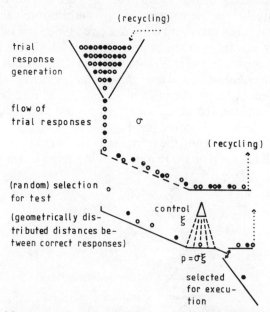

FIGURE 1. Memory search process model. σ, probability of a trial response being correct; ξ, probability of subject selecting and correctly identifying a trial response; $p = \sigma\xi$, probability of subject selecting a correct response in one working cycle of duration Δt. Recycling of missed alternatives may or may not be assumed.

bility p of a correct overt response in a short interval of time Δt, given that it has not occurred before, is the product of the probability of a trial response to be correct and the probability of selecting and correctly identifying a trial response. The waiting time or latency for the correct overt response (i.e., the number of trials to the first success) will be distributed geometrically (Albert, 1973; Feller, 1966; Johnson & Kotz, 1970; McGill, 1963).

Now let Δt, the duration of a single working cycle of the memory search mechanism (which is defined as the generation and testing of one trial response, if it has been selected), approach zero under the restriction that $p/\Delta t$ approaches a constant λ. Then the latency t becomes a continuous variable and the geometric distribution attains its limiting exponential distribution:

$$f(t) = \lambda \exp(-\lambda t), \qquad \lambda > 0, t > 0, \qquad \lambda = \lim_{\Delta t \to 0} p/\Delta t \qquad (1)$$

Also note that the expected value of the distribution is given as follows:

$$E(T) = 1/\lambda$$

The parameter λ is called the intensity (rate, hazard, or time constant) of the process because the density element $\lambda \cdot dt$ is the instantaneous conditional probability that the latency terminates in the brief interval dt following time t, given that it has survived t (Cox & Lewis, 1968; McGill, 1963).

A more modern interpretation of this process is based on a holographic memory model (Pribram, 1971; Weisstein & Harris, 1980). In one form of holography, monochromatic and monophasic light (e.g., a laser) is split into two beams. One of them, the reference beam, is led directly towards a photographic template; the other is directed toward and reflected by the object whose image is to be stored (see Figure 2).

The reflected wave front and the reference beam interfere and the pattern of interference is recorded on the template. If the object is removed and the

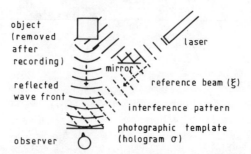

FIGURE 2. Holographic memory model. The pattern of interference is stored on the photographic template. If the transparent template is illuminated by the reference beam, the wave front reflected by the object is recovered and its image appears.

transparent photographic template illuminated by the reference beam, the observer behind the template sees a three-dimensional image of the original object. By varying the angle and/or wavelength of the reference beam, a large number of different images can be stored in the same storage space and each of them can be retrieved separately by using the appropriate reference beam. A holographic memory has tremendous capacity, is content-addressable, offers parallel access, and is associative. If part of the information on the hologram is destroyed, the image can still be recovered from the remaining fragment with overall structure intact, though with less detail. In the original mechanical memory model (Figure 1), the control instance can be substituted by the reference beam (ξ reflecting the ability of the subject to use the appropriate reference beam) and the flow of trial responses by the photographic template (σ reflecting the quality and amount of information stored on the hologram).

The exponential distribution of response latencies is compatible not only with a serial model but with parallel and stepwise models as well. Assume that the subject starts several parallel search processes at different places in his or her memory storage simultaneously. If their number is moderately large, the processes are independent, and their individual intensities λ_i (reciprocals of average latencies) are small, the waiting time to the nearest success approaches the exponential distribution (Feller, 1966). Further, McGill (1963) modeled a stepwise response generation process or serial search process with a random number of unobservable subresponses where the number of subresponses (partial solutions) is distributed geometrically and the component latencies are independent, identically distributed exponential variates. It follows that the total latency to the correct overt response is distributed exponentially. Thus there are a number of quite different process models leading to the exponential distribution, so that at the outset it can be considered a reasonable model for response latencies in typical speed test situations to a first order of approximation.

The intensity λ is constant over time for the exponential distribution. However, if more generally it is assumed that the subject may use systematic search strategies initiating the search at the most promising places in the search region or, on the contrary, successively advancing more and more promising regions, then the supply of adequate trial responses and consequently the intensity will not be constant but rather a function of time.

More formally, let $f(t)$ be the density and $F(t) = \text{prob}(T \leq t)$ the distribution function of a latency. Then $R(t) = 1 - F(t) = \text{prob}(T > t)$ is called the survivor function. Then $\lambda(t) = f(t)/R(t)$ is the intensity function and is proportional to the instantaneous conditional probability of a correct overt response in the short interval dt, given that the latency has survived t.

Simple special cases with monotone intensity functions are the Weibull distributions (Johnson & Kotz, 1970). The latency T of a Weibull distribution can be transformed into an exponential distribution by the power law transformation $T^* = (T - \tau_0)^c$, $c > 0$. The parameter τ_0 is a lower limit for the latency, which may be interpreted as a fixed unavoidable delay, and c is the shape parameter with $c = 1$ corresponding to a constant intensity and therefore to the exponential distribution. The intensity decreases monotonically if $c < 1$, it increases linearly if $c = 2$, and it gives a distribution very similar in shape to the normal distribution if c is in the neighborhood of 3.6. If c and τ_0 are known from the outset, simple systematic strategies can be included in the exponential reaction time model.

THE PSYCHOMETRIC MODEL FOR SPEEDED TEST DATA

Now let the same subject solve several speeded test items with varying easiness. Without loss of generality it can be assumed the intensities λ of the items to be given by $\lambda, \lambda + \varepsilon_2, \lambda + \varepsilon_3, \ldots$. If several subjects with varying ability solve the standard item the intensities can be assumed to be given by λ, $\lambda + \theta_2, \lambda + \theta_3, \ldots$. This suggests the psychometric latency model

$$f_{vi}(t) = (\theta_v + \varepsilon_i) \exp[-(\theta_v + \varepsilon_i)t], \tag{2}$$

where $\theta_v + \varepsilon_i > 0$.

Of course, it cannot be taken for granted that the subject parameters θ_v reflecting the efficiency of the search procedure and the item parameters ε_i reflecting the easiness of the task combine additively for all pairings of items and subjects. This, however, is a testable consequence of the model. Furthermore, the additive combination looks compensatory as if a hologram or a reference beam alone could be sufficient, separately, for a successful retrieval. Of course, a good image can be recognized quite well even with bad illumination.

From the considerations in the preceding section a multiplicative model would be expected. However, as scholars of conjoint measurement we observe that all parameters $\theta + \varepsilon$ have to be positive in the model, in Equation (2). If the scales are not fixed a priori, as is generally the case for parametric testing models, an additive and a multiplicative connection cannot be distinguished by only ordinal relations. There exists a simple monotone transformation converting multiplication into addition. Conversely, the substitution $\theta + \varepsilon = \ln \xi\sigma$ produces an equivalent multiplicative version of the model

$$f_{vi}(t) = (\ln \xi_v\sigma_i)(\xi_v\sigma_i)^{-t} \quad \text{for} \quad \xi_v\sigma_i > 0,$$

where $\ln \xi_v\sigma_i$ is only a normalizing constant.

Fischer (Fischer & Kisser, 1982) has shown that if the sum is required to be sufficient and if the reaction times depend monotonically on a subject and item parameter in an exponential latency model, then a transformation exists such that the subject and item parameter combine additively. More simply, the conjunction of the subject and item parameters has to be additive in an exponential latency model if the sum is required to be sufficient.

Suppose now that the items have been constructed and/or are administered according to the conditions of a given experimental design or that a psychological theory exists specifying the component processes involved in the tasks. Let (a_{il}) be a matrix of known constants specifying the frequency or amount to which each of the components l is present in every item i of the test. To each component is attached an easiness (or difficulty) parameter η_l. The following linear model is assumed to hold:

$$\varepsilon_i = \sum_l^m a_{il}\eta_l \tag{3}$$

where $l = 1, 2, \ldots, m < k$.

The model in Equation 2 together with Equation 3 is called the linear exponential model (LEM), as discussed earlier. Because there are (considerably) fewer unknown parameters η than ε, Equation 3 is an additional simplification of the model, resulting from additional knowledge about the structural components contained in the tasks. The theory embodied in Equation 3 and competing theories can be tested by conditional likelihood ratio tests.

An illustration of a linear theory is the simplest possible model for Posner's name versus physical identity paradigm. Suppose only three (compound) processes to be involved:

1. e = the perceptual encoding of two printed letters,
2. pc = the comparison of two internal perceptual codes, and
3. nc = the name association and comparison of two letter-name codes.

Let e correspond to the difficulty parameter η_1 and the task frequency constants a_{i1}; let pc correspond to the difficulty parameter η_2 and the constants a_{i2}; and let nc correspond to the difficulty parameter η_3 and the constants a_{i3}. The model for the basic types of tasks can then be summarized as in Table 1.

The linear model specified in Table 1 is one possible version in accordance with the interpretation of Posner's task given in the first section. Only one parameter is actually involved, as can be seen from the presence of only two classes of tasks (with Models 110 versus 111, respectively). Many alternative versions come to one's mind. For example, AA_n may be subsumed to the second class of tasks and/or the model of this class may be changed from

TABLE 1

LINEAR MODEL FOR POSNER'S NAME
VERSUS PHYSICAL IDENTITY PARADIGM[a]

Task	Correct response	Model		
		a_{i1} (e)	a_{i2} (pc)	a_{i3} (nc)
AA_p	Same			
Aa_p	Different			
AB_p	Different	1	1	0
Ab_p	Different			
AA_n	Same			
Aa_n	Same			
AB_n	Different	1	1	1
Ab_n	Different			

[a] p, physical identity condition; n, name identity condition; e, pc, nc, and a_{i1}, a_{i2}, a_{i3} explained in the text.

110 to 101. A closer empirical investigation may well reveal the necessity of a more complex model even for such a seemingly elementary paradigm.

ESTIMATION AND TESTING PROCEDURES

Parameter estimation and testing goodness of fit of the model are fully described in Scheiblechner (1979). The statistical procedures are characterized by the principle of specific objectivity (Rasch, 1960, 1961) or, equivalently, the principle of (minimal) sufficiency and conditional inference (Andersen, 1973).

First, the item parameters ε or component parameters η are estimated by conditional maximum likelihood (CML). The estimates are sample-free or specifically objective, that is, the estimates of the item parameters have the same invariant expectation regardless of the particular sampling procedure applied to the population of subjects (excluding degenerate samples and sampling only from the population for which the model is valid).

Second, in practice the subject parameters are estimated by ordinary maximum likelihood for reasons of economy. The specific objectivity of the subject parameter estimate means that the expectation of the estimate does not depend on the particular sample of items presented to the subject (excluding degenerate samples and sampling only from the task universe for which the model is valid). This is very important in practice because different subpopulations of subjects can be administered different subsets of respectively appropriate items, avoiding too-trivial items for the advanced subjects and not frustrating less able subjects by too-difficult tasks.

Third, in theory a powerful parameter-free test of the model can be derived. In practice, conditional likelihood ratio tests are performed testing the fit of the model (Equation 2) or testing linear assumptions (Equation 3) or comparing alternative (hierarchical) models.

The LEM is an attempt to open familiar results of latency modeling to speeded test construction and to base the measurement on a rational analysis of the process under investigation. The test construction phase has to be distinguished properly from test administration. For test construction, the separate measurement of each latency is required. However, once the test items and their parameters have been determined, the total time needed to complete the test is a sufficient statistic for subject parameter estimation in the power condition of test administration.

In Appendix II the subject parameter estimation procedure is derived for the speed condition and its equivalence to the estimator for the power condition is shown. The consequences of this equivalence for the appropriate choice of experimental conditions tailored to the specific group of subjects at hand and for the treatment of errors have been discussed earlier in the context of desirable properties of models for speeded test construction.

As a substantial consequence, the possibility of investigating true (i.e., completely testable) developmental growth curves ought to be mentioned. Subjects at low developmental levels can be given elementary and easy tasks, whereas for those at high developmental levels the tasks may be chosen to be quite complex and difficult. The subject parameter estimates will nevertheless be on the same scale because of the specific objectivity or sample-free property of the LEM model (of course, the validity of the model and a sufficient overlap of the sets of tasks at successive mastery levels must be assumed). In addition, low-level subjects can be given a long time limit and high-level subjects can be given a short time limit for work on the test without change of the measurement scale. No arbitrary equivalence conventions for the comparison of mastery level will be required, which is a logical prerequisite for a meaningful growth curve investigation.

The case of equal item parameters, not considered in the original formulation of the model, is treated in Appendix I. As a consequence a more robust CML parameter estimation algorithm is now available. Fischer and Kisser (1983) used the simple, however biased, joint maximum likelihood (JML) estimation procedure where equal item parameters cause no complications.

REAL TIME OR LATENT ADDITIVITY OF REACTION TIMES TO COMPOUND TASKS?

Reaction times to compound tasks very often are treated by Donder's classic subtraction method, made popular again in more recent years by the work of Sternberg (1970) and many others. The basic idea is very simple. Suppose the subjects need an average time X_1 for the correct solution of a given task. A new part is added to the otherwise unchanged task (e.g., the result has to be converted from yards to meters). If now the subjects need the time X_2 for solution it is concluded that the difference $X_2 - X_1$ is the time requirement for the new part. Typically, predictions are only made for averages and not for individual data.

The subtraction method is correct only if none of the components (parts) changes its character by recombination; that is, if the parts are invariant (and independent) under recombination. If a linear model (regression or analysis of variance) is fitted, then the invariance (and independence) hypothesis is confirmed by the absence of interaction. If probabilities for correct solution are considered, then the multiplication of the separate probabilities of success is the analogous method.

The simple additive (or multiplicative) model for real times (or probabilities) is typically true only for relatively elementary serial tasks (e.g., Mulholland, Pellegrino, & Glaser, 1980). The next level of complexity for modeling is to resort to conditional probabilities and conditional expected latencies for the components, conditional upon one or more preceding and notably future components (not to neglect foresight). For a linear model, this corresponds to the inclusion of interactions. At some order of conditionality or level of interaction the model is bound to be correct and eventually becomes trivial.

An alternative for an additive real-time model (or multiplicative observable solution probabilities model) is a latent additive model. The components may lose their invariance and independence by recombination. They may form a new supraordinate unit (or Gestalt) for the subject whose difficulties combine and have to be mastered simultaneously rather than sequentially, like the height and width of a hurdle.

For example, consider the slalom racer depicted in Figure 3. The racer has to start at a given point and pass through Gate 1. A difficulty component of Gate 1 cannot be discussed in the sense of real time needed or observed probability of success. The difficulty of Gate 1 depends on the gate that follows. Gate 1 is trivial if Gate 2 follows (because it affords no change of direction) but may become very difficult if something like Gate 2' follows. The gate acquires meaning only if it is clear where to start and which gate follows. The gates together form a new unit, a hurdle that must be

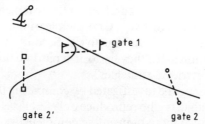

FIGURE 3. The combination of task components.

mastered at a single stroke. The multiplication of probabilities or the addition of component times does not make sense. A new unit can be formed by the addition of latent parameters—contrary to the gestalt principle that the whole is more than the sum of its parts. The important aspect of latent additivity is that the task has to be solved as one unit and not just by serial joining of parts.

This reasoning also conforms to a system-theoretic approach. Using Laplace transforms, the output function of a linear system is the product of the input and transfer function. The output function is not found by operation on real measurement values but by Laplace transformation, which is a latent representation and abstract form of operation.

This is not to say that a latent additive model like LEM or MPAM (which includes as a special case the real-time additive model) will always fit. But rather such a model should be tested as a simple and sometimes plausible alternative if a real-time linear model does not fit or leads to an undue degree of complication.

APPLICATION TO INTERRESPONSE LATENCIES OF A FREE RECALL EXPERIMENT

This experiment was performed by Meyer (1973) for an investigation of the list length effect. Lists of 10, 20, 30, and 40 German girl's names of approximately equal familiarity were presented once to subjects (students). The names appeared separately in random order for 3 seconds on a screen and were read aloud by the subject. Immediately after the last presentation the subject had to perform a numerical computation task for 40 seconds and thereafter started the free recall. The reproductions were registered by sound recording and the interresponse times between correct recalls were measured in milliseconds on an oscilloscript.

In addition to the list length effect (the relative decrease of correct recalls with increasing length of the list), two basic psychological questions for a memory theory arise. First, where do the subjects who do not recall the complete list fail? Do they learn and retain the complete list but does their reproduction fail to be exhaustive? Or is their learning and retention defective but their memory search exhaustive? Second, how do the subjects retrieve the information? Do they perform a random memory search or do they use systematic retrieval strategies?

The first question may be investigated by comparing the temporal course of reproduction of subjects who produce only few list elements with that of subjects who reproduce more or even the complete list. If reproduction is exhaustive, then a subject recalling 6 out of 10 should be in the same position as a subject recalling 10 after having reproduced 4. The temporal structure of the latencies of the short series should agree with the end of the longer or complete reproduction series. If retention is perfect but retrieval defective, then they should agree at the beginning.

For computation, the series of varying lengths were brought into line at the last position (backward alignment) to test the first hypothesis. The fit of the model was compared with the fit of the alternative alignment of the series at the first position (forward alignment).

The second question may be investigated by the study of the intensity function for single response latencies. If the memory search during the latency of a response is random, then a constant intensity or exponential distribution model must fit. If the subject uses a systematic memory search strategy such that the chance of a correct recall does increase with the length of the silence, then an increasing intensity or Weibull distribution model with exponent larger than 1 should fit. For a systematic search with decreasing chance of a correct recall, finally, a decreasing intensity function or Weibull model with exponent less than 1 should fit. These hypotheses were investigated by systematically varying the parameters of the Weibull distribution and comparing the fit of the models. These parameters are c, the value of the exponent, and τ_0, the constant delay.

The results for backward alignment of the reproduction series and the exponential model ($c = 1$) with a constant delay ($\tau_0 = 9$) are given in Table 2 and Figures 4 and 5. Table 2 exhibits satisfactory fit in all cases. In Table 2, about 15 subjects were observed for each list length. Twice the negative conditional log likelihood ratio (CLR) defined as follows:

$$CLR = -2(1_t - (1_l + 1_s))$$

The values 1_t, 1_l, and 1_s are the log likelihoods of the data for the total, long, and short series, respectively. In this example, CLR is distributed approximately as chi-square with degrees of freedom, as follows:

$$df = (df_l + df_s) - df_t$$

The degrees of freedom, df_l, df_s, dt_t, are the numbers of free parameters in the long series, short series, and total sample, respectively. Figure 5 repre-

TABLE 2

Tests of Fit of the Model $c = 1$, $\tau_0 = 9$ (exponential distribution with a constant delay) and Backward Alignment (exhaustive memory search) for List Lengths 10, 20, 30, and 40 Items

List	Number of correct responses		Chi square	df
	Long series	Short series		
10	8–10	7 o.1.[a]	2(421,908 − (164,874 + 256,140)) = 1,788	(8 + 5) − 8 = 5
20	12–17	11 o.1.	2(902,575 − (514,434 + 380,390)) = 15,502	(15 + 9) − 15 = 9
30	19–27	18 o.1.	2(1425,529 − (726,692 + 683,553)) = 30,568	(25 + 16) − 25 = 16
40	23–33	22 o.1.	2(1894,604 − (942,014 + 938,139)) = 28,904	(31 + 20) − 31 = 20

[a] o.1., "or less."

sents graphically the fit for list length 40 where the two outer values (i.e., Positions 27 and 14) are due to the algorithm not reaching final convergence, but do not seriously impair the overall fit. The long series includes 7 subjects with from 23 to 33 correct recalls, the short series 10 subjects with from 14 to 22 correct recalls.

The alternative models (not reported here) further confirmed these results. Backward alignment generally gave a better fit than forward alignment. An exponent c equal to or somewhat less but close to 1 gave a better fit than c larger than 1. The constant delay τ_0 could vary between 8 and 14.

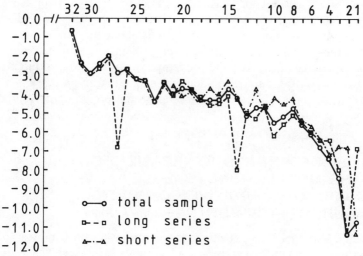

FIGURE 4. Graphic test of fit of the exponential model with a constant delay for list length 40 items. Ordinate: $\ln(\varepsilon_i + 0.00001097)$.

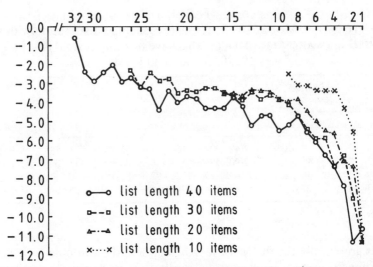

FIGURE 5.   Item (position) parameters for list lengths 10, 20, 30, and 40 items (plotted as in Fig. 4).

Thus the memory search can be considered random, with a constant delay, and exhaustive; that is, failures to recall are due to learning and retention but not to retrieval.

Figure 5 adds further (unexpected) evidence to these conclusions. The temporal pattern of reproduction as measured by parameters (not in absolute times!) is the same for all lengths of the lists. (There is some evidence that the shorter lists are reproduced with a somewhat steeper gradient, because all points for list length of 10 items lie above the curves for the other lists.) Thus a single model with essentially the same parameter values does fit for all lengths of the lists and the temporal course of reproduction does only depend on the number of elements still stored in memory at a given moment, and not on the number of elements presented or reproduced before.

SIMPLIFICATION AND GENERALIZATION OF THE MODEL: MONOTONE PROBABILISTIC ADDITIVE CONJOINT MEASUREMENT STRUCTURE (MPAM)

The LEM model can be generalized to a monotone probabilistic additive conjoint meaurement structure (MPAM). MPAM has several features that contrast with LEM. First, the dependent variable, reaction time, is only considered to be an ordinal measure. That is, a double reaction time is only interpreted to be a worse, but not just half as good, achievement. Second, no arbitrary and psychologically poorly justified distribution has to be specified in advance. The existence of some appropriate distribution simply has to be postulated, which is found a posteriori from the data. Third, the model still remains probabilistic. That is, it is not rejected by ubiquitous data variation and the fit can be tested by well-established statistical likelihood principles. MPAM combines the basic principles of parametric probabilistic measurement models and of axiomatic measurement models, but is released from the arbitrary scale and distribution assumptions of the former and solves the as yet unresolved error problem of the latter.

The following development was stimulated by critical comments of N. Verhelst on the exponential model (1981, personal communication):

Suppose the continuous variables t_{vi} to be dichotomized by introducing the new variables

$$a_{vi} = \begin{cases} 0 \text{ for correct responses within time } t_{vi} < t_0 \\ 1 \text{ for (right or wrong) responses with latency } t_{vi} \geq t_0 \end{cases}$$

where wrong and rapid responses either are neglected or eventually included in Category 1 and the time limit t_0 is arbitrary. The probability of $a_{vi} = 1$ then simply is given by the survivor function

$$\begin{aligned} P(a_{vi} = 1|\theta_v, \varepsilon_i, t_0) &= P(T_{vi} > t_0|\theta_v, \varepsilon_i) \\ &= \exp[-(\theta_v + \varepsilon_i)t_0] \\ &= \exp(-\theta_v t_0) \cdot \exp(-\varepsilon_i t_0) \\ &= \alpha_v \beta_i. \end{aligned} \tag{4}$$

Favored numerical values for the dichotomization point t_0 would be the median ($Mdn = Q_2$) and the first and third quartile (Q_1, Q_3) of all response latencies. Using one or more dichotomization points, very simple estimates of multiples of the parameters — and hence of the parameters θ_v, ε_i of the original model — can be found. If several points are dichotomized, a polychotomous (or multicategorical) model can be derived.

Reasons for dichotomization or polychotomization are simplicity, inexact measurement of latencies, or measurement errors. This reasoning also leads to simple controls of the model. Let the items be ordered in increasing order of magnitude of their marginal totals and the subjects be ordered likewise. Let Q_1, Q_2, Q_3 be the interquartile points of the total observed latency distribution. Let the entries $t_{vi} < Q_1$ be coded 1, $Q_1 \leq t_{vi} < Q_2$ be coded 2, $Q_2 \leq t_{vi} < Q_3$ be coded 3, and $t_{vi} \geq Q_3$ be coded 4. The pattern presented in Figure 6 should result.

In Figure 6 the triangular structure of the Guttman scale can be tested for each dichotomization point. If the original probabilistic model is maintained, some permutations of neighboring categories of course are allowed. In Figure 6, category h is defined by a correct response within the hth interval with lower limit t_{h-1} and upper limit t_h, $h = 1, 2, \ldots, K$ and $t_0 = 0$, $t_K = \infty$) and its probability is given by the difference of two survival probabilities.

The notion of a continuous dichotomization point leads to Spearman rank correlation coefficients between columns for item selection and between rows for eventual identification of divergent subject subpopulations. As overall tests, the corresponding Kendall coefficients of concordance can be computed. The model implies monotonically increasing rows and columns except for random permutations and nonnegative correlations. The level of the correlations depends on the sample, and the correlation between items gets larger as the subject variance gets larger. The correlations fall to zero if the individual differences vanish. More precisely, the model implies the conditions of a monotone probabilistic additive (conjoint) measurement structure, or MPAM for short.

Definition: A double indexed data set $((t_{vi}))$ is called an MPAM if scales θ and ε and a probability distribution function $F(t|\theta, \varepsilon)$ exist that conform to the data and satisfy the following conditions:

1. $F(t|\theta, \varepsilon) < F(t|\theta, \varepsilon + \delta)$ for $\delta > 0$
2. $F(t|\theta, \varepsilon) < F(t|\theta + \delta, \varepsilon)$
3. $F(t|\theta + \delta, \varepsilon) = F(t|\theta, \varepsilon + \delta)$

Conditions 1 and 2 express the monotonicity of the distribution function with increasing item and subject parameter. Condition 3 corresponds to the double cancellation condition of additive conjoint measurement structures

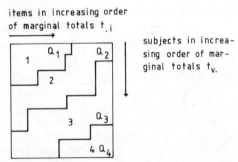

FIGURE 6. Polychotomization of latencies by quartile points where Q_1 is chosen such that $P(T < Q_1) = .25$, Q_2 corresponds to $P(T < Q_2) = .5$, and Q_3 corresponds to $P(T < Q_3) = .75$. (A dot in $t_{.i}$ and $t_{v.}$ signifies a summation over the corresponding index)

and expresses the postulate that equal increments to the item or subject parameter produce the same increment of the distribution function. Applying MPAM in practice, the scales θ and ε can be found from the data $((t_{vi}))$ by using one of the algorithms for additive conjoint measurement structures. When the appropriate scales have been constructed, the best-fitting distribution function can be found empirically (!) by principles of monotone regression and maximum likelihood estimation.

APPENDIX I
Equal Item Parameters

The model as stated by Scheiblechner (1979) required all item parameters to be different, $\varepsilon_i \neq \varepsilon_j$ for all pairs $i \neq j; i, j = 1, 2, \ldots k$. This assumption caused serious problems of convergence for the conditional estimation algorithm published by Scheiblechner (1978) if two or more item parameters came near to equality. The problem is evident, because several of the likelihood functions (e.g., compare Equation [4] in Scheiblechner, 1979) required the computation of the functions γ_v, for example

$$\gamma_v = \sum_{i=1}^{k} \exp(-\varepsilon_i t_{v.}) \prod_{j \neq i}^{k} (\varepsilon_j - \varepsilon_i)^{-1} \qquad v = 1, 2, \ldots, n \qquad (5)$$

where

$$t_{v.} = \sum_{i=1}^{k} t_{vi}$$

and where the product approaches infinity if one of the differences approaches zero. The author discussed the problem with N. Verhelst (1981, personal communication), who suggested considering the limit as one of the differences approaches zero. There is a very simple remedy for the problem, sufficient for all practical purposes, which simply is to exclude all but one of the items with equal or almost equal parameters from the conditional item parameter estimation and to reintroduce them for subject parameter estimation where they cause no complications (see Equation 11). The procedure might become tedious, involving trial and error, and is not satisfactory for theoretical reasons. Therefore, one should proceed by deriving exact distributions for the case of equal item parameters.

The simultaneous density of the separate latencies of $k \geq 1$ items with equal parameter ε is

$$f_{vk_\varepsilon}(t_{v1}, t_{v2}, \ldots, t_{vk}) = (\theta_v + \varepsilon)^k \exp(-(\theta_v + \varepsilon)t_{v+})$$

$$t_{v+} = \sum_{i=1}^{k} t_{vi} \qquad (6)$$

where t_{v+} is written to distinguish the sum over identical items from $t_{v.}$, the sum over arbitrary items. The density of the sum t_{v+} of the latencies of k identical items is obtained by computing the $(k-1)$-fold convolution integral over Eq. (6) and gives

$$f_{vk_+}(t_{v+}) = (\theta_v + \varepsilon)^k \exp[-(\theta_v + \varepsilon)t_{v+}]$$

$$\cdot \int_0^{t_{v+}} \int_0^{t_{v+}-r} \int_0^{t_{v+}-r-s} \cdots \int_0^{t_{v+}-r-s\ldots-z} dz \ldots du \, ds \, dr$$

$$= (\theta_v + \varepsilon)^k \exp(-(\theta_v + \varepsilon)t_{v+}) \cdot t_{v+}^{(k-1)}/(k-1)! \tag{7}$$

where $t, r, s, \ldots, z$ stand for the component latencies of the 1st, 2nd, $\ldots$, kth item, respectively.

Assuming next two identical and one divergent item to be given, the likelihood density of the sum of the latencies is obtained:

$$L\{t_{v.}|\varepsilon_1 = \varepsilon_2 = \varepsilon, \varepsilon_3\} = \prod_i^3 (\theta_v + \varepsilon_i) \exp(-\theta_v t_{v.})$$

$$\cdot \int_0^{t_{v.}} \int_0^{t_{v.}-r} \exp(-\varepsilon(r+s) - \varepsilon_3(t_{v.} - r - s)) \, ds \, dr$$

$$= \prod_i^3 (\theta_v + \varepsilon_i) \exp(-\theta_v t_{v.}) \int_0^{t_{v.}} u$$

$$\cdot \exp[-\varepsilon u - \varepsilon_3(t_{v.} - u)] \cdot du$$

$$= \prod_i^3 (\theta_v + \varepsilon_i) \exp(-\theta_v t_{v.})$$

$$\cdot [(t_{v.} - (\varepsilon_3 - \varepsilon)^{-1}) \exp(-\varepsilon t_{v.}) (\varepsilon_3 - \varepsilon)^{-1}$$

$$+ \exp(-\varepsilon_3 t_{v.}) (\varepsilon - \varepsilon_3)^{-2}].$$

Continuing with three identical and one divergent item produces

$$L\{t_{v.}|\varepsilon_1 = \varepsilon_2 = \varepsilon_3 = \varepsilon, \varepsilon_4\}$$

$$= \prod_i^4 (\theta_v + \varepsilon_i) \exp(-\theta_v t_{v.}) \int_0^{t_{v.}} s^2/2 \cdot \exp(-\varepsilon s - \varepsilon_4(t_{v.} - s))$$

$$= \prod_i^4 (\theta_v + \varepsilon_i) \exp(-\theta_v t_{v.})[(t_{v.}^2/2 - (\varepsilon_4 - \varepsilon)^{-1}(t_{v.} - 3(\varepsilon_4 - \varepsilon)^{-1}))$$

$$\cdot \exp(-\varepsilon t_{v.}) \cdot (\varepsilon_4 - \varepsilon)^{-1} + \exp(-\varepsilon_4 t_{v.}) (\varepsilon - \varepsilon_4)^{-3}].$$

For the general case assume k_1 single items, k_2 item pairs, and k_3 triples of items with identical parameters to be given. Let $I_1 = \{1, 2, \ldots, k_i\}$,

$I_2 = \{1, 2, \ldots, k_2\}$, $I_3 = \{1, 2, \ldots, k_3\}$, the index sets corresponding to singles, pairs, and triples, respectively. Let the $k = k_1 + 2k_2 + 3k_3$ items be indexed by $I = \{1, 2, \ldots, k_1, k_1 + 1, k_1 + 2, \ldots, k_1 + 2k_2, k_1 + 2k_2 + 1, \ldots, k_1 + 2k_2 + 3k_3\}$ and let ε_{2i} correspond to the parameter of the ith pair, that is, $\varepsilon_{2i} = \varepsilon_{k_1+2i} = \varepsilon_{k_1+2i-1}$; let ε_{3i} correspond to the parameter of the ith triple, that is $\varepsilon_{3i} = \varepsilon_{k_1+2k_2+3i} = \varepsilon_{k_1+2k_2+3i-1} = \varepsilon_{k_1+2k_2+3i-2}$; and let $I - I_{2i}$ be the index set of all items except the ith pair and $I - I_{3i}$, correspondingly, for triples. The likelihood density of the sum of latencies is given by

$$L\{t_{v.}|I_1, I_2, I_3\} = \prod_i^k (\theta_v + \varepsilon_i) \exp(-\theta_v t_{v.})$$

$$\cdot \left[\sum_{i \in I_1}^{k_1} \exp(-\varepsilon_i t_{v.}) P_{1i} \right.$$

$$+ \sum_{i \in I_2}^{k_2} (t_{v.} - S_{2i}) \exp(-\varepsilon_{2i} t_{v.}) P_{2i}$$

$$\left. + \sum_{i \in I_3}^{k_3} (t_{v.}^2/2 - P_{3i}(t_{v.} - S_{3i})) \exp(-\varepsilon_{3i} t_{v.}) P_{3i} \right], \quad (8)$$

where

$$P_{1i} = \prod_{j \neq i}^k (\varepsilon_j - \varepsilon_i)^{-1},$$

$$P_{2i} = \prod_{j \in I - I_{2i}}^k (\varepsilon_j - \varepsilon_{2i})^{-1},$$

$$P_{3i} = \prod_{j \in I - I_{3i}}^k (\varepsilon_j - \varepsilon_{3i})^{-1},$$

$$S_{2i} = \sum_{j \in I - I_{2i}}^k (\varepsilon_j - \varepsilon_{2i})^{-1},$$

$$S_{3i} = \sum_{j \in I - I_{3i}}^k (\varepsilon_j - \varepsilon_{3i})^{-1},$$

and the term in square brackets corresponds to the generalized function γ_v with pairs and triples of items with identical parameters.

Substituting the γ_v functions from Equation (8) into the conditional likelihood function for item parameter estimation (Equation [6] in Scheiblechner, 1979), the problem is essentially solved where for $n$tuples of identical items with $n > 3$ some items still have to be eliminated. At present, item parameters are set equal if their difference is smaller than $\delta = 10^{-160/k}$. The algorithm was programmed by Grüner (1982) using the STEPIT procedure by Chandler (1969). (In 3 cases out of 12, for up to $k = 32$ items the algorithm only gave approximate values not reaching final convergence).

APPENDIX II
Person Parameter Estimation for the Speed Condition and Equivalence to the Power Condition

Let c denote the constant time limit available for work on the test in the speed condition. A small number of subjects succeed in completing the test, and their total time needed is recorded by the experimenter. They actually have been tested under the power condition and for them the likelihood density is the likelihood of solving all k items of the test during time $t_{v.} = \Sigma_{i=1}^{k} t_{vi} < c$ (see Eq. [4] in Scheiblechner, 1979) and is given by

$$L\{t_{v.}|k\} = \exp(-\theta_v t_{v.}) \prod_{i}^{k} (\theta_v + \varepsilon_i) \left[\sum_{i}^{k} \exp(-\varepsilon_i t_{v.}) \prod_{j \neq i}^{k} (\varepsilon_j - \varepsilon_i)^{-1} \right] \quad (9)$$

For the other subjects the number x_v, for example, of correctly solved items within the time limit c is recorded. For them the time interval c is composed of two subintervals, for example the interval $t_{v.}$ in which they correctly solve x_v items and the interval $(c - t_{v.})$ in which they try in vain to solve the $(x_v + 1)$st item. The likelihood density of the two subintervals is the product of the likelihood of completing x_v items within the interval $t_{v.}$ and the survivor function of the $(x_v + 1)$st item at $(c - t_{v.})$. The likelihood of a total of x_v correct responses is the convolution integral over the foregoing product (summation over all possible lengths of the two subintervals that give the constant sum c).

$$L\{x_v|c\} = \int_0^c L\{t_{v.}|x_v\} R((c - t_{v.})|\varepsilon_{x_v+1}) \cdot dt_{v.}$$

$$= \int_0^c \exp(-\theta_v t_{v.}) \prod_{i}^{x_v} (\theta_v + \varepsilon_i) \sum_{i}^{x_v} \exp(-\varepsilon_i t_{v.}) \prod_{j \neq i}^{x_v} (\varepsilon_j - \varepsilon_i)^{-1}$$

$$\cdot \exp(-(\theta_v + \varepsilon_{x_v+1})(c - t_{v.})) dt_{v.}$$

$$= \exp(-\theta_v c) \prod_{i}^{x_v} (\theta_v + \varepsilon_i) \left[\sum_{i}^{x_v} (\exp(-\varepsilon_i c) - \exp(-\varepsilon_{x_v+1} c)) \right.$$

$$\left. \cdot \prod_{j \neq i}^{x_v+1} (\varepsilon_j - \varepsilon_i)^{-1} \right] \quad (10)$$

Comparing Eqs. (9) and (10) it can be seen that the first two factors are of the same form with the substitution of c for t_v and x_v for k, respectively, and they only differ by the term in square brackets, which, however, does not depend on θ_v. It follows from this that upon taking logarithms, differentiating partially with respect to θ_v and setting zero both give identical likelihood equations for maximum likelihood subject parameter estimation (see Eqs. [14] and [16] in Scheiblechner, 1979):

$$\frac{\partial \ln L}{\partial \theta} = \begin{cases} -t_{\alpha.} + \sum_{i}^{k} (\theta_\alpha + \varepsilon_i)^{-1} = 0 & \text{for } t_{\alpha.} < c, \\ & \text{power condition} \\ -c + \sum_{i}^{x_\alpha} (\theta_\alpha + \varepsilon_i)^{-1} = 0 & \text{for } x_\alpha < k, \\ & \text{speed condition} \end{cases} \quad (11)$$

Thus under speed and power conditions of test administration, the same estimator of the subject parameter results. It is interesting to note that the estimator in the speed condition in no way takes the (unknown) time spent in vain at item $x_v + 1$ into account, which therefore plays no role for the evaluation of the performance. The subject is treated as if the last answer were given just at the moment of the end of the time interval c. This is easily understood remembering the Markow or maximum entropy or lack of memory property of the exponential distribution (Feller, 1966; Johnson & Kotz, 1970; Rao, 1968). This property states that for the survivor function the relation $R(t + s|s) = R(t)$ is valid; that is, given that the latency has not been terminated before s seconds, the probability that the residual latency exceeds t seconds is the same that the latency lasts for more than t seconds from the beginning. The lack of memory property is just another expression of the constant intensity function. In terms of the memory model this means that the subject can gain no advantage from preceding ineffectual efforts. If confronted with the same item again, the subject would be in just the same position as at the first contact, and the solution time for the new trial would be distributed as if the subject never had seen the item before.

REFERENCES

Albert, D. (1973). Zur Theorie der retroaktiven Hemmung. (Theory of retroactive inhibition) Marburg-Lahn: *Berichte aus dem Institut für Psychologie der Philipps-Universität, 34.*

Andersen, E. B. (1973). *Conditional inference and models for measuring.* Copenhagen: Mentalhygiejnisk Forlag.

Chandler, J. P. (1969). STEPIT-Finds local minima of a smooth function of several parameters. *Behavioral Science, 14,* 81–82.

Clark, H. H., & Chase, W. G. (1972). On the process of comparing sentences against pictures. *Cognitive Psychology, 3,* 472–517.

Cox, D. R., & Lewis, P. A. W. (1968). The statistical analysis of series of events. *Methuen's monographs on applied probability and statistics.* London: Methuen.

Feller, W. (1966). *An introduction to probability theory and its applications* (Vol. 2). New York: Wiley.

Fischer, G. H., & Kisser, R. (1983). Notes on the exponential latency model and an empirical application. In H. Wainer & S. Messick (Eds.), *Principals of modern psychological measurement.* Hillsdale, NJ: Erlbaum.

Grüner, E. (1982). Computer program LEMNEU. Unpublished program description. Marburg-Lahn: Institut für Psychologie.

Hunt, E., Frost, N., & Lunneborg, C. (1973). Individual differences in cognition: A new approach to intelligence. In G. Bower (Ed.), *The Psychology of learning and motivation* (Vol. 7). New York: Academic Press.

Hunt, E., Lunneborg, C., & Lewis, J. (1975). What does it mean to be high verbal? *Cognitive Psychology, 7,* 194–227.

Hunt, E. (1978). Mechanics of verbal ability. *Psychological Review, 85,* 109–130.

Johnson, N. L., & Kotz, S. (1970). *Distributions in statistics. Continuous univariate distributions* (Vol. 1). Boston: Houghton-Mifflin.

McGill, W. J. (1963). Stochastic latency mechanisms. In R. D. Luce, R. R. Bush, & E. Galanter (Eds.), *Handbook of Mathematical Psychology* (Vol. 1). New York: Wiley.

Meyer, F. (1973). Untersuchung zum Problem des "Listenlängen-Effektes." [Investigation concerning the problem of the list-length effect] Marburg-Lahn: Institut für Psychologie der Philipps-Universität.

Mulholland, T. M., Pellegrino, J. W., & Glaser, R. (1980). Components of geometric analogy solution. *Cognitive Psychology, 12,* 252–284.

Posner, M. I., & Boies, S. (1971). Components of attention. *Psychological Review, 78,* 391–408.

Posner, M., Boies, S., Eichelman, W., & Taylor, R. (1969). Retention of visual and name codes of single letters. *Journal of Experimental Psychology (Monograph), 79,* 1–16.

Pribam, K. H. (1971). *Languages of the brain.* Englewood Cliffs, NJ: Prentice-Hall.

Rao, C. R. (1968). *Linear statistical inference and its applications.* New York: Wiley.

Rasch, G. (1960). *Probabilistic models for some intelligence and attainment tests.* Copenhagen: Danmarks Paedagogiske Institut.

Rasch, G. (1961). On general laws and the meaning of measurement in psychology. *Proceedings of the Fourth Berkeley Symposium on Mathematical Statistics and Probability, 5,* 321–333.

Scheiblechner, H. (1979). Specifically objective stochastic latency mechanisms. *Journal of Mathematical Psychology, 19,* 18–38.

Sternberg, S. (1970). Memory scanning: Mental processes revealed by reaction time experiments. In J. S. Antrobus (Ed.), *Cognition and Affect.* Boston: Little, Brown.

Weisstein, N., & Harris, C. S. (1980). Masking and the unmasking of distributed representations in the visual system. In C. S. Harris (Ed.), *Visual coding and adaptability.* Hillsdale, NJ: Erlbaum.

9

A Latent-Trait Model for Items with Response Dependencies: Implications for Test Construction and Analysis*

David Andrich

INTRODUCTION

The simple logistic model (SLM) of latent trait theory, generally known as the Rasch model (Rasch, 1960/1980), is used often now as a starting point for modeling responses to test questions. The SLM is suitable for this purpose because it is the simplest appropriate model for responses to test items that are scored in the simplest of ways, namely, dichotomously—as either correct or incorrect. Among the modifications or elaborations of the SLM, two are exemplified by the work of, first, Fischer (1973) and Spada (1977) with respect to the linear logistic test model (LLTM) and, second, Whitely (1980).[1]

In the first of these approaches, the difficulty of a dichotomously scored item is assumed to be composed of a set of difficulties of more elementary parameters. If the difficulties of each of a collection of items are composed of different combinations of the same set of elementary parameters, then these parameters can be estimated from the responses to the set of items.

* This research was supported in part by a cooperative Research Project between the State Education Department of Western Australia and The Department of Education, The University of Western Australia.
[1]S. E. Whitely is now S. Embretson.

Copyright © 1985 by Academic Press, Inc.
All rights of reproduction in any form reserved.
ISBN 0-12-238180-7

Among the advantages of the LLTM and the associated approach to item construction is that the number of elementary parameters is smaller than the number of items; therefore, an account of the data is more parsimonious than one using the SLM. In addition, the cognitive processes behind the responses can be studied more closely by considering the elementary parameters and the operations they are supposed to represent.

The approach by Embretson is similar; the response to any item is seen to be related to a set of cognitive processes she has called components. However, there are two differences between Embretson's approach and that associated with the LLTM. One is that the sequential nature of the operations that comprise an item can take various specified forms. This contrasts with the LLTM approach, in which only the operations for the successful execution of an item are postulated and no sequential or other dependencies are considered. The second difference is that Embretson's approach permits the person parameters, as well as the item parameters, to be composed of more than one component parameter. That is, the ability of each person with respect to each dichotomously scored item may itself be composed of different abilities, each ability corresponding to each component. In the LLTM, each person is characterized by one parameter and only the item difficulty parameters are resolved into more elementary parameters.

This chapter considers modifications to the SLM that, though having similar consequences to those just briefly described, are also different from them in an important way. The basic similarity resides in the reduction of the number of parameters required to characterize a set of dichotomously scored responses. The basic difference resides in the feature that instead of each difficulty parameter corresponding to a dichotomous response being resolved into a smaller number of more elementary parameters or components, the responses are clustered or pooled together, and in this way are characterized by a number of parameters that is less than the number of dichotomously scored responses.

One application of the model is to tests in which subsets of dichotomously scored items are deemed to belong together on some a priori grounds and as a result are treated as subtests. Another application is to tests in which the response to each item is of the extended form and in which different steps in the response are designated as correct or otherwise. Then each such item is treated as a single subtest. Both applications are illustrated in this chapter.

The model proposed for these two applications has two parameters for each subtest: One is the usual location or difficulty parameter and the second is the usual dispersion or scale parameter. An important aspect of the scale parameter is that it absorbs any dependence among the responses within each subtest. It accommodates, therefore, one of the more contentious assumptions of latent trait models, that of local independence. This topic is elaborated upon in the fifth section, following the derivation of the model in the next two sections and an elaboration of the contexts of its application in the fourth section.

THE RATING MECHANISM AND ASSOCIATED MODELS

The derivation of the model is approached from the point of view of a rating mechanism, and because this mechanism and its basic model have been presented in detail elsewhere (Andrich, 1978b, 1979, 1982a) only a brief exposition is provided here. The first stage in the derivation requires formalizing a threshold or cutoff point between successive categories on the latent rating continuum. The second stage involves making the assumption that the distances between successive thresholds are equal.

THE GENERAL RATING MODEL

The general rating model may be derived by taking the following key steps. For convenience, one can imagine that responses to Likert-style questionnaires are being modeled.

1. Assume that behind the rating mechanism are ordered thresholds τ_k, $k = 1 \ldots, m$, on a latent continuum that separate $m + 1$ successive categories.
2. Assume that in the first instance a judgment is made at each threshold giving a separate *dichotomous* response at each threshold.
3. Postulate the SLM for the response process at each threshold k according to

$$p\{Y_k = y; \mu, \tau_k\} = \frac{1}{\eta} \exp[y(\mu - \tau_k)],$$

where $\mu = 1 + \exp(\mu - \tau_k)$ is a normalizing factor, Y_k a Bernoulli random variable at the threshold k that takes the value of $y = 1$ if the threshold is exceeded and $y = 0$ otherwise, and $\mu = \theta - \delta$ the combined location parameter composed of θ, the person parameter, and δ, the item parameter. (In attitude measurement θ and δ represent, respectively, the person's attitude measure and the question's affective value, whereas in achievement testing they represent, respectively, the person's ability and the subtest's difficulty.

4. Introduce the random variable X, which takes the value 0 if the response is in the first category, 1 if it is in the second category, 2 if it is in

the third category, and so on until the last category for which it takes the value m.

5. Accommodate the restriction imposed by the *order* of the categories by limiting the acceptable subset of outcomes at each threshold, from the set of all possible outcomes, to those that conform to the pattern

$$
\begin{array}{lll}
(0, 0, \ldots, 0) & \text{for which} & X = 0, \\
(1, 0, \ldots, 0) & \text{for which} & X = 1, \\
(1, 1, \ldots, 0) & \text{for which} & X = 2, \\
\quad\cdot & & \quad\cdot \\
\quad\cdot & & \quad\cdot \\
\quad\cdot & & \quad\cdot \\
(1, 1, \ldots, 1) & \text{for which} & X = m.
\end{array}
$$

where the ordered m-tuplets reflect the outcomes at the respective thresholds. Clearly, this is the pattern of the Guttman scale (Guttman, 1954).

With these assumptions and definitions, the rating model takes the straightforward exponential form

$$
p\{X = x; \mu, \kappa, m\} = (1/\gamma) \exp[x\mu + \kappa_x], \tag{1}
$$

where $\gamma / = \Sigma_{k=0}^{m} \exp[k\mu + \kappa_k]$ is a normalizing factor and where

$$
\kappa_x = -\sum_{k=1}^{x} \tau_x, \quad x = 1, 2, \ldots, m,
$$

with $\kappa_0 = \kappa_m = 0$. The κ_x are the category coefficients expressed in terms of the m thresholds $\tau_1, \tau_2, \ldots, \tau_m$ on the continuum. From the definition of κ_x and κ_m, the sum of all the threshold values $\Sigma_{k=1}^{m} \tau_k$ is equal to zero. This restriction is algebraically convenient and can be imposed without loss of generality (Andrich, 1978b).

Though no interpretation of the category coefficients κ_x was provided, this model was derived by Andersen (1977) by assuming that the response categories have an order and that each person parameter θ has a simple sufficient statistic. The model, with the coefficients interpreted as just shown, has also been derived more recently in a slightly different way by Masters (1982).

Three further points should be noted. First, the coefficients of the location parameter μ are simply the successive integers commencing with 0. This means that the successive categories are *assigned* these integers and, therefore, are said to be *scored* by the integral scoring function. Second, because the threshold values are estimated, the scoring of successive categories with

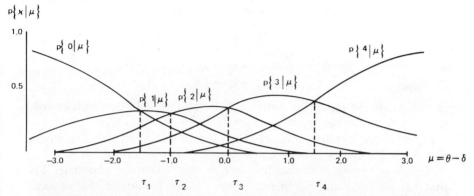

FIGURE 1. Category-characteristic curves for the integral scoring function and four un-equally spaced thresholds ($m = 4$) as a function of the difference between the person and item locations.

successive integers does not depend on any assumption regarding distances between successive thresholds. Figure 1 shows the category characteristic curves in the case where $m = 4$ and where the distances between successive thresholds are not equal. Third, each category coefficient is the opposite of the sum of the successive thresholds up to that particular category. Thus it involves an *accumulation* of the successive cutoff points on the continuum.

THE RATING MODEL WITH EQUIDISTANT THRESHOLDS

The basic model, Equation (1), can be used directly to analyze ordered response data (Andrich, 1978a; Wright & Masters, 1982). However, the emphasis here is on a specialization of this model in which the distances between thresholds are identical, so that $\tau_{x+1} - \tau_x = \tau_x - \tau_{x-1} = \lambda^* > 0$. With this assumption, the coefficients κ_x take on the following simple structure:

$$\kappa_x = \tfrac{1}{2}x(m - x)\lambda^* = x(m - x)\lambda,$$

where $\lambda^* = 2\lambda$, giving the model

$$p\{X = x; \mu, \lambda, m\} = 1/\gamma \exp[x\mu + x(m - x)\lambda]. \tag{2}$$

That $\kappa_x = x(m - x)\lambda = -\Sigma_{k=1}^{x}\tau_k$ can be readily illustrated with any value of m; $m \geq 2$. For example, consider $m = 4$, in which case there are five ordered categories. Then from $\kappa_x = x(m - x)\lambda$, $\kappa_0 = 0$, $\kappa_1 = 3\lambda$, $\kappa_2 = 4\lambda$, $\kappa_3 = 3\lambda$, and $\kappa_4 = 0$. Further, since $\kappa_x = \Sigma_{k=1}^{x}\tau_k = -(\tau_1 + \cdots + \tau_x)$,

$\kappa_x = \kappa_{x-1} - \tau_x$, so that $\tau_x = \kappa_{x-1} - \kappa_x$. Then, for $m = 4$,

$$\tau_1 = \kappa_0 - \kappa_1 = -3\lambda,$$
$$\tau_2 = \kappa_1 - \kappa_2 = -\lambda,$$
$$\tau_3 = \kappa_2 - \kappa_3 = \lambda,$$
$$\tau_4 = \kappa_k - \kappa_4 = 3\lambda,$$

in which case the successive distances between thresholds are, as required, given by $\tau_2 - \tau_1 = \tau_3 - \tau_2 = \tau_4 - \tau_3 = 2\lambda$.

Figure 2 displays the category-characteristic curves in the case where $m = 4$ and the distances between successive thresholds are equal.

A striking feature of the coefficient $\kappa_x = x(m - x)$ of the parameter λ is that it is *quadratic* and *symmetric*. Thus the first parameter, that of location, is scored *linearly* by successive integers and the second, that of scale, is scored *quadratically* by a function of the successive integers. Some general consequences that these properties have for the model have been articulated in Andrich (1982a).

Of specific interest is the new parameter λ and the roles it plays in the model. One important feature of λ, introduced as a scale parameter in terms of a distance between successive thresholds on a continuum, is that it also characterizes the dispersion of the responses. Thus, the more extreme the response the smaller the coefficient and value of λ, and vice versa. That the same parameter can be interpreted as both a scale and dispersion parameter is not surprising; it is a well-accepted relation in continuous distribution theory, where the scale is routinely transformed by a standardization of the variance. Because the model (M) characterizes the dispersion (D) of the responses through λ and their location (L) through μ, it is abbreviated DLM for convenience.

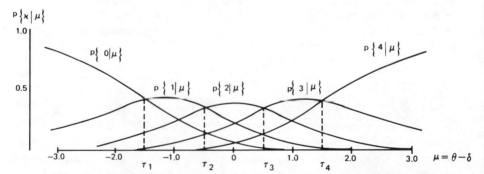

FIGURE 2. Category-characteristic curves for the integral scoring function and four equally spaced thresholds ($m = 4$) as a function of the difference between the person and item locations.

A second important feature, which will receive further elaboration, is that although λ is defined initially by $\tau_{x+1} - \tau_x = 2\lambda > 0$, it is possible to interpret both a value of zero and a negative value for λ. In the first case $\tau_x - \tau_{x-1} = 0$, and in the latter $\tau_x - \tau_{x-1} < 0$. The results may seem surprising, but they reflect the property that λ, being a coefficient of a quadratic function, characterizes the curvature of the function. Accordingly, it characterizes the curvature of the exponent in Equation (2) and therefore also the curvature of the distribution of this equation. More specifically, if $\lambda > 0$ the distribution is unimodal, if $\lambda = 0$ and conditional on the value of μ the distribution is uniform, and if $\lambda < 0$ the distribution is U-shaped. Consequently, the greater the value of λ the more peaked the mode; the smaller the value of λ, $\lambda < 0$, the sharper the U in the distribution.

Although it is convenient that the shape of the distribution, whether unimodal, uniform, or U-shaped, can be characterized by the same parametric structure, this in itself is not sufficient to understand the kind of data observed. In general, if λ is not positive, one may suspect that the rating mechanism is perhaps not working as intended (Andrich 1979, 1982a). This issue is not pursued here, though related points will be taken up later in the fifth section.

A third point to observe is that the linear and quadratic functions of the distribution are polynomials that correspond, respectively, to the first two principal components of the Guttman scale (Guttman, 1954). This result is consistent with the earlier observation that the permissable response patterns conform to a Guttman scale.

AN ELABORATION OF THE DISPERSION LOCATION MODEL

To consider explicitly a further elaboration of the DLM, it is instructive to introduce into the expressions explicit subscripts denoting persons and items. Let j denote a specific person and i a specific item. Then $\mu = \theta - \delta$ may be expressed more completely as $\mu_{ji} = \theta_j - \delta_i$.

A SCALE PARAMETER FOR EACH ITEM: THE DISPERSION LOCATION OF ITEMS MODEL

From $\mu_{ji} = \theta_j - \delta_i$, it is clear that the location of the response distribution is seen as a function of both the person and item locations. By analogy, one may consider that the *dispersion* of the distribution is also a function of both a person characteristic and an item characteristic. That is, some persons may tend to respond in extremes more than others, irrespective of the item, and some items may provoke more extreme responses than others, irrespective of the person. With this rationale, λ may be subscripted as λ_{ji}. Furthermore, and again by the analogy to the resolution of μ_{ji}, λ_{ji} may be resolved according to, for example, $\lambda_{ji} = \xi_j - \alpha_i$ where ξ_j characterizes the dispersion of the responses of person j and α_i characterizes the dispersion of responses to item i. In this form, with more than one parameter for both persons and items, the model resembles that of Whitely (1980).

This elaboration of the DLM, which is symmetric in the person and item parameters, will not be considered here. Instead, the scale parameter λ will be subscripted only by the index i, indicating that differences in dispersions among responses to items are assumed to be governed only by the items. This particular form of the DLM gives

$$p\{X_{ji} = x; \theta_j, \delta_i, \lambda_i, m_i\} = (1/\gamma_{ji}) \exp[x(\theta_j - \delta_i) + x(m_i - x)\lambda_i] \qquad (3)$$

which, because it has the dispersion parameter associated only with items (I), is abbreviated DLIM.

RELATIONSHIPS TO OTHER MODELS

In the original derivation and application of the rating model with thresholds (Andrich 1978a, 1978b) and earlier in this chapter, it was stressed that distances between thresholds were not required to be equal. However, it was assumed that the thresholds had the same values across all items. In the preceding modification of the rating model to the DLIM, the distances between successive thresholds are assumed to be equal for each item, but these distances may be different from item to item. In another modification of the rating model, Masters (1982) parameterizes each threshold of each item to give the model

$$p\{X_{ji} = x; \theta_j, \delta_i, \tau_i\} = (1/\gamma_{ji}) \exp[x(\theta_j - \delta_i) - \Sigma_{k=1}^{x}\tau_{ik}]. \qquad (4)$$

In this model the distance between successive thresholds within items are neither equal within an item nor equal across items.

In the form of Equation (4), the rating model is an alternative to the graded response model proposed by Samejima (1969). This latter model, which is a formalization of Thurstone's method of successive intervals (Edwards and Thurstone, 1952), assumes a single response process distributed either normally or logistically across all thresholds of the rating continuum. It is then postulated that the probability of a response above each threshold is either the area in a cumulative normal distribution or a logistic, where the latter is chosen usually because it is more tractable.

Applying the logistic, the probability p_x^* of a response above threshold x,

$x = 1, \ldots, m$ is given by

$$p_x^* = \frac{\exp[(\mu - \tau_x)/\sigma]}{\gamma}$$

$$= \frac{\exp[\alpha(\mu - \tau_x)]}{\gamma}, \tag{5}$$

where μ is the location as in the formulation of the rating model and σ is the variance of an underlying random process, with $\alpha = 1/\sigma$ called the discrimination. The probability p_x of a response in category $x, x = 0, 1, 2, \ldots, m$, is then given simply by the difference between successive cumulative probabilities, that is, by

$$p_x = p_x^* - p_{x+1}^* \quad \text{with} \quad p_o^* = 1 \quad \text{and} \quad p_{m+1}^* = 0.$$

While the same term, *threshold,* is used in both models for the cutoff point on the continuum, the thresholds are formalized differently and therefore have different values in the two models.

Another difference between the models in Equations (4) and (5) is in the way they accommodate the order of the thresholds. In the former, it is done by restricting the number of legitimate response patterns with the result that the successive thresholds are accumulated in the probability distribution. In the latter, the probabilities are accumulated directly across the successive thresholds.

A consequence of this difference in the way order is recognized is that the *estimates* of the thresholds in the rating model do not necessarily have to be in the assumed order. In the traditional model, Equation (5), the threshold estimates must be in the specified order. An advantage of the rating model is that it is possible for the data not to accord with the model, that is, it is possible for the data to refute the model with respect to the criterion of order on the latent continuum. In contrast, in the traditional model the order is a property of the model whether or not it is a property of the data. Thus, in principle, more can be learned about the rating continuum from the application of the rating model than from the traditional model.

A third difference between the two models is that whereas the rating model has sufficient statistics for its parameters the traditional model does not. Consequently, the estimation and related issues are much simpler in the former model, making it relatively easy to apply. However, and more importantly, the availability of sufficient statistics for the parameters indicates that the parameters are separable; thus, one set of parameters, such as the parameters of the items, can be estimated independently of the other set of parameters, the parameters of the persons. This feature places the rating model clearly within the class of Rasch measurement models. Advantages associated with these models have been described in a number of publications, but perhaps most rigorously and generally in Rasch (1961, 1977).

Another particularly relevant point to note regarding the DLIM of Eq. (3), which has a single location parameter for each person and both a location and a scale parameter for each item, is that it resembles the parameterization of the Birnbaum (1968) two-parameter model for dichotomously scored items. However, the DLIM cannot be applied to dichotomously scored items; it requires a maximum score of at least 2 or, equivalently, at least three ordered categories. Although this requirement is a constraint on the kind of data that can be analyzed according to the DLIM, it is the very feature that is exploited in the applications of the model.

As with the traditional model with ordered categories, the DLIM model and the Birnbaum model may be contrasted in that, unlike the Birnbaum model, the DLIM has simple sufficient statistics for its parameters. The set of sufficient statistics for the DLIM is simply $\{s_i, t_i, r_j\}$ where

$$s_i = \Sigma_j x_{ji}, \qquad t_i = \Sigma_j x_{ji}(m_i - x_{ji}), \qquad \text{and} \qquad r_j = \Sigma_i x_{ji}.$$

Before proceeding to the next section, it should also be noted that the rating models described here are consistent with those constructed within the framework of log-linear models for contingency tables analysis (Duncan, 1984; Goodman, 1981; Haberman, 1974). In addition, the DLIM and its implications are consistent with the substance of the paper by Holland (1981). Holland is concerned with possible dependencies among items of a subtest, and the DLM provides a means for operationalizing some of the theoretical ideas in that paper.

TWO CONTEXTS FOR THE APPLICATION OF THE DLIM (DLM OF ITEMS)

The derivation of the DLIM clearly was motivated by considering an established rating continuum with thresholds. Deriving the model in this way imposes no restrictions on applying the model to other possible contexts and response designs. The significant feature of the model that permits its ready application to the two alternative response designs to be discussed is, as already stressed, that the location parameter is scored with successive integers commencing with zero. Of course, the model must be compatible with these alternative response designs and its parameters must have corresponding interpretations.

Characterization of Dichotomously Scored Items as Subtests

The first test design for which this model is considered and subsequently applied is one in which a subset of items are deemed to belong together on some a priori criteria. Such a subset of items can be treated then as a *subtest*, and if the DLIM is applied each subtest is modeled by both a difficulty (location) and a scale (dispersion) parameter. While the items within the test, which are combined into subtests, may themselves be scored either dichotomously or polychotomously in ordered categories, the case being discussed involves items that are scored only dichotomously. Clearly, at least two dichotomously scored items per subtest are required. Thus if m dichotomously scored items are treated as a subtest, its possible total scores range from 0 to m, as required by the DLIM.

Both theoretical and practical reasons can be advanced for treating dichotomously scored items as subtests. Considering the practical aspects first, it is apparent that many tests already are constructed so that particular subsets of items belong together. Such a test is illustrated by the Australian Scholastic Aptitude Test (ASAT), which is taken by students aspiring to a tertiary education in some states of Australia. The test has relatively lengthy stems of information with which are associated four, five, and sometimes six dichotomously scored items.

Another variation of the same format is shown in many reading comprehension tests, where more than one question is asked for each passage read. Such test construction can be more efficient than one in which each dichotomously scored items has separate reading material, especially if more sophisticated content requiring extended reading time for each stem is required. Asking only one question per stem would not take full advantage of the time spent reading by the examinee, and using only one question may not reveal the possible different degrees of understanding of the material in the stem.

A second case in which some items may belong together is when they pertain to an area of content that is different in some way from the content of other items. For example, in elementary arithmetic tests questions on decimals may be more similar to each other than to questions on fractions, which in turn may be more similar to each other than to the questions on decimals. Variations on this test format are extremely common in educational settings.

While these test designs are common in educational settings and are used because of their practical efficiency, the analysis of the items usually does not take full advantage of the design structure. Instead, the dichotomously scored items are analyzed as if they were all equally independent.

By applying the DLIM, each subtest can be treated as a unit and character-ized by the two parameters. And for each subtest that has more than two dichotomously scored items, the parameterization is clearly more parsimo-nious than if each item were parameterized separately. This parsimony should make the parameter estimates of a subtest more stable than the parameter estimate of each item. Another practical advantage of such a parameterization is that usually when items do belong together, as in the ASAT, they will in fact continue to be kept together in subsequent applica-tions. Thus, in the construction of an item bank it is unlikely that the same stem would be repeated with each dichotomously scored item or that only one dichotomously scored item would be stored for each stem. Similar points can be made with respect to tests of reading comprehension.

In addition to the more practical concerns just considered, there is a major theoretical reason for applying the DLIM rather than a model that treats each dichotomously scored item separately. The reason is that the items of each pair within a subtest are, in some sense, more dependent upon each other than are pairs of items from two different subtests. This makes the universal assumption of local independence for such tests, which is made in all latent trait models for dichotomously scored items, questionable. It is shown in the next section how the DLIM takes this dependence into ac-count.

CHARACTERIZATION OF GRADED OR
EXTENDED RESPONSES

Before proceeding to the next section, and having indicated that the DLIM model can accommodate dependence among responses, the second test design for which the model is therefore appropriate is mentioned briefly. This is the design in which responses to questions are of the extended form and in which various steps in the response are scored as correct or incorrect. Samejima (1969) termed such response formats *graded*. There are also a number of variations on this type of design; these have been described by Masters (1982).

In some formats and scoring systems, a person may execute correctly any particular step even if a previous step has not been executed correctly. This scoring occurs frequently in responses requiring algebraic manipulations in which a correctly executed step, based on an incorrectly executed previous step, is acknowledged. When the model is applied to such formats, the total score does not indicate which steps have been executed correctly; therefore, the thresholds cannot be taken literally as cutoff points on the continuum that correspond to the actual sequential steps in the response. This feature is not necessarily a disadvantage, because in many extended response formats a correct total response may permit not only a different ordering of steps but also very different steps, depending on the approach taken. In such cases an interpretation of a total score in terms of the specific steps executed correctly cannot, in any case, be given.

On the other hand, there are formats in which failure on any step necessarily implies failure on succeeding steps. In such cases the scores and the specific thresholds do correspond to each other. The Likert-style rating format from which the models were derived originally produces responses of this kind.

The example considered in this chapter is of the former type in which a simple count of correctly executed steps, irrespective of order, is taken.

For consistency of terminology, in the remainder of this chapter both the dichotomously scored item and a dichotomously scored step within an extended response format are referred to as an *item*. A collection of two or more dichotomously scored items or an extended response having two or more dichotomously scored steps are referred to as a subtest. Obviously, a single item is also, in a certain sense, a subtest, but in this chapter the term is reserved for the case where the score of a unit of analysis is two or more.

THE DLIM AND DEPENDENCE AMONG RESPONSES

In order to appreciate the way the DLIM model accounts for dependence among responses, it is instructive to review first the score distribution when responses are independent. The best starting point is when the items of a subtest are not only *independent,* but also *equally difficult.* Then the scores are distributed according to the familiar binomial distribution.

THE BINOMIAL SCORE DISTRIBUTION: EQUAL ITEM DIFFICULTIES AND INDEPENDENCE

The binomial model, which corresponds to the amalgamation of dichotomously scored outcomes or Bernoulli trials with identical success probability, clearly corresponds to a particular case of the amalgamation of items described in the previous section. Further, the binomial distribution can be cast readily into the form of the DLIM. Thus if the SLM is taken to characterize the response to each of the m_i items of subtest i, and if all the items of the subtest are of the same difficulty and the responses are independent, then the so-called binomial logistic model (BLM) takes the form

$$p\{X_{ji} = x; \theta_j, \delta_i, m_i\} = \frac{1}{\gamma_{ji}} \exp\left[x(\theta_j - \delta_i) + \ln\binom{m_i}{x} \right]. \qquad (6)$$

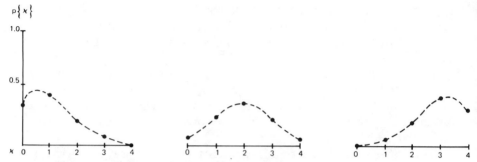

FIGURE 3. Binomial probabilities (●) with $m = 4$ Bernoulli trials and (a) $\theta - \delta = -1.1$, (b) $\theta - \delta = 0.0$, and (c) $\theta - \delta = 1.1$. For ease of visual inspection, the probability points have been joined by a curve.

Figure 3 shows the values of these probabilities for the three values $\theta_j - \delta_i = -1.1, 0.0$, and 1.1, with $m_i = 4$. That is, each diagram of Figure 1 reveals the probabilities of the scores $x = 0, 1, 2, 3$, and 4 when $\theta_j - \delta_i$ is fixed over four replications of a dichotomous response.

A Nonbinomial Score Distribution: Independence but with Unequal Item Difficulties

If one of the requirements for a binomial score distribution — that of equal item difficulty — is relaxed, then the distribution of the scores is peaked more than the binomial. Figure 4 repeats the distribution of Figure 3, but score distributions when the four items have the difficulty values $-1.5, -0.5, 0.5$,

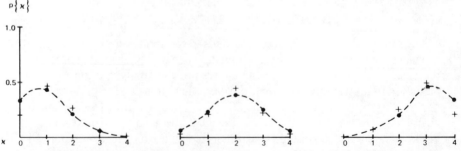

FIGURE 4. Binomial probabilities (●) with $m = 4$ Bernoulli trials and (a) $\theta - \delta = -1.1$, (b) $\theta - \delta = 0.0$, and (c) $\theta = \delta = 1.1$, as in Figure 1. Probabilities (+) where (a) $\theta = -1.1$, (b) $\theta = 0.0$, and (c) $\theta = 1.1$ and where four Bernoulli trials have respective item difficulties of -1.5, $-0.5, 0.5$, and 1.5 are also shown.

TABLE 1
THRESHOLD DISTANCES THAT CORRESPOND TO
BINOMIAL COEFFICIENTS

m				Thresholds				
1				τ_1				
				0.0				
2			τ_1		τ_2			
			-0.69	(1.39)	0.69			
3		τ_1		τ_2		τ_3		
		-1.10	(1.10)	0.0	(1.10)	1.10		
4	τ_1		τ_2		τ_3		τ_4	
	-1.39	(0.98)	-0.41	(0.81)	0.41	(0.98)	1.39	

and 1.5, respectively, are also shown. To correspond to the values of $\theta - \delta$ in Figure 1, θ takes the values $-1.1, 0.0$, and 1.1 in Figures 4(a), 4(b), and 4(c) respectively. It is evident from Figure 4 that the new response distribution is more peaked than the binomial, and it can be shown quite generally that for the amalgamation of independent Bernoulli trials, the binomial distribution with equal item difficulties for a fixed ability is the least peaked.

To clarify the relationship between the binomial and DLIM, the values of the thresholds in the DLIM that correspond to the binomial coefficient of Model (6), that is, when $\kappa_x = \ln\binom{m}{x}$, are shown in Table 1. It is evident from this table that the distances between thresholds are not equal for $m > 3$. This means that the DLIM with equal distances cannot be mapped into the binomial logistic model except in the case where a subtest is composed of either two or three dichotomous items. Nevertheless, the distances are not all that different from each other, as illustrated in the case $m = 4$. Thus a value of λ of the order of 0.45 for $m = 4$, shown in Figure 5, would indicate the possibility of a binomial response process. On the other hand, a value of λ much greater than 0.45, for example 1.00, would indicate the possibility of independent responses to items of different difficulty. Thus the scale parameter accounts to some degree for the variation in difficulties of the items that comprise a subtest.

A NONBINOMIAL SCORE DISTRIBUTION: EQUAL ITEM DIFFICULTIES BUT WITH DEPENDENCE

As indicated earlier, and even though it was motivated as a positive real number, the value of λ can in principle be any real number. With very low values of λ, such as those close to 0.0 or even negative, the interpretation of

p{x}

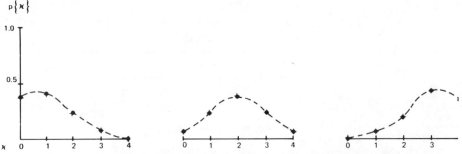

FIGURE 5. Probabilities (●) for the DLIM with $m = 4$, scale value $\lambda = 0.45$, and (a) $\theta - \delta = -1.1$, (b) $\theta - \delta = 0.0$, and (c) $\theta - \delta = 1.1$. For ease of visual inspection, these probability points have been joined by a curve. The corresponding binomial probabilities (+) are also shown.

thresholds as originally defined becomes difficult. However, the context of the binomial distribution becomes useful in appreciating what a small value of λ might mean in the two contexts being considered. Specifically, as λ becomes smaller the probability of responses in extreme categories gets larger. As a result, the distribution becomes flatter than the binomial. But one interpretation when the distribution of responses is flatter than the binomial is that the assumption of independence is violated. This can be appreciated by noting that dependence among responses to two items implies that getting one item correct affects the probability of getting a second item correct, with the further implication that scores of 0 and 2 across the two items will be more prevalent than is the case for binomial responses. With dependence, therefore, the distribution will be flatter than the binomial.

From the preceding analysis of the distributions in relation to the binomial, it can be seen that the parameter λ incorporates both differences in the difficulties of items of a subtest and some average of any dependencies among these items. In terms of the manifestation of these features in the response distribution, they operate *against* each other in that differences in difficulties generate a distribution more peaked than the BLM, whereas dependence generates one less peaked. As a consequence, if items have different difficulties and there is some dependence among responses, the observed distribution may look very much like the binomial. In other words, the dependencies and differences in difficulties may compensate or cancel each other. However, when the distribution is flatter than the binomial either the items are equally difficult but there is dependence, or the items are not equally difficult but there is so much dependence that differences in item difficulties do not compensate for the dependence. Therefore, a distribution flatter than the binomial implies some kind of dependence.

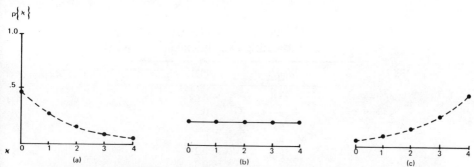

FIGURE 6.   Probabilities (●) for the DLIM with $m = 4$, scale value $\lambda = -0.0$, and (a) $\theta - \delta = -0.5$, (b) $\theta - \delta = 0.0$, and (c) $\theta - \delta = 0.5$.   For ease of visual inspection, the points have been joined by a curve.

Of course, the source of this dependence is not the abilities of the people or the difficulties of the items that are parameterized separately in the model; the source can be appreciated only by understanding the substantive and empirical relations among the items.   This is an issue for item and test construction.

Probability distributions associated with values of λ, which are 0.0 and -0.5, respectively, are shown in Figs. 6 and 7.   The distributions in Figure 6 are flatter than the binomial, whereas those in Figure 7 go beyond being simply flatter—they are U-shaped.

By considering the threshold values of Table 1 in relation to the preceding points, it is possible to formalize the available evidence for dependence.   It is possible because the bigger the distance between thresholds, the more peaked the distribution.   Table 2 provides the limit for λ below which its values

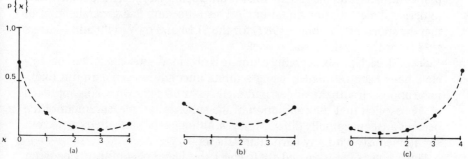

FIGURE 7.   Probabilities (●) for the DLIM with $m = 4$, scale value $\lambda = -0.25$, and (a) $\theta - \delta = -0.5$, (b) $\theta - \delta = 0.0$, and (c) $\theta - \delta = 0.5$.   For ease of visual inspection, the points have been joined by a curve.

TABLE 2
LEAST UPPER BOUND (LUB) FOR θ
Indicating Dependence

m	LUB
2	0.69
3	0.55
4	0.41
5	0.35
6	0.29
7	0.25
8	0.22

indicate dependence, with the scale value λ being the half-distance between thresholds.

For $m > 3$, the distances between successive thresholds are not equal for the binomial distribution. Therefore the half-distance between the closest pair of threshold values is taken to be the limiting value indicating dependence.

THE ILLUSTRATIVE DATA SETS

This section shows the analyses of two data sets according to the DLIM. The following general aspects of these analyses are important to note. First, the estimates of the two subtest parameters are carried out by considering the response of each person to each pair of subtests and then conditioning on the sufficient statistic for the person's ability. The person's ability parameter is thus eliminated and the general maximum likelihood procedure is then used to derive the estimation equations. This procedure is a generalization of that described by Choppin (1982) for the SLM and by Wright and Masters (1982) for the partial credit model.

Second, each person's ability estimate is obtained, after the subtest parameters have been estimated, using a direct unconditional maximum likelihood approach with the subtest parameters assumed known. This approach makes explicit that the calibration of the subtests and measurement of the persons are conceptually different stages, although they are often carried out simultaneously with any particular data set.

Third, a test of fit is carried out to check the degree of conformity between the model and the data. The test of fit used involves dividing the persons into class intervals on the latent continuum and then comparing, for each class interval, the observed total scores with those predicted by the model using the parameter estimates. It should be stressed that the chosen test of fit does not check all possible violations of the model. No test of fit provides conditions that are both necessary and sufficient for accepting any latent trait model. Thus every test of fit checks different possible model assumptions and violations.

The general test of fit used here shows whether or not the subtests operate in a consistent way across different positions on the latent trait. This is an important test because if the subtests operate differently at different points on the latent trait, the generality of the measures across the continuum derived from the subtests is seriously impaired.

The actual statistic calculated is taken to be an approximation to χ^2 on $[(G-2)(K-1)-1)]$ degrees of freedom, where G is the number of class intervals and K the number of subtests. This test statistic is based on that considered by Wright and Panchapakesan (1969) in relation to the SLM, and provides an indication of the overall conformity between the data and the model in relation to different intervals on the latent continuum. In general it is instructive to partition this statistic and identify the contribution of each subtest. The simple procedure used here involves considering that the contribution of each subtest to the total χ^2 statistic is distributed on $[(G-2)(K-1)-1]/K$ degrees of freedom. The probability value associated with the resultant nonintegral degrees of freedom poses no arithmetical problem in that both the χ^2 distribution and the subroutine used for the calculations accommodate any positive real number for the degrees of freedom. The subroutine using nonintegral degrees of freedom gives values that are similar to those when the statistic itself is corrected to correspond to the nearest integral degrees of freedom. Another point to note with respect to this statistic is that its approximation to a χ^2 is not very good for fewer than 20 dichotomously scored items. In the two data sets analyzed in this chapter, the equivalent numbers of dichotomously scored items in the subtests are 36 and 40, respectively. The statistic is satisfactory when taken primarily as an index of fit rather than as an exact statement of probability.

Fourth, a likelihood ratio test is conducted to test whether or not differences in scale values among subtests are significant. This is done simply by comparing the likelihoods of the data under the two assumptions of different and equal scale values. Unconditional likelihoods are used, and the usual transformation of $-2 \log (L_{H_0} / L_{H_1})$ is taken to be distributed as χ^2 on $K-1$ degrees of freedom, which is the difference in the number of parameters estimated under the two hypotheses. Rost (1982) provided evidence that unconditional likelihood ratio tests approximate the χ^2 distribution quite satisfactorily when the number of dichotomously scored items is 30 or more. The computer program written to carry out an analysis according to

TABLE 3
SUBTEST PARAMETER ESTIMATES FOR EXAMPLE 1

			Different $\hat{\lambda}_i$			Equal $\hat{\lambda}_i$		
Subtest	Total	Rank	$\hat{\delta}_i$	$\hat{\lambda}_i$	Rank	$\hat{\delta}_i$	$\hat{\lambda}$	Rank
1	848	2	−0.77	0.50	2	−0.73	0.41	2
2	802	4	−0.20	0.41	3	−0.33	0.41	3
3	640	8	0.89	0.34	8	0.73	0.41	8
4	688	7	0.42	0.58	7	0.42	0.41	7
5	587	9	1.17	0.27	9	1.03	0.41	9
6	793	3	−0.53	0.66	4	−0.25	0.41	4
7	757	5	0.13	0.41	5	0.01	0.41	5
8	747	6	0.22	0.38	6	0.07	0.41	6
9	869	1	−1.32	0.65	1	−0.94	0.41	1

Likelihood ratio test for equal scale values: $\chi^2 = 41.09$ on 8 *df*, $p < .00$.

the DLIM has been described by Andrich, De'Ath, Lyne, Hill, and Jennings (1982).

Finally, it is not the intent here to provide a comprehensive analysis of the tests themselves. Therefore, the two analyses presented involve only the main new features associated with the model. Thus, the analysis focuses on the interpretation of the scale parameters and the general implications their values have for any possible modifications to the tests. Specific details of the tests are not pursued, even though in the practical situation they would be important and not displaced by the introduction of the extra parameter. Clearly, the DLIM does not obviate the need for careful construction of test questions and the application of usual criteria found in most text books.

ANALYSIS OF ITEMS COMBINED INTO SUBTESTS

The first application of the DLIM model involves the responses of 264 ninth-grade students (approximately 14 years old) to 36 items of a 50-item basic numeracy test administered by the State Education Department of Western Australia. The 36 items comprised 9 subtests of 4 items, each relating to the following different topics: whole numbers, decimals, fractions, ratio and proportion, measurement (length, volume, and mass), measurement (area and time), algebra, geometry, and tables and graphs.

Table 3 shows the total score $s_i = \Sigma_j x_{ji}$ for each subtest and the parameter estimates with the full DLIM model and with the model where only one scale value is estimated across all subtests. It is evident from Table 3 that the scale values of the subtests are significantly different from each other.

TABLE 4
SUBTEST FIT STATISTICS FOR EXAMPLE 1

Subtest	Different $\hat{\lambda}_i$			Equal $\hat{\lambda}_i$		
	χ^2	df	p<	χ^2	df	p<
6	0.08	1.67	.93	5.45	2.56	.08
8	0.71	1.67	.61	0.96	2.56	.73
9	1.38	1.67	.40	0.21	2.56	.95
4	2.19	1.67	.24	1.38	2.56	.61
2	2.46	1.67	.20	2.57	2.56	.36
7	3.29	1.67	.12	4.40	2.56	.14
1	3.90	1.67	.08	5.34	2.56	.08
5	6.57	1.67	.00	9.91	2.56	.00
3	8.21	1.67	.00	10.94	2.56	.00
	28.79	15	.02	41.16	23	.01

It is also evident from Table 3 that the difficulty estimates $\hat{\delta}_i$ are not in the same order as the numbers correctly answering the items in a subtest when $\hat{\lambda}_i$ is estimated for each Item i. In particular, Items 2 and 6 reverse order. This reversal results from the different scale values and indicates that difficulties cannot be compared directly in the presence of different scale values for the subtests. When all items are assumed to have the same scale value, then the subtest difficulties are in the same order as the numbers obtaining items correct within the subtests. Thus the scale and location values are not independent, indicating that in selecting subtests on the basis of parametric values both parameters need to be considered, and not just the difficulty parameter. Once a subtest is characterized by two parameters, usual rules of order on a single dimension do not apply and the two parameters must continue to be considered jointly.

Before making too much of the parameter estimates, however, the quality of the fit needs to be examined. Table 4 shows the fit statistics for the subtests, both when all λ_i are estimated and when only one scale value is assumed. For ease of inspection, the subtests are displayed according to the fit order in the case where different scale values are estimated for the subtests. In calculating these statistics, four class intervals were formed.

The first observation that can be made from Table 4 is that the χ^2 statistic with the greater number of parameters estimated is smaller. However, the degrees of freedom are also smaller, and in relation to a reduction in χ^2 of $41.16 - 28.79 = 12.37$ corresponding to a reduction of 8 degrees of freedom, the gain is only marginal. Thus for the overall test of fit across all subtests and all class intervals, and according to the particular criterion,

TABLE 5

RESULTS OF SUBTEST 3 OF EXAMPLE 1[a]

Class interval	Size	Difference between observed mean and expected value	Standardized residual	Component^2
1	57	−0.02	−0.18	0.03
2	65	−0.03	−0.23	0.05
3	51	−0.19	−1.60	2.55
4	74	0.16	2.36	5.57

[a] Difficulty $\hat{\delta} = 0.89$, scale $\hat{\lambda} = 0.34$, $\chi^2 = 8.21$, $df = 1.67$.

scores are recovered about equally well by both models even though the scale values are significantly different. The indication is that both models do not fit very well, over all.

In examining the fit of specific subtests, it can be seen that Subtests 3 and 5, which coincidentally have the smallest scale values, fit most poorly. Indeed, they contribute sufficiently to the misfit that when they are eliminated from the analysis the χ^2 fit statistic on the remaining subtests is 15.36 on 11 degrees of freedom with $p < .14$, indicating adequate fit. Further, when these two subtests are eliminated and only the one common scale value is estimated, the χ^2 fit statistic has a value of 22.24 on 17 degrees of freedom. This is a more than adequate fit, with all subtests also fitting individually. The common scale value is 0.51 in this case, indicating that differences in item difficulties within subtests counterbalance any dependencies. For this particular set of responses, then, a common scale value is tenable, with the consequence that the model is very parsimonious.

Subtests or items should not simply be eliminated. They may be eliminated in terms of their original identity, but the information they have to offer should be retained. For any subsequent revision of the tests, it is entirely reasonable to try to modify the misfitting subtests while intending to elicit the same abilities. In fact, the intention should be to elicit and measure these abilities even more accurately than with the original form of the subtests.

To consider how the nature of the misfit may be investigated, further details of Subtest 3, the worst-fitting subtest, are shown in Tables 5 and 6. From these tables it can be seen that the performance of students in the class interval with the greatest ability is the major source of the misfit of the subtest. Significantly more students than expected answer all four items in the subtest correctly.

The specific details are not pursued here, although such an observation

TABLE 6
OBSERVED PROPORTIONS (OP) AND MODEL PROBABILITES (MP)

Class interval	Average ability		Scores					Observed mean	Expected value
			0	1	2	3	4		
1	−0.21	OP	0.39	0.37	0.18	0.04	0.00	0.85	
		MP	0.37	0.39	0.18	0.04	0.02		0.87
2	1.16	OP	0.03	0.20	0.35	0.29	0.12	2.25	
		MP	0.05	0.18	0.33	0.30	0.14		2.30
3	2.05	OP	0.00	0.06	0.18	0.49	0.27	2.97	
		MP	0.00	0.04	0.16	0.37	0.43		3.19
4	3.10	OP	0.00	0.00	0.00	0.18	0.82	3.82	
		MP	0.00	0.00	0.03	0.22	0.74		3.68

and a further detailed analysis of the items and response patterns would normally follow. Here only some aspects of the scale value are considered briefly. The estimate of 0.34 for the scale of Subtest 3 indicates dependence among responses, and it may be helpful to consider the difficulties of the individual items within subtests.

A separate analysis according to the simple logistic model where all items were treated separately was performed; the relative difficulties of the items in this subtest were 0.25, 0.63, 1.07, and 1.49. Relative to standard errors of the order of 0.16, the difficulties are significantly different from each other. These relative difficulties confirm that there is a dependence among responses in this subtest. From Tables 5 and 6, it appears that this dependence is not uniform either across the different items in the subtest or at different levels of ability; the dependence is greater at the higher levels of ability. Further examination of the content of the items in relation to the response patterns may indicate how a modification could be made to remove these differential effects.

Because the example is chosen primarily to illustrate an application of the DLIM the analysis of the fit will not be pursued further. However, one final point regarding this example to be made is that not only does Subtest 3 exhibit dependence among items within subtests, but so also do Items 3, 5, 7, and 8. Thus, five of the nine subtests show dependencies among items within subtests. This indicates that it might be important to retain the items together in subtests, not only from the perspective of the content they represent but also from the perspective of the statistical analysis, in which it might seem unreasonable to assume complete independence. The DLIM model reveals this dependence, and to a substantial degree accounts for it. With further modification of some items, dictated by their content and the response patterns, it should be possible to get better accordance between the model and the data without sacrificing any required characteristics of item content.

ANALYSIS OF EXTENDED RESPONSES TREATED AS SUBTESTS

The second example involves the responses of 211 students to 10 relatively elementary mathematics problems. These form a subset of a longer examination of 10th- and 11th-grade students at a suburban San Antonio high school in Texas. The response of each student was of the extended form in which the steps in the solution of the problem were shown. Of course, different methods for solving each problem were available; therefore, the solution of the problem, no matter what method was employed, was broken into four major steps. Each correctly executed step was counted to provide a score for each problem, here called a subtest. Tables 7 and 8, respectively, correspond to Tables 3 and 4 of the previous example, and again for the fit analysis four class intervals were formed.

As in the previous example, it is evident that the scale values for the subtests are significantly different from each other. Further, with an average scale value of 0.30 compared to 0.41, the limiting value for evidence of dependence, the dependencies among the dichotomously scored items within a subtest are greater than for the previous example. Because of the different formats behind the scores, the greater dependency among items of the extended response format would be expected.

TABLE 7
SUBTEST PARAMETER ESTIMATES FOR EXAMPLE 2

Subtest	Total score	Rank	Different $\hat{\lambda}_i$			Equal $\hat{\lambda}_i$		
			$\hat{\delta}_i$	$\hat{\lambda}_i$	Rank	$\hat{\delta}_i$	$\hat{\lambda}_i$	Rank
1	426	2	-0.47	0.30	2	-0.50	0.30	2
2	211	9	0.22	0.10	8	0.45	0.30	9
3	335	4	0.01	0.49	6	-0.12	0.30	4
4	500	1	-0.92	0.62	1	-0.75	0.30	1
5	315	6	0.24	0.62	9	-0.05	0.30	6
6	355	3	-0.20	0.28	3	-0.22	0.30	3
7	265	8	-0.01	0.02	5	0.20	0.30	8
8	293	7	0.12	0.35	7	0.05	0.30	7
9	126	10	1.18	0.37	10	1.02	0.30	10
10	327	5	-0.18	0.09	4	-0.10	0.30	5

Likelihood ratio test for equal scale values: $\chi^2 = 41.09$ on 8 df, $p < .00$.

TABLE 8
SUBTEST FIT STATISTICS FOR EXAMPLE 2

Subtest	Different $\hat{\lambda}$			Same $\hat{\lambda}$		
	χ^2	df	p<	χ^2	df	p<
1	1.45	1.7	.39	1.64	2.6	.56
4	1.96	1.7	.29	9.44	2.6	.00
8	2.22	1.7	.24	1.48	2.6	.60
3	2.23	1.7	.24	5.24	2.6	.09
7	2.23	1.7	.24	14.68	2.6	.00
5	3.77	1.7	.09	9.17	2.6	.00
10	3.85	1.7	.08	8.67	2.6	.00
6	6.11	1.7	.00	7.09	2.6	.02
9	11.71	1.7	.00	10.71	2.6	.00
2	28.74	1.7	.00	18.06	2.6	.00
	64.26	17	.00	86.17	26	.00

Next, it is evident from Table 8 that the data and model do not accord with each other. In this case, three subtests show a substantial degree of misfit. If these three subtests are excluded from the analysis, the overall fit statistic has the satisfactory value of $\chi^2 = 16.15$ on 11 degrees of freedom with $p < .11$.

In this case, however, with the assumption of equal scale values the fit is very unsatisfactory, with a χ^2 value of 57.79 on 17 degrees of freedom. Thus the scale values are clearly different from subtest to subtest, even when misfitting subtests are excluded from the analysis.

As discussed with respect to the previous example, it may be desirable to modify the misfitting subtests with the intention that subsequently they will conform better with the model. To indicate the direction of such modifications, further details of the analysis of the worst-fitting subtest, Subtest 2, are displayed in Tables 9 and 10.

It is apparent from these tables that, in traditional terminology, Subtest 2 does not discriminate satisfactorily. The weakest students in the first class interval scored much better than expected, and the strongest students in the last class interval scored worse than expected. The pattern of responses suggests that perhaps the first step is somewhat easy to execute, even for very poor students, but that very good students as identified by the test as a whole have trouble completing the final stage. A closer examination of the actual pattern of scripts and marks awarded may indicate simple adjustments, either to the scoring procedure or to a rewriting of the test question, so that it discriminates better and in a way that can be accounted for by the model.

On the whole, however, it is not expected that all subtests discriminate in

TABLE 9
RESULTS OF SUBTEST 2 OF EXAMPLE 2[a]

Class interval	Size	Difference between observed mean and expected value	Stanardized residual	Component^2
1	35	0.53	4.64	21.52
2	67	−0.08	−0.67	0.48
3	47	−0.07	−0.40	0.16
4	62	−0.41	−2.57	6.62

[a] Difficulty $\hat{\delta} = 0.22$, scale $\hat{\lambda} = 0.10$, $\chi^2 = 28.74$, $df = 1.7$.

TABLE 10
OBSERVED PROPORTIONS (OP) AND MODEL PROBABILITIES (MP)

Class interval	Average ability		Scores					Observed mean	Expected value
			0	1	2	3	4		
1	−1.29	OP	0.37	0.43	0.14	0.30	0.03	0.92	
		MP	0.72	0.22	0.05	0.01	0.00		0.39
2	−0.67	OP	0.48	0.36	0.16	0.00	0.00	0.68	
		MP	0.52	0.29	0.13	0.05	0.01		0.76
3	−0.34	OP	0.30	0.47	0.17	0.00	0.06	1.05	
		MP	0.38	0.30	0.19	0.10	0.04		1.12
4	0.07	OP	0.32	0.40	0.08	0.00	0.19	1.32	
		MP	0.21	0.25	0.24	0.18	0.12		1.73

TABLE 11
PARAMETER ESTIMATES AND TEST OF FIT FOR EXAMPLE 2
WHEN THREE SUBTESTS ARE EXCLUDED

Subtest	Different $\hat{\lambda}_i$				Same $\hat{\lambda}_i$			
	$\hat{\delta}_i$	$\hat{\lambda}_i$	χ^2	$p<$	$\hat{\delta}_i$	$\hat{\lambda}_i$	χ^2	$p<$
1	−0.30	0.30	0.64	.60	−0.33	0.33	1.62	.53
3	0.18	0.50	1.24	.41	0.06	0.33	4.45	.13
4	−0.77	0.64	1.51	.34	−0.61	0.33	9.88	.00
5	0.43	0.64	4.19	.05	0.14	0.33	11.75	.00
7	0.17	0.03	2.61	.17	0.40	0.33	19.60	.00
8	0.29	0.35	3.79	.07	0.24	0.33	3.10	.26
10	−0.01	0.09	2.17	.22	0.10	0.33	7.39	.01
		(11 df)	16.15	.11		(17 df)	57.79	.00

the same way. The dependencies between steps in the subtests clearly vary from subtest to subtest, and the scale parameter of the DLIM accounts to a great degree for these differences. To demonstrate this point further, Table 11 shows the parameter estimates and fit statistics when the three worst-fitting subtests are excluded.

DISCUSSION AND IMPLICATIONS FOR TEST CONSTRUCTION

In considering the DLIM for subtests, and the degree of success in applying it to the two sets of data used for illustrative purposes, it must be kept in mind that the tests were not constructed with the model in mind. Most tests are modified after initial analyses as empirical evidence demonstrates whether or not the tasks constituting the tests operate closely enough with expectation. Thus with modification based on the empirical evidence regarding the discrepancies between the model and the data, subsequent collections of data should conform better with the model.

This perspective implies that the model comes before the data. In a certain sense it does, but not in a naive way. The model is proposed in the first place on the basis of an appreciation of existing tests and patterns of responses to which other models have been applied. These other models have been found wanting, both conceptually and empirically, with respect to tests with a particular feature — namely, those having a dependence among items that is not accounted for by variations in the difficulties of the items and the abilities of the persons. The DLIM model is proposed to cater better to tests exhibiting these properties and is therefore a result of a conceptualization of test data. In this sense, the model arises from the substantive aspects of test construction and empirical evidence associated with it.

However, every set of test data that is collected and that can be analyzed by the DLIM should not be accepted without examination. A possible modification of the test, if it does not accord with the model, must be entertained. As indicated earlier, this perspective does not imply the simple elimination of subtests. Clearly, when the subtests are constructed it is expected that they will all contribute to the measurements. The modification of subtests in this way implies that the information they have to provide is taken advantage of and used in the modification of the test.

Although the scale parameter will account for dependencies among items, whatever the source of the dependencies, it cannot be expected to account for all variation in data beyond that accounted for by the location parameters of the persons and subtests, unless the tests have been collected with the model in mind. However, it is relevant to note that some empirical support is available already for the approach. Leunbach (1976) considered two tests jointly and estimated the complete set of coefficients κ_x for each of these tests. The respective ranges of the scores of the tests were $0-21$ and $0-16$. On completing the estimation, Leunbach attempted to summarize the coefficients by a polynomial. He found that the quadratic polynomial was quite satisfactory. The advantage of the approach using the DLIM over the approach used by Leunbach is that in the former the particular reparameterization of the quadratic polynomial can be interpreted in terms of the item difficulties and dependencies among items.

In addition to catering for dependence among subsets of items, the DLIM enlarges the basic unit of analysis. These units can be examined, then, both with respect to each other as they relate to the whole test and internally as they operate as units. With respect to the former perspective, the implications for test construction are similar to those used when the single item is the unit of analysis. That is, the subtests should span the continuum of interest and should be neither too easy nor too difficult for the persons tested.

With respect to the second perspective, the usual criteria and traditions for item construction are again relevant. However, the range of difficulties within a subtest should be narrower than is usual in whole tests, and thus should not cover the whole continuum spanned by the test. Although there should perhaps be some variation in item difficulties, the variation should not be so great that some of the items within a subtest are either too hard or too easy for examinees. If the range is too great, then the difficulty of the subtest as a whole does not represent adequately the difficulties of the items within it, with the consequence that treating the subtest as a unit to some degree misses the point. It is recommended therefore that subtests be constructed so that the stem, or the governing principle of the subtest, has a level of difficulty, and that the different items within a subtest be seen to reflect this difficulty. This perspective has particular implications for reading comprehension tests, in which the focus on difficulty, then, should be on the material read, rather than on the questions associated with the material. The questions should be of the same order of difficulty as the passage, with some variations, but the main differences in difficulties in a test should be from subtest to subtest.

An important feature of the DLIM, which has both a scale and a location parameter, is that it belongs to the class of Rasch measurement models, so the subtest parameters can be separated from the person parameter. However, as noted earlier, the two subtest parameters, while separable algebraically, have correlated estimates. Therefore, the scale parameter, which corresponds to the subtest discrimination, interacts with the difficulty. This means that in the selection of subtests in an item-banking context, both parameters should be considered. One subtest cannot be classified as unequivocally more difficult than another in the presence of different scale values because the position of the continuum being considered determines which is more difficult. Nevertheless, the values of the subtest parameters considered jointly should be free of the locations on the ability continuum.

The DLIM makes it also clear, through its relationship to the Guttman scale (which has been noted already), that the persons are characterized only by the first principal component. In general, this is the only component on which a formal distinction among persons is generally made. Although only the first principal component is considered with respect to persons, the first two components are considered with respect to subtests of items. By accounting for more components among subtests, more accurate person parameter estimates on the first principal component, and standard errors of those estimates, should be obtained.

How these properties may be demonstrated cannot be pursued here, but it is important to note that these issues, and others not covered in this chapter, do require further investigation. For example, it is necessary to understand how the scale parameter, which accounts for dependence, affects the standard errors of the estimates of person abilities. One feature shown in Andrich (1982b) is that as dependence increases, so does the subtest discrimination, which traditionally implies greater information. Yet, on the face of it, when items are dependent less information should be available than when they are independent. These apparently conflicting results, which are reminiscent of the attenuation paradox in traditional test theory, need to be formalized.

ACKNOWLEDGMENTS

Valuable suggestions arose from lengthy discussions with Graham Douglas, Peter Hill, Geoff Masters, Pender Pedler, and Benjamin Wright. The examples were provided by the State Education Department of Western Australia and Mrs. Loyce Collenback of San Antonio, Texas. Glen De'Ath and Alan Lyne wrote the computer program for analyzing data according to the model proposed in this chapter.

REFERENCES

Andersen, E. B. (1977). Sufficient statistics and latent trait models. *Psychometrika, 42,* 69–81.

Andrich, D. (1978a). Application of a psychometric rating model to ordered categories which are scored with successive integers. *Applied Psychological Measurement, 2,* 581–594.

Andrich, D. (1978b). A rating formulation for ordered response categories. *Psychometrika, 43,* 561–573.

Andrich, D. (1979). A model for contingency tables having an ordered response classification. *Biometrics, 35,* 403–415.

Andrich, D. (1982a). An extension of the Rasch model for ratings providing both location and dispersion parameters. *Psychometrika, 47,* 105–113.

Andrich, D. (1982b). *A multi-parameter generalisation of a model for ratings with implications for test construction and analysis.* Paper presented at the Conference of the National Council for Measurement in Education and the American Education Research Association, New York.

Andrich, D., De'Ath, G., Lyne, H., Hill, P., & Jennings, J. (1982). *DISLOC: A program for analysing a Rasch model with two item parameters.* State Education Department, Western Australia.

Australian Scholastic Aptitude Test. Australian Council for Educational Research, Melbourne.

Birnbaum, A. (1968). Some latent trait models and their use in inferring an examinee's ability. In F. Lord & M. Novick (Eds.), *Statistical theories of mental test scores.* Reading, MA: Addison-Wesley.

Choppin, B. (1982). The use of latent trait models in the measurement of cognitive abilities and skills. In D. Spearritt (Ed.), *The improvement of measurement in education and psychology.* Melbourne, Australian Council for Educational Research.

Duncan, O. D. (1984). Rasch measurement in survey research: Further examples and discussion. In C. F. Turner & E. Martin (Eds.), *Survey measurement of subjective phenomena: Vol. 2.*

Edwards, A. L., Thurston, L. L. (1952). An internal consistency check for the method of successive intervals and the method of graded dichotomies. *Psychometrika, 17,* 169–180.

Fischer, G. H. (1973). The linear logistic test model as an instrument in educational research. *Acta Psychologica, 37,* 359–374.

Goodman, L. (1981). Three elementary views of log linear models for the analysis of cross-classifications having ordered categories. In S. Leinhardt (Ed.), *Sociological methodology.* San Francisco: Jossey-Bass.

Guttman, L. (1954). The principal components of scalable attitudes. In P. F. Lazarsfeld (Ed.), *Mathematical thinking in the social sciences.* Glencoe, IL: The Free Press.

Haberman, S. J. (1974). Log-linear models for frequency tables with ordered classifications. *Biometrics, 30,* 589–600.

Holland, P. W. (1981). When are item response models consistent with observed data. *Psychometrika, 46,* 79–92.

Leunbach, G. (1976). A probabilistic measurement model for assessing whether tests measure the same personal factor. *Danish Institute for Educational Research.*

Masters, G. N. (1982). A Rasch model for partial credit scoring. *Psychometrika, 47,* 149–174.

Rasch, G. (1961). On general laws and the meaning of measurement in psychology. In *Proceedings of the Fourth Berkeley Symposium on Mathematical Statistics and Probability* (Vol. 4) (pp. 321–334). Berkeley: University of California Press.

Rasch, G. (1977). On specific objectivity: An attempt at formalizing the request for generality and validity of scientific statements. *Danish Yearbook of Philosophy, 14,* 58–94.

Rasch, G. (1980). *Probabilistic models for some intelligence and attainment tests* (expanded ed.). Chicago: The University of Chicago Press. (Original work published 1960).

Rost, J. (1982). An unconditional likelihood ratio for testing item homogeneity in the Rasch model. In D. Andrich & G. A. Douglas (Eds.), Rasch models for measurement in educational and psychological research. *Education Research and Perspectives, 9,* 7–17.

Samejima, F. (1969). Estimation of latent ability using a response pattern of graded scores. *Psychometric Monograph, 34*(2, Whole No. 17).

Spada, H. (1977). Logistic models of learning and thought. In H. Spada & W. Kempf (Eds.), *Structural models of thinking and learning.* Vienna: Hans Huber.

Whitely, S. E. (1980). Multicomponent latent trait models for ability tests. *Psychometrika, 45,* 479–494.

Wright, B. D., & Masters, G. N. (1982). *Rating scale analysis.* Chicago: MESA Press.

Wright, B. D., & Panchapakesan, N. (1969). A procedure for sample-free item analysis. *Educational and Psychological Measurement, 29,* 23–48.

IV

Test Design from the Test Development Perspective

10

Speculations on the Future of Test Design

Isaac I. Bejar

INTRODUCTION

I am grateful for the opportunity to write the final chapter for a book concerned with the improvement of test design. I do not envy for one moment the task of the contributors to this volume, for theirs is a difficult responsibility. By contrast, my task is to *speculate* on the future of test design, not so difficult a task when, as in this case, the contributors have provided such stimulating descriptions of their research programs.

The chapter is divided in two major sections. In the first section I identify three areas of test design that are bound to be significantly influenced by the increasing availability of technology. These three areas are computer-assisted test assembly, computer-assisted test administration, and computer-assisted test generation. All three will be significantly affected by the sheer presence of technology and thus there is the danger that they may be affected only in superficial ways. Contributions such as the ones presented in this volume will be largely responsible for effecting the hoped-for fundamental change. The second section argues that a fundamental change is more likely to come about by an integration of cognitive psychology and psychometric theory.

TECHNOLOGY AND TEST DESIGN

Future test designers will have at their disposal the ever-growing fruits of the information revolution. The evidence for this revolution is everywhere,

Copyright © 1985 by Academic Press, Inc.
All rights of reproduction in any form reserved.
ISBN 0-12-238180-7

but most significantly it is evidenced by the increasing presence of micro-computers at school, at home, and at work. For test designers, the increasing availability of technology is a mixed blessing. Although such growth creates the opportunity to develop better tests or administer them more efficiently, it also creates a pressure to computerize tests and use technology superficially. Three areas of test design that are vulnerable to these pressures are

1. Administration of tests by computers,
2. Computer-assisted test assembly,
3. The generation of items by computer.

ADMINISTRATION OF TESTS

The administration of tests by computers is no longer just a possibility, it is a reality. Moreover, it stands as one of the proudest achievements of psychometrics because the theory that would make adaptive testing a reality, Item Response Theory (IRT; Lord, 1980), was developed before computers were widely available. Had this theory not been developed, it is likely that in the current technological revolution computers would have been applied to testing in a shallow manner. That is, computers probably would have been used as automated answer sheets rather than as a means of delivering new kinds of tests or more efficient tests.

By the early 1970s computer technology had reached the point where it was possible simultaneously to test several examinees more or less economically. The pioneering efforts of Weiss (1974) capitalized on this event and on the availability of IRT to begin an extensive research program on the psychometric and practical issues of *adaptive* testing. In an adaptive test, the computer's job is not merely to present the item and score it but also to determine which item should be administered next, given the student's current level of performance. Although adaptive tests usually use multiple-choice items and thus give the impression that a paper-and-pencil test has been transferred to a computer, in reality different examinees are responding to different tests assembled by the computer for each examinee so that the resulting score may be most precise for an individual test taker.

It is tempting to say that adaptive testing became possible as a result of coupling computers and IRT. The fact is that Binet was doing pretty much the same thing at the turn of this century. Of course, then it was the psychometrician, not the computer, that was selecting and scoring the items. Adaptive testing is thus an efficient implementation of a long-standing idea. Nevertheless, it is still a significant achievement, especially considering what would have happened in the absence of IRT — namely, the blind transfer of items to a computer screen. That achievement is about to become a practical reality. The military and private testing organizations have both been seriously contemplating the practical implementation of adaptive testing systems. In some cases concrete steps have already been taken toward their implementation. Although it is too early to tell what success these initial efforts will encounter, computers are becoming so pervasive that not to give a test by computer may soon appear archaic. Chances are that there will thus be more computer administration of tests, although not necessarily because they are better psychometrically. It will therefore be up to the test designer to make the best possible use of the available technology.

While adaptive testing has been moving forward, technology, psychometrics and substantive theory have not remained static, and the integration of these three opens up additional opportunities. For example, most adaptive testing research has been limited to verbal items. This was so because until recently it was too expensive to display symbols and graphics on a CRT (cathode ray tube). That has changed and in principle test material can even be presented in the form of television images by means of videodisc players. A videodisc permits access to up to 54,000 television frames and, for example, language skills could be tested in very realistic contexts by presenting items as audiovisual sequences. On the psychometric front, models that go beyond the classification of responses into "correct" and "incorrect" have been formulated (e.g., Andersen, 1977; Bock, 1972; Fischer, 1973; Samejima, 1969; Embretson, Chapter 7, this volume; Scheiblechner, Chapter 8, this volume; Andrich, Chapter 9, this volume) but await tests that make use of their capacity. Finally, on the theoretical side, experimental psychologists have taken seriously Cronbach's exhortation (Cronbach, 1957) to unite experimental and differential psychology. As a result, there have been serious attempts since the 1960s to understand test performance in the light of substantive, not just quantitative, theories (e.g., Carroll, 1976; Embretson, 1983; Lansman, Donaldson, Hunt, & Yantis, 1982). In short, the materials are there not only to improve current practice but also to chart new courses.

COMPUTERS AND TEST ASSEMBLY

In the 1960s one would have predicted that the computer's first inroad into test design would be in assisting with the test development process rather than in administering tests. As just shown, however, test administration by computer is becoming a reality. By contrast, the possibilities of using computers for test assembly and test creation have hardly been exploited. Before speculating on how test assembly and item generation can benefit from the integration of psychometrics, technology, and psychological theory, I first review the state of the art.

A key problem in test development is maintaining a large item pool from which items may be drawn, according to some set of specifications, to assemble the final form. For the most part, item pools are kept in filing cabinets. When the time comes, however, to assemble another form it might be wise to sweep the floor, because often the test assembler spreads the cards on the floor to select (through an as yet unpublished procedure) a set of items. Typically, the items in the pool have been pretested, a requirement imposed by the actuarial nature of test development. Of course, that is not the end of the process. Once a tentative set of items has been chosen it goes through numerous revision stages in which some items are deleted and still others added. The criteria for reviewing items include the following:

1. Distribution of item statistics such as difficulty and discrimination,
2. distribution of distractors,
3. lexical overlap,
4. conceptual overlap,
5. content classification,
6. ethnic, gender, and racial bias.

Some of these criteria involve only surface characteristics of the items. Were it not for the fact that items are usually pretested, the test assembler would often have an erroneous idea of the difficulty and discrimination of the item (e.g., Bejar, 1983). It is in this sense that current test design is an actuarial science. Precisely because tests are assembled on the basis of surface characteristics, the process is amenable to computerization. Such computerization will take place if for no other reason than that it increases productivity.

For example, computers can, to the extent that the item pool permits, assemble a form to meet requirements just enumerated while simultaneously attempting to meet some psychometric criterion, such as the distribution of item difficulty and discrimination. The ideal system would be flexible enough to accommodate the styles of different test designers, and it would also be interactive. For example, the system should present the test designer with the option of either letting the computer suggest a form or allowing the test designer to assemble a form gradually. In either case the system should be interactive in the sense of allowing the test designer to ascertain how well the design goals have been met as often as the test designer desires. Naturally, the system should be powerful enough to access sizable item pools instantly, regardless of their graphic complexity.

Components of some of these ideas are being contemplated or in some cases have been implemented (e.g., Yen, 1983), but clearly there is room for improvement. For example, while the computer is in the process of selecting a set of items it may easily produce a report on the availability of different item types for the test designer — who, in turn, could take the necessary steps to replenish the item pool following the suggestions of the computer. It is at this point, however, that the actuarial nature of current test design makes itself obvious. If, for example, the computer reports that easy items of a certain category are running out the test designer can, at best, make the arrangements to pretest another batch of items and hope that among them there will be a large number of easy items.

A system to implement these ideas, to my knowledge, has neither been developed nor is it under serious consideration. It is, however, a question of time before the economics of the present labor-intensive approach becomes unbearable. Because substantial planning is required to develop such a system, it would be desirable to begin now before the need becomes urgent.

USING THE COMPUTER TO GENERATE ITEMS

Computers can be useful for test design because they can advise the test designer about the characteristics of *unpretested* items and, ultimately to generate items according to a prescription. These activities would, of course, be much more difficult to achieve; moreover, it would make the system described earlier unnecessary because in generating items the computer would make sure that they meet the required specifications. That is, rather than maintaining large item pools, as is now done, a point may be reached where submitting a prescription for a test to a computer that would produce a test meeting all the content and psychometric specifications would be feasible. Are we anywhere near the point where such feats are possible? A brief review of the state of the art is very much in order at this juncture.

The essence of the item generation process as it is currently practiced was described by Wesman (1971):

> Item writing is essentially creative — it is an art. Just as there can be no set of formulas for producing a good story or a good painting, so there can be no set of rules that guarantees the production of good test items. Principles can be established and suggestions offered, but it is the writer's judgment in the application — and occasional disregard — of these principles and suggestions that determines whether good items or mediocre ones are produced. Each item, as it is being written, presents new problems and new opportunities. Thus item writing requires an uncommon combination of special abilities and is mastered only through extensive and critically supervised practice. (p. 81)

Chances are good that the state of affairs described by Wesman will prevail in the immediate future. However, some efforts (e.g., Roid & Haladyna, 1982) are under way to make item writing more a science than an art. Many of the procedures outlined in the Roid and Haladyna work rest on a behaviorist foundation, which may make them incompatible with the cognitive turn that psychology and psychometrics have taken. For example, one item generation technique that has evolved is the *item form* (Hively, 1974). Hively defined an item form as a list of rules for generating a set of items. An item in turn is defined as a "set of instructions telling how to evoke, detect and score a specific bit of human performance. It must include the directions for (1) presenting the stimuli, (2) recording the response, and (3) deciding whether or not the response is appropriate" (Hively, 1974, p. 8).

From a psychometric and technological standpoint, item forms are attractive. They are congenial test development procedures for psychometric models relying on the assumption that the items in a test are a random sample from some universe of item. Generalizability theory (Brennan, 1983; Cronbach, Gleser, Nanda, & Rajaratnam, 1972) is the most prominent model based on that assumption. From a technological point of view, item forms are also attractive because they permit a computer to generate items. That is, the item form can be viewed as a program that in principle can enumerate all the items that belong to the universe. By the random choice of items from this universe a test can be formed that satisfies the random sampling assumption. Although item forms and generalizability theory are very compatible, the psychometrics of behavioristically oriented test design has often taken the form of very specific models (e.g., Harris, Pastorok, & Wilcox, 1977) rather than the broader foundation provided by generalizability theory.

In short, the closest we have come to using computers for item generation is through the notion of an item form from which a universe of items can be generated. In my estimation, that approach to item generation is too specialized. In practice, items differ with respect to a number of characteristics, and a useful generation scheme must have control over those characteristics. For example, a useful generation scheme should be able to generate easy items or hard items at will. I suspect that to build such systems it is first necessary to have an idea of what makes an item easy or hard. Some insights on beginning to do this can be found in efforts concerned with the development of computer programs that take tests (see, e.g., Evans, 1968; Green, 1964; Simon & Siklossy, 1972).

COGNITIVE SCIENCE AND PSYCHOMETRICS

A quick review of the history of psychology (e.g., Boring, 1950) shows that throughout the history there has been a tension between the study of consciousness and the study of behavior. As Boring put it, "in its simplest terms the basic problem about the data of psychology is this: Does psychology deal with the data of consciousness or data of behavior or both?" (Boring, 1950, p. 620). These tensions between opposing views often manifest themselves in psychology, as well as in other sciences, in the form of dichotomies (Newell, 1983). Within psychology, behaviorism once dominated the field. The pendulum has now swung and mentalism, in the form of cognitive psychology, now has the upper hand. It seems that psychometrics has swung along with the rest of psychology, as evidenced by the vigor of efforts to cognitivize psychometrics. Some of these efforts are represented in this volume. (The reader is also referred to Embretson, 1983, for an approach that encompasses not only test design, which she calls *construct representation,* but also an accounting of the relationship among scores from several tests, which she calls *nomothetic span.*)

It is not necessary to feel sorry for the behaviorist. When behaviorism was champion, psychometricians of that persuasion has their day, as demonstrated by the following excerpt from Osburn (1968) regarding test design.

> Few measurement specialists would quarrel with the premise that the fundamental objective of achievement testing is generalization. Yet the fact is that current procedures for the construction of achievement tests do not provide an unambiguous basis for generalization to a well defined universe of content. At worst, achievement tests consist of arbitrary collections of items thrown together in a haphazard manner. At best, such tests consist of items judged by subject matter experts to be relevant to and representative of some incompletely defined universe of content. In neither case can it be said that there is an unambiguous basis for generalization. This is because the method of generating items and the criteria for the inclusion of items in the test cannot be stated in operational terms.
>
> The time-honored way out of this dilemma has been to resort to statistical and mathematical strategies in an attempt to generalize beyond the arbitrary collection of items in the test. By far the most popular of these strategies has been to invoke the concept of a latent variable — an underlying continuum which represents a hypothetical dimension of skill. (p. 95)

The notion of criterion-referenced tests was popularized by Glaser and Nitko (1971) shortly thereafter, and for over a decade criterion-referenced tests enjoyed the endorsement of many psychometricians and clearly had an impact on test design (see Shoemaker, 1975). It is perhaps no coincidence that critics, once behaviorism ceased to be a major influence in psychology, began finding all sorts of problems in criterion-referenced tests. For example, Johnson and Pearson (1975) criticized criterion-referenced reading tests as being linguistically naive. They argued that by focusing exclusively on observable interpretations the usefulness of measuring instruments is diminished. Moreover, advocates of criterion-referenced measurement (e.g., Hambleton, Swaminathan, Algina, & Coulson, 1978; Nitko, 1980) have begun to accept construct validation as playing a useful role in the validation of criterion-referenced tests. This of course implies their acceptance of the legitimacy of using nonobservable constructs in test interpretation. Indeed, there is no reason why an emphasis on behavior and cognition cannot coexist in both an instructional and a psychometric sense (Greeno, 1978).

The more recent emphasis on cognitive psychology has at least two implications for psychometrics. One is the possibility of understanding test performance in terms of cognitive constructs (e.g., Sternberg, 1981). The other possibility is the exploitation of cognitive theory for the improvement and design of both current and fundamentally new tests. In the next section I discuss both possibilities.

VALIDATION OF TEST PERFORMANCE

The most likely immediate influence of cognitive science on psychometrics is as a source of constructs to validate test scores. Messick (1975) has eloquently argued for the necessity of construct validation, and the case need not be repeated here. It is sufficient to say that the availability of cognitive or information-processing constructs and the revival of construct validation have important implications for test design.

The validation of both aptitude and achievement tests has relied very little on cognitive constructs. In the recent past validation of achievement tests was strongly influenced by content considerations. This was in line with the behavioristic orientation of criterion-referenced testing that has dominated much of the thinking in the field. Similarly, the validation of aptitude tests, from the Scholastic Aptitude Test (SAT) to the Armed Services Vocational and Aptitude Battery (ASVAB) has relied almost exclusively on predictive validity, and this paradigm is responsible for the psychometric nature of procedures for improving validity. The alternative view is that understanding the nature of the relationship, as opposed to just its magnitude, puts test developers in a better position to increase validity. However, validation based on cognitive constructs, and for that matter tests developed from scratch based on cognitive theory, need not necessarily yield higher predictive validities. It is known from psychometric theory that the magnitude of correlation between a test and a criterion is determined by the proportion of variance in common between the two. Clearly, the test designer has control over the composition of the test but not over the composition of the criterion. Hunt (1983) anticipated this when he noted the following:

> The cognitive science view may lead to the development of new tests that are more firmly linked to a theory of cognition than are present tests. Such tests are yet to be written. There is no compelling reason to believe that new tests will be better predictors of those criteria that are predicted by today's tests. After all the present tests are the results of an extensive search for instruments that meet the pragmatic criterion of prediction. Theoretically based tests may expand the range of cognitive functions that are evaluated and certainly should make better contact with our theories of cognition. Theoretical inter-

pretation, alone, is not a sufficient reason for using a test. *A test that is used to make social decisions must meet traditional psychometric criteria for reliability and validity. No small effort will be required to construct tests that meet both theoretical and pragmatic standards* [italics added]. The effort is justified, for our methods of assessing cognition ought to flow from our theories about the process of thinking. (p. 146; Hunt, E., "On the nature of intelligence," *Science* 219 [14 January 1983], pp. 141 – 146, copyright © 1983 by the American Association for the Advancement of Science)

Moreover, from a social perspective, validation solely in terms of predictive validity is inadequate. A predictive validation strategy may have been appropriate when the primary object of testing was the identification of high-scoring individuals, but society's concern with equality requires a focus on low-scoring individuals also. As noted by the Committee on Ability Testing of the National Research Council:

> The relationship between problem solving on tests and everyday performance has taken on new relevance to public policy, as attention has come to focus . . . not on those selected, as was the case when tests were perceived primarily as identifying excellence, but on those not selected. This shift in focus has brought new prominence to the question of what is being measured by a given test or item type and has pointed up insufficiencies from a public perspective in validation strategies based solely on the demonstration of external statistical relationships. (Wigdor & Warner, 1982, p. 215)

This quotation and much of the litigation involving tests suggest that in the years ahead test designers will have to be more sensitive to the ethical implications of testing instruments. That is, test designers will have to take into account not just the psychometric and substantive base of tests but their consequences as well. Messick (1980) has suggested that the consequences of testing should be a component of the validation process rather than an afterthought. Just as construct validation consists of collecting evidence from many substantive perspectives, the procedure for incorporating consequences into the validation process consists of collecting information on the implications of using a test in a particular situation. However, such listing of implications cannot be fruitfully done in a psychometric vacuum:

> Appraising the possible consequences of test use is not a trivial process under any circumstances, but it is virtually impossible in the absence of construct validity information about the meaning and nature of test scores. Just as the construct network of nomological implications provided a rational basis for hypothesizing potential relationships to criteria, so it also provides a rational basis for hypothesizing potential outcomes and for anticipating possible side effects. (Messick, 1980, p. 15)

AN ILLUSTRATION

An example of construct validation in the context of an adaptive test is provided by Bejar and Weiss (1978). They postulated a nomological net to account for achievement in a college biology course and proceeded to test its

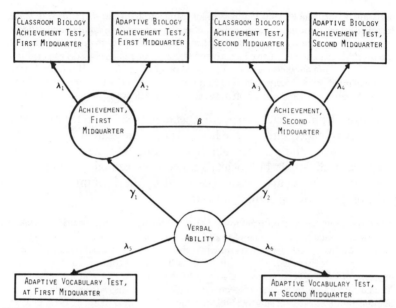

FIGURE 1. Nomological net accounting for achievement in a college biology course. Taken from Bejar and Weiss, 1978.

feasibility with a structural equation model (see Bentler, 1978, for a discussion of construct validation by means of structural equation models). The net is seen in Fig. 1. The rectangles represent the constructs postulated to account for the relationships among the six observable variables. The coefficients next to the arrows are those that need to be estimated. The direction of the arrow indicates that the variable at the head of the arrow is regressed on the variable at the other end of the arrow. Bejar and Weiss concluded that the postulated model indeed fitted the data and that although there were no major differences between the validity of paper-and-pencil and adaptive versions of the test, the adaptive test required 25% fewer items. At the time, such a reduction in the number of items, compared to the cost of an adaptive test, may not have been cost-efficient. By the 1980s, of course, the hardware cost per terminal could have easily been less than $1000, and the economics of adaptive testing may thus appear more attractive.

The net postulated by Bejar and Weiss was dictated more by the availability of scores rather than by an information-processing model of achievement. If measures inspired by cognitive science had been available they could easily have been used. Rose (1980), for example, developed a battery of tasks that are indicators of information processes. The use of that battery in the validation of the adaptive biology achievement test would have been consistent both with what has called cognitive correlates approaches to cognitive psychometrics (see Sternberg, 1981; Pellegrino & Glaser, 1979). In the cognitive correlates approach, the goal is to test subjects on several low-level tasks that are believed to be indicative of the subjects' efficiency in processing information. An example of a low-level task is matching whether two letters, such as $C c$, constitute a physical match or, as in this case, a name match. Because the tasks are easy, response latency, rather than correctness, is the outcome of interest on such tasks. In a cognitive components approach, the aim is to postulate a model of information processing and to test by obtaining data on the performance of subjects on testlike tasks. The outcomes from either approach can be used as part of a construct validation study designed to gain further understanding of the performance of students in a test.

Although it is beyond the scope of this chapter to consider achievement testing in detail (see Bejar, 1983), it should be noted that performance on an achievement test depends on both processing components and the storing of information. The cognitive components and correlates approach emphasizes the processing part but not the storage part, that is, the schema for representing information. Other researchers (e.g., Burton, 1982) have emphasized the storage part by elaborating constructs about how the students represent knowledge.

The Bejar and Weiss (1978) study, in addition to illustrating what Messick (1980) has called the evidential component of validation, also illustrated the consequential aspect of validation. Bejar and Weiss found evidence in their data of a medium effect. That is, it seemed that the medium of administration, whether it was paper and pencil or computerized, influenced the scores to some extent. If this medium effect can be replicated, the possible ethical consequences will be something for future test designers to worry about. For example, students from less-affluent homes are less likely to have been exposed to keyboards and CRTs and thus may obtain lower scores than they should. Because these students are also likely to have been exposed to a less-adequate educational environment, it would add insult to injury to test those students by computer without first ensuring that they are at ease with the computer as a medium for test delivery. The work of Snow and Peterson (Chapter 5 in this volume) has obvious implications for research on the detection of such problems.

TOWARD SCIENTIFICALLY BASED TEST DESIGN

In the previous section I discussed construct validation as a means to a better understanding of test scores. Although, no doubt, such information could be useful to a test developer, he or she may be at a loss on how to incorporate that information in the creation of new items or of entirely new tests. In this section I argue that from a test design perspective it is necessary to shift the focus of attention from the examinee to the item. That is, just as construct validation of test scores entails research to understand differences among examinees, construct validation applied to test design entails research to understand differences among items. More concretely, it is necessary to account for the differences among items with respect to their characteristics, especially difficulty. I suggest that cognitive science is an important source of ideas for accomplishing that goal. This integration of psychometric models and cognitive science, as reflected in the work of Embretson (1983) and Fischer (1973), is important not only for advancing the scientific status of psychometric instruments but also for creatively incorporating technological advances into the testing process. For example, if test developers are able to account for differences among items they may have captured the knowledge necessary to synthesize items of known characteristics (see Egan, 1979). They may, in short, be able to write a computer program capable of composing an item with known psychometric characteristics. The chapters by Sternberg and McNamara (Chapter 2), Pellegrino, Mumaw, and Cantoni (Chapter 3), and Butterfield, Nielsen, Tangen, and Richardson (Chapter 4), in this volume provide the basis for research toward that goal.

I would be the first to agree that synthesizing items, is not likely to be easy and that sustained research is required before practical results will be available. Nevertheless, adopting that effort as a goal puts test developers in the enviable position of simultaneously pursuing scientific and economic goals. That is, the ability to synthesize items is likely to improve the productivity of the test designer in much the same way that computers have altered the productivity of, for example, graphics designers in various industries. To reach that point, however, they will have to do considerable work to establish and validate a theory that explains the characteristics of items.

It is beyond the scope of this chapter to outline a detailed research program that will, in the end, allow the synthesis of items. However, a natural starting point is to account for the variability among existing items (see Carroll, 1979, for an attempt to do so). Unfortunately, this task is made difficult by the fact that most existing tests are of the multiple-choice variety. No doubt with such items the context in which the correct alternative occurs partially determines the psychometric characteristics of the item. This, unfortunately, makes the task more difficult than it ought to be because the multiple-choice item was invented to facilitate group testing, and thus its usefulness will presumably diminish as computers are used more and more in the administration of individualized tests. In the meantime, however, test designers must be ready to deal with the complications introduced by multiple-choice items.

Psycholinguistic theory is a rich source of hypotheses for the study of verbal tests such as reading comprehension tests and writing ability tests. Psychologists have devoted considerable attention to sentence comprehension (e.g., Kintsch, 1977). One early theory was postulated by Miller (Miller & McKeon, 1964) and is known as the Derivational Complexity Theory. According to this theory the comprehensibility of a sentence is determined by the syntactic complexity of the sentence. Complexity was measured as the number of transformations required to go from the deep structure to the surface structure of a sentence. Although this particular theory is not now well supported, it seems reasonable to suggest that if comprehensibility of a sentence is affected by some measure of syntactic and semantic complexity then psychometric difficulty of an item based on that sentence will to some extent also depend on the syntactic and semantic complexity of the sentence.

A test with items based on sentences is the Test of Standard Written English (TSWE), sponsored by the College Board and produced by the Educational Testing Service. One of the two item types in the test consists of a sentence that may or may not contain a grammatical error. The examinee's task is to determine whether the sentence as it stands contains an error; if it does, the examinee must select from several alternatives to correct the sentence. One way to apply these ideas to the TSWE is to obtain several measures of linguistic complexity on each item and study the relationship of those measures to psychometric difficulty. If a stable relationship is found, then, in principle, the resulting model may be used to predict the difficulties of new items and even to modify items so they will be easier or harder.

Although the preceding remarks are speculative, some research along these lines already exists. For example, the Degrees of Reading Power (DRP), sponsored by the College Board, is a reading comprehension cloze test. Unlike the usual cloze test, the DRP is a multiple-choice test; that is, the examinee is provided several choices for filling in the deleted word. The difficulty of those items can apparently be predicted on the basis of the readability index of the passage. Similarly, Swinton (personal communication) has experimented with verbal analogy items by forming different versions of the item in order to alter their difficulty.

The idea of synthesizing items of known characteristics has been implemented by at least one research team (Brown and Burton, 1978; Burton, 1982). They were concerned with the design of diagnostic tests of subtraction. Their goal was to infer what misconceptions may account for a student's error in arithmetic. To speed that process up it is necessary to synthesize items "on the fly" that are most informative with respect to the current set of hypothesized misconceptions: that is, a computer creates the items as they are needed rather than retrieving them from a pool of items.

One area that seems ready for the integration of cognitive theory and psychometric models is spatial ability. Spatial ability has been a subject of intense investigation. A well-established finding is that the response latency to problems that require mental manipulation is a function of the physical characteristics of the test stimuli. For example, the time it takes to determine whether two geometric figures are the same is a linear function of their angular disparity (see Cooper, 1980). This finding suggests that the psychometric difficulty of spatial items could be predicted from an analysis of their physical characteristics. A project investigating this possibility is under way at Educational Testing Service under the sponsorship of the Office of Naval Research.

CONCLUDING COMMENTS

In this chapter I have attempted to enumerate some of the ways in which the integration of technology, cognitive science, and psychometric theory can benefit test design. The state of the art is most advanced with respect to the administration of tests, with the notion of adaptive tests rapidly approaching operational implementation. As I have suggested, adaptive testing is a significant step forward. However, from a user's point of view, an adaptive test is just a multiple-choice test administered by computer because the improvements in efficiency and even the test's psychological advantages are not obvious to the naked eye.

I have argued that to move the state of the art forward it will be necessary to pay closer attention to the psychological foundation of tests. This effort calls, on one hand, for the construct validation of tests from both an evidential and consequential perspective. On the other hand, I have also argued that to improve the scientific basis of test design it is necessary to focus attention not only on variability among examinees but also on variability among items. In particular, a better understanding of why items behave the way they do is needed. From a practical perspective the payoff for doing so will be the possibility of ultimately being able to synthesize items of known psychometric characteristics.

REFERENCES

Andersen, E. B. (1977). The logistic model for m-answer categories. In W. F. Kempf & B. H. Repp (Eds.) *Mathematical models for social psychology.* New York: Wiley.

Bejar, I. I. (1983). *Achievement testing: Recent developments.* Beverly Hills: Sage Publications.

Bejar, I. I. (1983). Subject-matter expert prediction of item difficulty. *Applied Psychological Measurement., 7,* 303–310.

Bejar, I. I., & Weiss, D. J. (1978). *A construct validation of adaptive achievement testing* (Research Rep. 78–4). Minneapolis: University of Minnesota, Department of Psychology.

Bentler, P. M. (1978). The interdependence of theory methodology and empirical data: Causal modeling as an approach to construct validation. In D. B. Kandel (Ed.), *Longitudinal research on drug use.* New York: Halstead Press.

Bock, R. D. (1972). Estimating item parameters and latent ability when responses are scored in two or more nominal categories. *Psychometrika, 38,* 437–458.

Boring, E. G. (1950). *A history of experimental psychology.* New York: Appleton-Century-Crofts.

Brennan, R. L. (1983). *Elements of generalizability theory.* Iowa City: ACT Publications.

Brown, J. S., & Burton, R. R. (1978). Diagnostic models for procedural bugs in basic mathematical skills. *Cognitive Science, 2,* 155–192.

Burton, R. R. (1982). Diagnosing bugs in a simple procedural skill. In D. Sleeman & J. S. Brown (Eds.), *Intelligent tutoring systems.* New York: Academic Press.

Carroll, J. B. (1980). Measurement & abilities construct. In construct validity in psychological measurement. Proceedings of a colloqium on theory and application in education and employment. Princeton, NJ: Educational Testing Service.

Carroll, J. B. (1976). Psychometric tests as cognitive tasks: A new structure of intellect. In L. B. Resnick (Ed.), *The nature of intelligence.* Hillsdale, NJ: Erlbaum.

Cooper, L. A. (1980). Spatial information processing: Strategies for research. In R. E. Snow, P. A. Federico, & W. E. Montague (Eds.), *Aptitude, learning and instruction* (Vol. 1). Hillsdale, NJ: Erlbaum.

Cronbach, L. J. (1957). The two disciplines of scientific psychology *American Psychologist, 12,* 671–684.

Cronbach, L. J., Gleser, G. C., Nanda, H., & Rajaratnam, N. (1972). *The dependability of behavioral measurements: Theory of generalizability for scores and profiles.* New York: Wiley.

Egan, D. E. (1979). Testing Based on understanding: Implication from studies & spatial ability. *Intelligence, 3,* 1–15.

Embretson, S. (1983). Construct validity: Construct representation versus nomothetic span. *Psychological Bulletin, 93,* 179–197.

Evans, T. G. (1968). A heuristic program to solve analogy problems. In M. Minsky (Ed.) *Semantic Information Processing.* Cambridge, MA: The MIT Press.

Fischer, G. H. (1973). The linear logistic test model as an instrument in education research. *Acta Psychologica, 36,* 359–374.

Glaser, R., & Nitko, A. J. (1971). Measurement in learning and instruction. In R. L. Thorndike (Ed.), *Educational measurement.* Washington, DC: American Council on Education.

Green, B. F. (1964). Intelligence and computer simulation. *Transactions of the New York Academy of Sciences,* Ser. II, *27,* 55–63.

Greeno, J. G. (1978). Book review of *Human characteristics and school learning* by B. Bloom. *Journal of Educational Measurement, 15,* 67–76.

Harris, C. W., Pastorok, A., & Wilcox, R. R. (1977). *Achievement testing: Item methods of study.* Los Angeles: Center for the Study of Evaluation. University of California.

Hively, W. (1974). Introduction to domain referenced testing. *Educational Technology, 14,* 5–9.

Hambleton, R. K., Swaminathan, H., Algina, J., & Coulson, D. B. (1978). Criterion-referenced testing and measurement: A review of technical issues and developments. *Review of Educational Research, 48,* 1–47.

Hunt, D. (1983, January). On the nature of intelligence. *Science, 219* (No. 4581), 141–146.

Johnson, D., & Pearson, P. D. (1975, May). Skill management systems: A critique. *The Reading Teacher,* pp. 757–764.

Kintsch, W. (1977). *Memory and cognition.* New York: Wiley.

Lansman, M., Donaldson, G., Hunt, E., & Yantis, S. (1982). Ability factors and cognitive processes. *Intelligence, 6,* 347–386.

Lord, F. M. (1980). *Application of item response theory to practical testing problems.* Hillsdale, NJ: Erlbaum.

Messick, S. (1975). The standard problem: Meaning and values in measurement and evaluation. *American Psychologist, 30,* 955–966.

Messick, S. (1980). Test validity and the ethics of assessment. *American Psychologist, 35,* 1012–1027.

Miller, G. A., & McKeon, K. O. (1964). A chronometric study of some relations between sentences. *Quarterly Journal of Experimental Psychology, 16,* 297–308.

Newell, A. (1983). Intellectual issues in the history of artificial intelligence. In F. Machlup & U. Mansfield (Eds.), *The study of information: Interdisciplinary messages.* New York: Wiley.

Nitko, A. J. (1980). Distinguishing the many varieties of criterion-referenced tests. *Review of Educational Research, 50,* 461–486.

Osburn, H. G. (1968). Item sampling for achievement testing. *Educational and Psychological Measurement, 28,* 95–104.

Pellegrino, J. W. & Glaser, R. (1979). Cognitive correlates and components in the analysis & individual dependency. *Intelligence, 3,* 187–214.

Roid, G., & Haladyna, T. (1982). *A technology for test item writing.* New York: Academic Press.

Rose, A. M. (1980). Information processing abilities. In R. E. Snow, P. A. Federico, & W. E. Montague (Eds.), *Aptitude, learning and instruction* (Vol. 1). Hillsdale, NJ: Erlbaum.

Samejima, F. (1969). Estimation of latent ability using a response pattern of graded responses. *Psychometrika,* Monograph No. 17.

Samejima, F. (1972). A general model for free response data. *Psychometrika,* Monograph No. 18.

Shoemaker, D. M. (1975). Toward a framework for achievement testing. *Reviewing Educational Research, 48,* 127–141.

Simon, H. A. & Siklossy, L. (Eds.). (1972). Representation and meaning: Experiments in information processing systems. Englewood Cliffs, NJ: Prentice-Hall.

Sternberg, R. J. (1981). Testing and cognitive psychology. *American Psychologist, 36,* 1181–1189.

Wigdor, A. K., & Warner, W. R. (Eds.). (1982). *Ability testing: Uses, consequences, and controversies* (Part II). Washington, DC: National Academy Press.

Weiss, D. J. (1974). *Strategies of adaptive ability measurement* (Research Rep. 74–5). Minneapolis: University of Minnesota, Department of Psychology.

Wesman, A. G. (1971). Writing the test item. In R. L. Thorndike (Ed.) *Educational measurement.* Washington, DC: American Council on Education.

Yen, W. (1983). Use of the three-parameter model in the development of a standardized achievement test. In R. K. Hambleton (Ed.), *Applications of item response theory.* Vancouver: Educational Research Institute of British Columbia.

Author Index

A

Achenbach, T. M., 204
Albert, D., 226, *243*
Algina, J., 285, *293*
Andersen, E. B., 169, 171, 172, *191,* 230, *243,* 248, *273,* 281, *292*
Anderson, N. H., 28, *41*
Andrich, D., 169, *191,* 247, 248, 249, 250, 251, 252, 264, *274*

B

Baltes, P., 23, *43*
Barnes, G. M., 199, 211, 218
Battig, W. F., 210, *218*
Bejar, I. I., 282, 287, 288, 289, *292, 293*
Belmont, J. M., 160, *164*
Bennett, G. K., 47, 68, *76*
Bentler, P. M., 288, *293*
Bethell-Fox, C. E., 154, 158, *164*
Birnbaum, A., 254, *274*
Bishop, C. H., 5, *16*
Blow, F., 23, *43*
Bobbitt, B. L., 23, *42*
Bock, R. D., 6, *16,* 281, *293*
Boies, S., 13, *16,* 219, 220, *244*
Boring, E. G., 284, 285, *293*
Brennan, R. L., 284, *293*
Brown, A. L., 160, *164*
Brown, J. S., 291, *293*
Burton, R. R., 289, 291, *293*
Butterfield, E. C., 160, *164*

C

Calfee, R. C., 152, *164*
Campione, J. C., 160, *164*
Cantoni, V. J., 49, 53, *76*
Carroll, J. B., 46, *76,* 281, 290, *293*
Cattell, R. B., 28, *41*
Chandler, J. P., 242, *243*
Chase, W. G., *243*
Chi, M. T. H., 25, *41*
Choppin, B., 262, *274*
Clark, E. V., 29, *41*
Clark, H. H., 29, *41, 243*
Cooper, L. A., 45, 48, 67, *76,* 292, *293*
Cornelius, S., 23, *43*
Coulson, D. B., 285, *293*
Cox, D. R., 226, *243*
Crockett, L., 152, *165*
Cronbach, L. J., 3, *16,* 150, 151, 153, 159, 161, 162, *164,* 281, 284, *293*
Curtright, C. A., 211, *218*

D

Daalen-Kaptejins, M. M., van, 24, *41*
Donaldson, G., 23, *42, 281, 294*
Donlon, T. F., 163, *164*
Dorner, D., 190, *191*
Duncan, O. D., 254, *274*

E

Ebel, R., 5, *16*
Edwards, A. L., 252, *274*

Egan, D. E., 159, *165,* 290, *293*
Eichelman, W., 220, *244*
Ekstrom, R. B., 163, *164*
Elshout-Mohr, M., 24, *41*
Embretson, S. E., 4, 5, *16,* 195, 196, 198,
    207, 208, *217,* 281, 285, 290, *293*
Evans, T. G., 284, *293*

F

Federico, P. A., 150, 157, *166*
Feller, W., 226, 227, 243, *244*
Feng, C., 49, *76*
Ferrara, R., 160, *164*
Ferretti, R., 160, *164*
Fischer, G. H., 11, *16,* 169, 171, 178, 179,
    183, 184, 188, 191, *192, 193,* 209, *217,*
    229, 231, *244,* 245, *274,* 281, 290, *293*
Forman, A. K., 11, *16,* 179, *192*
Francis, W. N., 210, *217*
Fredriksen, J. R., 40, *41*
Frege, G., 27, *41*
French, J. W., 198, *217*
Frost, N., 23, *42,* 219, 220, 224, *244*

G

Gavurin, E. I., 150, 158, *165*
Gentile, J., 204, *217*
Gentile, K., 204, *217*
Glaser, R., 40, *42,* 46, 49, 53, 67, *76,* 78, 79,
    93, 94, 98, 101, 106, *147,* 157, 159,
    165, 199, 211, *217,* 285, 289, *293, 294,*
    323, *244*
Gleser, G. C., 159, *164*
Goodman, L., 254, *274*
Green, B. F., 6, *16,* 284, *293*
Greeno, J. E., 190, *192*
Greeno, J. G., 159, *165,* 286, *293*
Gruner, E., 242, *244*
Gustafsson, J. E., 169, *192*
Guthke, J., 188, *192*
Guttman, L., 248, 251, *274*

H

Haberman, S. J., 254, *274*
Habon, M. W., 179,ᐧ*192*

Haladyna, T., 283, *294*
Hambleton, R. K., 285, *293*
Hampton, J. A., 28, *41*
Harris, C. S., 226, *244*
Harris, C. W., 284, *293*
Hausler, B., 190, *193*
Hedges, L. V., 152, *164*
Heller, J., 205, *217*
Hevner, W., 178, *193*
Hively, W., 15, *16,* 284, *293*
Hoffman, L., 188, *193*
Holland, P. W., 254, *274*
Holzman, T. G., 78, 79, 93, 94, 98, 101,
    106, 123, *147*
Hornke, L. F., 179, *192*
Humphreys, L. G., 6, *16*
Hunt, D., 286, *294*
Hunt, E. B., 22, 23, *42,* 162, *165,* 219, 220,
    244, 281, *294*

I

Inhelder, B., 171, *192*

J

Jackson, M. D., 23, *42*
Jensen, A. R., 22, 24, *42*
Johnson, D., 285, *294*
Johnson, N. L., 226, 228, 243, *244*

K

Kail, R. V., 48, *76*
Kaplan, E., 23, *43*
Katz, J. J., 27, *42*
Kaye, D. B., 24, *42*
Keating, D. P., 23, *42*
Keil, F. C., 25, *42*
Kempf, W. F., 11, 12, *17*
Kessler, K., 204, *217*
Kintsch, W., 291, *294*
Kisser, R., 229, 231, *244*
Klahr, D., 150, *165*
Klauer, K. J., 179, *192*
Kluwe, R., 171, *193*
Koran, M. L., 161, *165*
Kotovsky, K., 9, *16,* 78, 79, 80, 93, 94, 100,
    108, 121, 126, 127, 128, *147*
Kotz, S., 226, 228, 243, *244*

Kubinger, K., 169, *192*
Kucera, H., 210, *217*
Kyllonen, P. C., 151, 157, 158, 161, *165, 166*

L

Lansman, M., 23, *42,* 281, *294*
Lesgold, A. M., 23, *42*
Leunbach, G., 272, *274*
Lewis, J., 220, *244*
Lewis, P. A. W., 226, *243*
Likert, R., 47, 49, *76*
Linn, R. L., 6, *16*
Lockheed, M. E., 163, *164*
Lohman, D. F., 45, 47, 48, 68, *76,* 151, 154, 157, 158, 161, *164, 165*
Lord, F. M., 280, *294*
Lucht-Wraage, H., 188, *193*
Luer, G., 191, *192*
Lunneborg, C. E., 23, *42,* 219, 220, *244*

M

McCarthy, K., 163, *166*
McClelland, J. L., 23, *42*
MacCorquodale, K., 196, *217*
McDonald, F., 161, *165*
McGee, M. G., 45, *76*
McGill, W. J., 226, 227, *244*
McKeon, K. O., 291, *294*
MacLeod, C. M., 162, *165*
McNamara, T. P., 29, *42*
Marshalek, B., 26, *42,* 157, *165, 166*
Marshall, S. P., *165*
Masters, G. N., 248, 249, 252, 256, 262, *274, 275*
Matarazzo, J. D., 22, *42*
Mathews, N. N., 162, *165*
May, R., 174, *193*
Mayer, R. E., 159, *165*
Meehl, P. E., 196, *217*
Messick, S., 286, 287, 289, *294*
Metzler, J., 210, *217*
Meyer, F., 233, *244*
Micko, H. C., 183, *192*
Miller, G. A., 291, *294*
Millman, J., 5, *16*
Mitchell, R., 23, *42*
Montague, W. E., 150, 157, *166*

Mulholland, T. M., 232, *244*
Mumaw, R. J., 49, 53, 67, *76*

N

Nahrer, W., 169, 171, 177, 179, *192*
Nanda, H., 159, *164*
Newell, A., 190, *192, 285, 294*
Nitko, A. J., 285, *293, 294*
Norman, D., 190, *193*

O

Osburn, H. G., 285, *294*

P

Panchapakesan, N., 263, *275*
Pastorok, A., 284, *293*
Pearson, P. D., 285, *294*
Pellegrino, J. W., 40, *42,* 46, 48, 49, 53, *76,* 78, 79, 93, 94, 98, 101, 106, 123, *147,* 157, 159, *165,* 199, 211, *217,* 232, *244,* 289, *294*
Pendl, P., 179, *192*
Perfetti, C. A., 23, *42*
Peterson, P. I., 150, *166*
Piaget, J., 171, *192*
Pinswanger, K., 179, *192*
Posner, M. I., 13, *16,* 23, *42,* 219, 220, *244*
Poulton, E. C., 152, *165*
Powell, J. S., 24, *42*
Pribam, K. H., 226, *244*

Q

Quasha, W. H., 47, 49, *76*

R

Rajaratnam, N., 159, *164*
Rao, C. R., 243, *244*
Rasch, G., 6, *16,* 169, 170, *193,* 230, *244,* 245, 254, *274*
Raven, J. C., 78, *147*
Reckase, M., 6, *16*
Reimann, P., 170, 190, *193*
Resnick, L. B., 150, 159, *165*
Revlis, R., 210, *217*
Rips, L. J., 28, *42*
Rockett, F. C., 154, *166*

Roid, G., 283, *294*
Rosche, E., 28, *42*
Rose, A. M., 157, *165,* 288, *294*
Rost, J., *16,* 169, 182, 184, 188, *193,* 263, *274*
Rumelhart, D., 190, *193*
Russell, B., 27, *42*

S

Samejima, F., 252, 256, *274,* 281, *294*
Scheiblechner, H., 11, 12, *16,* 174, 182, *193,*
    221, 230, 239, 241, 243, *244*
Schmitt, A. P., 152, *165*
Schneider, L. M., 169, *194,* 200, 201, 203, *218*
Schwartz, S. P., 29, *42*
Seashore, H. G., 47, 68, *76*
Sells, S. B., 210, *217*
Shepard, R. N., 48, 49, *76,* 210, *217*
Shoben, E. J., 28, *42*
Shoemaker, D. M., 285, *294*
Siklossy, L., 284, *294*
Simon, H. A., 9, *16,* 78, 79, 80, 93, 94, 100,
    108, 121, 126, 127, 128, *147,* 190, *192,*
    284, *294*
Smith, E. E., 28, *42*
Smith, W. F., 154, *166*
Snow, R. E., 150, 151, 153, 154, 157, 158,
    159, 161, 152, *164, 165, 166*
Solter, A., 49, 53, *76*
Spada, H., 11, 12, 16, *17,* 170, 171, 172,
    173, 174, 175, 177, 178, 182, 184, 188,
    190, *193,* 245, *275*
Spearman, C., 78, *147*
Steckler, J. F., 163, *166*
Steizl, I., 169, *193*
Sternberg, R. J., 7, *17,* 24, 29, 37, 40, *42,*
    150, 155, 157, 160, 162, *166,* 199, 204,
    211, *217,* 286, 289, *294*
Sternberg, S., 13, *17,* 219, 220, 232, *244*
Stiehl, C. C., 159, *165*
Stone, M. H., 169, *194*
Swaminathan, H., 285, *293*
Swiney, J. F., Jr., *166*

T

Taylor, R., 220, *244*
Thissen, D., 171, *193*
Thurstone, L. L., 9, *17,* 21, *42,* 47, 68, *76,*
    147, 197, 210, *217,* 252, *274*
Thurstone, T. G., 9, *17,* 47, 68, *76,* 78, *147,*
    197, 210, *217*
Tittle, C. K., 163, *166*
Toglia, M. P., 210, *218*

V

Vernon, P. E., 21, *42*
Vygotsky, L., 160, *166*

W

Weil, E. M., 162, *166,* 204, *217*
Weiss, D. J., 270, 287, 288, 289, *293, 294*
Weisstein, N., 226, *244*
Werner, H., 23, *43*
Wesman, A. G., 47, 68, *76,* 283, *294*
Whitely, S., *194*
Whitely, S. E., 11, *17,* 40, *43,* 157, *166,* 169,
    194, 195, 198, 199, 200, 201, 203, 211,
    215, 216, *218,* 245, 252, *275*
Wigdor, D. J., 287, *294*
Wilcox, R. R., 284, *293*
Willis, S., 23, *43*
Wittgenstein, L., 28, *43*
Wollenberg, A. L., von den, 169, *194*
Woltz, D. J., 158, *165*
Wright, D. B., 169, *194,* 249, 263, 266, *275*

Y

Yalow, E., 159, *166*
Yantis, S., 23, *42,* 281, *294*
Yen, W., 282, *294*

Subject Index

A

Achievement, 264–271, 287–289
  mathematical, 264–271
  science, 287–289
Adaptive testing, 6
Anagrams, 150–152
Analogy items, 204–208, 211, 215
Anxiety, test 152–155
Aptitude, *see* Intelligence
Aptitude treatment interaction, 10, 149–150
  compared to information-processing
    approach, 149–150
  contribution to test design, 10

B

Balance scale problems, *see* Concept
  learning, proportions

C

Cognition, relation to psychometrics,
  284–292
Cognitive component approach, 26–27,
  38–39, 46, 157–159; *see also*
  Information-processing
  review of, 157–159
  to spatial aptitude, 46
  special test scores, 38–39
  to verbal comprehension, 26–27
Cognitive contents approach, 159
Cognitive correlates approach, 22–23, 157
  definition, 157
  to verbal comprehension, 22–23

Component analysis, *see* Cognitive component approach
Component latent trait model, *see* Latent
  trait models
Computers
  administering tests, 280–281
  assembling tests, 281–283
  generating items, 132–133, 283–284
  impact on testing, 15–16
Concept learning, proportions, 171–178
Conjoint measurement structure, *see* Latent
  trait models
Construct representation, 3, 196–200
  definition, 3, 196
  model for, 199–200
  relationship to nomothetic span, 196–197
Correlational psychology, 3–4
Criterion analysis, spatial, 9, 61
Criterion-referenced testing, 285–286

D

Dispersion location model, *see* Latent trait
  models
Drawings, engineering, *see* Graphics

E

Expert-novice comparisons, 160

G

Graphics, 61–74
  processing drawings, 67–74
  representing drawings, 62–66

I

Inductive reasoning aptitude, *see* Series
  completion task
Information-processing, 22–25, 32–36,
  49–60, 67–76, 123–125, 155–156
  approaches to analysis of vocabulary, 22–
  25
  in graphics, 67–74
  model to classify test complexity, 155–156
  in series completions, 123–125
  in spatial visualization, 49–60, 74–76
  in vocabulary items, 32–36
Intelligence, 21–27, 157–160; *see also*
  specific aptitudes, such as Spatial aptitude
  approaches to studying, 22–27, 157–160
  implications from verbal comprehension,
  21–22
Item specifications, 5, 9, 78–82, 90–93,
  283–284
  for letter series problems, 78–82, 90–93
  role in test design, 5, 9
  for use in computer generation, 283–284
Item types, *see* specific types, such as
  vocabulary

K

Knowledge representation, 25, 27–32,
  62–66
  approach to analysis, 25
  in graphics, 62–66
  in vocabulary items, 27–32

L

Latent trait models, 10–14, 181–188,
  200–209, 225–231, 236–239,
  247–254, 257–262
  conjoint measurement structure, 236–239
  dispersion location model, 14–15,
  249–254
  estimation, 230–231
  general component, 11, 208–209
  for learning, 181–188
  linear exponential, 12–13, 225–230
  linear logistic, 10–12
  for linked items, 14, 257–262
  multicomponent, 11, 200–204

  rating model, 247–249
  for strategies, 204–208
Learning effects, 180–188, 233–236
  list recall, 233–236
  models of 180–188
  parameters for, 183–187
Linear exponential model, *see* Latent trait
  models
Linear logistic model, *see* Latent trait models

M

Memory, *see* Learning effects
Monotone probabilistic additive model, *see*
  Latent trait models
Multicomponent model, *see* Latent trait
  models

N

Nomothetic span, 3–4, 196–198

R

Rating scale model, *see* Latent trait models
Response time, 8–9, 12–13, 32–36,
  38–40, 53–57, 219–225
  additivity property, 232
  measurement model for, 12–13
  models for spatial visualization, 53–57
  models for verbal comprehension, 21–41
  need to measure individual differences,
  223–225
  relevance to cognition, 219–221
  role in group testing, 222
  using as test scores, 38–40
  versus error, 8–9
Rotation, *see* Spatial aptitude

S

Series completion task, 9, 77–132
  experiments on, 101–125
  generating by computer, 132–133
  psychometric versions, 126–132
  rule systems, 77–90
  theories for, 93–101
Spatial aptitude, approaches to analysis,
  46–47

Spatial visualization, 46–60
  experiments on, 49–60
  theories of, 46–49
Speed, 223, 242–243
  accuracy tradeoff, 233,
  versus power, 222, 242–243 *see also*
    Response time

T

Test complexity, model of, 155–156
Test design, 3, 37–38, 132–133, 150–152,
  162–163, 178–180, 196–200,
  209–215, 271–273, 289–292
  ATI research relevancy, 162–163
  by component difficulty, 212–215
  definition, 3
  to measure processing strategies,
    150–152, 215
  model for, 196–200
  of series completions, 132–133
  scientifically-based, 289–292
  by stimulus content, 209–212
  using component latent trait models,
    209–215

using the dispersion location model,
  271–273
using the linear logistic model, 178–180
of vocabulary analysis, 37–38
Training, information-processing skills,
  160–162

V

Validity, 40, 47, 75, 189, 196–200, 286–289
  impact of cognitive psychology, 286–289
  influence of cognitive components,
    196–198
  influence of learning, 189
  of spatial aptitude tests, 47, 75
  test design, relationship to, 196–200
  of vocabulary tests, 40
Verbal classification items, 200–201,
  203–204, 212–213
Verbal comprehension, approaches to
  analyzing, 22–27
Vocabulary items, 21–36
  experiments on, 27–36
  theories for, 21–27

DATE DUE

XXXXXXXXXXXXXXXXXXX

XXXXXXXXXX APR 18 '86 XXXXX

XXXXX 20 1984 XXXX

MAR 20 1989

APR 23 1997

MAY 1 4 2003

BRODART, INC.

Cat. No. 23-221

WITHDRAWN

3 1194 00291 1505

AMERICAN UNIVERSITY LIBRARY